AF531287

INTERNATIONAL ENCYCLOPAEDIA OF
SCIENCE AND TECHNOLOGY EDUCATION - 10

TEACHER TRAINING IN SCIENCE AND TECHNOLOGY EDUCATION

By

Dr. Digumarti Bhaskara Rao
M.Sc., M.A., M.A., M.Ed., Ph.D.
Reader & Research Director
R.V.R. College of Education
Srinivasa Nagar Colony
Guntur–522 006
(India)

DISCOVERY PUBLISHING HOUSE PVT. LTD.
NEW DELHI-110 002

Published by:
Namit Wasan
DISCOVERY PUBLISHING HOUSE PVT. LTD.
4383/4B, Ansari Road, Darya Ganj
New Delhi-110 002 (India)
Phone : +91-11-23279245; 23253475; 43596065
E-mail : discoverybooksindia@gmail.com
discoverypublishinghouse@gmail.com
namitwasan9@gmail.com
web : www.discoverypublishinggroup.com

Edition: 2020

ISBN: 978-81-7141-548-9 (Set)

ISBN: 978-81-7141-577-9

Teacher Training in Science and Technology Education

Printed at:
Infinity Imaging Systems
Delhi

Preface

Science and Technology have occupied almost all spheres of human life. The wonderful achievements of science and technology have glorified the modern world and transformed the modern civilization into a scientific and technological civilization. Considering the importance of science and technology, they have been incorporated in every stage of education.

This International Encyclopaedia of Science and Technology Education is developed covering a wide range of aspects related to science and technology education for the benefit of all those who are associated with science and technology education. This Encyclopaedia is consisting of eleven volumes, namely:

1. Science and Technology Education,
2. Science Education in Developing Countries,
3. Organizational Structure of Science,
4. Science Education in Asia and the Pacific,
5. Science and Technology Education for All,
6. Values, Ethics, Talent and Girls in Science and Technology Education,
7. Popularization of Science and Technology Education,
8. Science, Power and Society,
9. Information Technology,
10. Teacher Training in Science and Technology Education, and
11. Science, Technology and Society—A Curriculum Framework.

I convey my cordial thanks to UNESCO-PROAP, Bangkok, Thailand; UNESCO-ROSTE, Venice, Italy; UNESCO, Paris, France; IIEP, Paris, France; Commonwealth Secretariat, London, UK; UNCTAD, Geneva, Switzerland, Queen's University, Kingston, Canada; and Alberta Education, Edmonton, Canada for their kind co-operation in preparing this Encyclopaedia.

DR. DIGUMARTI BHASKARA RAO
Secretary
Academy of Communication Culture Education
Science and Service
GUNTUR (A.P.

Contents

Part V: Training of Trainers in Science, Technology and Mathematics Education: Regional Workshop Report

Part I

TEACHER TRAINING FOR SCIENCE AND TECHNOLOGY EDUCATION REFORM

Preface

This resource book is a product of a Regional Workshop on "Teacher Training for Science and Technology Education Reform." It was participated in by ten science educators and science teacher-trainers from India, Indonesia, Iran (2), Malaysia, Maldives, Pakistan, Philippines, Sri Lanka and Thailand; five resource persons, one from India and four from SEAMEO-RECSAM, and eight observers.

The Regional Workshop was convened by the UNESCO Principal Regional Office for Asia and the Pacific (PROAP) and was jointly organized by its Asian Centre of Educational Innovation for Development (ACEID) and the SEAMCO Regional Centre for Education in Science and Mathematics (RECSAM), Penang, Malaysia, 3-14 December 1990.

The designations employed and the presentations of materials throughout the publication do not imply the expression of any opinion, whatsoever, on the part of UNESCO concerning the legal states of any country, territory, city, or area of its authorities, or concerning its frontiers or boundries.

Introduction

This source book is compiled from the proceeding of the Regional Workshop on "Teacher Training for Science and Technology Education Reform" held in Penang, Malaysia 3-14 December 1990. It was jointly organized by SEAMEO-RECSAM and UNESCO/ACEID. This activity was part of UNESCO-APEID's 1990 Programme of Activities in Science and Technology Education, supported by the Government of Australia's Voluntary Cash Contribution to APEID. The list of participants, resource persons, observers and office bearers is found in Annex 1.

The Workshop developed exemplar training materials for science and technology education at the middle school level with emphasis on new competencies and skills required of science teachers, i.e. science process skills and its application to real life situations.

Based on the stated objective the workshop gave emphasis to:

(a) the new role of science teachers linked to the development processes in the Asian countries and towards meeting the comprehensive demands of learning and life.

(b) competencies and skills which must be learnt and practised by science teachers.

(c) changes in science teacher preparation programmes in the light of new role specifications and towards developing necessary teacher competencies.

(d) "evaluation" of science learning which takes into account both cognitive and affective domains effectively.

The Workshop was inaugurated by the Chairman of RECSAM's Governing Board, Tuan Hj. Nik Musa bin Nik Abdullah. In his speech he recognized the role of science and technology developments in the improvement of the quality of life, and that of a well-informed society in enhancing its own progress. He found the objective of this regional Workshop commendable for its relevance in this rapidly changing society. The sharing of country experiences and cross-fertilisation of ideas in the workshop are certain to influence the direction of change and refrom in science education in a large part of the world. He challenged the key educators present in this regional workshop to ensure that these changes and reform in science education are carried out in the countries they represent.

The welcome remarks was given by RECSAM's Director, Tuan Hj. Mohd. Khairuddin bin Hj. Mohd. Ashaari. In this remarks he welcomed all workshop participants to the UNESCO/APEID Workshop hosted by SEAMEO-RECSAM. He reiterated the commitment of SEAMEO-RECSAM to promote regional cooperation through education, science, and culture. The Centre has now come to be regarded as a viable development organization worth considering as a model for regional co-operation and solidarity.

He looks forward to a continued and closer collaboration and co-operation between UNESCO/ACEID and RECSAM in the years ahead.

This source book is composed of four chapters. Chapter One is on country experiences. The innovations and effects made in the preparation of teachers have been spelt out by the participants from the member countries. The major emphasis of their presentations are based on the four areas as stated in the workshop objectives. The end of the chapter presents a synthesis of the country experiences. The synthesis formed the basis for the development of chapters two, three and four of this book.

Chapter Two presents the trends and issues pertaining to teacher training for science and technology education reform.

Chapter Three presents the preparation of materials for the training of science teachers. Some exemplars developed are included in this Chapter.

Chapter four discusses the strategies for Evaluation of Teacher Competencies and Skills.

This source book is intended for use of science educators/ science teacher-trainers in developing programmes emphasizing the new roles/responsibilities of science and technology teachers.

1
Country Experiences

The innovations and efforts made in the preparation of teachers have been spelled out in this Chapter by participants from members countries. Major emphases of their presentations are based on four areas namely:

(a) the new role of science teachers linked to the development processes in the Asian countries and towards meeting the comprehensive demands of *learning and life;*

(b) competencies and skills which must be learnt and practised by science teachers;

(c) changes in science teachers' preparation programmes in the light of new role specifications and towards developing necessary teacher competencies;

(d) "evaluation" of science learning which takes into account both cognitive and affective domains effectively.

India

The New Role of Teachers of Science

(a) Shift to child-centred education in science which would help develop in the child, the scientific attitude and temper, technological competence and skills, self reliance, use of traditional skills and capabilities and making them enterprising, etc.

(b) Finding out the existing science talent and nurturing the talent.

(c) Involving the students in constructive project works.

(d) Exposing the students to real life situation, highlighting the effects of environmental degradation and imbalance.

(e) Emphasising the universal nature of science and hence including the component of international understanding and harmony.

(f) Involving the child in out-of-school, scientific activities like visiting science exhibitions, science-club activities.

Competencies and Skills Practised

(a) Encouraging participatory learning/teaching process in the classroom.

(b) Drawing illustrations from immediate environment, community.

(c) Actual demonstration of some activities—therefore, skill in designing and performing experiments—with locally available materials.

(d) Using and improvising teaching aids which facilitate the teaching-learning process.

(e) Designing activities for classroom teaching.

(f) Effective utilization of laboratory.

(g) competence in plugging in the gaps (in the instructional materials)—for the continuous learning of the students.

Teacher Preparation

(1) Pre-service Training

Pre-service training at primary/elementary level is conducted by Basic Training Institutions, several of which have not been concerted into District Institutes of Education and Training (DIET). This often is a two-year programme after Higher Secondary. For secondary schools, one-year pre-service training courses are conducted by colleges of education in the states, or four-year degree-courses after 12-years of schooling, organized by the 4 Regional Colleges of Education of National Council of Education Research and Training (NCERT). These lead to first degree in Education.

At the pre-service training stage, besides giving training in the methodology of teaching, the actual interaction with teaching situations is also imparted.

In actual training practices, the following are emphasized:

(a) Classroom practice teaching,

(b) Training for the education of handicaps (physical as well as mentally handicaps),

(c) Training in relation to community interaction and actual life situation—for example going to the villages; slums; hospitals; delinquent houses, and

(d) Use of ETV programmes for some abstract concepts.

(2) In-service Training

In-service training, i.e. the updating of practising teachers both in content as well as in methods of teaching is imparted through State Agencies.

A three-tier mode of transaction is practised.

(a) Key Persons Orientation

(b) Resource Persons Training

(c) Teachers' Training

State Level Agencies are State Council of Educational Research and Training (SCERT), State Institute of Science Education (SISE) and State Institute of Education (SIE). The District Level Agencies like DIET (District Institute of Education and Training)—around 260 in number at present—co-ordinate the work of in-service training. Now at the district level, District Science Resource Centres (DSRC) are also coming up. These Centres are operating under district level educational institutes (including semi-government or non-government) and helping in the in-service teachers' training programmes. DSRC is engaged, in general, in science improvement programmes.

Evaluation

As a policy decision, comprehensive continuous evaluation has been recommended up to lower secondary stage. However, the final decision are take up by State Governments and as such, depending upon their preparedness, the same is being implemented up to different grade levels. Generally speaking, practically all states have adopted it at primary stage, though in some cases at the end of the fifth year in school, a terminal examination is conducted with some internality. In grades VI, VII and VIII, normally schools conduct their own examination. They also practise comprehensive continuous evaluation throughout the year and it forms a part of annual examination.

This aspect is being given serious consideration and the National Council of Educational Research and Training (NCERT), is preparing experts at State Level who in turn will organize their multi-layer teachers' training/orientation in Comprehensive Continuous Evaluation Programmes.

Indonesia

A new science curriculum was implemented in 1986 in all primary and secondary schools. To improve the quality of teaching/learning, innovations such as student active learning and development of process skills were also implemented.

The science curriculum is intended to make the contents and topics relate to students' real-life needs, capabilities and environment. From Class I to VI a separate subject, General Science, is taught in primary schools. General Science is an integrated subject consisting of physics, biology, earth and space, health education and environment studies. At lower secondary level, science is separated into Physical Sciences and Biological Sciences.

The New Roles of Teachers of Science

- Providing a variety of learning.
- Using a variety of learning.
- Encouraging students as active participants in the learning.

- Encouraging students to be creative, discovering something by themselves, solving problems, deciding what to do.
- Improving better verbal interaction in classroom.
- Providing for individual differences.
- Using a variety of resources.
- Using the environment as resources for learning.
- Creating an attractive classroom that leads to student's active learning.
- Providing useful feedback.
- Assessing students' work in many ways.

Competencies and Skills Practised

The key teacher competencies related to activity-based learning have been identified. These are to:

(a) plan and manage the time available for learning more effectively;

(b) recognize and understand objectives relating to processes of thinking as well as concepts;

(c) recognize and provide for individual differences among learners, including children who are gifted, as well as children who are weak;

(d) organize and manage teaching and learning through a combination of class, group and individual activities appropriate to the needs of learners, the level of study, and the nature of the subject matter to provide a stimulating and effective environment for learning;

(e) use the environment and the children's direct experience as a resource for learning;

(f) use stimulating teaching and learning techniques (including questioning techniques) based on the use of process skills and leading towards more active and problem-centred approach to teaching and learning in science;

(g) provide better feedback to the learner and also to stimulate peer-group learning;

(h) evaluate the result of learning through the careful setting, monitoring, and assessment of children's output, not only through the work produced daily by the children in class but also through the attitudinal changes observed from time to time.

Active learning will be carried out successfully if supported with science-process skills. These skills are being developed in primary schools, such as:

- Observing objects or events.
- Raising question.
- Making a hypothesis which is a tentative answer to their question, and which they can test in a scientific way.
- Planning and carrying out an experiment to test whether the predictions from this hypothesis are correct or not.
- Observing experiments, interpreting the data collected and using them to decide whether or not their hypothesis was correct.
- Selecting the most appropriate way to communicate their findings to other people. It can be verbal, that is, using language in written and spoken form, as well as non-verbal by using conventional symbols, pictures, drawings, diagrams, tables and graphs.

Teacher Preparation

In-service teacher training programmes are available in Indonesia. For primary science teachers, nation-wide training, utilising the "multiplier effect" concept has been instituted in connection with the new curriculum. Key persons are trained in content as well as methodology of teaching science at the national level, who in turn, train teachers at the regional level, who conduct the training at the district level.

Science July 1990, for increasing the qualification of teachers who graduated from Teacher Training Senior Secondary School, a modular instructional system was provided. This programme is conducted by the Open University. At the same time pre-service teacher training for the primary school teachers is provided at the tertiary level by the Institute of Teacher Training and Education Services and Teacher Training Programme within universities. In-service teacher training for lower secondary teachers is being developed nation-wide. This includes the establishment of district level SANGGAR which develops materials to support the teachers' curriculum development efforts. Curriculum leaflets, distributed to the schools, contain the broad curricular objectives, and instructional objectives.

Evaluation

To evaluate concept and knowledge, currently that government made a decision to stress the test on analytical thinking. Different types of tests are being prepared by Centre for Development Examination systems. Observation sheets have also been developed to evaluate the affective domain.

IRAN

(A) New Role of Teachers of Science

The present society needs science as related to other areas of human activity. The science teachers must also keep in mind that:

(a) society needs economic and cultural upliftment through education for better life.

(b) they must assess community needs and demands.

The teacher prepares the students for needs/requirements of the society/community. The development of science and technology in Iran is very important in relation to society. It is necessary for science teacher to know the strategy of economy, industry and agriculture, as linked to science and technology. The effort is to achieve self-reliance in industry, health and agriculture. They must also appreciate fully the technological learning needs of children in order to fulfil their country's needs.

(B) Competencies and Skills

Competencies

(a) Teacher provides motivation and drive for the students—that science is important for the progress of a country.

(b) Students know about themselves and the environment. Science information must be *updated by* the teacher (latest knowledge). The students must be made to realize that science is a progressive subject and the latest ideas be taught.

Skills

(a) The teacher should learn and exercise skill of logical thinking; "what, why, how" problem-solving skills.

(b) Observing, collecting data, classifying and comparing,

Explanation skills

Making theories, concepts.

Students should be able to quantify the quality of environment, set examples, give estimates of distance without having to really measure perfectly.

(c) Problem-solving.

(C) Changes in Science Teachers Preparation Programmes

At present, the education system of Iran consists of:

(a) 5 years elementary school (6-10 years old)

(b) 3 years secondary preparatory school (11-13 years old)

(c) 4 years high school (14-17 years old)

In the teacher training programme, the teachers trained for elementary school, undergo two years of training for all subjects and some areas covered in science. Those trained for the secondary preparatory school undergo two years of training either in the Arts or Science subjects. While the teachers trained for teaching in the high school must be graduates and study four years in the University. These high school science teachers are specialized in one field only either Biology, Chemistry, Physics or Geology.

Suggested changes for science teacher training programmes:

(1) Improve the programme.

(2) During teacher training, trainees should be shown good examples of teacher teaching techniques and patterns.

(3) Emphasis on using educational technologies. There are at present teachers who do not have the skills to use scientific technologies and material and also others who do know but do not use/apply the same.

(4) The teacher-training programmes should be changed from theoretical approaches only to one that is practical and activity-oriented.

(5) Latest technology in science development, medicine, industry and agriculture in advanced countries should be adopted and adapted in the teacher-training programmes so that the teachers can disseminate these technologies in their school students.

(6) Organize workshops, conferences, seminars about teaching science to the teacher trainees.

(7) The teacher-training programmes should include in-service training for trained teachers who can undergo training while still working, for example, the teacher teaches in the morning and undergoes training in the evening.

(8) The programme should include an exchange of ideas and methods in teacher-training programmes from other countries either through country visits, conferences or educational magazines.

(9) The trainees should be taught how to make their own teaching aids from inexpensive materials.

(10) The trainees who have become trained teachers should be allowed to undergo continuous training or follow-up training to realize the progress in science; some trained teachers should also be allowed to further their studies to masters and doctorate degrees.

(D) Evaluation

At present, the evaluation programmes consist of evaluating the cognitive and knowledge parts only. What needs to be included in evaluation is the affective skills and attitudes. This can be done through interviews, practical tests (for skills) and written tests.

The evaluation of school students performance is through a common central examination. The teachers should be trained to evaluate their students effectively themselves and have the central examination system replaced. Evaluation should be a continuous process throughout the school life of the students and out not be made once a year at the end of the year.

Malaysia

In 1983, a new primary school curriculum was introduced called the KBSR. It emphasizes the basic 3 R's, communication skills, man and his environment as well as individual development. The KBSR stresses learning through group activities and introduces enrichment and remedial programmes.

The New Role of Teachers of Science

(1) Teacher as Facilitator

In the KBSR, the learning process is no longer restricted to "teacher tells, students accept". The teacher has to create an atmosphere whereby the students can investigate, question, discuss and seek guidance to come to a correct conclusion.

(2) Teacher as Designer and Maker of Teaching Aids

In carrying out the KBSR, science teachers have to equip themselves with a lot of teaching aids in order to succeed with the programme. In the training colleges, the trainees are trained not only in content and methodology, but also on various ways and means of creating their very own innovative teaching aids out of inexpensive materials.

Competencies and Skill Practised

(1) Creative in designing and producing teaching aids directly related to subject matter as well as being of inexpensive and lasting material.

(2) Skilled in creating an environment rich with potentials for students to investigate scientific phenomena/ concepts easily, with minimal guidance from the teacher.

(3) Skilled in applying science knowledge/facts taught in schools to everyday life, whenever possible.

Teacher Preparation

The following are suggested changes in preparation of science teachers in view of the new role specifications:

(1) Change in attitudes—the attitudes of trainees must be changed to that of being fully committed to their vocation.

(2) The training colleges must be able to produce teachers who throughout their careers will be willing to experiment and explore in search of better methods and techniques.

(3) Before communication skills can be developed between the teacher and his primary school students, these skills must first be developed and practised between teacher trainer and trainee in order for the trainee to emulate and further enhance these skills when he becomes a teacher.

(4) Lecturers have to be continually updated on the latest development in teaching requirements, strategies and skills before they can impart these to the trainees.

Evaluation

Evaluation in the cognitive domain is well known to all teachers but it is in the affective domain where the problem crops up. In Malaysia, trainees have to include dissemination of good values during a lesson. Wherever possible, the values should be directly related to the subject concerned. Evaluation of the effective domain can therefore only by qualitative.

Maldives

Science and technology play an important role in assisting national development goals. Taking into account the present-day trends and in view of training Madivians for the 21st century, developing science and technology is vital. The national educational goals emphasize the provision of science education which is relevant to the local environment.

Competencies and Roles of Science Teachers

Three key factors are kept in mind in developing effective training programmes for Maldivians. These are:

(1) Familiarising with upgraded content and the ability to acquire more knowledge.

(2) Grasp of educational methods.

(3) Practising of acquired skills.

Competencies in the teaching of 'Environmental Science' includes understanding of ecological principles, economic theories, national and international resources, study of man and his biosphere, awareness and implementation of public environmental policy and the role of every citizen in the process.

Educational competencies include the acquisition and use of information for behaviour and attitude formation; an understanding of the social relations of the school, trends and problems in education.

Skills required are mainly environmental problem-solving, handling of values and controversial issues, use of materials and the local environment.

Competency in methods require an understanding of its aims and objectives, identification and use of resources, understanding of assessment and feedback, identification and solution of environmental problems.

The teacher plays a multiple-role in the classroom. These are:

(1) as a model.

(2) as a psychological whether-maker in determining the social climate of the classroom.

(3) as a question-poser to stimulate thinking and interest.

Teacher Preparation

Pre-service programme

Teacher training courses in the field of pre-service education contains a methodology course and content up-grading course.

Methodology course is designed to equip teachers with the required skills and methods of teaching environmental studies in primary grades. The study and application of the scientific method is stressed in the course. Time allotted is 70 hours.

Content up-grading course is designed at improving their science background knowledge, thus giving them more confidence in teaching the content effectively. Time alloted is 60 hours.

At middle school stage, teaching is mostly conducted by expatriate teachers and local teachers trained abroad.

In-service Programme

In-service training courses in science and other subjects are presently carried out for trained and untrained teachers. These are mainly face to face training—either the trainees being brought to a particular location or the trainer moving to a particular location. The training period for such programmes is mainly two weeks. On-site teacher training is now in practice with a teacher educator being posted at a particular location for a longer period.

The changes in the curriculum, the varying patterns of science education and the national development goals together have determined the nature and scope of the science teaching programme. The revised curriculum for use in teacher training emphasising scientific skills, attitudes and values has been implemented from 1989. Furthermore, this curriculum would be reviewed in early 1991 in light of the problems and shortcomings experienced.

Other changes in the aspect of teacher education includes further training for science teacher educators, developing teacher education texts, strengthening of information network in science and technology and the realization of the urgent need for training of middle school teachers.

Evaluation

Evaluation in primary schools is mainly done through continuous assessment. However, in Grades 4 and 5 cognitive objective type tests are given in addition to it. Rating scales are prepared, having in mind both the cognitive and affective domains.

No particular instrument is yet formulated in middle school to evaluate pupil achievement in the affective domain. The instruments used at present are mostly cognitive.

Pakistan

Science Education is the most important area among the factors that influences the growth and development of very country.

In Pakistani schools, Science is taught in two stages:

(1) Primary and Middle Level (I-V and VI-VIII): Science is taught in an integrated form.

(2) Secondary Level (IX-X): Science is taught independently in 4 subjects.

Science education reform is carried out through:

(1) continuous training of teachers in a phased manner through refresher courses for 4 to 6 weeks, with emphasis on:

   (i) Developing an understanding of professional knowledge.

   (ii) Developing an understanding of educational theory to help in professional judgement and actions.

   (iii) Developing a knowledge of relationship between educational and psychological aspects of learning.

   (iv) Developing technical skills through training and practical experiences.

   (v) Developing an ability to make best use of community resources.

(2) popularization of science and technology through science museums, science clubs, science fairs, science poster contests, computer based science instruction scheme, audio-cassette textbooks.

(3) provision of optimum physical facilities and manpower resources.

(4) implementation of modified curricula, textbooks, and instructional materials.

(5) development of teaching-learning strategies.

(6) development of feedback mechanisms for effective evaluation of training programmes.

New Roles of Teachers of Science

In view of these reforms in science education, some of the science teachers' roles have been recast and modified, others have been reinforced, while new ones have evolved:

(1) a professional who continues to improve his knowledge;

(2) an educational theorist who exercises professional judgement and actions about science education and its reform;

(3) a technologist whose technical skills are most needed for teaching aids and equipment improvization;

(4) an educational psychologist with an in-depth knowledge of the relationship between educational and psychological aspects of learning;

(5) an active member of the community who makes best use of community resources;

(6) a campaigner/advertiser who popularises science and technology through science museums, clubs, fairs, camps, computer-based instruction, and audio cassette textbooks;

(7) a nurture of science talent who guides the sciences talented students to higher levels of accomplishment;

(8) an evaluator who continually seeks effective evaluation.

Competencies and Skills Needed by Science Teachers to Efficiently Perform their Roles

(1) learning skills—to process and learn new knowledge.

(2) technical skills—to productively use technological equipment and apparatus in constructing/improvizing teaching aids and devices.

(3) organising skills needed for organising in-school and out-of-school science activities.

(4) competence in using knowledge in curriculum work, instruction, evaluation, developing strategies.

(5) pedagogical skills needed for teaching practice and use of instructional materials.

(6) evaluating skills needed to evaluate science learning, identify the science talented, evaluate science programmes and projects.

Teacher Preparation

(1) Pre-Service Training

It is managed before the teacher enters the department as a regular teacher and provides a basic knowledge of teaching. The courses offered are:

- Primary Teaching Course (PTC)—to teach at the Primary School Level (Classes 1-5)
- Certificate of Teaching (CT)—to teach at the Middle Level (Classes 6-8)
- Bachelor of Science (B.Sc.) or/and Bachelor of Education (B.Ed.) to teach at the Secondary School Level. The teacher receives training either through a 14+1 model to get a one-year degree; a 12+3 model a acquire a B.Ed. after 3 years. The teacher seeks specialization in 2-subejct combinations: (a) Physics-Chemistry, (b) Physics-Mathematics, (c) Chemistry-Biology. At the end of the training course, the pre-service trainees is required to give at least 2 practice teaching lessons, 1 in each subject of specialization.

No new programmes have been instituted lately.

(2) In-Service Training

•Training is provided to teachers in service to update their knowledge of content, methods of teaching, and new developments in curriculum.

In-service training courses ranging from 1-4 weeks, or with a crash programme or yearly plan basis are offered both by the Federal and Provincial Government, subject to the availability of funds.

The newly established Institute for Promotion of Science Education and Training (IPSET) arranges special seminars, conferences, workshops for teachers, students, parents and general public.

Evaluation

New techniques of identifying and evaluating the science talented students have developed through the out-of-schools science activities (e.g. science fair, science camp, science contest, etc.).

The IPSET has taken, as one of its objectives, the development of new assessment procedures including aptitude tests, achievement tests, and attitude tests.

The in-service training is a means of providing feedback on the quality and scope of the pre-service training.

Philippines

Emerging Roles and Competencies of Science Teachers

The educational reform and current national goals are envisioned to recast the Philippine educational system more qualitatively than structurally, resulting in the emergence of new roles for teachers, particularly science teachers.

The new roles of the science teacher require him/her to become:

(1) Updated and competent in:

- facilitating the growth of scientific literacy among the general populace, which should, in turn, hasten modernization and economic progress;

- nurturing science talent for development into future manpower for science and technology.

(2) A socially-oriented teacher, who:

- works for social equity, justice, and peace through scientific development;
- strives to develop in students, participatory and decision-making skills needed for the solution of issues and problems.

(3) An environmentally-oriented science teacher, knowledgeable and skilful in:

- typing up science concepts to real-life local and global conditions;
- devising/selecting appropriate within-school activities that facilitate comprehension for more complex and higher-level ecological concepts;
- developing values and attitudes that are strongly pro-conservation and contribute to the enhancement of the environment;
- promoting participation and public action against the environmentally harmful applications of science and technology.

(4) A science teacher, knowledgeable in the psychology of learning and the intricacies of interpersonal relationships in the classroom, so as to competently:

- create an enjoyable learning atmosphere;
- inspire students to give forth their best and to develop their full potential.

(5) An ingenious and resourceful lesson planner and organizer, who:

- matches content with appropriate strategy;
- employs motivation schemes that catch and hold the interest of students;
- designs and improvises devices and equipment out of available materials.

(6) An articulate and efficient lesson presenter, who:

- by appropriate selection of language and teaching devices, facilitates learning;
- makes the lesson appear easy and enjoyable;
- accomplishes the objectives of the lesson.

(7) A perceptive evaluator, who:

- constructs test items to evaluate comprehension of science content and science methodology, laboratory skills, and development of the students' affect (feelings, interests, concerns, sense of responsibility, attitudes and values).
- is capable of translating scores and other forms of evaluation into grades.

Teacher Preparation

For admission into the teaching service at the elementary school a Bachelor of Science in Elementary Education and, in the secondary school, a Bachelor of Science in Education (B.S.Ed.) degree is required. A qualified science teacher is one who has majored in Physics, Chemistry, Biology, or Integrated (General) Science for which at least 36 units of credit have been completed.

A workshop sponsored by the Bureau of Higher Education has recommended the installation of new courses, such as Environmental Science, Earth Science, and Science and Society; the updating of textbooks and other resource materials; and the increase of hour-credits for such courses as Botany, Zoology, Chemistry and Physics for some teacher-training institutions.

Alternative strategies to increase the number of science majors in the Bachelor of Science in Education (B.S.Ed) programme are presently under consideration. One strategy is to make available for science majors a number of government scholarships. Another strategy is to organize consortia of proximally located teacher-training institutions which offer science majors programmes, with each unit offering the course as is best capable to the programme.

Evaluation

The past decade saw a great deal of improvement in test construction and test administration in science teaching. It is common place now to end a science lesson with a 3-item or 5-item quiz to find out roughly how well the students have learned the lesson. This practice compels the teacher to focus the teaching-learning transaction on the objectives of the lesson. The end result is increased effectiveness and efficiency. However, the evaluation has concentration on the cognitive domain.

It is only lately that some inroads have been made into the evaluation of the affective domain. This has come about in the form of a few workshops on test item construction such as that conducted by the National Educational Research and Testing Center (NERTC), and a more recent one conducted by the University of the Philippines, Institute for Science and Mathematics Education Department (UP ISMED). On the whole, however, paper-and-pencil testing of the affective domain of science teaching is not a common classroom practice as yet. More commonly, the science teacher makes intuitive and qualitative assessments of the students' interests, concerns, attitudes and values in science. These are written by the teacher in the students' report cards.

Sri Lanka

Science is compulsory at Junior and Senior secondary levels. It is a "science for all" and a "Science for citizens". The emphasis of the learning process of science is to learn science scientifically. The objectives of science education at this stage, in terms of learning by pupils, are to:

(1) Understand the methods and procedures followed by scientists in solving problems, and using them where necessary.

(2) Develop the scientific knowledge, skills and attitudes necessary for day to day life.

(3) Develop the knowledge, skills and attitudes required for a good personal health as well as good public health.

(4) Recognize local resources and acquire the scientific knowledge, skills and attitudes to use them efficiently.

(5) Understand the problems and dangers arising due to new technological developments, and appreciate the importance in selecting a suitable technology for Sri Lanka.

(6) Understand the impact of mankind on the environment and appreciate the importance of the equilibrium of nature.

(7) Appreciate the service of scientific institutes in developing the country and get the assistance of those institutions where necessary.

(8) Develop competence in assessing critically the information given by communication media.

(9) Develop creativity and originality.

(10) Use science efficiently in hobbies.

(11) Understand concepts and patterns in the integration of science.

(12) Build up educational foundation for further education in life.

But what is taught in school is directly linked with the examinations, which test only the knowledge component. Teacher education is one aspect where changes are possible.

The Competencies and Skills

The following need to be developed by science teachers:

(1) Understanding and appreciation of the importance of science education in building up an inquiring mind.

(2) Understanding the nature, process and procedures of science.

(3) Acquiring scientific skills and attitudes by means of activities within the laboratory and outside.

(4) Knowing the content and the objectives of grades (6-11) science syllabus and familiarizing with the handbooks, teacher guides, etc.

(5) Acquiring knowledge, developing skills and building attitudes to teach grades (6-11) syllabus and to fulfil given objectives.

(6) Using necessary psychological principles in teaching.

(7) Constructing teaching aids and improvising apparatus using low cost resources from the environment.

(8) Recognizing and using the resources available in Sri Lanka relevant to grades (6-11) syllabus and using them as required.

(9) Acquiring the skill to handle the laboratory equipment and instruments properly, efficiently and carefully.

(10) Using the environment and resources without damaging them and appreciating their conservation.

Teacher Preparation

The institutes which prepare and implement the teacher education programmes are:

(1) Teacher Colleges

There are two teacher colleges out of the seven colleges in the country. Trainees are selected from non-graduates with the qualification G.C.E. O/L and A/L with teaching experience. The training period is 2 years.

(2) Colleges of Education

Colleges of Education were started in 1985 as pre-service education institutes. The trainees are selected from G.C.E.A./L. The training consist of two-year residential and one-year internship periods.

(3) Institute of Teacher Education

The Institute of Teacher Education (ITE), under the National Institute of Education, conducts teacher-in-service training separately for trained teachers and untrained teachers.

In 1985 a new teacher education curriculum was prepared for colleges of education which emphasized the improvement of skills and attitudes of the teachers in science. In this new curriculum

(1) more time is given for laboratory and field work.

(2) a new subject area called "Education Practice" was introduced.

Evaluation

The evaluation process consists of continuous and terminal assessments. Observations, interviews and assignments are the bases of the continuous assessments.

Fifty per cent weightage is given to manipulative skills in science practicals.

Thailand

New Role of Teachers of Science

Thailand has emphasized the utilization of science and technology as the key factor for the social and economic development of the country. Thailand placed emphasis on three areas:

(1) Genetics Engineering and Biological Technology.

(2) Electronics and Computers.

(3) Material Science.

With the intention of becoming a semi/newly industrialized country, with development plans in accordance with natural resources, Thailand needs qualified manpower. The general populace needs to possess minimal skills and knowledge that will enable them to lead quality life. Then decision-makers need to have basic knowledge and understanding of science and technology and comments to the search for more information in order to make wise decision. Finally a certain percentage of high calibere manpower is needed to produce and invent technological products so that the country will be able to be self-sufficient.

In response to the country's needs, the Ministry of Education will implement the revised curricular structure nationwide in May 1991. The structure calls for more emphasis on the learning process at all levels. Also, at the secondary level, more time is allocated for effective courses. In addition, an expansion of 3 more years of education in primary schools is now being tried out in certain pilot schools.

Science teachers, the key factors to successful manpower development, need to change their roles to be more dynamic, flexible and more global.

The science teacher's expected roles are also follows:

(1) Facilitator: facilitating development of science process skills, scientific attitudes and ethics in science;

(2) innovator: being innovative in.choosing things available and putting them together and promoting scientific message using real life situation/problems;

(3) curriculum developer/implementor: develops teaching-learning materials/activities that are relevant to local development;

(4) stimulator/inspirator: stimulate students and bring about their potentials;

(5) evaluator: needs to evaluate students progress in all aspects and provide feedback to them and oneself;

(6) leader: in promoting critical thinking and decision making among students and community especially in the issues concerning local/national development that might have adverse effect on people;

(7) learner: willing to learn about changes taking place around and attempt to interpret and utilise these.

Competencies and Skills to be Learned and Practised

"Open competence" first put forward by the "Study Group Meeting on Science Curriculum and Instructional Materials Development" (UNESCO, Bangkok, November 1981) need to be acquired by/should be required for science teachers. This includes: science process skills (13 skills illustrated by SAPA) Knowledge: Ideas/concepts and applications of science and technology Way(s) of thinking: analytical, synthetical, divergent, imaginative and creative scientific attitudes ethics and values in science decision making.

Teacher Preparation

(1) Pre-service Training Programmes

Presently there are 2 degree programmes being offered.

(1.1) A 4-year education programme for high school graduates whether from universities or teachers' colleges. The programme varies from place to place. There have been no major changes in terms of the programme structure. Nevertheless, when implementation of new science curriculum occurs, time is allocated for training the student teachers before they complete the programme. More time should be allocated for:

- courses in ethics in science where is effects on human beings and their environment are heavily discussed.
- discussions and looking into development plans at the national as well as local levels.

(1.2) A 2-year education programme for diploma graduates offered by teachers' colleges.

(2) *In-service Training Programmes*

Occasional in-service training programmes are conducted in various forms:

(2.1) Face-to-face training programmes done at the institution/cluster/school-based, in response to the teachers' needs and administrators' needs.

(2.2) Distance-training programmes

These are conducted formally and informally through televised educational programmes of the open universities; newspapers; radio; television; resource books/materials, such as programmed instruction materials, videotapes. In the near future, the Institute for the Promotion of Science Teaching (IPST), in co-operation with the office of Primary Education Commission, Universities, and Teachers' College will set up a scheme for in-service training programmes for primary teachers who are mostly untrained in science teaching.

Evaluation

At present most of the evaluation is conducted internally. Science teachers at secondary level are required to assess students' behaviour in effective domain and recorded the assessment in a report card. Science process skills, unfortunately, are seldom assessed at both levels although efforts are being made to make sure that these skills are emphasized in the curriculum objectives as well as in the teaching-learning materials.

However, with the implementation of new curricular structure which provides opportunities for students to take more elective science courses, there is a trend that assessment will emphasize more on science process skills and scientific attitudes. This is due to the nature of the elective courses developed by IPST which calls for development of science process skills and scientific attitudes in students.

(Examples of these elective courses are: Various scientific toys, Mechanical and electrical toys, Science and problem-solving, Let's begin with science project, Fun with electronics, Science projects and quality of life).

Synthesis of Country Experiences

The discussions following each presentation of country experiences and the summaries presented by the participants from the member countries provided the basis for coming up with the following syntheses.

Scientific and technological developments and the aspirations of people for their further growth and influence on industrialization efforts have led to reform in science education, in most countries in Southeast Asia. Reciprocally, a reformed science and technology education plays an important role in achieving national development goals. The reform consisted in changes in approaches, strategies, and points of emphasis in the science curriculum of the elementary and secondary schools which resulted in new roles and competencies/skills demanded of science teachers, changes in science teacher education programmes, and laid emphasis on evaluation in science teaching at all levels.

New Roles of Teachers of Science

Science education reform demands that science teachers perform new roles. The science teachers' roles have increased in number and complexity. The new roles listed below have been drawn from papers on the subject submitted by the eight participating countries in this workshop.

The new roles of science teachers are as follows:

(1) Life-long learner—continuously strives to learn science and technology developments, educational and psychological developments, and local/global issues and events;

(2) innovator—sees familiar things, events in new ways; acts as change agent in school and community; is convinced of the need to change if the quality of education and of life is to be improved; must be able to adapt materials and methodologies to the local situation;

(3) implementor/developer of curriculum—interprets curriculum and translates it into student learning activities; draws ideas from the physical/biological/ cultural environment for use in interactive learning of students;

(4) perceiver of children's needs/development—is concerned with the growth and development of children; considers their needs when planning lessons;

(5) planner—plans the sequence and emphasis of the lesson;

(6) resource manager—selects and mobilizes locally available teaching materials, equipment and facilities; identifies and mobilises human resources to enhance student learning;

(7) facilitator of learning—facilitates growth of scientific literacy through the development of science process skills and the acquisition of scientific literacy;

(8) interpreter and communicator—interprets and communicates to students the concepts, processes, and the philosophy of science as stated in the curriculum; interprets and communicates to the general public the goals and activities of science education;

(9) supervisor of children's growth and development—supervises activities and tasks that provide opportunities for intellectual and physical growth of children;

(10) developer/promoter of values, attitudes, feelings, and social responsibility—develops scientific values and attitudes; must be skillful in developing the value not to abuse science so that it is harmonious with society and the value of environmental conservation;

(11) evaluator of learning outcomes—assesses the cognitive, affective, and psychomotor learnings of students in science; constructs test items; devises instruments and procedures for evaluating the affective domain and psychomotor domain;

(12) effective member in community development-initiates/ participates in projects that develop and improve the community; links science and school to the community; possess the commitment to improve the quality of life in the community.

Competencies/Skills Required of Science Teachers

The proper performance of the science teachers' new roles requires the acquisition of certain competencies and skills. Competencies and skills needed for effective teaching cut across several roles that teachers perform. These competencies and skills are listed below:

(1) science-process skills

(2) instructional skills

(3) information-processing skills

(4) decision-making skills (ethics and values in sciences)

(5) managerial skills

(6) creativity

(7) evaluating skills

(8) scientific values and attitude development skills

Changes in Science Teacher Training Programmes

Science and technology education plays an important role in assisting national development efforts. Taking into account the present day trends, the communication patterns of science education, and national developmental goals together have helped determine the nature and scope of the science teacher training programmes. With the effort to produce a need-based and culture-based science curriculum, the elementary school science curriculum has resulted in major revision. Science-kits have been introduced to be used in implementing the curriculum. With major changes in the curriculum, the need for curriculum renewal in teacher education programmes at in-service level has become an immediate and urgent need.

In general, pre-service teacher training programmes include students with 12 years of schooling, who undergo one to two years of teacher training. In some cases, it is further supplemented by one year of internship programme. Few exceptional cases are of countries having to accept 7 to 10 years of schooling, supplemented by two years and one year of teacher training respectively. This is in the case of an urgent need for teachers to fill in the role of expatriate teachers and untrained teachers.

Earlier, the trend in teacher training in science has included training in methods of teaching only, whereas the present, day training includes training in content and methods of science education. Mastering only in methods has not helped in effective transfer, due to lack of confidence in teachers themselves. Hence, content up-grading in science has been realized as an urgent need for effective teaching of science. Emphasis is greatly laid on learner-centred and activity-based approaches. Hence, laboratory practices, classroom demonstration, active participation by the students whenever possible, and field interactions have become major components of the course.

Present-day education stresses on giving equal opportunities to all students—slow learners, gifted and handicapped.

Pre-service training has a component of community interaction. That is, the would-be-teachers go to the actual situations such as mentally-related children's homes/schools; slum; factories; mines; etc. to access the need for the special-education in all such cases.

Technology education plays an important role in meeting the demands of learning and life. Familiarization of tools and improvization of tools, providing field level experiences, developing new technological materials have become important components of teacher training.

Science cannot be learnt in isolation of the environment. An understanding of the environment and ecological principles, conservation are areas included.

New institutions, either in the form of organizations or resources centres, have further supplemented training programmes. These have been established at National, Provincial or District level, depending on the numbers of teachers.

Utilization of available resources in all fields help to enrich the on-going programme in science education and provide it with more meaningful, in relation to daily life.

The above changes in science training makes it evident that students are more sensitive to the environment and to the community.

In-service training is imparted in a number of ways. It includes summer classes which is planned to coincide with school holidays. This can be one of the methods of face-to-face training. The other type of face-to-face training is, instead of removing teachers from their attached schools, teachers educator/trainer are being sent over for a fixed period to provide training.

Distance education has proved one of the most effective ways is imparting in-service education in countries especially where transportation is difficult due to geographical locations.

In case of in-service training involving large number of trainees, this has resulted in weak results or dilution of what was imparted initially, so direct training is always more fruitful than using a mediator.

It is virtually impossible to give training to an exceptionally large number of practising teachers by one organization. This not only faces the constraints of the resources but also it is unmanageable.

Therefore, help of different institutions are sought fast. Most commonly the 3-tire in-service programme is in practice:

Orientation of Key Persons or Master Trainers; Training of Resource Persons, and Training of Teachers.

Attempts have been made to provide locally relevant materials for use in teacher training. Materials printed in local language would serve as useful teaching materials in enriching their knowledge.

Evaluation

Changes in curriculum often receive a setback due to the rigid examination systems. Essay type of test has led on to objective type tests with no change in the level of testing, still leading to testing of knowledge at the cognitive level.

Several countries seem to accept continuous evaluation. But this, too, has proved difficult to implement due to teacher unwillingness or unpreparedness. The most important reason is pupil/teacher ratio being very high, multi-grade teaching catering to a large number of different abilities and age groups, and also teachers having to teach in more than one shift.

Societal perception has also to be considered in finalising a method of evaluation. Parents' and societies' concern for students to do well in school is almost common everywhere. Hence, their expectation and an understanding of the method of evaluation is necessary. Any sort of evaluation tool prepared, need to be well understood and perceived by the society.

Abolition of annual examinations, contrary to expectations, had a decrease in achievement level of students. These examinations have acted as motivators to learning on the part of the students' and the teachers' efforts input in the teaching-learning process being greater to get the desired outcome from the evaluation.

Changes in the curriculum can be further supplemented with improvements brought about in the methods of teaching and for effective results, the evaluation methods for implementation need to be improved upon further.

2

Teacher Training for Science and Technology Education Reform: Trends and Issues

Introduction

National development in third world countries is closely dependent on the availability of literate and capable manpower. Development is no longer perceived in isolation to scientific and technological process. Consequently, elementary education is no longer viewed as mere learning 3R's or obtaining a certificate from an institution. These nations need a broad base of talents nurtured in a rational and scientific climate and environment. The pace of development is closely linked to the extent of assimilation of scientific and technological developments, growth of scientific temper and national capabilities to develop appropriate indigenous technologies. Towards this, a basic understanding of specific developmental needs is to be appreciated. It is now appreciated that no growth model can just be transplanted from some developed countries into a developing country, and more importantly, only higher level technological and scientific personnel alone are not sufficient for universal distribution of the benefits of scientific and technological developments. It is these realizations which prompted the third world countries to consider seriously the need for providing science education to all children up to elementary/secondary level.

This has been a very bold and positive development in the context of the countries which were and several still are, struggling to universalize basic education itself. These nations are still facing obstacles in terms of resource crunch, including economic, social and cultural handicaps.

It may appear intriguing to recall at this stage that just a few years ago, girls were not expected to study mathematics and science even in elementary classes. There were situations when boys were compulsorily required to study mathematics but the same was optional for girls. This illustrates the path traversed by the present-day science education, now being remodelled as science and technology education. The perceptions of science have changed amongst the teachers and the perceptions of science from the community are also now very different. Science is no more for the elites; it is for all. It no longer prepares pupils for next higher class or grade, but for life. And once this is accepted, science can no longer be a distant and difficult jargon of laws, rules and hypotheses only, but of everyday assistance in improving the quality of life through judicious understanding and appropriate utilization. Science and Technology education has now to be oriented, reshaped and linked to comprehensive national development goals. Content of science and technology is to be determined by a large variety of expectations that the society has from it. Each country has to ensure availability of trained manpower, develop self-reliance in science and technology capability, encourage innovations in basic science as well as relevant technologies appropriate to national socio-economic objectives and needs. They have to prepare a much wider base of people equipped with basic appreciation of scientific approach, scientific temper and enhanced creativity. This could be achieved by science for all, technology being accepted, adopted, adapted and utilized by all. In developing countries, the demand on and from science and technology is essential of amelioration of human conditions, as a necessary ingredient to enable all people to contribute to national development.

A. The New Role of Teachers of Science Linked to the Development Processes in the Member Countries and Towards Meeting its Comprehensive Demands of Life and Learning

Consequences of rapid developments in science and technology and their impact in socio-cultural life may include considerable impacts on the human approach to life itself. The problem before each one of us in the future would be how to make gainful use of these developments. We can certainly visualize the exploitation of knowledge, its management, universalization and transfer of the relevant and useful developments to the next generation. The last one obviously is largely the prerogative of the teacher and for valid reasons of the science teacher. He has to handle new inputs in curriculum, larger numbers of pupils in the classrooms and meagre resources to manage these. Even within these constraints, he has to nurture the potential of his pupils towards their all-round development. He 'teaches' to enable the young ones

- to react to changing environment with rationality and scientific temper;
- to foresee the future environment, newer technologies and their impact, and identify such elements as are likely to contribute to it significantly; and
- to anticipate such contributions on their own part, as would influence the future environment in a positive direction.

This obviously cannot be achieved by teachers, so long as the mere transfer of knowledge is taken by them as their major professional obligation. There is no dearth of such learned individuals who opine and see a neck-to-neck race between the present-day education and catastrophe. The only way to salvation instead of catastrophe is again geared to the above-mentioned objectives.

Practically, every nation has attempted revision in teacher education programmes, particularly in science teacher preparation during the last few decades. These changes in teacher education are part of the comprehensive changes in educational structures, curriculum revision/renewal, strengthening of institutions, including training institutions and other efforts in professional development of teachers. As the curriculum development is a continuous process in all stages of education, so is the process of curriculum renewal in the teacher education programmes at pre-service as well as at in-service stages. Probably, the changes in teacher training require greater insight and in-depth appreciation of all other changes, to make these programmes more effective. In the teacher is not fully equipped and trained to handle the new curricula, the curriculum transaction would be weak and, consequently, the learning in schools inadequate. Teacher education institutions have to continuously update their understanding of the curriculum-renewal processes as well as the demands and expectations from the community on the educational system. The training strategies have to be governed by both these considerations. The science teacher is, however, no longer a mere transactor of curriculum in the classroom, but much more than that.

Science teaching was conceptually replaced by learning science, learning by doing, activity methods, child-centred approach and others. All these were attempts in the right direction and could be considered as the outcome of past experiences in science teaching and appreciation of the current learning needs of children. As indicated above, the science teacher prepares children to face real life situations and not only for getting good grades or marks in annual examination. He is preparing the child for an adult life which is closely and intimately related to the changes taking place in his immediate environment. Further, he has to be prepared to receive continuously such changes, developments and their impacts in his adult life in the future. Scientific and technological developments are not divorced form social, cultural and behavioural aspects. Consequently, skills and competencies like making a point in conversation, making adjustments, information-processing, communication, group behaviour and management are crucial to teaching and learning of science and consequentially for the science teacher.

Teachers' Own Initiative

Without going into the technicalities, let us attempt to perceive steps which the teachers of science and technology can initiate themselves without much external assistance.

Some of these probably could be listed as:

- The teacher must observe his own way of work and analyse the same to incorporate such changes he considers expedient.
- The teacher must be convinced of the need to change; his approach, style, habits, and even personality.
- Teachers must appreciate the necessity of not only teaching but also 'talking' to his pupils and effectively listening to them. Listening could be a positive reinforcement in the style and approach of the teacher.
- The activities involving a pupil's attitude required extra effort. Resource mobilization and its appropriate utilization also depend upon this willingness.
- A basic understanding of the behaviour and background of the pupil is as necessary in science teaching as in any other discipline. In imparting instruction in science at the elementary stage, one has to break several barriers.
- No one else can give the teacher a methodology suitable in all aspects to handle a particular topic, particular group of pupils or specific situations; he himself has to evolve the same. He must by prepared for modifications at each stage and through every source.
- Science teaching and technological skill development has to be interesting, understandable and human. No approach, style or methodology can afford to neglect this aspect. Efforts are to be made to link it to the individual's life and his environment.
- The science and technology teacher must understand and appreciate the role of the appropriate language in his effort. Ability to communicate in a language within the reach of the child is a must.
- The teacher must guard against becoming a weak teacher as he grows in years and experience. He has to remain open to new experiences and learning situations to requip himself with all available sources.

- The science teacher has a distinct role and he has to know about this himself as well as make others realise the same.

Identification of Teachers' Specific Role

Identification of the roles of a teacher could be viewed from different angles. There is no dearth of those who are sincerely convinced that their job is to teach (only). On the other end are those who find it hard to single out positive attributes which a teacher could safely avoid. The list of expectations from teachers becomes alarmingly long, often probably beyond the reach of individual human beings.

As we examine the role of a teacher in developing countries, several of them still struggling to universalize elementary education, we find justification in a much broader and wider role expectation of the teachers by communities and learners. Where else is the other resource? We discuss some of the more pronounced roles of teachers.

(i) Curriculum Developer

From a centrally prescribed curriculum, usually available in term of textbooks and official instructions, this is a revolutionary change. Not only are teachers being involved in the process of centralized curriculum development, they are being provided the opportunity and responsibility to develop their own curriculum, relate it to real life situations, design locally-relevant activities, utilize local resources and encourage children to bring in their life experiences and relate them to the curriculum. The teacher is the designer of activities himself. He is not only the implementor of the curriculum but its developer as well. He organizes activities, arranges community expertise available to school, improvises wherever necessary and organizes the entire activity.

(ii) Motivator

The teacher is often in situations where resources are inadequate and need to be mobilized. No innovative teaching-learning situation could be conceived unless the teacher is keen to innovate. Once he has thought of requisite resources and designed an innovative situation, his job gets confined to motivating the target group. What better method could be to motivate than to motivate by example. He could visualize interesting and rewarding learning situations, expose children to materials that would generate curiosity, explain natural phenomenon and provoke children to discover more. There could be no limits if the children are motivated to know things around them, observe them, analyse and bring their own interpretation and learning to the teacher. The teacher could also be a partner in such investigations.

Only a motivated teacher could be a motivator of students or of a community. To provide motivation to others, he himself has to be an investigator and explorer.

(iii) Teacher as Learner

A teacher is a life long 'student'. Teaching is one profession which could literally be enjoyed by the practitioners as they have practically all decisions regarding methods, strategies, techniques of curriculum transaction to be decided by themselves individually. With his pupils, a teacher is totally and completely autonomous. It is his latent potentialities which could convert the learning process into really enjoyable and interesting, burden-free situation for the children and for himself also. Naturally this requires much homework on the part of the teacher. He has to constantly update himself, learn from all possible sources available to him. He has to keep his eyes and ears open. The best learning that comes to a teacher is from his pupils. Pupils' reactions, questions, interventions, degree of interest and rapport with the teacher could be converted into potential instruments of evaluation of the teacher's own learning. A sensitive teacher, fully conscious of his responsibilities is bound to make all efforts to learn more and more. The situations now are such that without willingness to learn, no teacher can remain even at 'average' performance level and is destined to become a week teacher. The system has to provide necessary motivation and opportunities for all teachers to continuously become more equipped teachers.

(iv) Community Collaborator

This reflects best the changing demands on the teacher and the widening of his roles and responsibilities. He is the resource person for the community, and the parents as well. They know he shapes the future of their children. They go to him to help them find solutions to their own problems as well as to interpret for them the new changes that are affecting their lives. To perform this role, the teacher needs to understand himself, the existing socio-economic and cultural scenario, perceive the possible impacts of technological changes and prepare the community to accept only those which would not only provide short-term gains but would be of lasting benefit. Several of these situations would require a good number of precautions to be taken. Only the teacher could explain, demonstrate and convince regarding its necessity.

Here is a chance for the teacher to establish a close working relationship with the school and the community. This would mean mutual accountability, which in turn, would really contribute in the effective functioning of the school.

(v) Evaluator

Evaluation no longer remains a simple routine activity. It requires in-depth understanding and adequate preparedness. The objectives of evaluation are no longer confined to testing of cognitive attainments; it includes cognitive and equally importantly, the affective domain. In view of the drastic change in the very objectives of curriculum transactions, the learning in affective domain has become very prominent as the majority of learners are not going for higher education but are being prepared for life. As such, it is implicit to evaluate their interest, attitudes, values and ability in decision-making. On the psychomotor side, the manipulative and laboratory skills are to be developed and consequently evaluated.

In majority of the situations, the teachers are to conduct formative evaluation which provides diagnostic feedback to the teacher himself. The summative evaluation could be conducted the same as it has been in practice for long, though its techniques and procedures would be different now. However, it is the formative evaluation which requires the teacher to be ready to investigate, pose his own questions; identify and select situations and problems; design activities; and finally, make decision to enable him to assess what he, in fact, desires to assess. It is this continuous evaluation of pupil achievement which could help teacher in decision-making at various stages to improve learning.

B. Competencies and Skills which must be Learnt and Practised by Science Teachers

The new role expectations demand new skills and competencies of science teachers as they are, in addition to their curriculum oriented roles, supposed to be the guides of the community in terms of new developments taking place in the fields of agriculture, medicine, communication, household technological gadgets, and others. This implies that they need competencies and skills that with equip them to meet the demands of the community which is striving everywhere to improve their quality of life. While individual teachers have played such roles on their own initiative, the sheer pace of transformation makes it implicit on teacher-education programmes to equip all teachers with such skills that would enable them to meet the comprehensive demands of learning and life. Initially, when science became part of school curriculum, it was perceived as something meant only for a select few; those who would go for higher education and become scientists. This is no longer the case now. It is fully realized that science has to be "science for all" and as such its content, methodology, and objectives need a thorough redefinition. This has been attempted or is being attempted. At present we have gone at least one step ahead and it is now not only 'science for all' but 'science and technology for all'. From universalization of elementary education, we have moved to universalization of science education.

In terms of the science teaching competencies, it would be desirable to specifically identify the requisite skills for each stage/area, as no one particular set of the same, may be universally applicable everywhere. Wherever a curriculum development, or renewal process is taking place, the requisite competencies have to be identified and classified. This in fact, helps in the renewal of teaching-learning material for teachers and teacher-educators. This would include self-learning material for teacher-educators, hands-on experience and also for developing analytical process skills among the teacher-trainees. Genuine problem-solving situations are rarely visualized in such training programmes. While theoretically we might have brought it in textbooks, it is rare to find exercises where teacher-educator and teacher-trainees work together to find solutions to the problems for which solutions are genuinely not known to both; as otherwise, the exercise often becomes a routine repeat performance to the teacher. The teacher-trainees are to be given an opportunity which would allow full play of divergent thinking required to anticipate the problem situations, and identify alternative strategies to find different solutions. There is indeed an intense need to develop this aspect of teacher-training process, in the context of which the question of competencies has been often discussed. In the Study Group Meeting on Science Curriculum and Instructional Materials Development in 1981, it was observed that" . . . in order to adapt to the rapidly changing and progressing age and to contribute to the socio-economic progress, it is important for all the students to acquire certain competencies and attitudes to solve problems, processing appropriately fast expanding information and to think creatively. For education to assist in this, school science education programmes will have to provide for teaching-learning experiences through a variety of methods which will help develop concepts and skills which are flexible and applicable to a wide variety of situations rather than limited in scope." The requisite competencies and attitudes were subsumed under four major processes, namely:

- Information-processing
- Problem-solving
- Creativity
- Decision-making.

These and a few other alternative formulations were discussed by the group in detail. It was agreed upon that it would be rather artificial to attempt separate classification of skills and competencies. While these could be technically distinguished, none could overlook the wide extent of overlap in each case. The group then proceeded to discuss some of these skills/competencies considered essential for the lower secondary stage.

(i) Information Processing and Utilization

The textbook or the teachers guide/manual are no longer sufficient to equip the teacher of science. So much more is available, changing and affecting the learners; which just can no longer be ignored. The developmental sectors are producing materials relevant to the community and hence to the teacher. The mass media is influencing not only the technological front but also the social and cultural fronts. The situation before the teacher is manifold. First, he is supposed to identify and locate sources of information, establish necessary channels to procure these and then proceed to sieve out the relevant and useful components.

The primary sources often do not provide information within the comprehension of the target group. The teacher here becomes the interpreter of the same to the groups of his concern. Most of these would pertain to the fields of medicine, agriculture, industry, energy, nutrition, health and these could expectedly change the quality of life of the children as well as adults. The salient and relevant aspects of these newer technologies will have to be internalized by the teacher as only then can he do justice to his efforts.

In their actual life, opportunities for school teachers in access to information include first hand evidence in real situations, e.g. school surroundings, problems in the community, information from secondary sources such as newspapers, magazine, radio programmes, T.V. programmes, etc. and information from tertiary sources such as data centres, information centres. It is essential that teachers' skills be developed in effectively selecting appropriate information to be used in their teachings.

(ii) Creativity

All children are endowed with this natural gift. The objective in developing this skill would provide situations which would nurture creativity. These would be the settings that provide full opportunity to develop the inherent creative talents of children. When a young child visits a sea shore for the first time, his imagination, resulting out of his observations, immediately proceeds to establish concrete relationships, find solutions and explanations. Even the list of observations alone would be unending. The teacher could in turn, always keep at list of such creativity-promoting settings.

A bullock cart, horse driven carriage, makes noise. Greasing or oiling are the solutions. What is beyond that? Could everyone afford it? Is it readily available? Identification of such unsolved problems which have multiple solutions and are linked to community needs is one right approach for the teachers. In the curriculum context it could provide themes for discussion of multi-disciplinary nature within the classroom as well. Accepting new challenges (problems help in this approach) also prepares children to handle 'risky' situations and problems.

It is implicit that in creativity nurturing activities, probing, analytical and open-ended questions could not only lead to solutions but also permit full scope for the children to formulate alternative solutions.

The technological developments, reaching every habitation and community, provide ample scope for identifying creativity-promoting settings. Episodes from history of science, particularly the way scientists work, could infuse new enthusiasm. This could also exploit the idealism and desire to do something "big" which is inherently present among all children.

One major point which deserves serious attention on the part of the teachers is his assessment of pupils' response. As an example, consider a child who comes forward with few alternative solutions patterned similarly while another, after a thoughful consideration, comes forward with only one solution. The child's solution is away from routine thinking and establishes new connections. Needless to say, the child has provided much pronounced evidence of creativity than the other. The distinction is to be utilized by the teacher to determine his inputs.

(iii) Managerial skills

More often than not an elementary teacher works under constraints and handicaps, such as lack of resources and teaching/learning materials. On his own professional side, opportunities for updating himself with new development, techniques and technologies rarely make an appearance before him in terms of in-service education or orientation programmes. For children, the teacher is a 'Mr/Miss Know All' and mobilizer of all resources apart from being a fountain-head of knowledge and must answer to their curiosities and questions. How could this situation be managed effectively?

The school education systems mostly attempt to play a supervisory role, collect certain data or utilize teachers for performing other roles, as in elections, census, etc. These systems rarely provide professional support, and consequently, the teachers are left to fend for themselves. Only he can help himself. His role as a resource mobilizer comes into play at this stage. He needs to utilize community support, expertise and skills available with others to be utilized for the benefit of the children. A visit to a small industrial establishment could provide much more insight and education than what could be achieved over weeks in classroom situations. To anticipate learning in such situation, to arrange for the same by co-ordinating with different agencies and individuals require a well-developed skill of persuading people to utilize their inherent tendency to help children and contribute as a societal obligation.

The other aspect would be to organize learning materials, tools, science kits, often from the school education system itself. Subsequent replacements, improvizations would need particular attention. This phenomenon has been observed in several countries when the limited enthusiasm towards activities dies down to 'wear and tear'.

A very major role in the total management of the school is played by teachers. However, the head of the school, his commitment, rapport with other teachers and willingness to apply himself to the tasks ahead plays the most vital role. He must be fully conversant with the needs of science teachers and the demands on or expectation from them.

(iv) Decision-making

The development activities and their consequences have brought in sharp focus the need for critical level decision-making from local level to international level. The degradation of environment is one case in point that indicates the damage resulting out of decisions aimed at short-term gains which were fated to result in long-term damages. Use of insecticides, pesticides, chemical fertilisers, location of industries and numerous others require a sharp decision-making preparedness of the young persons. It is a need, not only for the individual's own situations, but may also help in initiating or participating in people's actions and community decisions.

The first skill required towards decision making is that of information processing, judging to ensure accurate and adequate information and recognizing the consequences of the alternative possibilities that may exist in a certain situation. The objective assessment of short-term or long-term, consequences will not often be easy to assess and may call for collective decision-making. The teacher may be the person to present objectively, the information, possibilities and alternatives before community. His intervention would carry weight and hence enhance his responsibility further. His communication skills would also be brought into action in these situations. He has to have a basic understanding of group behaviour, particularly in societies which do not find consonance among traditions, beliefs and technological impacts. Social sensitivities make objective decision-making complex. Mature and sensitive handling becomes expendient.

What a teacher does in the classroom situation is the preparation for the above. He may not be handling 'mature' individuals but he is amongst dynamic, creative, free-from-prejudice minds which could definitely be much more objective in individual and collective decision-making. Once prepared to do so, they may give better evidence of objective decision-making in the future.

(v) Science Process Skills

One of the aims of science teaching and learning is to develop within the learners the scientific capabilities of which science process skills may be the most explicit components.

Science process skills, as prescribed by the AAAS comprise the basic skills and the integrated skills, to be presented by pupils.

The pupils learn to develop their basic skills in:

- Observing
- Using space/time relationship
- Classifying
- Using numbers
- Measuring
- Communicating
- Predicting
- Inferring

The integrated skills make use of the basic skills in the development of more sophisticated processes of:

- Formulating hypothesis
- Controlling variables
- Intepreting data
- Defining operationally
- Experimenting

Behaviourally, pupils should be able to perform the following to demonstrate their science process skills:

(a) Basic Skills

- *Observing*—"Identify and name/find out properties of an object or situation by using their senses."
- *Using space/time relationships*—"Construct drawings of common 3-dimensional shapes."
- *Classifying*—"Identify and name observable properties of objects which could be used to classify the objects."
- *Using numbers*—"State and apply rules for expressing the mean of a set of numbers, rates as ratios, and the decimal equivalents (or approximations) of ratios."
- *Measuring*—"Demonstrate the use of simple measuring instruments to measure length, mass, and time."

- *Communicating*—"Describe the properties of an object in sufficient detail so that another person can identify it."
- *Predicting*—"State predictions by interpolating between observed events or extrapolating beyond the range of observe events."
- *Inferring*—"Identify inferences that should be accepted, rejected or modified on the basis of additional observations."

(b) Integrated Skills

- *Formulating hypothesis*—"Construct a hypothesis that is a generalization of observations or of inferences."
- *Controlling variables*—"Identify and name variables which were not held constant in the description of an investigation, although they varied in the same way in all treatments or were randomized."
- *Interpreting data*—"Describe certain kinds of data, using the mean, median, and range; construct predictions, inferences, or hypotheses from this information."
- *Defining operationally*—"Construct an operational definition which adequately describes a procedure, concept, object, or property of an object in the context in which it is used."
- *Experimenting*—"Construct a question to be answered, construct a test that will provide data to answer the question, identify variables to be controlled, construct operational definitions, demonstrate the test, and collect and interpret data from a given set of observations. Construct a report of the experiment."

It is essential that science teachers also acquire and be able to demonstrate science-process skills. Moreover, they must have a clear and systematic view of how scientific capabilities may be developed. They must also have a clear cut and systematic view of teaching competence in conducting activities for the development of these skills.

C. Changes in Science Teacher Preparation Programmes in the Light of New Role Specifications and Towards Developing Necessary Competencies

Programme Objectives

The curriculum changes and renewals in member countries have also resulted in perceptible changes in the objectives, structure and contents of science teacher preparation programmes. A broad overview would indicate that, generally speaking, the following are included in the objectives of teacher preparation programmes:

- develop an understanding of the nature of science and take a holistic view of science.
- acquire sound scientific literacy and appreciation of social and ethical aspects of science and technology.
- analyse the content in terms of concepts, activities and applications.
- plan suitable activities, mobilize appropriate resources, and organize activities.
- design, identify and implement strategies aimed at developing science process skills.
- relate learning experiences and learning activities to the developmental stage and the age of the learner.
- design and organize activities to help children with specific needs, i.e. slow learners, gifted, physically and mentally handicapped.
- encourage learner-centred and activity-based approaches.
- utilize learning experiences from life and immediate environment of the learners.
- develop suitable outlines, procedures and methods of evaluation and provide feedback for remedial action.
- identify real-life situations, solutions of which are undertermined and probably could be obtained by teacher and learner working together.

- improvize, handle and utilize low-cost teaching learning aids to make the learning experiences and environment joyful.
- appreciate the use of educational technology and also encourage the children to utilize the same.
- familiarize himself with the curricular changes taking place.
- equip himself to act as interpreter of new ideas and technologies to the community.
- find out the relationships of science and technology with health, agriculture, industry, nutrition and other aspects of living.
- use the scientific knowledge in correcting false beliefs, prejudices and practices.
- develop decision-making and problem-solving skills and utilize these in daily life situations.

Programme Structures

Structures of programmes vary in member countries depending upon several factors. Eleven or twelve years of school education followed by one, or two or four years of pre-service education summarizes the different programmes and trends. In some cases this includes internship of varying durations. There are instances when two years of teacher education is followed by another year of supervised teaching in actual school situations.

There is another very significant aspect to teacher preparation programmes which concerns teaching of science in remote and far flung areas and also to children of deprived, depressed and underserved people. These numbers are not small. Teachers who are trained in pre-service programmes are unwilling to serve in these areas. Even if rarely some of them agree, they find themselves alien in the social and cultural climate and as such their stay is cut short by circumstance if not by unwillingness.

Certain bold decisions have been taken to cater to the needs of these groups. Minimum entrance qualification has been reduced to ten years from twelve years. Young children from the concerned areas are given preference at the time of entrance to elementary teacher-training institutions. Certain incentives are also provided to them. To look after the girls education, which deserves top priority in view of their abysmally low literacy rate, certain short term strategies have been evolved. Girls from these communities are encouraged to complete eight/nine years of education and then provided intensive orientation and upgradation by the state to enable them to serve their own communities and provide education to the children. They are encouraged to enhance their qualifications through correspondence enrichment programmes and also by being provided with opportunities to join regular schools.

The importance and need for in-service education for teachers, who joined schools after receiving pre-service teachers training, is now fully realized and infrastructures have been set up to cater to this aspect. The programmes normally focus on teaching methods and approaches, educational technology, child-centred and activity orientation of curriculum transaction strategies, development of vocational skills, improvization and design of low cost equipment, community interactions and others. Wherever numbers are large, a multiple tier strategy in terms of training of master trainers, resource persons, and finally the teachers is adopted.

Institutional Infrastructure

Countries have developed national level institutions catering to the changing needs of practically all aspects of school education. Those with larger population have corresponding institutions at state level and also at district level. It is increasingly being realized that there is a need to have comprehensive elementary level teacher training institutions for such a viable area or number of teachers, which could be easily accessible to them and meet the demands of pre-service as well as in-service education of these teachers. Such an institution could perform the following illustrative functions:

1. Training and orientation of the following target groups:

- Elementary school teachers (both pre-service and in-service education)
- Head masters, Heads of clusters schools, and Officers of Education Department dealing with elementary education.
- Instructors and supervisors of non-formal, part-time education (induction level and continuing education).
- Members of education communities at various levels in the area, community leaders, youth and other volunteers.
- Resource persons who will conduct suitable programmes for the target groups mentioned above.

2. Academic and resource support to the elementary education system in the district in other ways, e.g. by:

- extension activities and interaction with the field,
- provision of services of a resource and learning centre for teachers and instructors,
- development of locally relevant materials, teaching aids, evaluation tools, etc., and
- serving as an evaluation centre for elementary schools and programmes of non-formal and part-time education.

3. Action research and experimentation to deal with specific problems of the area in achieving the objectives in the areas of elementary education. Assessment studies in community needs, attitudes, environmental changes, and external influences.

Such an institution needs to be provided with well-equipped laboratories and well trained staff. Its unit-wise structure could be on the following suggestive patterns:

- Pre-service Teacher Education Branch—consisting of faculty members in the "Foundations" area as well as in various school subjects (excluding work experience).

- Work Experience Branch, including technological skills training.
- Area Resource Unit for Part-time and Non-formal Education.
- In-service Programmes, Field Interaction and Innovation Coordination Branch.
- Curriculum, Material Development and Evaluation Branch.
- Educational Technology Branch.
- Planning and Management Branch.

To be really functioning and dynamic, basic essential facilities need to be provided for. Some of these could be listed as follows:

- Library and documentation.
- Methods laboratories for Physical and Life Sciences.
- A work-shed and garden/farm for work experience activities.
- Equipment for Education in Visual and Performing Arts.
- Playgrounds and equipment for Physical Education and Sports.
- Audio-visual aids.
- Computer Room.
- Equipment for education of the handicapped.
- Special materials and equipment relevant for Part-time and Non-formal Education.

These institutions will run regular programmes of pre-service, in-service and the staff would be fully acquainted with the local area-level situations, the community needs and would relate the learning to local resources and needs. The trainees would be familiarized with changes taking place in the quality of life, both positive and negative, and shall be helped to prepare for 'life.'

Specific Strategies for Training of Science Teachers

An institution like the one suggested above would be fully equipped to look after the training needs of all elementary teachers including science teachers. However, it may be worthwhile to discuss in some detail as to how the stage to train the teachers of science ought to be arrived at. The development of curriculum, science kit and tool kit, and training of teachers are to be viewed comprehensively and attempted sequentially. A core co-ordination group could start the process of curriculum renewal through an academic group including curriculum developers, subject teachers, teacher educators and practising teachers. Simultaneously, the other group consisting of technical experts, skilled persons as well, may begin the exercise of identifying technical and manipulative components. The two groups could interact regularly. While the first one would proceed to develop textbooks, teachers guides and supplementary materials, the second would be ready with a science kit and tool kit, along with production details. Both outputs could be tried out in schools simultaneously and the tryout would lead to comprehensive co-ordinated revision on both sides, resulting in their being ready for use in teacher training, likewise the textual materials and also the kits. Training programmes must precede the use of the materials and kits in schools. At the same time, there is always a need to ensure that adequate number of such materials are available in schools by the time the teacher is back from the orientation.

Teacher Transformation

The teacher is the principal means for proper implementation of educational programmes and appropriate transaction of curricula within the classroom and outside the classroom. Expectations from teachers are very many. The changing times have enhanced their roles and responsibilities. It is, as such, imperative that the teacher preparation programmes take due cognisance of the changing scenario and provide such education and training to the trainees that will equip them to meet the new challenges. While pre-service programmes are very important, equally significant are the in-service programmes which can really update the teacher and keep him abreast with the new developments, particularly in the field of science and technology relevant to the community. The teacher has to remain 'aware and awake'. Apart from training programmes, this would also depend upon his own interest, aptitudes, and creative abilities. Rational and scientific thinking will definitely keep him dynamic and make him receiver of new ideas, techniques and technologies.

The structure and content of elementary level teacher education programmes, at pre-service stage and also at in-service stage need to be examined with respect to the components, contents and methods of science education, skill and technical training. There are still programmes at elementary education level which practically provide no training in science and skill components. Unless and until these are provided to all the teachers, they may not be in a position of develop requisite scientific approach, rational outlook, willingness to change and capacity to analyse, interpret and accept change.

In countries where the number of institutions and children are pretty large, mobilization of community resources is a must. To achieve this, there is greater need for understanding the demands of the community by the school. Equally important is the need to prepare the community to provide for the needs of the school. This is a situation of mutual accountability of the learning systems and the community where the teacher becomes the prime mover on both sides. Towards this, it would be necessary to have well-equipped learning centres, school complexes, institutes of training, fully equipped to train in techniques, technical skills and technologies. These institutions should be willing to open their facilities to the community and accept their problems. These facilities need to be available to all the teachers on a regular basis. Further, it may be worthwhile to encourage individual teachers to take up innovative, experimental and action research projects which need to be assisted in various ways. This would generate self-confidence of teachers and achieve teacher transformation which is the basic aim of all teacher education programmes.

D. Evaluation in Science which Takes into Account Both Cognitive and Affective Domains Effectively

The understanding of 'assessment' in schools has grown over the years, from the narrow knowledge of 'terminal examinations' to much broader area, evaluation of the pupils

TRAINING TEACHERS OF SCIENCE AND TECHNOLOGY

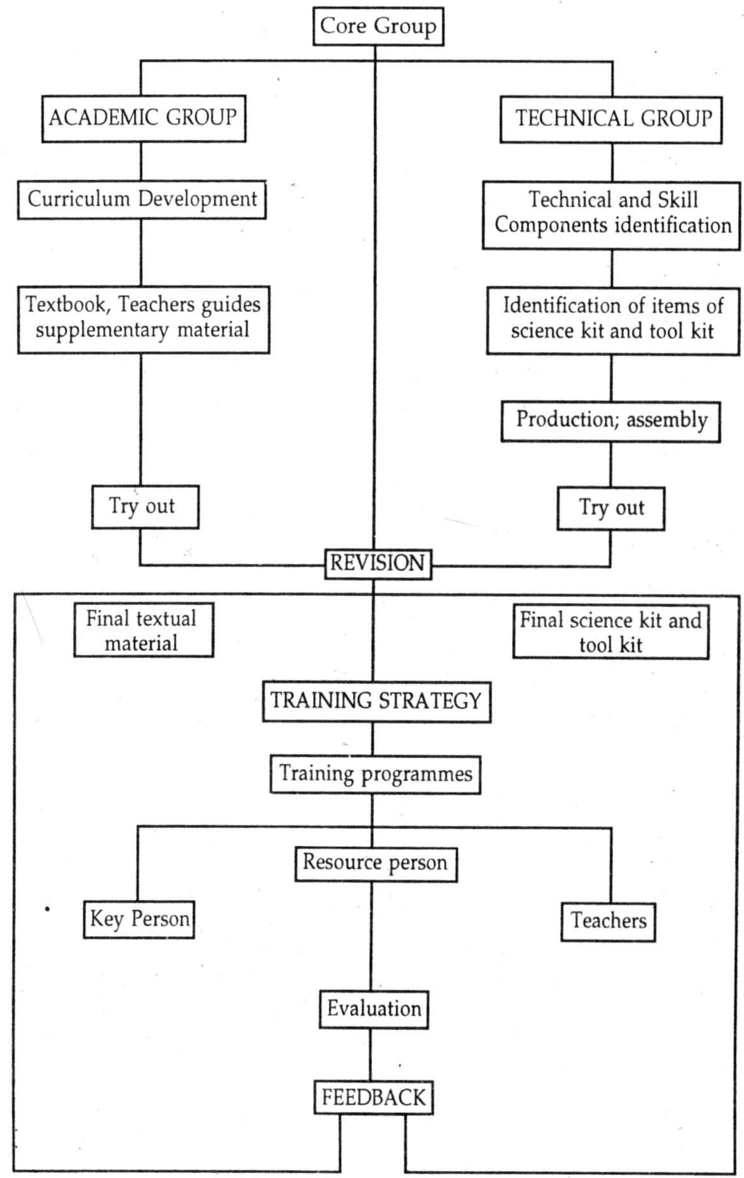

'achievements'. These are then compared to expected achievements pertinent to the stage of the learner. At this stage, rather through this exercise, the teacher foresees and visualizes remedial inputs, whenever considered necessary.

The most visible demonstration of assessment could be seen in any active and alert classroom situation. The way teacher responds to queries, questions or answers of a child indicates an 'evaluation' to the child. The child notices whether his intervention was liked, discouraged, used as an idea in developing the lesson, or simply ignored. These provides definite indicators to the learners. These could also be equally, if not more significantly, important to the teacher, who in fact 'sees' the levels of achievement of each individual learner. The situation could be termed as 'child referenced' and provides immediate feedback—both to the teacher and the learner. Situations where standardized tests are administered, the basis is the 'average' expected learning for the particular stage and the outcomes of such a test indicate relative achievements of the learners. This, unfortunately, is the most prevalent practice and is equally responsible for the negative image of evaluation; hence the need for multifarious efforts to improve upon the methods, practices and procedures of assessing the learning outcomes.

The Objectives

It is now universally accepted that the purpose of assessment is essentially to help learning. Once it is so, it ipso facto becomes a part of teaching-learning process, being carried within the school or outside the school. Learning does not take place in the presence of teachers only. However, they are in a much better situation to observe more closely and could provide feedback not only to the learners but also to parents and others interested in keeping themselves abreast of the progressive attainments of the learner. The concept of continuous comprehensive evaluation is a consequence of these considerations.

In practice, there are few success stories of continuous comprehensive evaluation. There are situations where terminal evaluation has been discarded in favour of continuous comprehensive evaluation which has not yet taken off. The learning of the children has obviously suffered in these situations. Without going into technical and theoretical aspects of evaluation, it may be worthwhile to discuss what actually can be 'ascertained' and 'obtained' by the teacher out of the regular teaching and learning situation in and outside the classroom. In an activity based learning situation, the following could help the teacher to know—

(i) how children proceed

(ii) how they progress at different stages

(iii) the way they derive inferences at various stages by interpreting situations

(iv) the initiatives for further activities that some from them

(v) the relevance of the activity to real life situations as perceived by the learner

(vi) concrete suggestions for changes and for applications.

This could only be a suggestive list. In fact, it is the teacher himself who is to determine the points of 'observations' and 'participation'. He 'knows' what to look for, how to get the requisite details, match it to the stage of progress of the child and finally to utilize it to help the child.

The Teacher Prepares

The teaching and learning of science in the present context has brought upon the teachers of science added roles and responsibilities. He has to be more equipped and better prepared before a learning interaction/activity takes place. The teachers need to ensure the following, as prior self-preparation:

- He is fully aware of the possible learning outcomes.
- Ensures availability of sufficient materials, equipment that are in a fit condition to be handled by learners.
- Know the points of intervention for himself particularly in group learning situations.
- Willing to learn from the children's ideas and ready to listen to them with patience.
- Talks only that much which is sufficient.
- Has equipped himself fully well in the area under study not confining only to textbooks or teachers guides but

having consulted other resource material which may even have to be arranged.

- Has prepared his talking points in a language within the comprehension of the children.

The Child Proceeds

Before any particular activity is undertaken by the child and the teacher together, they normally interact at the initiative of the teacher. After this and before the actual activity begins the following may be relevant for the teacher to ensure that the child:

- is clear about what he is proceeding with
- has understood the teacher well
- knows the points which need further clarification
- knows why is he performing the activity.

While the activity is on, the teacher may like to observe the following:

(i) 'Peer' group interaction—its extent and quality of participation by each and individual learner.

When children are in groups, those attempting to remain 'withdrawn' are to be encouraged for enhanced participation. This could be done by assigning specific tasks within the total activity to a particular individual—'Rajan—why don't you record the temperature variation—you are such a keen observer'.

(ii) Handling of Equipment

There certainly would be children who would avoid handling equipment, particularly if it is delicate or breakable. The teacher is supposed to provide assurance and impress the need for every one to separately handle the equipment. It generates interest in the equipment.

(iii) Observation during experimentation

This requires alertness and skill of recording with precision. There are situations where help may be needed from others. The teachers' role is to encourage learner to be precise, cautions, accurate and follow a systematic approach in recording observations.

(iv) Measurements, if any

The way measurements are made indicate learning and development of proper attitudes and honesty of purpose. At this stage, children often come forward with the possible inaccuracies and deficiencies in their measurement. This is to be treated as normal expectation.

(v) Inferences, hypothesis

This, too, is a skill development exercise and prepares children to play a very significant role in adult life. Obviously, it could also play a major contributory part in case they go for higher levels of learning science.

(vi) Interpretations

Observations and results have a meaning if these lead to the development of a analysis of situations and interpreting all that is evident through observations and data, and what could be derived out of it. In fact, so much is to be interpreted in future life!

(vii) Correlations, connections

Learning through activity-based science gains added importance if the learner could relate it to real life experiences and situations. The emphasis is now shifting towards developing curriculum from the experiences of the child. It is definitely going to be the in thing in years to come.

(viii) Applications

Every activity must lead to appreciation of its possible applications. The concepts learnt must be seen to be applicable in different situations. It would be preferable if these are easily identifiable.

(ix) Utility

This has to be viewed from the angle of science, technologies and societal acceptance of changes. It is not necessary that every activity should lead to utility. Some way indicate negative aspects as well. Use of pesticides, insecticides could be converted into several learning activities few, of which, may indicate negative effects.

Each one of the above indicates either the learners approach, attitude, interest, skill, competence or capacity. The extent of peer group interaction could communicate total dependence on others or capacity to work with others, share ideas and learn from others. Only the teacher's keen observation and involvement could make a distinction.

Classroom Situation

Imagine the change in the classroom interactions and consequent pleasure both to the teachers and their pupils when at the end of the lesson, they carry out different processes of thought on the same concept. Consider the following sample terms:

1. Analysing
2. Applying
3. Assembling
4. Checking
5. Collecting
6. Classifying
7. Discovering
8. Defining
9. Dismantling
10. Degeneralizing
11. Hypothesizing
12. Limiting
13. Locating
14. Mathematizing
15. Outlining
16. Quantifying
17. Reformulating
18. Selecting
19. Summarizing
20. Telling
21. Transferring
22. Validating
23. Verifying
24. Writing

Utilising Assessment Results

The way a teacher reacts to his own assessment of different aspects of the learning behaviour of the pupil is crucial. Let us take a few examples.

- The child has not proceeded in his/her activity as per the perceptions of the teacher. Now it is the turn of the teacher to understand the 'perception' of the learner and then analyse the way the child proceeded further. Here the teacher may like to analyse his own role while assigning the activity to the child and sieve out as to what were the weaknesses in the interaction. Language could be one.

- Understand the way children learn and develop their ideas. No idea need to be brushed aside without asking for, and understanding the way they arrived at it. Was there an alternative way possible?
- All achievements are to be discussed with learners in positive ways. However, in doing so, the teacher may also like to reinforce certain technique, approach or ability that would help the child next time.
- In group discussions, those who appear withdrawn need to be encouraged, if necessary, by providing sufficient provocation.
- Provide children a chance to test their own ideas. Let them be prepared to challenge assumptions and ideas whenever they differ with others.
- Encourage him to go further. Whenever the child feels that job is completed, he needs encouragement and also further motivation to find out alternative uses, utility and application of the job considered complete.

Comprehensive evaluation could become a practical idea only through the total involvement of the teacher and learner in the school situation. Prior to it, the complete and thorough understanding of evaluation needs by curriculum developers would be a prerequisite. Evaluation conducted in the right spirit could certainly help the learner in nurturing his talents, creativity and enterprise.

Teacher Evaluation

This has all along, been a neglected aspect. While one could readily identify efforts in examination reforms and evaluation procedures for children in practically all countries, one rarely comes across anything other than the terminal examinations at the end of pre-service teacher training courses; when it comes to evaluation of teachers. It is no doubt a sensitive issue but it no longer could be ignored. The need for professional updating of science teachers has been realized and as a consequence, different strategies for the same have been evolved. These include face-to-face interaction, correspondence education or a combination of both. However, there rarely is a built-in mechanism. In isolated cases wherever it has been attempted, teachers have either avoided participation or ignored returning the 'response sheets'.

There is a need to study and analyse in-depth the evaluation needs of teacher education programmes. At pre-service, this analysis should concentrate in bringing about necessary changes, particularly in the affective domain. In case of in-service programmes, the need is to develop a pattern or a system which would be acceptable to participating teachers and would also bring forth the gaps that still need to be looked after by programme planners. This deserves serious consideration.

An Illustrative Case Study

In order to have a practical idea of roles performed by individual teachers, it was considered relevant to scrutinize a specific study presented before the group. The intention was to identify, on the basis of this scrutiny, the roles, skills, and attitudes which could be attributed to the teacher concerned. The study is given below.

Teacher-Community Relationship

The teacher-community relationship has a long and healthy tradition. It is possible to locate teachers and communities with mutual concern and consideration in abundance. The teacher is also a guide, helper, interpreter of new technologies, apart from being a 'teacher'. In times of need, the community looks toward the teacher. There are teachers who themselves identify the community needs and proceed to find solutions. Obviously, there are limitations of various types but these never deter enterprising individuals. Identification and dissemination of such stories may be undertaken by teacher preparation institutions. One such case is that of Shri Chandra Shekhar Lohumi, an elderly primary teacher from the northern hills of India. He had no formal training in science but developed a scientific outlook and concern for the community.

Lantana camera has been rated as one of the world's ten worst weeds. It is an attractive member of Family Verbenacea and is a native of South and Central America. It was introduced by the English to Indian gardens around 1809 as an ornamental plant. The English have left-but the gift they brought has resisted all efforts and forces of eviction. An aggressive invader, this problem weed is found almost in all the States of India but is more common in certain parts of Rajasthan, Punjab, Uttar Pradesh, Himachal Pradesh, Assam, Bihar, Kashmir and Delhi. It spreads to wider areas where cattle grazing is a major concern. It resists cutting, stumping, burning and even spraying. The seeds are disseminated by birds and animals. It blooms throughout the year.

Lantana competes with the crops for space, food and water, overruns forest plantations and it also harbours injurious insects, including the malarial mosquito. The leaves and berries are toxic to animals and humans as it causes photosensitization due to hepatocellular damage.

Shri Chandra Shekhar Lohumi, a school teacher since 1932, when posted in the village Naukuchiyatal, was deeply touched by the plight of the village people, their cattle, their crops because of the overgrowing Lantana, locally called Kuri. He remembered having heard somewhere about a similar situation in Australia and recollected that they had introduced an insect to control cacti plantations. Ever since this thought occurred to him, he was on the lookout for such an insect which could be feeding on Lantana. He began his search by observing the bushes around his own house. He also discussed the problem with the local farmers. After a fruitless search of several days, he was once told by a fellow villager about a withering bush of Lantana which was a rare phenomenon. Although he was unable to discover any insect on that bush, he was very optimistic that he was close to his discovery. And finally he discovered some insects on Lantana leaves on 26th of December 1967. What followed was a systematic collection, observation of plants and the bugs, seasonally and regularly. He spread populations of bugs on Lantana and useful crop plants and studied the effects. He also observed that the population of the bug is affected by the extreme seasonal changes which were favourable for its growth. The adult insect is formed within 12 days from the egg. Its age is from 21 to 25 days. His study and record of the life cycle of the bug was found highly scientific, logical and rational by research scientists.

Shri Lohumi contacted the nearest Agricultural University in Nainital to ensure that the scientists there also were appraised of the problem and his solution. He was very particular to ascertain that there is no adverse effect of the spread of the bug on other useful crops. Only then Shri Lohumi started raising the insect population and distributed these to the local farmers, as well as the neighbouring villages and again made systematic observations. The discovery made by Shri Lohumi was researched by several scientists and his findings confirmed that this insect is an effective control for Lantana. He was given a special prize by the Indian Council of Agricultural Research in the year 1980.

Discussion

This is a typical case where a concerned teacher, proceeding systematically and rationally, arrives at a solution which helps the community. The teacher ensures that the solution arrived at is examined in its aspect, particularly concerning any other harmful effects. The following roles of the science teacher were identified, in addition to his normal classroom teaching.

(i) Innovator
(ii) Helper
(iii) Interpreter
(iv) Problem identifier
(v) Coordinator
(vi) Researcher
(vii) Observer
(viii) Problem Solver

Skills were identified as

(i) Sensitivity (to situation)
(ii) Information processing
(iii) Communication with community
(iv) Commitment with community
(iv) Commitment to change
(v) Decision making
(vi) Creativity

Essentially, it is the positive attitude to life that leads such an individual to perform his social and community obligations, dutifully at each stage of life.

3

Preparation of Materials for the Training of Science Teachers

Introduction

The influence of science and technology has been so pervasive that most aspects of life, even the realm of the abstract; and almost all sectors of society have in some ways been changed. A large part of the global population sees this influence and change as mostly beneficial, leading to a letter quality of life. But society has to keep in step with Science and Technology while putting controls on it to prevent/minimise its abuse and misuse if it is to derive benefits from it. Reforms in science education are means to do so.

Science education reform should be evident in the class and classroom. We expect a classroom that is undergoing science education reform to have a display of updated illustrations, charts, maps and equipment. We should see tools, improvised equipment, and materials being used by children. We also expect much interactive learning taking place not only between teacher and students but also among students in an atmosphere of sharing. We should find the teacher eliciting and accepting questions, suggestions, and comments from students. The students' behaviour should be determined by self-discipline rather than teacher-control. Students should be eager to discover and learner by themselves, seeking confirmation of their school learning in the real world and bringing these experiences to the school. The lessons should include community problems thus extending the classroom into the community and availing of its resources.

Science education reform should make it possible for the students and community to benefit from each other at the instance of the teacher.

Teacher Training Materials

Pre-service Teacher Training Materials

Materials for use in pre-service training usually come in the form of textbooks, modules, and/or loose-leaf hand-outs. Textbooks and modules are often prescribed for specific courses by the instructors of the course. In general, they are authored by specialists and written for a discipline or a specialized branch of a discipline and NOT for a specific course. For example, "Teaching Science and Technology in the Secondary School" could be a published textbook that has been approved for use in a pre-service course entitled "Methods of Teaching Science in the Secondary School" in Teacher Training Institution A, but is titled "Strategies of Science Teaching, Secondary School" in Teacher Training Institution B. The author could be the instructor himself, or someone else, possibly not known to the instructor of the course. Loose-leaf handouts are usually culled from several sources or written by the instructor to supplement the content of textbook or the module. They are usually given out a few pages at a time, throughout the term as needed for discussion or task performance.

In-service Teaching Training Materials

In-service training materials are written for or reprinted as readings for specific training courses. They are intended to provide for specific identified needs of trainees. For instance, if in a needs assessment conducted by the in-service coordinators and lectures, the majority of teachers in a locality were found deficient on knowledge of local applications of science principles and ideas, then a training manual may be prefaced. The manual may include, among others, background information for teachers on local applications of science and technology.

In-service training manuals for science teachers are generally characterized by a curious mix of some or all of the following different kinds of content:

1. educational foundation topic which in view of the trainers and coordinators would answer some expressed need of the trainees;

Example: An educational psychology topic such as cognitive development of adolescents.

2. Science/technology/mathematics topics for which the trainees have expressed a need for upgrading;
3. topics on strategies of teaching science which may be conducted along the micro-teaching demonstration-cum-post demonstration discussion;
4. exemplar lessons for teaching the students of trainees;
5. instructions on the production of trainee output which may take the form of:
   (a) an action plan to conduct a project, echo a seminar, or a school-base training for other science teachers.
   (b) a part of a curriculum material that may be used in the school of the trainee.
   (c) in improvized equipment or teaching device.

(6) instructions on the performance of a required task such as peer teaching, or full length lesson demonstration in a real class, or planning and carrying-out a scientific investigation to develop science process skills.

Preparation of the Exemplar Lesson

The exemplar lesson has become a major feature of many teacher training manuals. It functions as a guide to lesson preparation for classroom teaching and exemplifies in print the strategies and subject matter reflecting science education reform. A thorough presentation on the preparation of exemplar lessons is in the succeeding parts of this chapter.

Lesson Preparation—The foregoing in an exercise on lesson preparation

A major task of the science teacher is lesson preparation. A successful performance of this task demands the use of skill which the teacher is expected to learn.

In writing a lesson in science a teacher may go through the following steps:

- selecting a topic drawn from a real life situation
- stating objectives of the lesson
- selecting strategies and resources to use in teaching the lesson
- writing out a plan for a science lesson
- illustrating the selection of a topic drawn from a real life situation

1. Given a prescribed science curriculum objective "To identify environmental problems in the community", choose a topic drawn from a real-life situation that you can use to plan a science lesson that would enable students to attain the prescribed objective.

Example: Utilization of pesticides and fertilisers in farms and households.

2. Find out how suitable your selected topic is by answering the following questions.

- Does your topic deal with a serious problem of the community?
- Will the topic develop science learnings that are beneficial both to the students and the community?
- If you answered YES to both questions, then you have chosen wisely. If one or both of your answers is NO, then look for another topic.

A follow-up discussion should bring out the following points:

- the seriousness with which the problem is regarded by the community.
- using the topic as a means of teaching science concepts.

- using the topic as a way of teaching environmental consciousness and social responsibility.
- using the topic to teach several science ideas.
- the applicability of the topic to both farming and urban communities.
- the interest of the students on the topic.

3. Look up the list of teacher competencies/skills specified in Chapter 2. Which of them must you possess to successfully pursue a science lesson?

4. Look up the list of teacher roles. Which role do you perform in selecting this topic for teaching. Explain your answer.

A discussion should bring out the following ideas:

- teachers perform various roles as they do various tasks for and in teaching
- the roles of the teacher have increased in number and complexity as science and technology education continues to develop
- teacher skills are varied; they make various roles possible
- awareness of the roles and skills improves performance.

Stating Objectives of the Lesson

All lessons are likely to become effective if both teachers and students are aware of the objectives. The objectives of each lesson must be explicitly stated in terms of learning outcomes which would facilitate evaluation of the effectiveness of the lesson. The lesson objectives could be cognitive, affective, and/or psychomotor.

Discussion

- cognitive objectives—those that aim for the development or refinement of knowledge; those that aim for the development or refinement of how to acquire knowledge.

Example: To identify the various types of pesticides used by a community.

- Affective objectives—those that concern feelings, interests, appreciations, attitudes and values.

  Example: To develop a feeling of concern for the undesirable effects of pesticides.

- Psychomotor objectives—those intended to develop and refine action, motion and behaviours.

Example: To collect different kinds of pests in a squaremeter of cropland.

The suggested steps in integrating the three objectives are as follows:

1. Write lesson objectives for the topic chosen.
2. Identify which objective or part of an objective is cognitive; which one is affective; which one is psychomotor.

Based on the given topic in Task # 1, the following are examples of objectives:

- To state the problem brought about by the use of pesticides and fertilisers.
- To find out by a survey of a community (by asking parents, neighbours and farmers) what different kinds of pesticides and fertilisers are used, how they are used, and what are their effects.
- To set up an experiment to identify the most potent pesticide and fertiliser used by a community.
- To decide using role playing in a class if the sale and use of certain pesticides and fertilisers should be controlled or totally banned in a community.

Discussion—Bring out the following points:

- lesson objectives give direction to the lesson; strategies, resources, and evaluation are based on it.

- lesson objectives can be stated in terms of science process skills (e.g. observe, predict, hypothesize, infer, etc.)
- lesson objectives can be stated in terms of knowledge to be learned (e.g. to gain understanding of ..., to clarify, to differentiate ...)
- lesson objectives can be stated so as to include the teaching strategies (e.g. to design an experiment..., to conduct a survey...)

3. Identify the skills needed to write the lesson objectives of your topic.

Consider the needs of students in relation to the topic, the objectives, and the strategies.

Students as growing adolescents in a community have certain needs. These needs must be considered and provided for, if they are to benefit maximally from the lesson.

1. How did you make your strategies more suitable to your students' age level?
2. How did you provide for the development or verbal skills in your students?
3. How did you provide for the development of higher level thinking skills in your students?
4. How did you provide for attitude and value development of your students?
5. What skills do you need to do all of the above?
6. What role do you perform in taking into consideration numbers 1-4?

Selecting strategies and resources for the lesson

1. Based on your chosen topic, decide what strategies and resources you will use in teaching the lesson.

Discussion

- the strategies must fit the objectives and resources and vice versa.

- whenever possible, focus on strategies that develop science process skills, values, and attitudes.

2. Are the strategies you have chosen for your lesson suitable? How can you tell?
3. Are the resources to be used with the strategies appropriate?

Discussion

- focus on resources available within a community.
- resources should include teaching aids, equipment, instruments and references.
- require students to improvize tools and equipment.

4. What skills are needed to choose the appropriate strategies and resources for your lesson?
5. What role is performed while selecting a particular strategy and a resource?

Writing out a lesson plan

1. Assemble the topic you have chosen, the objectives written, the strategy and resources identified and write out a lesson plan from them. Arrange them as follows with all their details:

   Topic:

   Objectives:

   Concepts/subconcepts:

   Procedure/Strategy:

   Methodology:

   Resources:

Lesson Presentation

Objective—to present a prepared lesson to students by:

1. motivating them to perform activities and tasks relevant to learning,
2. supervising their activities,

3. conducting interactive sessions with them,
4. evaluating the learning that occurred.

Motivating Students to the Lesson

The teacher should be prepared to engage his students' interest right at the very start and maintain this interest. This part of the lesson is the motivation scheme.

To give examples of motivation schemes using the topic "pesticides and fertilisers":

- Present to the class newspaper clippings reporting illnesses and death caused by household or farm pesticides; degradation attributed to excessive use of fertilisers.
- Show film/slide/transparencies/video of illnesses attributed to pesticides, and of the effects of fertilisers on soil and water.
- Discuss to explore student knowledge on the subject matter.
- Present to class containers of pesticides and fertilisers and invite students to look at skills and crossbones sign, the stated chemical components, and the instructions on how to use them.

1. Based on the prepared lesson, describe briefly the motivation to be used in teaching the chosen topic.
2. Suggest two other alternative motivation schemes for your lesson.

Discussion

Although motivation is always suggested at the start of a lesson, continuous motivation should be provided through activities, use of equipment and teaching aids, and stimulating verbal interaction in class. Consider:

3. the competencies and skills to use to motivate the students;
4. the role to be performed when motivating students toward the subject of the lesson.

Supervising Student Activities

The teacher is most needed in class during the performance of student activities. The teacher sees to it that:

- the procedure is given in simple, easy to understand language
- the activities provide opportunities for learning
- the activities proceed with little or now waste of time
- the safety and well-being of the students are provided for
- materials and equipments are correctly used to prevent breakage and wastage.

The following activities are suggested:

1. Briefly describe the activities students will perform during the lesson.
2. State reasons for choosing the activities.
3. Identify the competencies and skills needed to supervise student performance of the activities.
4. The roles performed by the teacher when supervising the student activities.

Conducting Interactive Sessions with Students

Interactive sessions with students are largely varbal. Lectures in which only the teacher talks in class is NOT an interactive session. An interactive session in a science class is characterised by the following:

- Both teacher and students talk, exchange ideas, refine, modify, reinforce, restate each others' ideas.
- Science ideas are interacted on.
- The teacher tactfully and affectionately encourages the shy and reticent student to share their ideas.
- The teacher's manner of asking and responding to questions influences the students' manner of asking and responding to questions.

- No single person monopolises the sessions.
- A summary of the main points discussed can reinforce students' learning.
- A resource person (external to the class) may be invited to share his/her expertise on the subject but much time should be allotted for interaction (questions and answers) with the students.

In our example of a lesson on pesticides and fertilisers the following science ideas may be discussed during the interactive sessions:

- the problems regarding the use of pesticides and fertilisers
- their effects on health
- their effects on the environment
- the lack of knowledge of users about the chemicals
- components of the substances they use
- the inability of users to follow instructions on how to use
- the carelessness of users in applying and storing
- certain pesticides and fertilisers are intended for specific pests and specific soil condition, i.e. NOT all pesticides kill all kinds of pests, and NOT all fertilisers are good for all kinds of soil
- different kinds of pesticides should be applied at different concentrations for different purposes, therefore the instructions on the package must be read and carefully understood
- individuals have different reactions to the same kind of pesticide or fertiliser
- application of a particular type of pesticide kills not only the pest for which it is intended but also some other organisms
- there is a right time for a profitable application of fertilisers

Some procedural matters on the strategies used in the lesson may also be interacted on, such as:

- in the survey, the same set of questions should be asked by the students in the class (of their neighbours and friends, or other members of the community)
- some words of caution on the tactful manner of asking questions in a survey should be formulated, so as not to offend the respondent
- the need to consolidate the data obtained in the survey by the class
- how the analysis and interpretation of the consolidated data shall be conducted
- deriving the conclusion and its implication
- in the class hearing, where role play is the strategy to be used, how assignment of roles are made
- how long is the preparation time for these taking major roles in the hearing (role play)
- where and how sources of information may be obtained

The questions that the teacher may reflect on are as follows:

1. Using the lesson topic, what science ideas are expected to be brought out in the interactive session?
2. What procedural matters concerning the strategy used would need further discussion?
3. What kind of learning outcomes are to be expected from the interactive session?
4. What skills are to be developed in conducting the interactive session on the chosen topic?
5. What roles are performed by the teacher in carrying out the interactive sessions on the chosen topic?

Resources: This refers to all the materials to be used in teaching the lesson. It includes charts, maps, globes, instruments, equipment, chemicals and other consumable materials, films, videos, tapes, transparencies, and reference materials.

In selecting resources, consider the following:

1. the age level of the students for which the resources will be used,
2. the sufficiency of the resources to motivate and maintain the interests of the students,
3. whether the use of the resources will help in devolving the science ideas and objectives aimed for,
4. whether resources will be easy enough to use under the classroom conditions available in the school,
5. weather it be possible to allow students to handle and operate/manipulate/use these resources,
6. whether students will be safe in using these resources?

Essential aspects of lesson preparation and presentation have been attempted in this specific case. While such preparation is an essential pre-requisite; equally important is the understanding that a truly creative lesson takes its final shape only during the classroom transaction. The teacher trainer has to have the preparedness to absorb new ideas, assimilate these in his plan and conduct the classroom transaction comprehensively.

TEACHER TRAINING EXEMPLAR ON DEVELOPMENT OF SCIENTIFIC ATTITUDES, VALUES AND ETHICS

Introduction

Traditional approaches of teaching science can no longer meet the learning needs of the children. These needs impinge upon every aspect of human life and behaviour as the impact of science and technology is gradually permeating social, cultural and ethical contexts as well. The last one, though very sensitive, is equally crucial and deserves delicate handling. The learners need to develop rational thinking, scientific methods of analysis and arriving at results. Further, they need to learn to apply these in their real life situations with full awareness of short and long term consequences. The teacher training could help in this by suitably developing these attributes among learners.

In order for teachers to comfortably bring in the attitudinal, value and ethical aspects of science and technology to their science teaching, the teachers need to possess skills and competencies which can be developed through certain activities.

To assist the teacher trainees develop such skills and competencies, a series of activities are suggested as follow:

1. experiential session
2. reflective thinking session
3. planning and development of strategies/activities for children.

Topic

Effects of pesticides in farms and households

Training Objectives

After the training, the teacher trainee should be able to:

1. express/show awareness of ethical and social dimensions, particular of the problems resulting from the effects of utilization of pesticides in farms and households;
2. develop a feeling of concern for victims and would-be victims of the careless use of pesticides and social responsibility to disseminate correct information about pesticides;
3. present, after discussion and reflection, a view of the interplay of competencies and skills needed to develop the scientific attitudes, values and ethics in children;
4. relate teacher competencies and skills to strategies and activities development to be used with the children;
5. acquire skills in developing feelings of concern and social responsibility in children;
6. evaluate one's own knowledge and affective behaviour.

Activities

1. Experiential Session

1.1. Presenting Incidents/Problems Related to the Effects of Pesticides

To motivate teacher trainees to become interested in the subject matter, several strategies may be employed:

(a) Present and read to class newspaper reports on illness and deaths caused by pesticides.

(b) Asking students to explore their experiences or what they hear from friends and neighbours about it.

(c) Present to class, containers of pesticides and invite students to look at the skull and crossbones signs and read the words of caution on the labels. Discuss the implications of these.

(d) Show films, slides, video on information about pesticides.

Examples of Reports that can be presented:

1. There was a report of the death of a 29-year old man who worked as a pesticide sprayer in a banana plantation. He was doing this job for the last three years. Earlier, when he first began to work in the plantation, he was not provided with complete protective suit. Later on, however, the company, under pressure from outside, did provide him and other workers with protective suits.

   It was reported that his death was the result of his being exposed to the pesticides for a continuous period of time. The pesticides affected his brain, and later he became paralyzed. It also caused organ-system malfunctions.

2. A farmer was brought to a hospital in Manila after having been taken to a provincial hospital because of vomitting and giddiness. The doctors tried their best to save him. Unfortunately, he died. It was reported that the man was mixing pesticides in a large amount by dipping his uncovered hands and arms in it. Only the following day did he start to develop certain symptoms which got worse as time passed. He, then, was taken to the hospital.

1.2 Discussion

Discussion among teacher trainees are conducted under the guidance of a teacher-educator who needs to prepare certain questions in advance to start a discussion. At some points during a discussion, trainees should be given some time to search or seek for information to be used for discussion. At any rate, a discussion is meant to stimulate thinking on scientific attitudes, values, and ethics which will hopefully lead to the development of such attitudes values and ethics.

Questions to ask concerning the reported incidents:

- Pesticides have been in use for years. What do you think went wrong in these incidents?
- What agencies are responsible for regulating/controlling the use of pesticides?
- If you were a member of the family of the victim, what would you have done as soon as you heard of the incident?
- What can be done to prevent similar incidence in the future?

1.3 Extending the learning

Conduct a debate or discussion on the subject of utilization of pesticides with emphases on the following questions. This again is meant to enhance the development of scientific attitudes, values and ethics.

Utilization of pesticides in farming

- What are we really trying to do when we use pesticides?
- What are some advantages of the utilization of pesticides?
- Are there risks in doing so? If yes, what are these risks?
- How do you perceive a balance between providing sufficient food for human beings and protecting their environment?
- Can we keep the balance between desired and undesired products in this case? If so, how?
- Can we justify the use of pesticides to increase food production in order to alleviate the problem of starvation?

- What problems of storage and possible accidents, that may occur because of it, can you foresee?
- When making decisions about safety of pesticide utilization, is it permissible (or inevitable) to allow some risks? Why?
- Are there any alternatives to pesticide utilization which are beneficial to human beings as well as the environment?

Utilization of Pesticides in Household

- What are we really trying to do when we use pesticides in the home?
- What are some advantages of household utilization of pesticides?
- Are there risks in doing so? What are these risks?
- Are there any alternatives to the household utilization of pesticides? If so, what are these alternatives?

1.4 Evaluation of Trainees by Teacher-educators

- Attitudinal test items concerning this particular issue can be prepared and administered to the trainees before and after the session.
- Essay tests can be given to the trainees after the experiential session. For example, trainees can be asked to respond to certain statements such as:

  "Household utilization of pesticides should be banned." Explain why.

  "Research and production of more potent pesticides should be encouraged since pests develop resistance to pesticides." Provide explanation to your pro or con answers.

2. Reflective Thinking Session

Upon completion of the experiential session, reflective thinking session is required as a follow-up activity. It is assumed that the teacher trainees now have acquired competencies and skills required for development of scientific attitudes, values and ethics. They have also learned how a discussion is guided. There are times when discussions may lead to no conclusions. And there are times when discussions may just help them think divergently, analytically and synthetically.

Here at this point, the trainees are asked to do some reflective thinking through individual thinking or some group discussion on the following points:

- From the beginning until the end of experiential session, what competencies and skills are required?
- To what extent does the experiential session help you develop scientific attitudes, values and ethics?
- If you were to acquire a higher level of scientific attitudes, values and ethics, what other strategies can and should be implemented?

Note:

Competencies and skills most needed during the experiential session may be as follows:

(a) Science-process skills

- communicating, interpreting data and making conclusion.

(b) Information-processing skills

- identifying, locating and utilizing information
- classifying, analysing and utilizing relevant information
- searching for ways to understand scientific information from primary sources
- always update oneself on scientific and technological information, as well as information in other areas.

(c) Decision-making skills

- selecting reliable information and classifying values, ethics
- identifying alternatives

- predicting the consequences of each alternative
- weighing the pros and cons of each alternative
- ordering the alternative
- taking actions consistent with the stated values
- accepting possible consequences of the actions taken.

At this point, the teacher educator may need to provide explanations and examples concerning such competencies and skills. Moreover, the trainees may need to be given more exercises to practice such competencies and skills.

3. Development of Strategies/Activities for Children

The teacher trainees should discuss among themselves (with guidance of teacher educator) about strategies/activities to be used in real classrooms in order to bring about the development of scientific attitudes, values, and ethics.

Certain points need to be taken into consideration during this session. They are as follows:

- establishment or enhancement of the relationship between children, schools and community.
- level of children (maturity level, as well as, intelligence level).
- linkage with real-life activities.
- integration of science process skills.
- access to sources of reliable information.

Possible outcomes (for grade 8/9 students)

The teacher and the children discuss possible activities they can undertake in order to learn more about the subject. Eventually they decide on one or two. They then proceed to plan in detail how to carry it out.

Suggested Activities are:

(a) Use of newspaper clippings about pesticide cases.

(b) Research (collection of pamphlets, books, articles from magazines and from journals).

(c) Record observations in the community—use logbooks, scrapbooks, etc.

(d) Field trips/visits by the whole class

(e) Student reports

(f) Film shows

(g) Survey of community members or people's knowledge, practices and observations—whether they use pesticides, what kind of pesticides, frequency of use, noticeable effects on humans, do people read labels and instructions.

(h) Role playing of a public hearing situation—the features and functions of each role should be made clear so as to avoid the wastage of time and to facilitate interaction among role players.

(i) Community service—the service must be beneficial to the majority of students and is approved by members of the community.

4. Evaluation of Classroom Students

This can be done in various ways.

4.1 *Through observations*—what to observe (event); whom to observe (individuals, small group); when to observe (short period of time); how to observe (checklist, notes).

Example of assessment sheet

Could either be a remark sheet or a checklist.

Name of Students	Remarks or Checklist on Scientific attitudes, values, ethics				
	Rational	Open-minded	Honest	Social responsibilities	Belief and apply process of science

Observation can be done regularly throughout a semester. What to look for?

Rational

- always provide reasons or evidence to support the ideas.
- judgement is usually based on information

Open-minded

- accept other people's ideas that are different from oneself's
- willing to change one's idea if more information are provided
- willing to listen to others

Honest

- sincerity of observation, accuracy, commitment all combine together to indicate the honesty of effort or activity.

Social responsibility

- think collectively (always take into consideration the factors concerning community or group)
- take action (if need be) for the benefit of community/ society/group
- concern for others

Belief and apply process of science

- recognize the value and importance of the process of science (scientific method)
- apply process of science in daily living (tackle problems systematically)

In addition, observations can be done as the activities proceed. Children's behaviour can be observed through the following questions:

- Does the child show interest in the activity?
- Does the child co-operate and participate actively?
- Does the child initiate/lead in planning and carry through activities?

- Is the child developing manipulative skills as the activity proceeds?

4.2 Through paper-pencil tests

- Attitudinal test items can be administered before and after the course to partly measure the development of scientific attitudes, values and ethics.
- Essay type of test can be administered after the course. For example, some statements such as those given in 1.4 or stories can be given in a test and students are asked to express their ideas as a response to given statements.

4.3 Evaluation by parents and community

- Parents and community can be asked to evaluate students' performance regarding their involvement in family and community activities.

TEACHER TRAINING EXEMPLAR ON TEACHER AS A FACILITATOR AND A MOTIVATOR OF LEARNING AND A COMMUNITY COLLABORATOR

Introduction

The exemplar teaching-learning materials are intended for teacher trainees. These trainees will be prepared not only to play the roles of facilitator and motivator of learning, and community collaborator as well as conscientions members of society and who will serve as teachers in different environmental situations (rural, urban, agricultural, industrial, etc.).

It is assumed here that the teacher trainees have studied science at least up to the elementary stage. This exemplars thus, provides for the development of a teacher with the necessary knowledge, skills and attitudes. It is envisaged that the roles, as mentioned earlier, are performed, and relevant skills and competencies are developed, through science activities, discussions, demonstrations, lectures, field work, project work and assignments.

The skills relevant to a subject are acquired through practice work, observations, act. The subject matter must be based on real life situation and, wherever possible, it should give the idea that education in science is a quality for living and not merely for acquiring knowledge.

Objectives

The following are the objectives of this training material:

1. To develop an ability in teacher trainees to become innovators/facilitators/motivators of learning and community collaborators, as well as a conscientious member of society.
2. To develop competencies/skills and positive attitudes in teacher trainees, which would finally lead to the development of scientific skills and positive attitudes of pupils in order to prepare them to be citizens with scientific temper.
3. To use different modes/strategies for evaluating pupil performance.

To attain the above stated objectives the following exemplar lessons are presented for teacher trainees who will teach science at the elementary level; to demonstrate to them the roles of the science teachers and the competencies and skills (especially science process skills) through the science activity, relate science to real life situations (problems which a trainee may deal with when he goes to the classroom) and illustrate alternative strategies in lesson presentation. It also includes suggested strategies on assessment of student performance.

Exemplar: Teacher as a facilitator, and motivator of learning

Competencies and skills to be achieved

Observation

Improvization

Science Process Skills: Observation, experimentation, inferring, hypothesizing, confirming the data, generalizing

Creating a joyful class learning environment

Science Activity

Corrosion and its prevention

Grade Level: Class VIII

Concepts to be developed

Corrosion is wasting away of metals layer by layer by electrochemical action

Metals corrode faster when exposed to moist air

Protection of metal surface prevents corrosion

Teaching Strategy

Activity-based teaching learning method; Field trips

Time allocation: Approximately 3 hours. 6—periods

Objectives

1. To be able to identify and observe the process of corrosion
2. To be able to identify the causes of corrosion
3. To be able to take steps which would prevent corrosion and protect metals
4. To be able to select materials which are not liable to be corroded easily.

Teaching Hints

Introduce the lesson by requiring from the class what are the various metals that they use in daily life. Help students recall at least five different instances where metals are used.

Discuss the care taken to ensure the proper functioning of the metallic parts. Let students experience, that a shining metal surface is smooth when touched, whereas a metal which is dull and tarnished is not smooth.

Student Activities

A. Observation Done during Class Period

Student Activities

1. Boil water in an aluminium kettle. Remove the water when cooled. Observe what happens to the inner surface of the kettle.

   (It becomes dull gray or gets tarnished because oxygen dissolved in water reacts with aluminium to form an oxide layer.)

2. Observe that happens when iron nails, screws, and pipes, are exposed to moist air. (On standing, all develop a fine reddish brown-coating called rust which is responsible for the corrosion of iron).

3. Observe that on longer exposure, copper and silver also lose their shine, copper at times might develop a green deposit and silver may get blackened. (Copper reacts with carbon dioxide and forms greenish copper carbonate, ruhite silver reacts with hydrogen sulphide and gets blackened due to coating with silver sulphide).

4. Observe whether polishing helps to regain the metallic luster. (Showing that the corrosion occurs layer by layer.)

5. Observe the aluminium and iron vessels (a) in regular use (b) not in regular use.

6. Galvanise iron nails by dipping them into molten zinc. (Zinc is resistant to corrosion by air.)

B. Observations Made Over a few days

8. Apply a coat of oil or grease on the iron tools. Expose to moist air for a few days. Record observations (Rusting is not there).

9. Paint the iron rods, door hinges with white paint. Record observation.

   (No corrosion is observed even during heavy rainy season).

Discussion

Allow for class discussion to arrive at the following concepts:

- moisture and air are responsible for corroding metals
- corrosion is prevented by avoiding contact with air or moisture
- boilers and machine parts can be protected from wear out by regular oiling
- community members use material metals specific to their needs
- damage by corrosion of metals cause heavy loss to the nation's economy
- plastic-coated metal sheets will not corrode and therefore, are used in construction of buildings
- anodization process prevents corrosion of aluminium.

Questions to answer after the lesson and for further class discussion:

1. During rainy seasons metallic door hinges make creaking sounds.
   (a) What could be the reason?
   (b) What is done to restore the normal functioning of the door hinges?
2. Why are chrome-plated or nickel-plated objects more resistant to corrosion?
3. Give reasons why silver gets easily tarnished?
4. Does polishing of metals take away the outermost surface layer?
5. Is it safe to eat acidic food served in brass plates? Why? Why not?
6. Why do we recommend that pickles be stored in ceramic vessels only?

Further Activity

1. Field Trips

Make trips to

(a) the cycle repair shop and see how the different parts of a bicycle are greased to prevent corrosion;

(b) a shop where nickel/chrome/copper plating is done;

(c) a factory where galvanization of iron wares/sheets is done.

2. Assignment

Observe an electrician at work. (Why does he use the rough sandpaper to clean the wire surface before making any connections?)

3. Observe how the hand pumps, agricultural tools, the swings, etc. are oiled. Inquire from the farm mechanic why agricultural tools need occasional oiling. (Oil is used for lubrication as well as for prevention of corrosion.)

Exemplar: Teacher as a facilitator, motivator of learning and a community collaborator.

Competencies and skills to be developed

Science process skills: observation, experimentation, problem identification, communication

Science Activity: Soil Structure

Grade Level: Class VII

Objectives of the lesson

1. To be able to identify different soil structures.
2. To be able to select soil suitable for planting.
3. To be able to relate the concept of soil structure to daily life situation.

Concepts to be developed

1. Soil is made up of different structure.
2. Loosening of soil structure helps in planting.
3. Different soil structures are needed for different purposes.

Teaching Strategies

Experimentation, Group discussions, Field trips

Time allocation: Approximately 7 hours

Procedure

1. Identify and visit places in the surrounding environment having different soil structure.
2. Observe what happens on pouring equal amounts of water to different selected areas with different soil structures, in terms of time required for water to percolate through. Take students out to these selected spots in the field. Let them perform the experiments on water percolation and see how much time it requires for the water to pass through in different cases. Back in class, encourage the pupils to discuss their observations, and also help them to think of problems related to their observations.
3. Involve students in discussion on topics like "water passes more easily at some places than at others."
   - Guide students' discussion wherever it is necessary.
4. Allow students to perform different experiments found in the syllabus about soil structure and their percolation properties. Discuss results with the entire class members.
5. Allow students to interview community members on the importance of soil structure in farming (farmers), construction of buildings and houses (engineers), etc.

Assignment

Find out what type of soil structure is needed for constructing a cement flooring.

Follow-up Activities

Prepare a resource folder for extra readings, taking newspaper clippings about research and experimentations carried out on soil structure, especially relevant to a community.

Assessment of Learning Outcome

1. Observation of students in the field and in the classroom activities. A check-list has to be prepared in terms of students participation in group discussion, whole class discussion, participation in field activities, use of science process skills, awareness about learning concepts of soil structure related to daily life situations.
2. Project work on role of soil structure in development activities which are on-going in the community, e.g. building construction, cementing of roads, etc. and how the results could influence policy decision made for the community.

4

Strategies for Evaluation of Teacher Competencies and Skills

This task is to be performed by teacher educators. It should also be assisted by teacher trainees. The present position, as discussed earlier remains wide open for modification and changes in view of new role expectations of teachers and new skills and competencies that need to be acquired, the hence evaluated. The shift in emphasis to affective competencies and behavioural changes demands new approach to evaluation practices, and consequently, new techniques and instruments are to be thought of and validated. These achievements could be judged through the following areas:

(i) Classroom techniques and methods as evidenced through actual observation of practice in teaching lessons.

(ii) Analysis of cognitive learning through report writing, test sheets, assignments and interaction with teacher educators.

(iii) Manipulative skills through improvization of equipment, mobilization of resources, uses of educational technology, preparation and use of models, charts, teaching aids.

(iv) Attitudes acquired through interaction with community, commitment and sense of responsibility, willingness to take responsibility and evidence of managerial capabilities.

(v) Professional development through self-learning, by peer group interaction and ability to find sources of new knowledge and technologies.

(vi) Social skills as judged by interaction with parents and members of the community.

(vii) Self image to be judged by participation in social, cultural and community activities and through willingness to accept new responsibilities in these areas.

The above list is only indicative and should be rewritten by every teacher educator himself as per his perceptions. So far, maximum concentration in evaluation was in cognitive attainments (tested through essay type answers, mostly) and cursory observations of the classroom teaching situations where the trainee is usually unnerved more when the teacher educator enters the classroom to observe his performance. It is most amusing situation. While the teacher educator's presence prevents normality of the teacher trainee, the learners (children) know that 'sir' (the trainee) is being examined and usually enjoy themselves. It may not be desirable to state that the situation becomes comic if not farcical.

In such a situation, the need for fresh approach becomes imminent. While proceeding to develop instruments of evaluation certain suggestions are listed below and these could be utilized as guidelines, along with others, to formalize the evaluation tools and techniques.

Classroom Situation (Practice Teaching)

(i) Asks questions
- frequently
- infrequently
- appropriately
- inappropriately
- rarely
- never

(ii) Responds to the students response

- encouragingly
- cautiously
- indifferently
- ignores
- get unnerved (becomes nervous)

(iii) Response to students ideas

- praises pupil ideas
- incorporates ideas in discussions
- discourages their ideas
- ignores them completely
- discourages all interventions

(iv) Participatory teaching learning

- ensures participation of all
- neglects some
- forgets about pupil participation
- encourages participation of talented only
- unfamiliar with the technique of participatory teaching/learning

(v) Conducts activities

- prepares well-thought-of design
- comes unprepared
- is unsure of objectives
- avoids conduction activities
- mobilizes resources
- gives too many directions
- is indirect in guiding

(vi) Communicates

- at a level beyond learners
- too fast
- conscious of learners' comprehension
- knows the technique and ensures comfortable transaction to learners

(vii) Nurtures creativity

- never
- rarely
- instinctively/compulsively
- is himself not creative

(viii) Classroom environment

- pays attention to it
- neglects it
- makes it enjoyable
- makes learners disinterested
- remains serious throughout

(ix) Achieve objectives

- concerns only with the cognitive transfer of knowledge
- ensures learning
- is more concerned about how children learn than the final 'product'
- allows no digression to his planned lesson
- changes transactions incorporating learner ideas during the progress of the 'lesson'

(x) Provokes

- new thinking and connections
- more learner ideas
- greater participation

- more activities
- peer-group learning

(xi) Uses education technology

- never
- adequately
- infrequently
- frequently
- appropriately
- inappropriately

(xii)Focuses on

- concept development
- skill development
- relationship to real-life situations
- utility
- applicability

And beyond classrooms

(i) Decision-making

- avoids
- takes quick decisions
- slow in decision-making
- incapable of decision-making
- confused
- depends on others

(ii) Management of resources, time and activities

- committed manager
- resourceful
- utilizes time gainfully
- makes activities challenging

- concerns only with 'teaching'
- leaves these aspects to others

(iii) Community collaborator

- avoids meeting people
- has ego problems
- meets people pleasantly
- pleasing manners
- understands their problems
- earns their confidence

(iv) Interaction with parents

- communicates assessment to them
- seeks their collaboration
- avoids meeting them
- is concerned
- commands respect from them

(v) Attitudes

- rational
- chauvinistic
- principled
- committed
- concerned

(vi) Personality

- likeable
- friendly
- unapproachable
- dynamic
- dull
- dependable
- undependable

(vii) Relations with school authorities

- unconcerned
- cordial
- strained
- business-like

It may indeed not be desirable to make a sharp distinction between classroom and classroom-plus-outside-the-classroom assessments as the two are closely interlinked. However, on the lines suggested above, an evaluation instrument can be developed and standardized or validated by teacher educators themselves.

Evaluation of Instructional Methods and Behaviours in Science Classroom

(a) *Pre-service training programme*

The ultimate goal of pre-service teacher training is to have the trainee teachers gain competencies and skills in teaching. An evaluation of the classroom practices is a way to investigate the teacher's competence and skills as applied in teaching. This could also be done by peer-group teaching, teaching practices and teaching demonstrations. Responses could be obtained from the teacher trainers, peers, classroom students and even from the trainee through self-evaluation.

Evaluation of the trainee's classroom practices can be made by using a checklist on types of instructional methods applied by the trainee (see List I), together with observation questionnaires on teachers' and students' behaviours in the science classroom (see List II).

List I: Types of instructional methods applied by science teachers

1. Question-and-answer methods for presenting information to the whole class.
2. Lecture to the whole class followed by questions from individual students.
3. All students do the assignment, working from their textbooks or other printed materials.

4. The class is divided into smaller groups who work together on the same assignment or different assignments, including practical/laboratory work.
5. Students follow individualized programmes, which have include individual printed materials and laboratory work.
6. Presentation of audio-visual materials to the whole class: for example, slides, films, TV.
7. The whole class goes on field trips or excursions in connection with the science programme.
8. Students in groups, visit industries, research institutions, botanical/zoological parks and places of scientific importance. They are exposed with the details, processes and methods therein. They relate these to scientific concepts and grasp the actual processes and methods.

List II: Teachers' and students' behaviours in science classroom

1. At the start of each science lesson, the teacher reminds the students about the work they covered and concepts and ideas learned during the previous lessons.
2. At the end of each science lesson the teacher gives a summary of what was learned in the lesson.
3. The students are allowed to make their own choice of science topics to study.
4. The teacher uses students' ideas and suggestions when planning science lessons.
5. The teacher does demonstrations to help explain scientific ideas.
6. The teacher makes science lessons interesting for students.
7. During science lessons, the students copy teacher's notes from the blackboard.
8. For science homework, students' reports of their laboratory and practical work.

9. The teacher explains have the science that the student are learning relates to their own life.
10. The teacher discusses possible careers in science with the students.
11. Students have tests on what they have learned in science.
12. The science teacher helps students who have difficulties in learning science.
13. Students do field work outside the classroom as part of their science lessons.
14. Students do practical work (experiments) as part of their science lessons.
15. The science class is divided into small groups of students to do practical work (experiments).
16. When students perform experiments, the teacher gives instructions about what to do.
17. When students perform an experiment, they use a practical book or other written instructions on how to perform it.
18. In their practical work, students identify their own problems and then the teacher helps them to plan experiments to solve problems.
19. When students do experiments, the teacher provides them with problems to solve and then leaves students to work out their own methods and solutions.
20. In their practical work, students identify their own problems and work out their own methods to investigate the problems.

(b) *In-service training programme*

Although huge investment has been made on the provision of in-service training programmes for science teachers, the evaluation of these programmes has been neglected. In the actual situations where in-service education programmes are offered to a large number of teachers, and that the "multiple-tier technique" is applied, it was found that such training programmes faced a number of limitations, like lack of essential equipment and materials. Rarely, systematic evaluation was incorporated. This situation creates a lot of possible losses which may affect the quality of the in-service education programmes offered for science teachers. Thus, in many instances, certificates awarded at such training programmes were just of attendance, and not of the quality of the learning. In these situations, extreme care must be taken to ensure the quality of the training programmes, so that the huge amount of efforts, time and money, both from the government budget and from other sources which are continuing to be spent in many countries are effectively used.

Guidelines for the Teacher Educators in Using Checklist Prepared for Evaluating Teacher Trainees

In assessing the role of the elementary science teacher as a facilitator the following points are to be observed and assessed:

1. The science teacher should be well familiar with the science concepts. The fluency with which he deals with students' questions and the competence with which he organizes to impart the science learning and important aspects.
2. The science teacher needs to be aware of the prior knowledge of the student. He should be able to relate the new concepts to the prior knowledge of his students.
3. In his role as a facilitator, the science teacher should encourage children's inherent curiosity. Problems and issues related to the natural phenomena and questions concerning these could be considered as an encouragement on the part of the teacher.
4. It is important that the science teacher feels free and works along with the pupils. How he joins in with pupils to solve their problems and how he guides them in trying out different activities are aspects that can be observed.

Figure 1: Possible Loss Throughout Stages In Teacher Preparation Programme

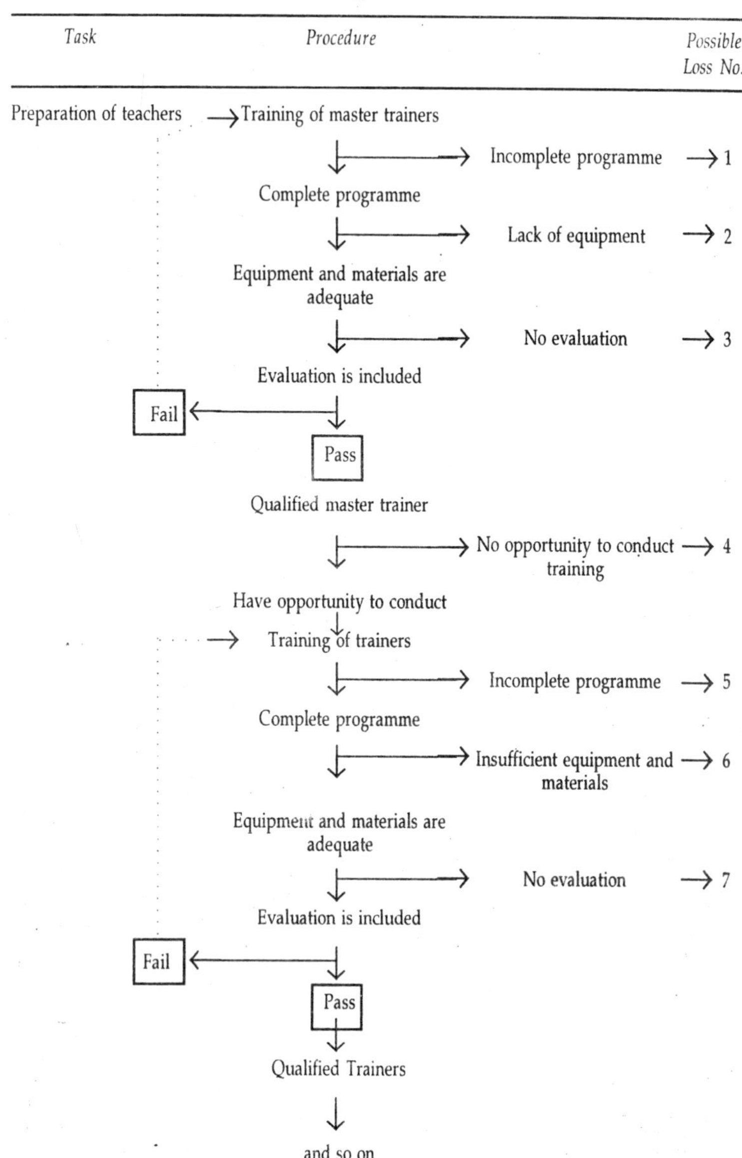

5. The science teacher continuously learns from his day-to-day experiences. In this, his interaction with students play an important role. He should be willing to listen to children's ideas and suggestions, and learn from them, as well.
6. Science learned with no relation to daily life may give the students the idea that science is a difficult or abstract subject. Hence, science should be related to daily life situations to make it more meaningful to the students.
7. The teacher has to play an important role in encouraging students through activities and suggestions which relate the science concepts to identifying and solving community problems.
8. The science teacher should help and guide students to link science with other subjects. In questioning and formulating activities, consideration has to be given to link science with other subjects.
9. The science teacher should motivate students to ask questions relevant to their observations. This could be mainly done through reinforcement and student appraisal.
10. Science education should be thought of as a continuous process. This stimulates pupils' interest to initiate their own projects related to learning and would encourage continuity and further learning.
11. Different ability groups have to be taken into consideration by all teachers and more so by science teachers. Hence the teachers' ability to organize, plan and cater for different ability groups has to be considered.
12. Effective communication can occur only within the comprehension level of the students. Communication is an important process of learning, and cannot be ignored.
13. Learning based mainly on curriculum tests restricts scope of wider learning. Utilization of all available resources whether they be human, natural or

environmental should be considered by all science teachers.

14. Interaction takes place in every single learning process. The interaction varies for different activities, making it impossible for the same classroom organization to be successful for all activities. The activity whether it be carried out in the class or outdoors has to be thought of in terms of the interaction expected to occur and well-planned before hand.
15. Evaluation is a major component of a teaching/learning process. Continuous evaluation using different modes has to be a built-in process in the science teaching programme.
16. It is in terms of the possible learning outcomes that the science teacher can carry out self-evaluation or evaluation of the students. A full awareness of the possible outcomes is a competency required of a science teacher.

Checklist to Evaluate Science Teacher Trainees by Teacher Educators

Role: The Science Teacher as a Facilitator of Learning

Direction: Tick to what extent the teacher has developed the competencies and skills.

Competencies/Skills	Most		To		Least
	A	B	C	D	E
The science teacher,					
(1) demonstrates confidence in science concepts.					
(2) relates new concepts to prior science knowledge that the students possess.					
(3) encourages children to be more curious about natural phenomena.					
(4) joins with pupils in solving problems and trying out different activities.					
(5) listens to children's ideas intently.					

Competencies/Skills	Most		To		Least
	A	B	C	D	E
(6) relates science concepts to daily life situations.					
(7) encourages children to relate science concepts that they learn in school to solve community problems.					
(8) appreciates the role that science plays in solving community problems.					
(9) helps to link science with other subjects.					
(10) reinforces student answers to motivate them to ask questions relevant to their observations.					
(11) encourages pupils to initiate their own science projects related to what they learn in school.					
(12) handles pupils of different scientific ability					
(13) communicates effectively within the level of comprehension of the children.					
(14) uses suitable resources for every science learning activity, e.g. human, natural, environmental resources, etc.					
(15) organizes for desired interaction in science activities					
(16) assesses pupils performance in science using different modes of evaluation, e.g. observation, paper and pencil, test assessment and practical skills, project work, etc.					
(17) adjusts to the situation to get the desired or possible learning outcomes.					

Exemplar Evaluation Material

For any project or activity to consistently improve, a systematic way of arriving at a basis for improvement must be devised. Evaluation is one such systematic device. A well-planned evaluation system should be able to identify the flaws and weaknesses (if any) of an activity or project and give direction to attain the desired change.

A teacher training programme, immersed as it is in a continually changing social, cultural, political and economic environment, must necessarily change, if it is to remain in harmony with its environment.

Evaluation for a training unit or lesson, as a component of

a training programme, can take many forms; oral, written, essay test, objective test, attitudinal test, content test, etc. A single evaluation instrument cannot assess all aspects of instruction. However, an evaluation instrument can be designed to assess a particular domain of instruction, for instance, the competencies and skills being developed. We have attempted to design a few strategies and instruments to evaluate teacher competencies and skills as shown in the foregoing.

1. Self Evaluation (by Trainee):

Each trainee can and should evaluate himself on his or her performance. This can be done after each teaching practice unit. A checklist form provided below is meant to be an example. Modification should be done in accordance with the situations.

Competencies/Skills		Level of Acquisition (least) (most)				
		1	2	3	4	5
Information processing skills	identify, locate and utilize information					
	classify, analyse and utilise relevant information					
	search for ways to understand scientific information from primary sources					
	always update oneself on scientific and technological information					
	select reliable information and clarify values, ethics					
Decision-making skills	identify alternatives					
	predict consequences of each alternative					
	weigh the pros and cons of each alternative					
	order the alternatives					
	take actions consistent with stated values					
	accept possible consequences of the actions taken					
Instructional skills	use a variety of resources					
	use, improvise, develop teaching aids					
	design certain activities					
	effective utilization of laboratory and instruments					
	stimulate/arouse students interest					
	bring in real-life situation to class and vice-versa					
Science process skills						

2. Evaluation by Teacher Educator:

2.1 Systematic observation throughout the training

The sheet below lists only skills that are mostly required for development of scientific attitudes, values and ethics, and as an example on how a grading can be done. The performance of the trainee is rated from the least which is 1, to the highest point which is 5.

Competencies/Skills		Planning			Presentation		Evaluation		
		Choosing Topic	Writing Objectives	Selecting Resources	Motivating	Facilitating Students Activities	Providing Feedback	Collecting Evidence	Interpreting
Information Processing skills	identify, locate and utilize information								
	classify, analyse and utilize relevant information								
	search for ways to understand scientific information from primary science								
	always update oneself on scientific and technological information								
Decision-making skills	select reliable information and clarify values, ethics								
	identify alternatives								
	predict the consequences of each alternative								
	weigh the pros and cons of each alternative								
	order the alternative								
	take actions consistent with the stated values								
	accept possible consequences of the actions taken								
Science process skills (observing, classifying etc.)									
Instructional skills	use a variety of resources								
	use, improve, develop of teaching aids								
	design certain activities								
	effective utilization of laboratory and instruments								
	stimulate/arouse students interest								
	bring in real-life situation to class and vice-versa								

Comment on the competencies/skills a trainee has acquired including the strength and weaknesses.

____

____

____

____

____

____

____

2.2 Open-ended questions: reactions to situational problems

This type of evaluation is an exercise to develop an appreciation of ethics and values in the trainees with regard to the application of science in real-life situations. The format is as follows:

1. a brief description of the present real-life situation is given.
2. questions are posed to the trainees to debate among themselves.

Real-life problem situations presently occurring in the region are recommended for the discussion, among which are:

1. pollution (air, water, soil)
2. alternative energy resources (nuclear power)
3. utilization of chemicals in farms and households (pesticides, fertilisers)
4. deforestation
5. health

Problem 1

The construction of dams to provide water is inevitable to ensure a continuous supply of water to an ever-increasing population. But before the construction begins, vast deforestation has to be carried out. This results in floods and droughts and destroys the ecosystem of the area. Erosion due to land clearance and construction activities may lead to situation of the rivers. Vegetation clearance increases temperature and reduces rainfall. Once the dams are constructed, more forest land will be destroyed as it becomes submerged with water for the reservoirs.

Questions

1. Is there any way we can increase water supply to populated areas without having to destroy vast areas of forest?
2. Do you think the benefits of a dam outnumber its disadvantages?

Problem 2

It is found that approximately only 10 per cent of total petrol sold in Southeast Asia is lead free. Lead has the effect of decreasing the body's metabolism and has an adverse effect on the liver. Incomplete combustion in most vehicles also results in soot, haze and poisonous gases being emitted which includes the killer gas carbon monoxide.

Question

Is there any way to reduce air pollution caused by vehicles?

Problem 3

A very poor woman was being slandered and ostracized by people in town for auctioning one of her kidneys in order to ensure food for her children.

Questions

1. Do you agree with the people in town?
2. What were the rights and wrongs of a very poor mother in doing so?
3. Are there alternatives to this?

Problem 4

While an airplane was spraying pesticides an a plantation, strong guests of wind blew the pesticides over to a field where small farmers were ploughing. The farmers became very seriously ill and had to spend many weeks of suffering in a hospital.

Questions

1. To what extent should plants be protected at the cost of human welfare?
2. If the plantation gives farmers compensation, would they be free from blame?

Problem 5

A woman needs a large amount of money for taking care of her aging sick mother. She agrees to become a surrogate mother for a couple, who in return, provides that large amount of money she needed. The contract was signed. Upon delivering the baby, the woman refuses to hand over the baby to the couple because she feels attached to it during her pregnancy. She was forced by the court to hand over the baby to the couple.

Questions

1. Do you agree with the court's verdict? Why?
2. Should surrogacy be legalized?

3. Evaluation by Peer Group

During teaching practice, a trainee can also be evaluated by peer group, as well. Informal observation can be done by using a form of checklist as illustrated below:

Competencies/Skills	*(low)*				*(high)*
	1	2	3	4	5
1. uses a variety of resources available 2. designs non-traditional activities (child-centred) 3. brings in real-life situation to class 4. integrates controversial issues related to science and technology 5. encourages students to think divergently, analytically, systematically 6. leads a discussion impartially 7. encourages students to search for relevant information 8. encourages student to hold their final judgement until there is sufficient information					

Competencies/Skills	(low) 1	2	3	4	(high) 5
9. encourages all students to participate in discussion					
10. assists students to be willing to listen to others					
11. motivates students to ask more questions					
12. accepts the possible learning outcomes					
13. is able to handle students' different ideas					
14. encourages students to think of alternatives					
15. encourages students to weigh the pros and cons of each alternative					
16. encourages students to take actions consistent with the stated values					
17. arouses the students' awareness to accept possible consequences of the action taken					
18. assesses students' performance by using various methods					

Comments

The suggestive checklists and other indications attempted in this Chapter are to be re-examined and refined by individual teacher educators and teachers. No exhaustive list of competencies and skills could be prepared as the same has to be developed in each institutional/regional situation, depending upon the general and specific expectations from the teachers. No doubt there would be considerable commonality and the presentation here is an attempt in the same directions. It incorporates possible curriculum transaction situations, teachers' skills and competencies needed for this transaction, the groups which could assist in evaluating the outcomes and finally how each assessment could be utilized as remedial input for enhanced learning outcomes, both in cognitive as well as in the affective learning. Learning is important for the trainee. It is equally significant for the trainer.

Concluding Remarks

The sharing of experiences amongst the group brought out clearly the concerns of member countries in imparting science and technology education at elementary level which is very crucial in the life of young learners. While the limitations were noted, potentialities in each country were also found adequate to proceed further and strengthen the science and technology education. It was agreed upon that there were some very prominent areas that need immediate attention, strengthening and assignment of specific roles to institutions. While practically every country has developed some expertise, produced materials linked to real life situation and have modified their teacher education programmes, shifting emphasis to practical training, they still need to strengthen the links between school and community and establish a visible mutual accountability between the two. To achieve this, it was felt that there was a need to strengthen or establish comprehensive teacher training institutions, fully equipped to look after the training needs of teachers of science and technology in a particular area or region. Resource institutions at state level or national level, which exist in all countries may concentrate on resource-person training and production of exemplar materials. Sharing of experiences through workshops, seminars within the country and also on bilateral basis among countries should be regularly organized and attempted. UNESCO may also continue to provide more opportunities for sharing of experiences at international level.

Part II

EDUCATION FOR TEACHING SCIENCE AND MATHEMATICS IN THE PRIMARY SCHOOL

Introduction

The concern of this small publication is to explore the extent to which there is common ground in the approach to the education of primary school teachers in science and mathematics. To the extent that this is the case it may be possible for there to be some economy in time and effort and some increase in effectiveness in teacher education programmes. Given the greater emphasis on these areas of the primary curriculum in all countries, and the concern that this causes to teacher education, such possibilities are well worth serious exploration. But the arguments go beyond the pragmatic to the essential nature of the subjects and the value of defining differences and commonalities so that the identity of each subject is respected even in the early stages of children's learning. We have been careful to respect the integrity of the mathematics and science whilst arguing that there is much in common about the approach to learning the subjects at the primary level.

Two things are best made clear at the start. First, that it is not our concern to advocate an integrated approach to science and mathematics in school teaching. Second, that we are neither advocating nor not advocating an integrated approach in teacher education; our purpose is to raise and explore relevant issues. We would not have embarked on this study, however, if there were not reasons to consider that there exist major areas of similarity and real possibilities of improvement in teacher education that may result from considering the similarities and differences between science and mathematics in teaching and learning at both school pupil and teacher education level.

A major area of similarity is the view of learning of the subjects and the way in which this is conveyed in teacher education. It is recognized that a view of learning is communicated to teachers or student teachers not only overtly, through providing information, but as a message implicit in the way in which courses are conducted. The particular view of learning which is shared in mathematics and science education and by the authors emphasizes the importance of taking the learner's initial ideas as a starting point and the participation of the learner in modifying and extending ideas in the light of experience. If this constructivist view of learning, perhaps as one of others, is to be embedded in the training of teachers, there are significant consequences for training programmes. Of similar importance is the way in which the nature of the subjects is conceived. These factors seem to the present authors to be of such fundamental importance that we have used them as the basis for the structure of this publication.

We have begun, therefore, in Chapter 1, presenting a model and a rationale for the significant influences on teaching. What is significant in teaching necessarily identifies important foci for teacher education. Consistent with the important role we have ascribed to the view of the subject and of the nature of learning in science and mathematics, the next two chapters are concerned with these matters. Chapter 4 addresses the vexed question of the knowledge of science and mathematics that primary teachers need. The emphasis here is on an adequate basic grasp of different aspects of the subjects rather than on advanced mastery of an academic kind.

Assessment is a third major influence on teaching. This is addressed in Chapter 5, where emphasis is laid on assessment as a formative part of teaching. The implementation of the constructivist view of learning, which underpins the thinking in this publication, depends on assessment of pupils' ideas and skills. Chapters 6 and 7 discuss more directly the content and methods of teacher education programmes. Chapter 6 offers lists of the opportunities for professional development which might be provided at pre-service in-service stages. What is learned, however, depends not just on the content of courses but on the methods used in training, matters which are taken up in more detail in Chapter 7.

To reiterate an earlier statement, these chapters do not offer solutions or lines of action to be followed. Their purpose is to provoke thinking and discussion of issues relating to the education of future teachers of primary science and mathematics. In writing them, we ourselves found that we raised many questions which we are not able to address and identified areas where further research and development are needed. We hope that by listing these at the end of the booklet the publication may more easily be used as a discussion and study document by others. To further this purpose, we also include an annotated bibliography of sources which others may find as useful as we have. Whilst there is a degree to logic to the order of the chapters, sequential reading is not essential. To aid 'dipping', each chapter begins with a brief summary of its contents.

The production of these chapters has been a combined effort of the contributors. The publication began as an idea discussed among representatives of UNESCO, ICMI and ICSU-CTS in March 1989. Writing began in earnest after a workshop held in Liverpool in February 1990 and subsequent drafts were further discussed and refined at a meeting in Edinburgh in October 1991. Certain members of the group have taken the main responsibility for writing various chapters and are identified by their initials at the end of each chapter. During the whole process and particularly at the final meeting, comments from others helped to shape the contents of chapter and often to modify and add to them. In addition, a firm editorial hand had been applied to try to produce a coherent and readable whole.

1

A Model for Discussing Teacher Education

A Model for Classroom Decision Making

Observations of teachers in their daily work in classrooms indicate a consistency between how teachers go about their work and their views of learning. This has been recognized through research and is described as teaching style of approach[1,2]. One teacher will prefer to provide a range of activities for children, perhaps covering the whole curriculum, and will give the children a considerable amount of responsibility for choosing and completing their work. Another will keep the class as a whole for most of the time so that they will share the maximum amount of the teacher's attention. Yet another may encourage groups of work together and expect a cooperative product in some appropriate form. When asked about why they choose one approach rather than another, the reasons teachers give are in terms of their views of what they want children to learn and what they think is the best way of helping children to learn it. Each conscious decision about how to arrange the class, what kinds of activities to provide, how to bring children into interaction with the materials supplied, the kind of help the teacher gives and how success is to be assessed, will be consistent with the teacher's view of what and how children should be learning.

For example, suppose that a particular teacher's view of learning is that it is a matter of rote memorization. This teacher will provide learning experiences which expose children to accurate facts and encourage them to memorize procedures and algorithms. To do this efficiently the teacher will probably provide the information in digestible packets, each to be mastered before the next is attempted. The class will be arranged to optimize exposure to information from the teacher, from the blackboard and from books, and to minimize interference from non-authoritative sources, such as other children. The teacher's role will be seen as being to ensure attention, to present information clearly and to reward accurate recall; the pupils' role is to attend, to memorize and to recall; resources may be used to illustrate applications of fact already learned or just to add interest and prevent boredom. Of course, the evaluation criteria will be defined in terms of how well the children can recall or reproduce information. This teacher will be doing a good job of rote teaching; all the classroom conditions are consistent with rote learning and support its implementation.

If the teacher has a different view of learning, along the lines suggested in the Introduction and described in more detail below, where the learner is active in creating understanding and in testing and modifying initial ideas, then the classroom provision consistent with it will clearly be quite different from that described for rote learning. Now the experiences provided will enable pupils actively to seek evidence through their own senses, to test their ideas, to take account of others' ideas through discussion and using sources of information; the class organization will facilitate interaction of pupils with materials and pupils with pupils; the teacher's role will be to help children to express and test their ideas, to help them to reflect upon evidence; the pupils' role includes some responsibility for learning and taking part in generating ideas; the materials have a central role in providing evidence as well as arousing curiosity in the world around. The assessment criteria must include reference to developing and using skills and ideas and not neglect development of related attitudes.

The model below (adapted from Harlen and Osborne,

1985)[3] is an attempt to convey this relationship between the kinds of learning experience teachers try to provide for their pupils and the kind of learning they want to bring about. Their decisions about implementing this, in terms of the role they take as teachers, the role they allow for the pupils and the way in which they use resources, are made so as to be as consistent as possible with the intended learning experiences. The success of the teaching and learning is judged against criteria which in turn are related to the view of what should be learned and how it should be learned. Feedback from evaluation brings the planned experiences and their implementation more closely into line with the kind of learning intended.

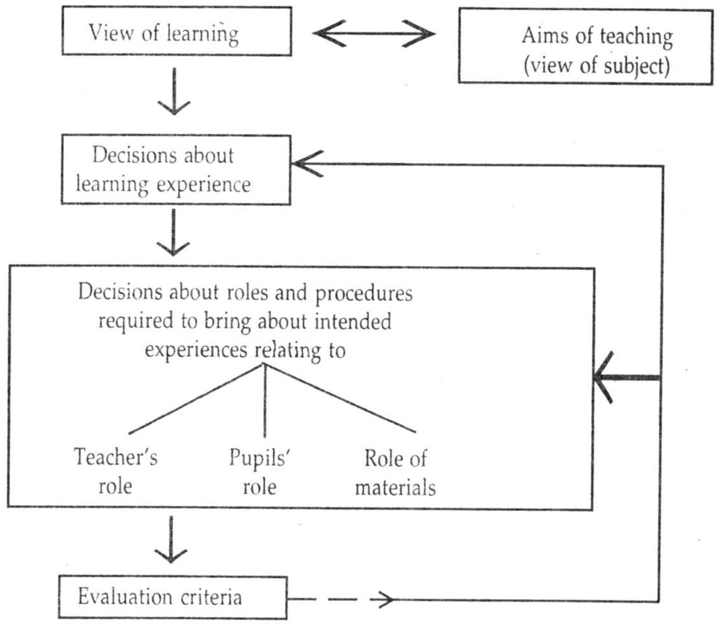

The classroom of the teacher who values rote learning and that of the one who takes a constructivist view would clearly be very different learning environments. Assuming that we do not favour rote learning, a question for in-service teacher education is: how can be turn the first one, arranged for rote learning, into a different one, perhaps more like the second? At this point we must admit that we have ignored the inevitable constraints on teachers imposed by conditions such as class size and the provision of materials and basic facilities, which are not available to all teachers. Where teachers lack the conditions which would enable them to teach in the way they would like, the solution has to be sought through other channels than teacher education.

However, if the teacher is free to choose and has chosen to teach by rote, the answer to our question about how to change the learning environment (s)he has created is certainly not by telling him or her to recognize the class so that, for example, the children sit in groups. Nor will it be by merely providing different books, since a devotee of rote learning can turn anything into an exercise of memorization. What is required is for the teacher to become re-educated as to the nature of learning. Only when the teacher is convinced that role learning will not lead to understanding and is equally convinced of the value of children taking an active part in their learning will he or she be prepared to make the effort to organize the class, the materials, and to make the time, for children to learn in a way consistent with this view.

Teacher Education: Determining the View of Learning and Teaching

The above model proposes that the views of learning and of the subject are the keys to the learning opportunities that a teacher provides for the children. It therefore follows that these views must be given a high profile in teacher education. The major question in the present context is: to what extent are the views of learning relevant to primary school mathematics and science the same?

Let us consider the constructivist view of learning as an example, first taking its application in science and, later, in mathematics education. This is a view of learning which holds that the learner, in trying to make sense of new events or objects, begins from relevant existing ideas or models and tests the extent to which the new phenomena can be explained using these existing ideas or models. If predictions based on a related existing idea or model fits the new observations, than the range of application of the idea or model is extended; if the evidence does not fit the prediction, however, this may mean that the idea or model has to be modified or rejected in the light of the new evidence.

Science encompasses the first-hand use of physical and mental skills to generate and test reliable knowledge and generalizations. In learning science, these skills (referred to as the process skills) are involved in using and testing existing ideas. It is through processes such as observation, questions raising and hypothesizing that ideas are used in trying to explain new evidence; it is through processes such as prediction, planning, experimenting and interpreting that conclusions are drawn as to whether the ideas fit the evidence. If these process skills are not carried out in a rigorous and scientific manner, then the emerging ideas will not necessarily fit the evidence. Ideas may be accepted which ought to have been rejected, and vice versa. Thus, the development of ideas depends crucially on the processes used. While the facts or data and generalizations are important, how we come about them and what makes us believe them are of equal importance. It is important that they derive directly from the phenomena themselves, that careful planning, observation and recording are done, and that the conclusions drawn are bases for further investigation and verification.

It follows that attention needs to be given to the way in which children test out their ideas in primary science, that is, to the development of the process skills. However, this cannot be done effectively by direct teaching any more than the understanding of abstract scientific concepts can be taught directly. Experience of attempting to give instruction in observation, or prediction, as such, using content-free activities (meaning trivial content, since there has to be some) is that the skills are not transferred to use in scientific enquiries as hoped. The usefulness of the skills in helping understanding has to be experienced. So a pupil who recognizes that finding a pattern in observations has helped in making a useful prediction is likely to try this in another situation because of its value in helping understanding and not just because (s)he knows how to do it. The continual interweaving of knowledge and process skills in the investigation of natural phenomena is an essential characteristic of science education.

Science also involves using the knowledge that has been generated through process skills to create and continually refine testable models of nature that help us to describe, explain, predict, and to conceptualize observable phenomena of nature. In this model building of science, the approach is first-hand enquiry built around experience and experimentation and the focus is the phenomena themselves. The models at first will be approximations that are improved or revised or discarded in the light of additional data that comes available as children's experience expands. Children, like scientists, must be ready to reject ideas when the evidence requires this. In this way ideas gradually change and develop to be more encompassing, more generalized and more abstract.

In the type of learning just described the learner collects the evidence and does the reasoning; makes the ideas his or her own. This is what we may call learning with understanding. Learning without understanding, as in rote memorization, does not require the use of process skills. Learning with understanding helps children to feel at ease with science, to know its strengths and weaknesses, to realize how ideas emerge from human activity, which is important in their education even if they are not destined to practise science.

In mathematics education these same arguments apply in relation to devolving children's knowledge, say of arithmetical operations, and to developing skill in selecting appropriate operations, knowing when to add and when to subtract. Children are often taught to know how to add, subtract, multiply and divide, but may still be unable to decide which to do when faced with a real problem. Without experience of taking part in the construction of an algorithm in solving a problem the procedures have to be learned by rote, without understanding. They lack the understanding of what the process means in real terms and the ability to move from a verbal description of a problem, say of dividing a sum of money equally between a number of people, and the appropriate mathematical algorithm.

As in science, the aim in mathematics education is to stimulate and support learning with understanding. The interweaving of knowledge development with process skills and the resulting creation of models of the nature of things are elements that we believe should be at the centre of science and mathematics education.

This, then is the kind of learning which we aim to bring about in children through the education we give the teachers. To do this for teachers already in schools, through in-service education, it is often necessary to produce a quite radical change in their view of what teaching is and how children learn. This will not happen quickly or without some considerable effort on the part of those concerned. The status quo acts to moderate attempts at change and to establish new patterns and move to a new status quo takes a matter of years rather than the months over which in-service activities are usually spread. In the case of teachers in initial training the position is not so different, since these aspiring teachers will have spent up to 12 years in school through which they will have developed quite firm ideas about teaching and learning which may well have to be changed.

So, because of the existing ideas and experiences which teachers or student teachers bring with them, in teacher education we are concerned with changing ideas, not just planting new ones in virgin soil. Producing change is notoriously difficult. In the context of curriculum development it has been a matter of concern since the early days of curriculum projects, in the 1960s. In the 1970s, Kelly[4] and Rudduck and Kelly[5] carried out studies of implementation of innovation in which they distinguished between translocation (just getting new materials to teachers), communication (getting a message over), implemen-tation (using the new materials) and re-education (developing real understanding and commitment to the new approach embodied in the materials). Their work has been followed by many other studies which have shown that producing materials and ideas alone is not sufficient to change practice and that this cannot be done without the active participation and cooperation of teachers.

The Particular Problems of Science and Mathematics

Most of the points made above, although illustrated in terms of science and mathematics education, apply equally to most other areas of the curriculum. In science and mathematics, however, particular problems are encountered. Many, perhaps most, primary teachers have received from their own education a legacy of failure or at least dissatisfaction in relation to science and/or mathematics. Thus their overriding requirements are for confidence, an appreciation of the nature of scientific and mathematical activity and enthusiasm for teaching the subjects.

These pervading aims have implications for the conduct of a teacher education programme, since they concern attributes which cannot be engendered through specific content but only in the way of dealing with that content (which may mean, for example, not lecturing to a large group of students as the predominant style of a course). In meeting these needs it is as important not to do certain things as it is to do other things. For instance, it would seem important not to teach teachers the science and mathematics background they need in the same way as they were taught previously and which dismally failed. Neither should we underestimate the value of their everyday knowledge, which may be implicit, rather than explicit, but could be greater than assumed. Further, we should not treat them as if they had not existing ideas of their own about teaching, learning and about the subject matter to be taught.

Mathematics and science suffer from the popular perception they are difficult, remote from the understanding of most people and only for the 'specialists'. Teachers, as members of the society in which these views are embedded, tend to share these perceptions. They stand, therefore, to benefit from actions which are taken towards creating a more positive popular attitude towards mathematics and science. More positive attitudes of teachers will influence the perception of these subjects by their pupils, the future citizens, and thus break into the present vicious circle in which unconfident teachers pass on their negative attitudes through the way they teach. Thus the moves to popularize mathematics and science are to be welcomed. For example, a study by ICMI[6] has provided both general considerations and concrete examples around the notion of presenting mathematical ideas of various level of sophistication to a wide audience.

A further problem particular to science and mathematics is that the majority of primary teachers in most countries are women. Like many women, they have suffered from the 'masculine image' of science and mathematics. By this is meant the reputation these subjects have of being 'cold and calculating', objective, concerned with facts and accuracy, impersonal and excluding emotions and feelings. Such characteristics do not, as a generality, seem attractive to girls, leading to a high rate of drop out and a sense of failure and alienation from these subjects. Many theories have been put forward to explain this situation, relating to the psychological origins of personality, in-born differences in spatial ability, social conditioning in early life, etc.[7,8].

A growing body of opinion is looking at the nature of the subjects and the way they are portrayed in schools, rather that at the supposed deficiencies of girls, for the source of the problem. It has been suggested, in the case of science, for example, that "process-based science is likely to project a more human view of science and to involve learning experiences that engage the thinking, imagination and interest of pupils as well as leading to an understanding of key concepts and principles. The aim of this approach is for pupils to learn with understanding, through development of their own ideas, which are taken seriously and not ignored in favour of the 'right answer.' This type of learning is more likely to appeal to all pupils."[9] The same may be said of mathematics. If such a view of these subjects could be transmitted in teacher education it could play an important part in generating the confidence and enthusiasm which so many teachers lack. The importance of not reinforcing old prejudices follows clearly from this.

REFERENCES

1. Galton, M.J., Simon, B. and Croll, P. (1980) *Inside the Primary Classroom*. London, Routledge and Kegan Paul.

2. Bennett, N. et al (1976) *Teaching Styles and Pupil Progress*. London, Open Books.

3. Harlen, W. and Osborne, R. (1985) A model for learning and teaching applied to primary science. *Journal of Curriculum Studies*, vol. 17, no. 2, 133-146.

4. Kelly, P. J. (1975) *Report to SSRC on the Curriculum Diffusion Research Project*. Mimeo. Centre for Science Education, Chelsea College, London.

5. Rudduck, J. and Kelly, P.J. (1976) *The Dissemination of Curriculum Development*. NFER, Slough, UK.

6. Howson, A.G. and Kahane, J.-P. (eds) (1990) *The Popularisation of Mathematics* (ICMI Study Series). Cambridge University Press.

7. Burton, L. (ed) (1986) *Girls into Maths Can Go*. London, Holt, Rinehart and Winston.

8. Kelly, A. (ed) (1987) *Science for Girls?* Milton Keynes, Open University Press.

9. Harlen, W. (1989) Education for equal opportunities in a scientifically literate society. *International Journal of Science Education*, vol. 11, no 2, 125-134.

2

The Interface Where Science and Mathematics Meet and Mingle

Introduction

Science and mathematics are often mentioned in one breath, which indicates that people associate the one subject with the other quite readily. This is not surprising since many scientific observations can be quantified in numerical expression, in measured magnitude, or proportional relationship. Somewhere along the line of a scientific investigation, a switch is made from objective physical observation to mathematical processing of obtained data. The dividing line between the two subjects is crossed with ease, but is not so clearly drawn. Particularly in physical science, though not exclusively, one can benefit greatly from mathematical systematization, logical consideration of possibilities, and clear questioning. Mathematical attitude and scientific disposition almost coverage here.

It is little wonder, then, that there have been attempts to integrate science and mathematics as school subjects, in conversation or discussion as well as in intended practice, particularly at primary level. However, the conversation and discussion have proved easier than the implementation in practice. Where the attempt has been made to integrate the two subjects consistently, difficulties have arisen, emphases have been biased, and interests have clashed. Without a serious attempt to coordinate and align the differing subject matter of mathematics and science, the uneasy marriages have broken up all too easily.

Distinct Disciplines, But . . .

Science and mathematics are, after all, two distinct disciplines, each having its own characteristics. Using the work 'discipline' in close association with 'disciple' gives it the meaning of 'gathering information' or rather, 'a process of building knowledge'. 'Knowledge' is then taken in the sense of a framework, or network, of interrelated concepts or ideas. The difference of obtaining and processing concepts and ideas distinguishes the resulting bodies of knowledge, in this case science and mathematics. The distinction, however, does not erase the obvious relationship between the two disciplines. Consider some examples where the two ways of gathering knowledge run together.

A Mathematical Problem may be Evoked in a Scientific Context

Children take a daily measurement of their growing maize plant. However, over the weekends the school is closed and no measurements are taken. How much did my plant grow on Saturday? How much on Sunday? This is now a mathematical problem. Keeping careful daily measurements on the weekdays, enables the children to employ the mathematical skill of graphing these, so they can interpolate the most probable lengths of the plants on the weekend days. Alternatively they can use their measurements to calculate an average rate of growth, and use this per diem proportion to figure out the unmeasured magnitudes.

A Scientific Problem may be Approached in a Mathematical Context

Where would my maize plants grow faster, inside the classroom or outside in the garden? An experimental situation as suggested by the question should be set up. Measurements need to be taken at regular intervals, both inside and outside, and the quantitative results compared. For more accuracy the daily rate of growth in both situations may be calculated and compared. For still greater accuracy a number of plants may be grown and measured, inside as well as outside, and average results may be determined and compared.

As these examples suggest, science often provides a framework, or context, for mathematical activity. The primary teacher who teaches the children both subjects ought to be aware to this, not so much from the point of view of designing a curriculum of mathematics, but in order to be ready to jump at every good opportunity to make the children apply their mathematical skill and knowledge in a situation of reality which happens to be meaningful to them. This places the children in a situation where they need and want maths. It enlivens the exercise, and provides sound motivation, for it carries within itself the reward of satisfaction.

Mathematics is often called 'the language of science', for it enables the young as well as the older scientist to generalize, to summarize and to communicate in clear and concise mathematical terms, formulations and equations. This is a great assets, and one more reason to insist on letting the children grow and develop in this most useful subject and apply it wisely. This simply means: teach the children mathematics with integrity and science with integrity. Instead of attempting to integrate what in essence stands apart, the two subjects are to be presented in a working relationship of interdependence where this is relevant and useful. In this way they become a most powerful educational 'tool' giving meaning and depth to the expression 'science and maths education'.

The use of mathematics as a toolkit for science makes it by no means subordinate to science, and certainly not when one considers that everybody's science would be severely crippled in its progress without mathematics.

Mathematics deals with quantities and magnitudes which are specific properties of physical objects and materials. Whereas mathematics systematically loosens itself from the bedrock of concrete, physical objects and their quantitative properties in order to pursue pure mathematical patterns and laws in the abstract regions of numbers, spatial relations and algebraic structures, science keeps returning to the reality of physical objects, their interactions and working systems. The flight of a scientist into mathematical abstraction is always related to some physical, down-to-earth, concrete, matter of fact observation, which poses a problem and asks for understanding.

Archimedes shouted 'EUREKA' because he found a mathematical construct to express (and find) the specific gravity of materials. Thus he could distinguish the specific gravity of the metal from which the king's crown was moulded. By comparing the magnitudinal properties of the pieces of matter Archimedes used a mathematical way to come to a reliable scientific conclusion with regard to the quality of the king's crown. His prediction was based on mathematical insight and physical experience.

Returning to the primary school, we find children who are taking their first steps in orderly scientific investigation. The essence of their scientific activities is 'encounter and interaction'. Children encounter (or are purposely confronted with) real objects, living or non-living, which by their colour, texture, shape or behaviour invite or challenge the children to explore and investigate. This interaction between the children and the object of their immediate attention may be free and exploratory, but it can soon be given order and system by good science education when a good suggestion given by the alert teacher turns the free exploration into a purposeful investigation, whereby the children are encouraged and helped to develop and employ various scientific process skills. Observation, questioning, trying to explain, or hypothesizing, predicting and verifying by experimentation, are readily mentioned as typically scientific process skills. However, quantifying data, measuring and related calculation or computing, belong to the category of scientific process skills, too. These, by nature mathematical activities, are now applied to the solving of scientific problems. Certain scientific challenges call directly for specific mathematical activity, which provides a motivation as well as an opportunity to initiate and develop, through practice, these mathematical skills.

Example: Constructing a Scientific Model

These overlaps of maths and science should not go undetected by the experienced teacher, and the teacher in training should be given the opportunity to develop this detective eye, for this is the interface we are talking about. The following example illustrates where science and maths meet and mingle.

Strips of pegboard, with holes at equal distances, can be made into remarkably accurate balances. With sturdy paperclips as units of weight countless experiments can be done to find equilibrium. By simple trial and error combinations, of weights at various distances on either side of the balance arm, can be found which bring both arms in equilibrium.

However, when the teacher intervenes to help the children to bring order into their investigations, and to quantify their findings, the errors diminish, and the trials turn into direct experiments. A simple way of recording data is suggested whereby the relation between weight and distance on either side, or arm, of the balance is noted down in a systematic may. A worksheet with a series of problems like the one below is at the same time a model of good recording.

6W at ?D	=	?W at 3D
	=	2W at ?D

The question marks are to be replaced by the actual numbers (of distance to the fulcrum or of units of weight). If the balance is in equilibrium, it indicates that the figures are right. Initial trial and error is still in order. However, it will not take long before the children being to suspect some relationship between weights and distances, and they use their suspicion, which by now has become a hypothesis, to predict the outcome of a possible combination of weights and distances on either side of the balance.

Slowly a pattern emerges which, often with some help of the teacher, can then be formulated and understood as:

The sum of Weights times Distances on the Left equals the sum of Weights times Distances on the Right.

Once this mathematical construct has been mastered, the children can make countless combinations without touching the balance. Besides, this 'moments bar formula' enables them to find the unknown weight of other objects (pocket knife, pencil sharpener) by balancing them on their balance and then turning the algebra of the formula into a equation to be worked out by simple calculation.

The continuous interaction between science and mathematics is there in the primary school. In the case of the balance we find the science in the way the balance responds to changes in weight or of distance in an ordered and consistent way. There is a pattern in the way in which the forces, acting on either side of the balance, influence its behaviour. This pattern in turn can be expressed (or summarized) in a mathematical formula which applies in all physical circumstances. There is also an element of technology in this example of the balance. The instrument, simple though it is, must be made precisely and the weights must be cut to equal size, or volume.

The activities can be presented to pupils in a simple way. A series of 'worksheets' can set them going, giving the teacher a chance to pay attention to individuals, as the examples on the following pages may indicate. These examples were chosen from a unit called *Children and Balances*.[1]

Quantitative View

Developing a quantitative view of the world around is an objective of both science and mathematics education. This 'quantitative view' induces children (and adults) to find ways of measuring or otherwise quantifying things whenever this helps to solve a problem or whenever it would reveal some (new) relationship.

The mathematical requirements of the young primary scientist may be simple and straightforward, the necessary skills must well be mastered before any creative use can be made of them. Primary mathematics must take its own flight into more abstract working with quantities and magnitudes simply because it has an educational value of its own. It offers a different, if not a wider, context of application than science.

Example: Constructing a mathematical model

Constructing a scientific model of equilibrium with the help of simple experiences of balancing weights and measuring

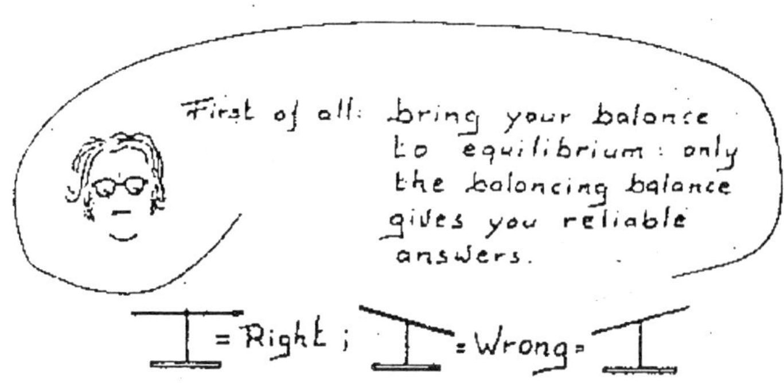

these are examples of what to do and how to record it: Put 1 unit of Mass at Distance 14, on the left side, and 1 unit of M. at D. 14 on the right-hand side

	Left		Right	
	M	D	M	D
	1	14	1	[14]
	[2]	6	1	[12]
	2	4	[1]	8
1	1	14	2	[ ]
2	2	14	1	[ ]
			[ ]	4
3	[ ]	10		
	1	[ ]	3	11
4	3	[ ]	2	12

This is one problem!

The "Law" of the balance:
or: What makes the balance balance?

The following course of action can be undertaken by older children (age 12 - 81).

By solving some simple, direct problems - to which the balance "knows" the answers - you are led to a general conclusion: a generalisation, a "rule", a "law", which can be expressed in a formula.
(This process is called: induction.)

Understanding this formula enables you to solve new problems by deduction.

Provide enough balances with a peg-board strip as balance arm, suspended from the centre, top hole.

14 13 12 11 10 9 8 7 6 5 4 3 2 1 0 1 2 3 4 5 6 7 8 9 10 11 12 13 14

Number the holes as shown above.
These numbers indicate the distances (D) measured from the centre (0). This is the fulcrum, or turningpoint.
(The amount of holes may be 14, 12 or 10.)

Use sturdy paperclips as "weights", as <u>units of mass</u>. One paperclip is: <u>1 M</u>

Per hole you can use more than one unit of mass, of course; more than one paperclip.

For instance, you are instructed to place "3 M at D8".
This means that you must place 3 paperclips in hole number 8.

Before you start, make a small rider out of bent wire, or a tiny paperclip, so that you can bring your balance arms into perfect equilibrium: only then can your balance give you faultless answers.

distances, which primary children can appreciate, was illustrated in the example given above. This finds its parallel in mathematical model building at primary level in the field of number work and algorithms.

Long division and its rules might have confused those of us who were, at onetime, given these rules without supporting experiences. The following example attempts to illustrate possible steps to avoid this confusion by building a mathematical model which makes sense to primary children.

We can present the children with what may be for them rather a complex situation of seating 81 people at the occasion of a parents' meeting in the assembly hall of the school. There are tables available, each accommodating 6 people. How many of these tables will be need to make all 81 parents comfortable? In most cases the children would start by drawing a sketch of the situation and try and solve the problem by the means they have at their disposal: counting, adding, and trying to find short-cuts in their calculations. The problem may be approached at various levels:

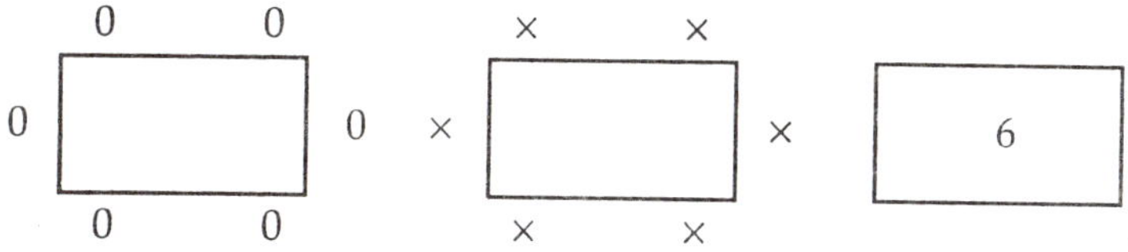

0 0 / 0 [ ] 0 / 0 0   × × / × [ ] × / × ×   [6]

6 + 6 + 6 + 6 + 6 + 6 + 6 + 6 + 6 + 6 + 6 + 6 + 6 + 3

$\underbrace{6+6+6+6+6}_{30}$ $\quad$ $\underbrace{6+6+6+6+6}_{30}$ $\quad$ $\underbrace{6+6+6+3}_{21}$

60 + 6 + 6 + 6 + 3

So, at various levels, places are counted and grouped and added to reach 81 available places to match the 81 expected parents at a specific number of tables each seating 6 people at the time. Although they may use rather roundabout ways, the children will eventually find a solution to the problem. But it is all rather messy and disorganized.

So, next time a similar problem may be approached in a somewhat more sophisticated manner. A new problem is presented in the following way. "Freddy finds a box full of marbles in the attic. He takes the box outside where his brother Joe is playing with his friends Bernard, Hubert, Ed, Geoffrey and David. They are going to play at marbles, but want to start off with an equal amount each. How would they divide their treasure?

This time the teacher places a box full of marbles on the desk, and leaves the children to divide this (as yet unknown) number of marbles fairly among the six boys. However, the process of dividing the marbles is now recorded onto the blackboard by the teacher, closely following, and thus describing, what happens:

Freddy	*Joe*	*Hubert*	*Bernard*	*Ed*	*David*
10	10	10	10	10	10
10	10	10	10	10	10
10	10	10	10	10	10
5	5	5	5	5	5
5	5	5	5	5	5
2	2	2	2	2	2

Three marbles are left over. Now they can talk about the sharing of the marbles and how fair it was. The figures on the board help them.

The next step is to move into a more theoretical problem: There are 324 marbles in a box to be divided among four boys. How many should each get? This is a problem in words without real boys or marbles, so in this case we must find another way to figure it out ... Small worry: we can now follow the example of tabulating the numbers on the blackboard as it was done before:

	Peter	Bruce	Jim	John
324 – 40	10	10	10	10
284 – 200	50	50	50	50
84 – 80	20	20	20	20
4 – 4	1	1	1	1

Nor marbles are left over.

Some important questions have now have tackled:

- How many marbles were there?
- How are they to be shared?
- Are there enough (for each to get a fair share)?
- How many are left (if any)?

As a last step in this stage of horizontal mathematising a problem like the following can be raised: "Linda has invited 12 friends to her birthday party. Before departing each one of them is to be given a bag of sweets. Mother has bought 425 sweets to be divided over the 12 bags. How many sweets will go into each bag?" This time the whole story is translated into numbers on the blackboard, and work out in an interactive way together with the children:

	U	U	U	U	U	U	U	U	U	U	U	U
425												
– 12	1	1	1	1	1	1	1	1	1	1	1	1
413												
– 120	10	10	10	10	10	10	10	10	10	10	10	10
293												
– 240	20	20	20	20	20	20	20	20	20	20	20	20
53												
– 48	4	4	4	4	4	4	4	4	4	4	4	4
5												

. . . But who does not get tired of doing all this on the blackboard? The need to find a short-cut is now keenly apparent. From now on the notation scheme becomes the object of study, and the improvement on it makes the way to the solution of problems shorter and more efficient. This is *vertical mathematization*. The problem might, in words, read as follows: Six girls divide 432 coloured beads among themselves for each to make a necklace. How many beads will each girl get? But . . .

who, at this stage, needs girls or beads? The teacher will write numbers on the blackboard and will use only one pot now:

6	432	
	–60	6 x 10
	372	
	–60	6 x 10
	312	
	–300	6 x 50
	12	
	–12	6 x 2
	0	

The "50 x 6", of course, is 5 x 10 x 6, which, being a sensible estimate, is a big step towards a short-cut in calculation. So, in the end, girls and sweets and beads and boys are left out altogether, and a purely mathematical construct, or model, or algorithm to work with remains. Now they can work out the answer to a mathematical problem on a more abstract level:

18	3866		
	–1800	100	
	2066		
	–1800	100	
	266		
	–180	10	
	86		
	–72	4	
	14	214	(rest 14)

This mathematical model now reflects fair division, and is understood as such.

These illustrations show how short-cuts in problem solving are looked for in both science and in mathematics.[2]

There are many instances where science and mathematics meet and mingle. So, when some science activity makes the children ask for anything mathematical, their interest is alive, and the never-to-be-missed moment has arrived, where the teacher and the children are to select the most appropriate mathematical tool. Recognizing these interactive situations, and even setting them up purposely, belongs to the art of teaching and so finds a place of priority in the training of future elementary school teachers.

REFERENCES

1. Harlen, W. and Elstgeest, J. (1992) UNESCO *Source Book of Activities for Primary School Science Teacher Education*. Paris, UNESCO.

2. Streetland, L. (ed) (1991) Realistic Mathematics Education in the Primary School. Paper given on the occasion of the opening of the Freudenthal Institute, Utrecht.

3

Children's Learning in Science and Mathematics

Introduction

Learning and its theory have a long history. In this century the study of learning, initially mainly a concern of psychology, gained ground in the context of learning and teaching in school. A prominent theme in this history is an increasing emphasis on 'activity', that is, on the activity of learners. In science and mathematics education the emphasis on activity, on 'learning by doing', stands out particularly.

In the next section the key concepts of active learning will be identified through consideration of learning in general. Then these key concepts will be our guideline in elaborating children's learning of science and mathematics. Designing instructional materials and teaching in both fields, making connections between the subject areas but also keeping them distinct, requires knowledge of both similarities and differences.

The Study of Learning in a Wider Context

The behavioural psychology which dominated the study of learning at the beginning of this century has given way to cognitive psychology which emphasizes the role of mental activity, as opposed to unthinking 'response' to stimuli, in determining behaviour. At the same time it has been recognized that studying learning in controlled laboratory conditions gives little information about learning inside and outside schools. Gradually the view has emerged that learning depends upon what is learned, in what contexts and with what motivation. So educational psychologists have taken a position closer to the disciplines and to school subjects and as a consequence closer to pupils and their learning activities.

The recognition of the role of the activity of the learner led to the notion of learning by discovery, the desire to give pupils the excitement of finding things out for themselves. In science this approach, also known as the heuristic method, was advocated at the end of the last century, but was only widely adopted in the 1960s. Its deficiencies in practice were soon apparent. It was extremely difficult for pupils to arrive at accepted generalizations through their own observations and investigations. Thus the notion of 'guided discovery' was introduced, giving the teacher a role in structuring the learning situation. However, a more fundamental criticism of discovery learning, whether guided or not, was that it makes no explicit reference to pupils' own ideas.

The notion of activity in learning, implicit in 'discovery', also appeared from Eastern Europe as well as from the West. But it was highly structured and left little room for learners' own constructions. Western educators and learning theorists stressed personal involvement in the learning process more and more; experiential, participative and cooperative learning became popular terms. Particular value was placed on problem solving, using realistic and relevant problems.

But in practice it was soon realized that 'activity' of itself is not necessarily accompanied by learning. What could be done to transform an activity into a learning activity? One of the convincing answers came from the designers of 'Problem Based Learning" curricula[1] in which students create their own learning activities starting from a relevant problem. In the initials steps relevant prior knowledge will be brought to bear in tackling the problem and will be restructured as new knowledge is acquired. Throughout the whole process time is spent on reflection. Working in cooperative task-group stimulates interaction in which individual constructions can be shared. The necessity to put mental images into words appears to support reflection and arguably raises the standard of thinking.

Children's Learning in Science and Mathematics

The common thread in a large number of studies of learning in science in the last two decades is that children bring to their new experiences existing ideas formed as a result of earlier experiences, formal and informal, processed by their own ways of reasoning. These ideas make sense to the children, often more than the accepted scientific views of things, which they thus reject. The recognition of the existence and nature of children's own ideas led to the realization that it was frequently ineffective simply to attempt to teach the 'right' concepts. Attention thus turned to different ways of teaching which took account of existing ideas. Several strategies have been proposed. An early and still popular one is to introduce an event or phenomenon which is discrepant or conflicting with the pupils' view in the expectation that this will cause a modification in thinking.

At a theoretical level, Piaget's notion of provoking disequilibrium in order to bring about accommodation of the mental framework to encompass new experience suggests that new experiences should challenge existing ideas. However, there has been much discussion of the nature of the dissonance between the pupils' ideas and those required to understand the new experience. Too small a gap means that pupils assimilate the new experience into existing ideas (perhaps with minor modifications); too great a gap means that the new experience makes no connection with existing ideas which are left unchanged. The different ways proposed for using 'discrepant events' in the classroom include following the event with groups discussions[2], brainstorming and then debating ideas[3], charting all the ideas coming from the class[4], and 'interpretive discussion'[5].

There have been warning notes, however, about the effectiveness of discrepant events in practice, since children may be less concerned about having their ideas challenged than adults would be. In addition an objection on more ideological grounds suggests that the notion of a conflict between ideas and the subsequent decision as to which one 'wins' is unsound as a basis for learning. Certainly it would not seem to aid pupils' ownership of ideas. It can be argued that these objections have particular force at the primary level, where it is important to take children's ideas seriously. Finding out what children's ideas are in order to 'confront' them is not the same as requiring children to use and test their ideas, as a result of which the ideas may be modified or perhaps abandoned in favour of ones which they decide are better fits for the evidence available.

This process bears close resemblance to the way science has been constructed during the history of mankind; mathematics too was constructed likewise in different cultures and in different places. In the so called 'genetic' approach of teaching the historical development of the subject, the ontogenesis, students are offered opportunities to 're-invent' what mankind invented earlier[6]. Materials for learning and teaching in the domains of science and mathematics have been designed with this genetic approach[7].

In the current view of learning in science and mathematics the core concept is activity[8] and, according to modern science and mathematics educators, learning is 'learning by doing science and mathematics'. Learning by doing is the device but by no means the whole story.

What students do should be intrinsically motivated, perhaps through presenting a realistic problem-situation and an opportunity for investigation, cooperative and interactive, using prior knowledge. Learning by doing requires reflective thinking and creates opportunities for personal constructions. What has to be learned ought to become a personal mental property, integrated in what was acquired before. It becomes, so the speak, 'owned' by the learner.

Together with knowledge and skills in the field of science and mathematics, pupils acquire a specific attitude towards identifying, tackling and solving problems. It is this attitude that supports continuous learning, even in situations a long way from classrooms or when the schooldays have been left behind. Further, by doing science and mathematics students will develop a very specific and personal view of these disciplines. The approach reflected in this publication will embrace a concept of science and mathematics as a process, in contrast with science and mathematics viewed as a collection of rigid facts, procedures and rules.

Science, as portrayed by prominent philosophers, is seen as the construction of explanatory models that encompass wider and wider ranges of phenomena. This is not all that different from the learning of science seen as the construction by pupils of ideas about the world around and tested against their own experience. Thus these two advances are regarded as connected and as leading towards a new science of learning with great import for the learning of science[9].

Points of Special Attention

Having traced the roots of 'learning by doing' in educational psychology, we now use the identified key concepts to look more closely at learning in science and mathematics.

Activity

On a variety of occasions environments change into learning environments. In can be an event, a problem, a phenomenon or an argument that raises questions and asks for investigation.

The situation can be mathematical by nature, in which case investigation means mathematizing, horizontally first (in order to put the problem into a mathematical context) and then vertically (using mathematical tools). Other important activities include organizing, describing, mapping, using suitable schemes and models, ordering the raised questions and systematically searching for answers.

For example the 'scheme' of the empty number line has been found very helpful in assisting mental arithmetic. Take the following problem, to be solved by pupils in grade 3[10]:

A book has 64 pages.

I have read 37 pages.

How many pages are left for me to read?

The line is a thinking model to represent the book:

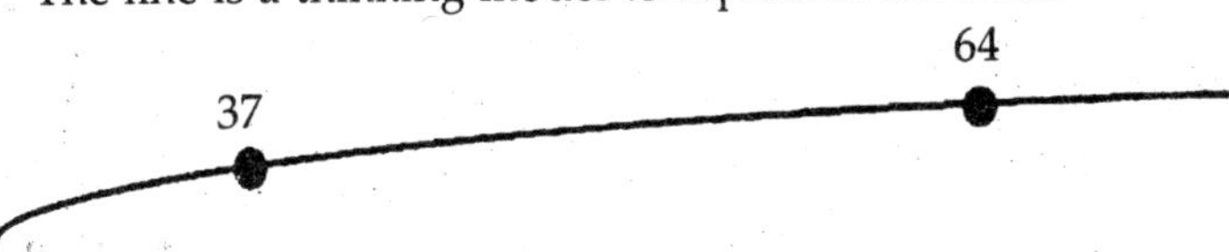

One approach is to work forwards in steps, this way:

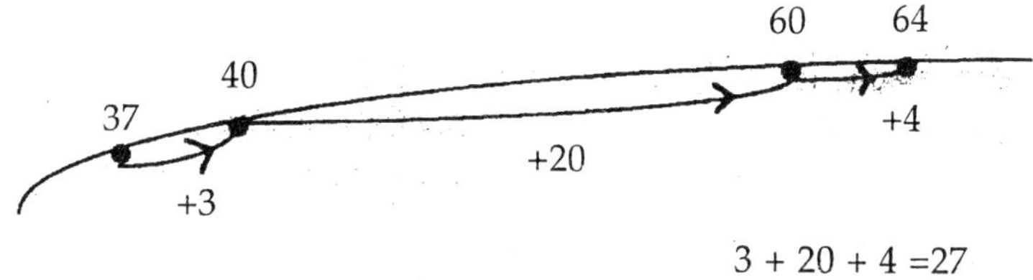

Another is to go beyond the end to an easy point, which does not exist in reality but can be considered as an extension of the line:

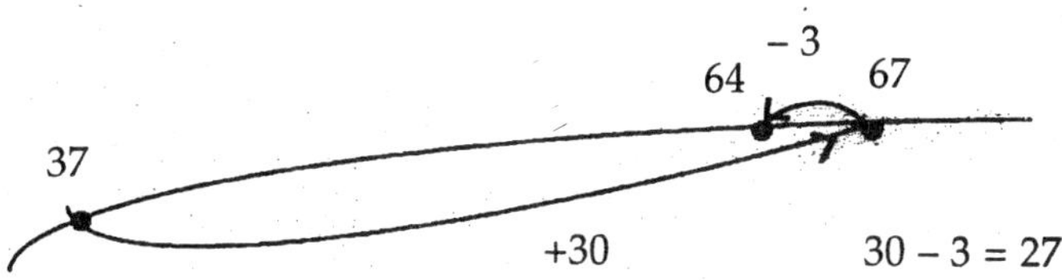

In this kind of activity prior knowledge and intuitive notions are used and new knowledge and notions are developed. The need for being efficient supports the invention of short-cuts, a way to establish mathematical procedures like algorithms.

In science, 'activity' is characterized by the use of process skills, observing and detecting, raising questions, formulating hypotheses, making predictions, and reporting the findings, simultaneously communicating and discussing them.

Realistic Situations and Contexts

Realistic means realistic to pupils. In other words it is not just daily life, but play and imagination are also realistic for (young) children. Context means what comes into mind because of a situation: intuitive notions, pre-concepts, misconceptions, experiences, (ir)relevant memories, successful trials, a nice solution, an unforgettable failure etc.[11]

Realistic situations and contexts are essential conditions for the learning of science and mathematics because:

- applications are met, learned and practised from the very beginning

- well known situations motivate, pupils recognize usefulness
- in realistic situations prior notions and pre-conceptions are easily brought in
- some contexts become exemplary and can develop into general models[12].

It is not easy to create realistic situations designed to become learning environments which meet these conditions. Whilst the imagined division of a pizza appears to offer a good orientation on fractions, and a yoghurt-cup telephone can provide a useful exploration of the phenomenon of sound as a vibration, it is more problematic to introduce 'kinetic energy' through the realistic context of 'windmills generating electricity' and in a context of 'banking' the multiplication of negative numbers will not become clear. There is often a conflict between the detail of the reality and the requirements of the disciplines.

Interaction

We may say that 'activity' in the field of science and maths becomes 'learning activity' if, among others, fundamental notions are constituted, concepts are developed, new views arise, skills are practised, procedures are developed and models are acquired. Just doing is not sufficient: what has been done needs to be put into words. This activity of formulating and expressing their ideas needs reflecting and anticipation; reflection on their own learning process and anticipation of how other learners need to be told to understand what they have learned. Working together with other learners creates the necessary stimulation. Interaction is more than communication; pupils learn to understand each other, they learn to listen, to immerse themselves in the thinking of peers and teacher, to feel for others' efforts and to realize that they must given access to their own thoughts. Meanings that initially have been constructed individually will be shared and completed by interaction.

Personal Constructions and Productions

Science and mathematics bring worthwhile knowledge and skills if (and only if) these become an integral part of an individual's 'common sense'. By common sense we mean the approach which makes sense to the individual and which s/he uses to tackle problems in daily life. Common sense can be developed to various levels and on this depends the extent to which the subject matter, understandings and skills can be used.

Research and practical wisdom show the inadequacy of school knowledge which exists only in artificial settings and remains isolated from everyday applications. Children cannot use this knowledge and so often revert to more primitive procedures, such as counting instead of multiplication. The procedures used go back to pre-school learning and are so to speak 'true to nature'; sometimes similar to those which can be recognized in primitive stages of the ontogenesis of the discipline. The research literature on 'ethno-mathematics' provides examples of this phenomenon and suggests that pupils' intuitive and natural approaches to problems[13] are a worthwhile starting point for learning. In mathematics a similar ontogenesis has been found in different locations and in different cultures[14]. It goes without saying that children should be enabled to construct their own (primitive) notions and procedures, as happened in the history of mankind, of course, without imitating the big blunders or simulating the long periods of stagnation. Reinvention is the term used; children are stimulated to invent their own mathematics.

Here is an example of reinvention by a child in tackling this subtraction sum:

$$\begin{array}{r} 324 \\ -\,187 \\ \hline 263 \end{array}$$

3 minus 1 equals 2
2 minus 8 equals 6 short
4 minus 7 equals 3 short

200–60–3 = 140–3 = 137

Most interesting are children's free productions as answers to 'classroom tasks' such as:

- make a manual for this calculator to be used by pupils of grade (n-1)
- think of a test on doing this for your friends

- write a book about the number 1 million
- invent all kinds of sums with the answer (3/4)
- tell younger children how to graph the growth of a bean
- how would you explain that a big piece of styrofoam is lighter than a small stone?
- devise a test to find which (of three given samples of) paper would be best for covering books?

Children create their personal science notions as well[15]. As in mathematics the teacher has to intervene so that pre-conceptions are adjusted rough checking 'common sense' ideas against the evidence of nature.

It seems to be evident that in both subjects 'learning by doing' needs teacher's support and intervention. Core questions posed at well chosen moments stress the essentials. In maths, for instance, the suggestion to use a particular scheme or model can open doors. The skill of reporting accurately (orally in discussion, as well graphic, in writing and diagram, graph or sketch) becomes important here.

So it is not only the investigating which needs support; important stages need to be concluded by reflective summarises or to be anticipated by advance organizers and specific tasks have to given in order to memorize and practise skills.[16]

In science any of a range of interventions may be used. For example the following have been proposed by the SPACE project[17].

(i) Enabling Children to Test their Own Ideas

This will involve children in using some or all of the process skills of science: observing, hypothesizing, predicting, planning and carrying out fair tests, interpreting results and findings, communicating. It is an important strategy which can, and should, be used often. Implicit in the suggestion of using process skills is the notion of developing them, for example, through greater attention to detail in observing, more careful control of variable in fair tests and taking all the evidence into account in interpreting.

(ii) Encouraging Generalization from One Context to Another

Does an idea which has been proposed for explaining a particular event fit one which is not exactly the same but which involves the same scientific concept? Other contexts might be suggested by the teacher or by the children. The application may involve discussing the evidence for an against, or gathering more evidence and testing the idea in the other context, depending on familiarity with the events in question.

(iii) Discussing the Words Children use to Describe their Ideas

Children can be asked to be quite specific about the meaning of words they use (whether 'scientific' or not) and to provide examples in action where possible. They can be asked to think of alternative words which have almost the same meaning. They can discuss, where appropriate, words which have special meaning in a scientific context and be helped to realize the difference between the 'everyday' use of some words and the 'scientific' one.

(iv) Extending the Range of Evidence Available

Some of the children's ideas may be consistent with the evidence presently available to them but could readily be challenged by extending the range of evidence. This applies particularly to things which are not easily observed, such as slow changes, or those which are normally hidden, such as the insides of things. Attempts to make these imperceptible thing become perceptible, often using secondary sources, helps children to take a wider range of evidence into account.

(v) Getting Children to Communicate their Ideas

Being required to express ideas in one way or another—through writing, drawing, modelling and particularly through discussion—means that they have to be thought through and often rethought and revised in the process.

Differences

Having mentioned a number of similarities between learning in mathematics and science, we now thus to the possibility of differences. A first difference comes up when we consider the way a situation is organized for solving problems in mathematics. As was shown in Chapter 2, in relating to the creation of an algorithm for division, the organizing of the sharing situation become a organization model for doing future divisions and eventually it becomes kind of mental model to do the calculations without the need for further reference to real things. In science, however, the eventual check is always against reality, not internal logic, as it is in mathematics.

A second difference is that mathematics distinguishes itself from science in respect to the concept of 'being certain'. What given direction to the process of problem solving in mathematics classrooms, is the search for certainty.

Seven persons go into a double decker bus. Some are going upstairs, some are staying downstairs. How many possible distributions can you find?

There is a certainty implied here that there is indeed a single solution and that no-one can find a greater number of distributions. This specific kind of certainty is missing in science investigation, where the possibility always exists of an alternative answer which fits the evidence.

But the validity of differences between the subjects depends to some extent on whose judgement is being used. While it is clear for the general public that there is rapid development at the frontiers of most sciences, the same can hardly be said about mathematics. There are possible many roots for such a misconception. On a somewhat anecdotal level, the mere fact that there are Nobel Prizes related to various sciences, but none in mathematics, may suggest to the lay person that nothing 'new' is happening in mathematics. Perhaps more to the point is the fact that while the vast majority of today's adults will have learned mathematics for many years in the classroom, the mathematics they have then encountered is for the most part centuries old, be it in arithmetic, geometry, algebra or even calculus. In contrast to the science teacher who can find many occasions to relate aspects of the curricula to recent developments, the mathematics teacher is usually working with a curriculum that can only reinforce the image of mathematics as a static discipline.

Implications

For the general public, mathematics is concerned essentially with calculations and formulas, a view strongly supported by both the standard primary and the secondary school curricula and related to the traditional conception of mathematics as the science of number and shape. The recent developments in electronic technology have created a situation which may suggest to the public that a shift in emphasis could—and should—happen. While in certain historical or sociological contexts the ability to perform, say, arithmetic calculations might have rightly been considered a high-level skill, this is on longer the case, now that calculators are available—almost universally—to evaluate these routine operations.

So emphasis in the primary school curricula must change, for instance, for calculating skills needed for the exact evaluation of more or less complex arithmetic expressions to the decision-making skills enabling one to chose the appropriate arithmetic operations corresponding to a given situation and to assess the reasonableness of the answer. In other words, a shift from purely algorithmic skills to more complex interpretative ones.

There has been recently a strong movement to revamp the public perception of mathematics by presenting it not merely as the science of number and shape, but rather as the science of structure, of order, of patterns of all sorts18. Such a view, while not negating the fact that numbers and forms are at the very heart of mathematical activities, clearly stresses the idea that it is not the ability to manipulate such mathematical objects that is crucial, but rather the ability to use them in a proper way. Much of the computational drudgery can now be safely left to the calculator (or the computer), which allows for more attention to be given to the mathematical process *per se*.

Developing skills in the execution of arithmetical algorithms has always dominated the traditional primary school curriculum. It is probably safe to say that any algorithm of such basic importance that it should be included in the primary (or even secondary) school curriculum will have been programmed and made available on computers (if not on calculators). So placing the sole emphasis on performance in algorithmic computations is definitely not the best way to prepare the pupils adequately for the mathematical needs of the twenty-first century.

Does this imply, say with respect to the primary school arithmetic curriculum, that there is no more a place for the study of basic calculation techniques? Surely not! But the education process should promote the acquisition not of 'mechanical' abilities, for which the machine is superior but of more 'human' abilities pertaining to the choice of an appropriate mathematical model, the planning of the operations, the development of number sense allowing one to check, through mental approximation, the order-of-magnitude of the results (not the exact value!) and to interpret those results intelligently. All these results in quite a different agenda from the traditional goals of primary school mathematics. While the exact nature of the learning experiences needed for the development of the new skills is still to be assessed, such skills will surely require a thorough understanding of the fundamental principles on which is built the new practice of mathematics. The key issue does not thus concern whether the teaching of fundamentals is to be included in the primary school curriculum, but rather which fundamentals should be included and how they should be presented to the pupils.

This leads us into the next chapter where we consider the knowledge that teachers require in order to produce this learning in primary pupils. Later, in Chapter 7, the implications for training are spelled out.

REFERENCES

1. Schmidt, H.G. (1982) Problem-based learning: rational and description, in *Mathematical Education*.

2. Erickson, G.L. Children's conceptions of heat and temperature, *Science Education*, 63, 221-230.

3. Nussbaum, J. and Novick, S. (1981) Brainstorming in the classroom to invent a model: a case study. *School Science Review*, 62 (221), 771-778.

4. Shapiro, B. (1988) What children bring to light: towards understanding what the primary school science learner is trying to do. In P.J. Gensham (ed) *Directions and Dilemmas in Science Education*. Falmer, Brighton.

5. Baird, J.R. and Mitchell, I. (eds) (1986) *Improving the Quality of Teaching and Learning*: An Australian case study. Melbourne, Monash University Printery.

6. Freudenthal, H. (1973) *Mathematics as an Educational Task* Reidal, Dordrecht.

7. Wagenshein, M. (1970) *Ursprunglisches Verstehen und Exactes Denken I.* Stuttgart 1965, Vol. II Stuttgart.

8. Christiansen, B. and Walther, G. (1986) Task and Activity, in Christiansen, B, Howson, A G and Otte M, *Prespectives on Mathematics Education*, Reidel, Dordrecht 1986, 243-308.

9. Novak, J.D. (1988) Learning science and the science of learning, *Studies in Science Education*, 15, 77-101.

10. Streefland, L (ed) (1991) *Realistic Mathematics Education in Primary Schools*, Freudenthal Instituut, Utrecht, p. 41.

11. Krabbendam, H. and de Vries, M. (eds) (1990) *Goals and Methods in Science, Mathematics and Technology Education in the Netherlands* Report of a conference in the framework of the OCED project 'Science, Mathematics and Technology Education', SLO Enshede. Chapter 3: The theme 'Settings and Methods'.

12. Gravemeijer, K., van den Heuvel, M. and Streefland, L. (1990) Contexts, Free Productions and Geometry in *Realistic Mathematics Education*, OW & OC, Utrecht.

13. d'Ambrosio, G. and Bishop, A. (1988) in the volume of ESM, produced on the occasions of ICMI in Budapest.

14. Bishop, A. (1988) *Mathematics Enculturation. A cultural perspective on mathematics education* Klumer Adacemic Press, Dordrecht.

15. Watt, D. and Russell, T. (1990) the Science Process and Concept Exploration project: 'Sound', Research Report, Liverpool University Press.

16. See among others Reigeluth, C.M. (1987) *Instructional Theories in Action* Lessons Illustrating selected theories and models, Hillsdale.

17. *SPACE 1993 Project Handbook* Collins, London.

18. Steen, L.A. (ed) *On the Shoulders of Gaints: New Approaches to Numeracy*. National Academy Press, USA.

4

What Should Teachers of Primary Mathematics and of Primary Science Know?

Introduction

"Teachers should know more than the children they teach." This is the simplest, the quickest and the most meaningless answer one can give. Although it sounds like 'common sense', it requires distinguishing degrees of knowledge the nature of which remains obscure. Having followed a more advanced course in mathematics or science or, indeed, having passed an exam at a higher level, is of little or no relevance unless it results in teachers having ready, usable knowledge at their fintertips. In other words, we discuss not what they should have had, neither what they should have passed, but what they should have made their own: *an intellectual structure of interrelated concepts on which they can draw with confidence when placed in a problem situation.* This knowledge concerns science, mathematics and education. It includes the disciplines of the subjects, the subject matter, as well as the complications of helping children to learn. Altogether this forms a many-faceted construction, which is considered further in Chapters 6 and 7.

A Triple Interaction

Children learn best when they occupy themselves fully with the 'things' that make up the subject of their learning. In science education these 'things' are real, concrete, touchable living and non-living objects or materials which are found or placed in a variety of situations. It could be a seedling growing on blotting paper and another one growing in soil. It could be a magnet picking up pins. It could also be a small community of living organisms growing, or moving about on a square metre of ground (a 'minifield') at the edge of the garden or somewhere in a piece of wasteland, or it could be a mealworm in a box given a choice between heaps of sand, sawdust and cornmeal.

In mathematics it could very well mean the same things, but then in some quantitative relationship on a slightly more abstract level: e.g. the daily rate of growth of the seedlings; the number of pins the magnet picks up; the measuring of equal distances between the mealworm and the three heaps of its choice; or the different sets of living things found within the 'minifield', or their coordinates for placing them on a map. But even if the 'things' of maths occupying the children are of a more abstract character, such as the symbols they use for numerals and signs of operations, or the planimetric figures they draw, these are still a self-created reality with which the children work.

In occupying themselves with their subject matter, be it the very concrete things of science, or the partly abstract symbols of maths, children go beyond mere encounter. They enter into a 'dialogue', an interaction with the object of their immediate attention, and they manipulate it in such a way that it reveals something of its own essence. This may be a property, or a 'way in which it works', or a sequence of 'things I can do with it', or something that has been uncovered, or that has been invented or even re-invented.

The 'revelation of something of its own essence' is nothing else but the formation of a concept in the mind of a child. This may be a new concept altogether, or some change or refinement of an already present concept. It could also be the rejection of some preconception which is now suspected as false. Finally, it might be a new association with some previous concept(s) so that a relationship is established which deepens understanding and insight.

The teacher who wants to engross the children in the subject matter of science and mathematics through real things and representative symbols which the children can handle, must himself have undergone, or undergo, the excitement and joy of learning, and so share it with the children. Only then can the teacher appreciate a learning situation, assess its value, judge what next step should be taken, create new learning experiences, and foresee where the renewed investigation can lead.

Foreseeing what a learning experience can lead to implicates an interaction of the teacher with the subject matter at hand on the level of an adult, someone who has learned, through experience and study,

(a) to place a new concept in a wider framework of existing knowledge;

(b) to use a familiar concept in the wider context of one's (own) existing knowledge;

(c) to retrieve an old concept and to see its relevance in a new situation.

With this more mature intellectual potency the teacher can approach both the subject at hand and the querying, learning children, and so interact with them, being sensitive to their needs or wants, and helping them with word as well as with deed, so that they can see relationships and understand an explanation. The teacher's interaction with the children and with the subject matter may assist the children to recognize and make use of a relationship which they had learned already, so that they find or discover their own explanation of what they were puzzling about, or gain a new insight.

Now we can summarize the tripartite interaction which is in evidence in good education:

(1) The child interacts with the 'subject matter' at hand (e.g. germinating seeds, darkness seeking woodlice, an isosceles triangle, or some quantity to be divided). At the same time the child interacts with the teacher who with word, deed, or other intervention (or, indeed, by just leaving the child quietly alone) helps the learning.

(2) The 'subject matter' (which, broadly taken, comprises the 'stuff of to be learned', the things to be handled,

the sources being tapped, and the problem situations into which the children are placed) interacts both with the children to whom it presents a challenge, and with the teacher to whom it once was, or may now still be, a challenge.

(3) The teacher, in turn, interacts with the querying children as well as with the object of their query, namely the 'subject matter' at hand.

It is with this triple interaction pattern of education that we should seek for what teachers of primary mathematics and science ought to know in order to be good and confident in their teaching[1].

Knowledge

The world 'knowledge' does not simply represent a clear, unambiguous and unequivocal concept. By different people, or in different circumstances, it may be given various shades of meaning.

Popularly stated we distinguish:

(1) A '*How-is-it-called-knowledge*' which relates mainly to the formulation of factual information, the right name, the appropriate word. It helps of show that you know what you are talking about, yet does not guarantee it. Learning by rote tends to lead to this form of 'knowledge' and go no further.

Because this aspect of knowledge is easily assessable, it may be associated with what is referred to as 'school knowledge', and as such be given undue desirability.

Yet we should not underestimate the value of 'communicating knowingly' as it creates permanence in one's own mind as well as intelligent intercourse among communicating humans. Perhaps we ought to refer to this aspect of knowledge (which for a great deal fills our intellectual 'archive' called 'language') as 'social knowledge' since it covers words and terms, conventions and rules, established and agreed upon by society, which we can only learn by social contact with others by word of month or, otherwise, in writing.

As examples one could mention: 'Naming the parts of the flower', or 'Naming the internal and external features of the frog'. Nomenclature is an obvious example. In mathematics one could think of the names of counting numbers, the names of geometrical figures, or of algebraic symbols.

(2) A *'How-it-appears-to-be-knowledge'* which refers to direct experience. It is a knowledge emerging from interaction between an observer and the object under observation. It embodies properties or observable behaviour of real objects and their possible or actual interactions with other objects, or with the observer/learner. It is checkable knowledge, based on experience, observation, experimentation, research, induction. This makes it also changeable knowledge, adaptable, in as far as it can be adjusted by new experience or investigation, revealing new evidence. Therefore, it is often imperfect, biased, open to discussion. It may also possess a certain degree of probability.

This knowledge makes 'prediction' possible: it stretches ahead. When you see lightning, you can expect a thunderclap; when multiplying any number by two results in an even number. Since the evidence supporting this knowledge is searched for in the physical world—in the nature of things as they are—it may, perhaps, better be called 'physical knowledge'.

(3) A *'How-does-it-relate-knowledge'*. This conception signifies a higher order of abstraction in which relationships between concepts become evident: generalizations, conclusions and patterns inferred from repetitive experiences or experiments. It may also be deduced from pure thought processes in which existing concepts, at various degrees of abstraction, are related to each other, or are recognized as related to each other. Even reflecting on such thought processes may form new knowledge which, in the sense here elaborated, comes close to being identical with 'insight' or 'understanding'. A better name to indicate this knowledge would be: 'logical knowledge'. It is at this level of knowledge that

we talk of insight and understanding, because it has been 'processed' to fit into a person's total store, or 'web' of acquired knowledge, beyond pure experience undergone at first hand.

(4) A *'How-it-should-be-done-knowledge'* which comes close to an ability to do things. However, it goes beyond the physical ability or skill in as far as it incorporates not only the remembered sequence of operations, but also the foresight to create, to invent, to lay out, and to plan a succession of processes or operations in order to compose things, to put things together, to calculate, to compute, to programme, to experiment, or to run an investigation. It has to do with algorithms, with rules of thumb, with safety precautions, with operations, physical as well as mathematical. This knowledge precedes skills and abilities, and motivates to do the necessary exercise to acquire these. One could call this 'technical knowledge' but then in a more than purely mechanical sense. Above the levels of imitating and the grasping of procedures one needs insight and inventiveness in order to be able to organize an experiment or an investigation. Resourcefulness belongs to this aspect of knowledge.

(5) Finally there is a *'How-to-find-your-way-about knowledge'* which makes a person resourceful enough to tackle any problem in the most effective way possible. (Tackle, not necessarily solve!) It consists of a knowledge of resources and their accessibility. It is the knowledge of how to make use of any level of existing knowledge within oneself, coupled with the knowledge of where to look for and obtain the new information, advice, or resources one needs. One knows where to look for things, situations, people, books, scripts, charts, maps, archives, tables, computer ware and whichever other modes of storing information may be useful. This is the knowledge which leads directly to self-reliance in searching and in learning. It is the knowledge of the professional and could, perhaps, aptly be called 'professional knowledge'.

Distinctions, Not Levels

It should be emphasized that the five distinctions described above are not five different kinds of knowledge, nor even levels of knowledge. Knowledge is an intellectual relationship of a person with the world of thought and reality, and is in this person one and undivided. The actual development and actualization of a person's knowledge may, however, be biased towards one or more of these five aspects of knowledge. This may enhance or impair its quality with regard to insight and understanding (of, for instance, mathematics and science) and so determine its use or usefulness.

The Knowledge Which a Primary Teacher (of Science and Mathematics) Should Cultivate

Without going into details of the content of possible maths and science courses in primary teacher training institutions, we can indicate and state that one should strive for as close a balance as one can accomplish between the five outlined emphases, or aspects, of knowledge. In mathematics as well as in science the teachers should become fluent in the appropriate language and use of symbols. They should be rich, and become richer still, in direct experience by a very active and totally involving (workshop) approach. Through reasoning in discussion, reflection on action and thought processes, and wide related reading and discourse, they should gain in comprehension, so that they build up a framework of insightful understanding on which they can rely in their work as well as in their further personal development, with confidence.

Successful teaching of children in mathematics and in science requires a knowledge of the basics, the elements of the subjects. This knowledge requires a deeper understanding than many teachers seem to achieve in their training courses. This seems to indicate and imply that the elements of the primary school's subjects matter refers to what lies at the foundation of the sciences, and these foundations are dug deeply. 'Elementary' is therefore by no means to be identified with 'childlike' or 'easy'. These elements, then, are to be pursued in depth in the training courses, rather than superseded by 'more advanced subject matter', whatever that may be.

Apart from having 'necessary' knowledge it is important for the teacher to be aware of having a distinct view of the subject. Is science an accumulation of facts to be conquered by gathering factual knowledge? Or is science itself a way of learning: the operative skill of acquiring knowledge by the intellectual processes of observing, questioning, hypothesizing, experimenting and reasoning? An answer to either of these questions will express the teacher's view of science and profoundly influence his mode of teaching the subject. Many people tend to accept that acquiring knowledge of the facts of science is the purpose of science teaching, and would consequently emphasize the orderly organization of these facts in graded packages for learning, if necessary by rote, but supported by demonstrations and illustrations, according to the assumed intellectual capacity of children in different classes. However, the view of science as an intellectual process of active learning is adhered to by a growing number of educators, and this results in a way of teaching which we could characterize as 'problem posing teaching promoting problem solving learning'[2]. Similarly, the teaching of mathematics requires some flexibility of approach where mathematical processes enter the picture. For instance, in teaching computation there is more than one way of familiarizing the children with algorithms. If teachers tend to teach only 'their own' algorithms, they should become aware that there are many different models, some of which may be invented by the children. The consideration and conscious appreciation of a different algorithm, or indeed any other mathematical model, reaches beyond pure computation and calculation, and helps the children really to understand mathematical processes. The example of constructing a mathematical model given in Chapter 2 illustrates how this kind of mathematization can occur in a primary classroom.

It is insight and intelligence that should be challenged in the future teacher. It should touch upon all the facets of the teacher's knowledge that we have emphasized above. It should not be unduly overbalanced and directed to one particular aspect, as often happens in rote learning. Teacher training courses that move away from the kinds of knowledge that matter leave students bewildered and battered, sighing: 'This science (or this maths) is not for me', in which case neither will it be for their children.

Teachers need delight and enthusiasm in their own learning, their own formation of knowledge. By being totally immersed and involved in the process of 'making' their own basic knowledge of science and mathematics, they learn to help the children work toward making their own knowledge, too, for there is truth in the remark that teachers tend to teach the way they themselves were taught. Let either be appropriate and efficient.

REFERENCES

1. Hawkins, D. (1967) I, thou, it. In *ESS Reader* Newton, MA: Education Development Center, 1970.
2. Elstgeest, J. (1978) Teaching Science by Posing Problems, *Prospects*. Vol. VIII, No.1, UNESCO.

5

Education for Assessment as Part of Teaching

Introduction

The model of decision-making in teaching, proposed in Chapter 1, suggests that assessment, carried out in a manner which is consistent with the teacher's views of the subject matter and of learning, provides feedback as a basis for adjusting pupils' learning experiences. An interaction between the views of learnıng and of the subject, the decision about classroom activities and assessment was thus identified. In theory the assessment procedures follow from the decisions about learning experiences which are related to the curriculum goals. However in practice the situation is often different and the assessment procedures come first and may dominate what is taught and how it is taught.

The extent to which the assessment leads the curriculum rather than vice versa depends upon the importance given in a particular context to assessment and testing in primary education. It will be affected by whether their is an end-of-primary school examination and whether progress from one year to another is determined by end-of-year tests set within the school. If assessment has a high profile it will tend to lead the curriculum in all subjects which are assessed. Those subjects not assessed are likely to be neglected in all but lip service. In these contexts, the success of any innovations will be limited by existing procedures for assessment and testing. Thus it is necessary to develop appropriate assessment procedures relating to any innovations of curriculum content, methods or goals. It follows that training in these procedures has to be included in teacher education courses, otherwise teachers will fall back on established assessment methods and will adjust their teaching to these.

It cannot be emphasized too much that appropriate assessment methods have to be devised and made available to teachers if there is to be any chance of implementing changes in children's learning experiences. Developments in the last few year have meant that it is no longer acceptable to claim that process skills and understanding (as opposed to knowledge of facts) cannot be reliably assessed; the techniques are now widely known. Indeed it is becoming accepted, perhaps reluctantly, that to change assessment is perhaps the swiftest way of bringing about change in teaching. It was certainly in this way that process-based learning was given a firm foothold in secondary science in schools in England.

This is not the only argument for giving new procedures in assessment a prominent position in teacher education courses. There are many other reasons, perhaps the most important being that assessment is an essential component of putting into practice the constructivist approach to learning that is endorsed in this document. It is possible that some teachers do not recognize the role of assessment in their teaching, or regard it as too informal and not 'proper' assessment, which they see as formal and separate from learning activities. A change of attitude towards, and understanding of, assessment purposes and procedures is signalled for these teachers.

Meanings and Roles of Assessment

The view of assessment that we are adopting here is that it is a process in which information is collected about performance, compared with some standard, criterion or expectation and a judgement is made on the extent to which there is a match. In this view, assessment results in a record or response which replaces the actual behaviour (which can only be preserved if the pupils' work is preserved or video-recordings are made). It follows that there is always some selection and some information is lost. Results of assessment are not 'the real thing' and cannot tell the whole story. This must be kept in mind in interpreting and using the results of assessment.

The various ways in which information is collected and the various bases for judging it create the variety of different kinds of assessment. These include standardized tests, where information is gathered whilst children are tackling carefully devised tasks under controlled conditions and, in contrast, ongoing assessment, carried out almost imperceptibly during normal interchange between teacher and pupils.

A major distinction is to be made between tests (and examinations) and other forms of assessment. Tests are specially devised activities designed to assess knowledge and/or skills by giving precisely the same task to pupils who have to respond to it under similar conditions prescribed by those who devised and trailled the test. However the distinction between tests and non-test assessment is not always all that clear. Some 'tests' can be absorbed into classroom work and look very much like normal classroom work as far as the children are concerned and so they cannot always be regarded as 'formal'. Whether formal or informal, of course, tests are only part of assessment.

Pupils are assessed for a number of reasons and the method chosen should suit the purpose. The main groups of purposes are:

- to help teaching (formative assessment)

  To be effective in this role the assessment must be planned, recorded and used.

- to provide a record of achievement (summary)

  This record is used in ongoing discussion with pupils, in producing a summary of progress and achievements for discussion with parents, and providing information to receiving teachers.

- as a contribution to school effectiveness measures
  The information here will be about the performance of groups of pupils and should be only one part of the information about the school.

- to provide national performance survey data

> This may be used to compare performance across various groups of pupils with national targets, to make comparisons from year to year and between sub-groups.

In the present context we will confine discussion to the first of these purposes since it is the one which has most impact on the teacher's day to day work.

Assessment as Part of Teaching

For pupils to have opportunity for learning with understanding they must have chance to apply the ideas and skills they bring with them to a new experience, and to take part in changing their ideas through using process skills (which are thereby developed). This is the essence of active learning by the child and involves mental and physical activity. The outcome will be ideas which make sense to the child and can be described as being 'owned' by the child.

For there to be the chance of this kind of learning the teacher must find out what are the ideas and skills that children bring to their learning experiences. This is the second step in teaching for understanding, the first being to provide the opportunity for children to engage with materials and problems in an informal way a which will allow their ideas to be elicited. These first and the subsequent steps are represented as follows (derived from the primary SPACE[1] project).

Providing opportunity for exploration and involvement

↓

Finding out ideas

↓

Interpreting

↓

Helping children to develop their ideas and process skills

Assessing change in ideas and process skills

Where work continues on the same topic, the second and fifth steps become the same, both being concerned with ascertaining children's ideas at a particular time. The step of 'providing opportunity for exploration and involvement' ensures that children's thinking is engaged before ideas are sought. When introducing a new topic this initial step will merge into that of 'finding out ideas' where the teacher should be able to choose from range of assessment methods, including open questioning, asking children to draw and annotate their drawings, encouraging children to write about or talk about their ideas, and at all times listening to what the children have to say.

The 'interpretation' is an important step which may be very short or quite long, depending on the teacher's experience and the nature of the ideas which come from the children. It involves reflecting on the experience which may have lead children to their current ideas and the kinds of reasoning that they are using. It is these things which are the basis for deciding the best way to help children in the next step. For example, if a child expresses the idea that growth only happens at certain times and is not continuous, the problem may be lack of evidence and the teacher will try to provide new experience which would challenge a view of discontinuous growth. On the other hand, if a child's ideas are highly bound to particular contexts (such as having different explanations for evaporation in different situations) it may not be new evidence which is required, but a discussion of the reasoning, or perhaps the words, being used about evidence already available.

For the step of 'helping children to develop their ideas' the starting point is the ideas which the children have, whether or not these ideas are along the 'right' lines. 'Development' means heightening, extending and strengthening useful ideas as well as challenging ones which are not useful in explaining things. One of the main ways of doing this involves Children in devising and carrying out investigations to test their ideas, but some activities may be less extensive, such as asking children to provide examples of what they mean by certain words they use, encouraging them to apply ideas they use in one context in trying to explain another one, providing a greater range of evidence (including the use of secondary sources) and encouraging reflection and communication. During these activities there are likely to be opportunities for assessment of any change in children's ideas, using the same range of techniques as in the 'finding out' step.

The way in which the steps are described and characterized varies to some extent according to different interpretations of constructivism (see Chapter 3), but the important common feature is that assessment is embedded in the teaching. It is something that has to be given as much attention in planning as are the materials and the initial activities. Indeed the way in which the materials are used and the nature of the learning experiences will depend on the information gained in the initial assessment.

For example, a teacher planning a lesson on the energy value of different foods started by asking children to look at the information about energy value given on food wrapping and containers. When they began talking about food, the teacher found that many children and not connect food with energy at all. In fact it was sometimes the reverse; they reported feeling sleepy and not at all energetic after a big meal. Their ideas were simply that 'Food keeps us alive. You die if you don't eat.' The teacher then modified his plan and led a discussion on the different reasons the children could find for eathing. These were gathered from the family at home, from claims made in advertisements, from the school cook. Then they discussed what happened if people did not eat, as well as the reasoning behind the views they had collected. After a few weeks the children had linked food and energy in their minds and so that teacher suggested the investigation of differences in this respect since this had become a real issue for the children.

Similarly a teacher finding children interpreting 1/2 x X as X divided by a half would recognize that the meaning of multiplication by a fraction needed to be established by practical examples before the rule for dividing by a fraction was introduced.

The Particular Problems of Assessing Active Learning

It follows from the above discussion that for assessment to have a role in teaching it must comprehensively encompass all learning aims, whether of skill, concept or attitude development. This and other points made so far apply to all subjects, but there arise some particular problems shared by mathematics and science Active learning, where mental and physical skills are being developed, and where how things are done is as important as what things are done, poses a challenge for assessment. Whilst much can be done through study of the products of children's work, it is also important to obtain information about, for example in a mathematics problem, how results were arrived at, whether the appropriate mathematical model was used, how operations were planned, what checks were carried out. In science the equivalent matters include whether tests carried out were 'fair', whether necessary variables were controlled, whether all evidence was taken into account and valid conclusions drawn form it.

Experienced teachers pick up this information during their normal interaction with children as part of teaching, but it poses considerable problems for novice teachers or for those who are introducing active approaches to learning in their classrooms for the first time. These teachers need help to use assessment in the pursuit of active learning, for which conventional methods of assessment are inadequate.

The help teachers need in relation to assessing active learning includes guidance in these three matters:

- what to assess
- how to collect information systematically
- hot to involve children in the process.

Our discussion of these, whilst focusing on science and mathematics, has relevance to assessment in other parts of the curriculum.

What to Assess

Assessing children during active learning is not just a matter of seeing whether or not they are observing, hypothesising, selecting appropriate models, checking, etc. Such broad judgements would have little value for helping the children's learning and in any case could not be made without first thinking through what it means to observe, hypothesis and so on. A first step, therefore, is to have some general indicators or what children are doing when carrying out the processes. The form these might take is best suggested through an example. At a workshop for science teacher educators[2], the following indicators were among those identified for process skills:

Observing

- using the senses (as many as safe and appropriate) to gather information
- identifying differences between similar objects or events
- identifying similarities between different objects or events
- noticing fine details that are relevant to an investigation
- recognizing the order in which sequenced events take place
- looking for patterns that may exist in observations
- etc.

Finding Patterns and Relationships

- putting various pieces of information (from direct observation or secondary sources) together and inferring something form them
- using patterns or relationships in information, measurements or observations to make predictions
- identifying trends or relationships in information
- realising the difference between a conclusion that fits all the evidence and an interference that goes beyond it
- etc.

Hypothesising

- attempting to explain observations or relationships in terms of some principle or concept
- applying concepts or knowledge gained in one situation to help understanding, or to solve a problem in another

- recognizing that there can be more than one possible explanation of an event
- realizing the need to test explanations by gathering more evidence
- etc.

Raising Questions

- asking questions which lead to enquiry
- asking questions for information
- asking questions based on hypotheses
- realising that they can find out answers to some of their questions by their own investigation
- putting questions into a testable form
- recognising that some questions cannot be answered by enquiry
- etc.

Devising Investigations

- deciding what equipment, materials, etc. are need for an investigations
- identifying what is to change or be changed when different observations or measurement are made
- identifying what variables are to be kept the same for a fair test
- identifying what is to be measured or compared
- considering beforehand how the measurements, comparisons etc. are to be used to solve the problem
- deciding the order in which steps should be taken in the investigation
- etc.

Attitude indicators can be defined similarly[3]:

Respect for Evidence

- reporting what actually happens even if this is in conflict with expectations

- querying and checking parts of the evidence which do not fit into the pattern of other findings
- querying a conclusion or interpretation for which there is insufficient evidence
- treating ideas or conclusions as provisional and as being open to challenge by further evidence

Critical Reflection

- willingness to review what they have done in order to consider how it might have been improved
- considering alternative procedures to those used
- identifying the points in favour and against the way in which an investigation was carried out or its results interpreted
- using critical reflection of a previous investigation in planning and carrying out a later one.

A valuable workshop activity is for groups of teachers to work out these indicators for themselves. In doing so they will be clarifying the meaning of the process skills and attitudes and acquiring some ownership over the common definitions to be used. The indicators have to become part of the mental framework the teacher carries in his/her head, used in gathering information through watching children, listening to them, discussing with them what they are doing, as well as from any products in the form of writing, drawings or artefacts.

In use the general indicators have to be translated into the context of specific activities. What will children be doing or saying as evidence of the skills and attitudes when they are investigating vegetation along a transect, working out prime numbers, finding the relationship between masses on a balance— or investigating the melting of ice?

A class of 7 and 8 years old was entranced by a very large block of ice (made by filling a balloon with water and putting it in freezer for a few days) floating in water[4]. In their interaction, discussion and related investigations they showed evidence of—

Observing

- they pointed out details of 'lines' and air bubbles in the ice and places where it was opaque
- they used their sense of touch to feel the 'stickiness' of the ice when just out of the freezer
- they noticed the sequence in which parts of the block started melting.

Finding Patterns and Relationships

- they linked together pieces of information in finding that the larger pieces which they broke off slid down a slope more easily than smaller pieces
- they found a pattern relating the size of pieces of ice to how quickly they melted
- they noted that the parts of the block in the water were melting first but showed caution in saying that 'it isn't everything that will melt more quickly in water than in air'.

Respect for Evidence

- they reported evidence contrary to their ideas: 'moisture still forms on the outside of the tank when there is a cover on it, but I thought it wouldn't'
- querrying whether there is air in the bubbles in the ice: 'we don't know the bubbles are air, we think they are'.

Critical Reflection

- criticizing their investigation of the effect of size on rate of melting: 'it would have been better to start with some larger pieces, then the difference would have shown up more'
- criticizing a comparison of melting in and out of water: 'we should have held the piece in air above the table so that they weren't sitting in the water when they melted'.

Again, practice in 'translating' general indicators into evidence in the context of particular activities can be usefully carried out in teachers' workshops, were added value comes from considering the potential for learning in various activities. The importance of maintaining rigour in the assessment has to be emphasized; the indicators are the criteria against which children's performance is assessed. Whilst the particular ways in which the skills and attitudes are made evident vary infinitely in various activities, it must be possible to show that they are all variants of the behaviours described by the general criteria.

Assessing Systematically

Teachers new to the idea of assessing children during their activities can be overwhelmed by the scale of the task. How can all the children be observe all the time? They can't be, of course. What is required is for the teacher to plan to observe and make notes about one particular group during an investigation, which could spread over several sessions. The teacher would not be standing and watching this group for long periods; indeed the special focus in his/her mind should not be apparent to the children. The difference should be in the identification of particular kinds of information which the teacher is gathering during interaction with the group and in the notes (mental and perhaps written) made at the time about each child in the group. This is not in practice as demanding as it may at first seem, as the example of the ice block activities may have indicated.

In a subsequent investigation another group of pupils would be the 'targets' of observation and so on until all the members of the class have been assessed. A benefit of planning the assessment in this way is that information is gathered about all children, not just the ones who claim most of the teacher's attention. A consequence of this approach, however, is that pupils will be assessed on the same skills but when engaged upon different activities. The questions as to whether this matters takes us back to the point about careful application of criteria. It is a useful focus for discussion in a workshop, as is the development of skill in assessing individual pupils working within a group. Ideally teachers or students should try out suggestions in classes in between workshop sessions.

Involving Children in their Own Assessment

Involving children in assessment has several benefits. It can ease the teacher's burden of assessment, but perhaps more importantly enables the children to take a positive role in their learning,. But it means that children must know what are the aims of their learning. Communicating these aims is not easy since directly telling about complex learning objectives and is not easy since directly telling and complex learning objectives and criteria of achievements is unlikely to be successful. So self-assessment skill has to be developed slowly and in an accepting and supportive atmosphere. It takes time to work through several stages before children are able to apply to their achievement anything like the criteria which their teacher would apply.

The process can begin usefully if children from about the age of eight are encouraged to select their 'best' work and to put this in a folder or bag. Part of the time for 'bagging' should be set aside for the teacher to talk to each child about why certain pieces of work were selected. The criteria which the children are using will become clear. Whatever they are, they should be accepted; they may have messages for the teacher. For example if work seems to be selected only on the basis of being 'tidy' and not in terms of content, then perhaps this aspect is being over-emphasized.

At first the discussion should only be to clarify the criteria and children use 'Tell me what you particularly linked about this piece of work?' Gradually it will be possible to suggest criteria without dictating what the children should be selecting. Through such an approach as this children may begin to share the udnerstanding of the objectives of their work and will be able to comment usefully on what they have learned. It then becomes easier to be explicit about further targets and for the children to recognize when they have achieved them. This is part of building confidence in pupils that their part in assessment is valued and that it can make their learning more enjoyable.

Using a somewhat similar approach to teachers in training has the same value for them as learners. Regularly they should be asked to comment on what part of their course they enjoy most—and least—and why. They should also be asked to identify what they have learned, as distinct from what they have done, and to reflect on the circumstances which affected their learning. They will then realize, from their own experience, the value of being asked to assess their own work and may then be more likely to give their pupils this opportunity.

REFERENCES

1. *SPACE 1993 Project Teachers' Handbook*. London: Collins.
2. Commonwealth Secretariat/UNESCO *Primary Science Teacher Training for Process Based Learning*, Report of the Workshop held in Barbados 1987.
3. Harlen, W. 1992, *The Teaching of Science* London: David Fulton Publisher, pp. 42-44.
4. Ovens, P. 1987, Ice balloons, *Primary Science Review*, No. 3, pp. 5-6.

6

The Training Needs of Teachers

Introduction

In Chapter 1 we presented a model of teaching and learning which, in a very telescoped way, indicated the decisions teachers have to make in providing learning experiences for their pupils. The particular point then made through this model was that these decisions were strongly related to a view of the subject, a view of learning and the evaluation of progress in learning. This indicated three priorities for teacher education courses: to ensure that teachers will receive a thorough understanding of how children learn, insight into the nature of scientific and mathematical activity and the ability to assess progress in all the objectives of learning and to use this information in providing learning experiences. These are such key points that we have devoted the three previous separated chapters to them.

Although these are essential, they are not, of course, sufficient as a preparation for teaching. Teachers also need knowledge of how to plan programmes, of what teaching and learning materials are available and how to choose and use them, of the pros and cons of different curriculum and class organizations, of the school and local authority organization and the part they play in them. They need skills of managing their classroom and its resources, of responding to children's questions, of encouraging children, of intervening, of standing back, of assessing and keeping records, of matching demands to children's abilities to respond to them. They need attitudes of caring and responsibility, self-criticism, reflection, enthusiasm and optimism.

In this chapter we consider how to express these needs and propose a list to initiate discussion. It is neither a syllabus nor a set of objectives. The approach to identifying needs through specifying the skills, attitudes, knowledge and understanding required for teaching has certain attractions but also has dangers. Like the objectives approach to developing classroom programmes, the danger lies in the likelihood of identifying only what is easily definable, narrowing the range to what we are able to specify at present. In the case of classroom activities it is often found that we can with confidence recognize and specify worthwhile classroom experiences but yet not say precisely what learning we expect to arise from each experience. Similarly, it may be best to express the requirements for training as opportunities which have to be provided, which relate to the tasks teachers have to carry out, rather than to attempt to list specific learning outcomes. In any case, the training opportunities have to be identified for any action to be taken and so need to be identified at some stage, whether or not outcome objectives are also stated.

The Balance Between Pre-service and In-service Teacher Education

Recognizing that all the aims of training cannot be achieved in an initial course, it may be helpful to distinguish between what should be provided in pre-service courses and what could or should be provided through in-service courses. In attempting to draw this line there will inevitably be contention about what is essential as a 'basic minimum' for the beginning teacher and the matter will generally be decided in specific cases by the constraints of time and the consideration of the context of the training.

Time is necessarily limited in initial teacher education courses, especially where, as is usually the case in primary education, the teachers are being prepared to teach all subjects right across the curriculum. The timing and structure of pre-service cruises also limits what can be achieved for the development of certain attributes of effective teaching requires experience of a sustained relationship with children and colleagues, and perhaps also with pupils' parents, which is generally not available at the initial stage. Therefore, where these attributes are not essential for the beginning teacher, their development need not be an aim of an initial course designed for the regular classroom teacher.

In this argument, however, there is an assumption about the provision of opportunities for continued professional development which should be available. The pace of change in teaching and the need to maintain the relevance of curriculum of children's everyday lives mean that in-service education is essential for other reasons than complementing pre-service education. However, if it is not available as an entitlement, then more than the base-line minimum has to be included in the initial course. What is possible in this respect varies with course structures. For example, courses where students spend a large portion of the time in schools will differ from those which are mainly institution based.

With these points in mind, then, we propose the following lists for discussion.

Proposals for core opportunities to be Provided in Initial Teacher Education Courses

- experience of the nature of scientific and mathematical activity
- experiences which generate an enthusiasm for science and mathematics
- activities which supplement personal knowledge and understanding of the subjects to a level beyond that expected of the children they are to teach
- experiences which inculcate the scientific attitudes of willingness to tolerate uncertainty, respect for evidence and open mindedness, and the professional attitudes of empathy, willingness to take responsibility and integrity
- activities which develop personal understanding of science processes and mathematical thinking

- studying the development of scientific and mathematical understanding and relating it to learning in general (i.e. developing a view of learning)
- studying and practising assessment of pupils during regular work and through structured tasks
- using the information so gained to match activities to pupils' progress
- planning the content and organization of science and mathematics activities for children within a given school programme
- observing, evaluating and practising strategies for classroom control, with particular reference to practical science and mathematics activities
- studying a range of teaching styles and practising some of them
- acquiring familiarity with the required syllabus and with available published resources
- identifying and using criteria for selecting and adapting available classroom material
- experience of selecting and improvising simple equipment
- experiences designed to develop skill in handling and using productivity children's questions
- studying and practising ways of encouraging children's communication and recording for various purposes and audiences
- making use of information technology in science and mathematics activities
- experience of techniques for, and encouragement of the habit of, self-appraisal
- study of where and how science and mathematics can usefully be combined in integrated or cross-curricular topics and approaches

- recognizing and avoiding sources of bias or inequality of opportunity relating to gender, ethnicity, and physical handicap.

Additional Opportunities Which May be Provided Through In-service Programmes

The needs of teachers for continued professional development and the extension of responsibility beyond their classroom requires opportunities for

- further development of all skills, attitudes, knowledge and understanding indicated in the above items
- studying ways of catering for children with special needs
- experiencing programme planning at the whole school level
- developing skills of working with colleagues and of liaison with other schools, both primary and secondary
- interpreting and using records and results of assessment
- reporting to parents and to school board members (if appropriate)
- communicating to parents and the local community the objectives of the school and dealing with queries
- selection and organization of equipment and resources
- continued development of the use of information technology in teaching and learning science and mathematics
- developing classroom research skills
- incorporating science and mathematics experiences into the curriculum of pre-school children.

The Learning of Teacher Trainees

In discussing children's learning in Chapter 3 we have made much of the importance of taking their earlier experiences and ideas derived from it as the starting point. This applies to all learning at all stages, to adults, to teacher trainees, as well as to children. Few of those entering teacher training courses will, in their own education, have had experiences which enable them to understand science and mathematics in the way we have suggested. Instead they will have notions of school and of these subjects, ingrained during up to twelve years of first hand experience, which conflict with the notions advocated here. It will, then, be as little effective just to tell them about a different view of education as it is just to tell children what are the 'right' ideas when their heads are full of their own ideas derived from their experience.

Trainee teachers' ideas of teaching are, therefore, likely to have to be changed, but changed in a way which gives them ownership of the new ideas. This means that the ideas make sense in terms of experience and reasoning, both of which have to be provided in the training course. Thus the course must give them the opportunities for realising the nature and the value of the kind of learning which leads to ownership through themselves learning in this way.

So, for example, when learning about the nature of scientific and mathematical activity, they should be working in the same way and it is intended that they work with children; being active physically and mentally. There should be some time in which they can undertake simple scientific investigations and mathematical tasks in a way which creates the excitement and enthusiasm of finding solutions through their own activity. After experiences of this kind, however, as adults and teachers, they can stand back and consider what they have been doing and examine their learning. They will then be able to think out for themselves how to make these sorts of experiences available to children. Then their previous assumptions about teaching will be challenged and their ideas changed.

This way of learning in teacher education does not have to be restricted to developing personal knowledge of science and mathematics and considering appropriate activities for children. It can and should be applied in all the experiences listed above. It means using the ideas which are already present in trainees as the starting point, whether these are about how to answer children's questions, about how to assess children's understanding, about class organization or about using equipment. In all these cases active learning can be implemented, producing an atmosphere where evidence and logical reasoning is used and everyone's ideas are respected and openly discussed.

A further advantage of this approach is that it fosters positive attitudes such as respect for evidence, open mindedness, tolerance and willingness to review actions and arguments critically. Recalling that attitudes are caught not taught, however, means that this has implications for the training of teacher educators.

The Possibilities for Some Integration of Mathematics and Science in Teacher Education Courses

The fact that a single list of opportunities covering both science and mathematics has been proposed here, suggests that there are many similarities in what is required by primary teachers in relation to these subjects. The possibility of time-conserving cooperation appears to be present, but nevertheless it would be perfectly logical to run two separate courses, with one providing the opportunities in relation to mathematics and the other having the same function for science. Course structure often determines the extent to which the teaching of science and mathematics can be studied together or in cross-curricular topics. Many courses begin from study of separately identified subjects so that these can be recognized in integrated topics which are introduced later; other begin in a more holistic way which requires considerable collaborative planning on the part of those involved in a primary teacher education course.

Since national or local curriculum guidelines usefully exist as subject based documents, if integration is desired then it is important for teacher education to avoid further reinforcing the subject divisions through its course structures. This joint planning and shared sessions in many areas of professional development would not only assist in the 'litre into the half-litre pot' problem, but would be the best means of educating primary teachers—as opposed to teachers who change personae from 'science teacher' to 'maths teacher', from one part of the day to the next.

The way in which the teacher education course is organized may well have to strike a balance between what the logic of the two subjects dictates and what is expected in the schools (which does not always follow this logic). Teachers will need not only to consider but to experience some integrated work in their initial training if they are to practise it with understanding. It will only deepen their understanding of the subjects to consider the points of similarity and difference such as have been brought out in earlier chapters.

This matter is leading us from the subject of what opportunities are needed, which has been the concern of the present chapter, to the next chapter, in which the how is considered. In comparing the various approaches described in the next chapter, the sorts of experiences identified here have to be borne in mind. It is also necessary to remember that we wish to engender in teachers understanding and commitment, which must involve a process more appropriately described as 'education' rather than 'training'.

7

Teacher Education Approaches

'Activity' as the Key Concept

The history of learning theory shows an increasing attention to learners' activities. Olsen, a Norwegian mathematics teacher educator, uses the word 'Activity' with a capital A to stress that teal learning takes place when situation, problem and activities have a 'political' value for the students[1]. What they do must be of importance to their own lives, they must experience an improvement of circumstances because of their learning activity. The concept of 'ownership' has similar import. This is what student teachers should experience in their courses; activities which are important to their professional life, as teachers-to-be now and eventually as teachers in their own classrooms.

Close to the concept of activity are 'interaction'[2], 'reflection' and 'production'. Working together in small cooperative groups stimulates those actions in which intuitive notions, beliefs, former experiences, pre-conceptions and informal procedures can be brought in, discussed and accommodated. Meanings are developed and shared as participants put their ideas into words to explain them to others. To do this, reflection (thinking about your own activity, even about your own thinking) appears to be necessary.

Teacher educators, who teach this view of learning in their courses, cannot neglect it in designing their own teacher education. This means that in the courses there must be room for cooperative work in which attention is paid to the students' subjective theories, their own learning-histories, their beliefs and conceptions with regard to the school-subjects they study, and their philosophy of the disciplines behind these subjects. It also means that teacher education courses must provide room for production, reflection and interaction in situations, and with problems to solve which future teachers recognize as real problems and which strongly motivate them. Sometimes conflicts arise, for instance, when personal theories do not fit into new ideas about learning and teaching. In this case the teacher educator is challenged to create a learning environment for students in which interaction, reflection and their own ideas set the course.

Three Dimensions of Activity in Teacher Education

Many primary teacher students have received form their own education a legacy of failure, or at least dissatisfaction, in relation to mathematics and science. Therefore, their first and foremost requirement is to acquire confidence, to gain an appreciation of the nature of scientific and mathematical activity, and to develop enthusiasm for teaching mathematics and science. The educator of teachers who is guided by this idea creates opportunities for participation and investigation by the students and thinks in terms of 'learning environments'.

Students must be active in the learning environment, in relation to the (school) subject matter, to the pedagogy of the subject and to what is going on in classrooms when this subject is being taught. Within this we can identify three dimensions of activity in teacher education:

(i) studying the (school) subject means that the student teacher's own knowledge and ability is brought up to the required level. If possible the studies extend around the subjects so that further relationships and deeper insight into the discipline emerge. Sometimes the history of science and mathematics can contribute, particulars when developments in the past given cues for learning in classrooms now. Mastery of the subject for teachers does not mean advanced study beyond the basics.

(ii) developmental work and research in both domains contributes to the body of pedagogical knowledge. This knowledge becomes the subject of activity in teacher education. There, is the (school) subject comes to life closer to classroom practice, students are further stimulated to improve their own standards of knowledge, but now from the perspective of being a teacher.

(iii) classroom practice is viewed as an experimental field in which learning and teaching can be investigated, designed and practised.

If we compare science and mathematics in the framework of these dimensions, similarities and differences emerge. For example, with respect to the first dimension, in primary mathematics the teacher's own skill in calculation play a more important role than in science. It is that instrumental character of mathematics (Bishop speaks of 'symbolic technology'[3]) that makes a difference in the pedagogical dimension as well. Student teachers often have to work hard to acquire the basic skills of mathematics, which they should have memorized during their own years of primary school, but often did not do. In, science there is less need for memorized factual knowledge.

In both subjects a large amount of psychological research has taken place from which many contributions of pedagogical knowledge have come. Together with the results of developmental projects, this means that a considerable amount of knowledge is available with regard to both subjects.

Science and mathematics are also very close in the third dimension. Learning to teach in the classrooms requires a study of learning processes, knowing how to start those processes and how to support and supervise them and what materials can be used.

Activity in Teaching Workshops

A workshop is a direct way of providing a learning experience in which the learner creates meaning or understanding through his or her mental or physical activity. What is provided as a basis for this action can be objects or materials to investigate or use, or problems to solve, or evidence to examine and discuss, or all these together. The outcome may be an artefact, a solution to a problem, a plan, the recognition of a new relationship between things, a critique or a set of criteria. Perhaps the most important product, however, is a greater understanding of how to achieve such results.

Workshops of this kind have been well developed in science.[4] Not only is the scientific phenomenon at hand the subject of investigation, but so are the investigators and the investigation itself. All those involved stand back from their involvement and reflect on their role, their interaction with each other and with the materials and consider the role of the materials used and the educational setting. These workshops in science have the three characteristics of the learning environment for student teachers, mentioned earlier.

This kind of workshop is in many respects quite similar to what in mathematics is called a 'mathematical-didactical' workshop. Student teachers cooperatively and thus interactively solve mathematical problems at their own level, similar to the way children would do it at their levels. All the three dimensions are taken care of, so that not only the mathematical subject matter, but the pedagogical knowledge and the learning and teaching of this subject matter become issues of study as well. A few examples illustrate specific workshops, for

- mathematical problem solving
- explaining mathematics
- analysing concrete materials for use in primary schools
- educational design
- creating help for low achievers.

But learning to teach mathematics requires more than just the mathematics to be considered[5]. The educator of primary mathematics teachers must pay particular attention to issues like:

- studying children's strategies in acquiring number concepts and the way school books teach it
- observing children's learning of algorithms and the way school books teach it.

Investigating the Differences

'Learning to the science' and 'learning to teach mathematics' are to be distinguished. There are essential differences in the nature of knowledge in the subjects. The following will illustrate this point of view.

Take the activity of 'organising', which in both, science as well as in mathematics, is considered as basic and fundamental. But, as we shall see, it has in each subject a very different interpretation and application. In the science workshop organising (the investigation) means to gather data systematically in order to get knowledge about the object of the current investigation, to be able to make a clear description of the phenomenon, to create possibilities for investigating details, to ask better questions, to manage the answers in order to check earlier hypotheses etc. Organising in science workshops serves the investigation.

Organising in mathematics not only facilitates the problem solving activity, but it also affects the way in which the knowledge is organized in children's minds. A specific organization of 'situations of division' leads to a specific algorithm constructed in the children's minds. Using a city plan to organize multiplication-situations affects the way a related thinking model (in this case the grid model) arises in the minds of the pupils. This means that in mathematics organising structures the knowledge itself and, because such knowledge could be strongly context-bound, it is necessary to investigate other contexts with a similar structure (isomorphic problems) that permit the same organization. From a broader point of view all kinds of organization can be seen as part of 'mathematising'. In all particular situations mathematising stands for organization, discovering a structure, creating a useful notation schema, inventing short-cuts. All these activities affect and structure of developing personal knowledge. (An example of organising in mathematics, is given as an Annex to this Chapter.)

The Communities

In the foregoing paragraphs a number of similarities between primary science and mathematics passed in review. Summarising we conclude that learning to teach both subjects in primary school

- demands opportunities for students teachers to overcome dissatisfaction from the past and to create new perspectives on the subjects
- needs activity with interactive, reflective and productive participation in investigation

- has to take into accounts students' own ideas and personal, subjective theories
- must pay much attention to children's learning processes in science and mathematics
- is organized in a 'reflective model' of teacher education[6].

A 'Mixed Economy'

Balancing the differences and similarities it becomes possible to draw some conclusions. When designing teacher education it must be possible to realise collaboration between science and mathematics, but recommending total integration of both domains in teacher education, would be unwise. The identified differences ask for a clear distinction, the existence of fundamental commonalities suggest a carefully thought-out 'mixed economy', certainly not only to save learning time, but because a mixed economy of science and mathematics teaching in the colleges of education really can be richer than teaching the subject areas separately.

A mixed economy in teacher education for instance means combined science and mathematical pedagogic workshops, with maths activities in a science context, as starting points for a study of learning and design practice.

This mixed economy may be the best from the teachers' point of view. If the differences are clear and the teacher has enough self-confidence to teach both subjects 'actively', it will be worthwhile sometimes to use mathematics in order to deepen science understanding or to use a science context to develop a mathematical skill. Between the separated approach and the advanced integration of the two, many variants are possible. At the secondary school level one subject is used as a field of practice for the other. At the primary level the similarities in pedagogy weighs more heavily than the need to reflect the distinctions between the disciplines. These differences should be considered by both teacher educators and trainee teachers in relation to their own teaching.

The role of teacher education is to provide the knowledge and awareness which will support a greater proportion of integrated work. If students and teachers encounter mathematics and science only in separate compartments, their ability to combine the two is unlikely to grow. Some of their work should be clearly focused on each subject so that the identity of mathematical and scientific activity can be in no doubt, but some should be integrated so that points of contact can increasingly be recognized.

REFERENCES

1. Olsen, S. M. (1987) *The Politics of Mathematics Education*, Reidel, Dordrecht.
2. Bishop, A. and Goffree, F. (1986) Classroom organization and dynamics. In B. Christiansen, A. G. Howson and M. Otte (eds) *Perspective on Mathematics Education*. Reidel, Dordrecht (309-356).
3. Bishop, A. (1988) *Mathematical Enculturation. A cultural perspective on mathematics education*. Kluwer Academic Press, Dordrecht.
4. UNESCO (1985) *The training of primary science educators*, a workshop approach. Paris, UNESCO.
5. Skemp, R. R. (1976) *Relational understanding, instrumental understanding*, Mathematics Teacher.
6. Schon, D. A. (1984) *The Reflective Practitioner*, Basic Books, New York.

Annex

The six-column Erathostenes sieve.

The idea of building a sieve in order to identify all the prime numbers up to a certain pre-determined limit (e.g. up to 90) is a rather natural one: it uses only the concept of prime number per se and the idea of getting rid' of all those numbers that are multiples of smaller ones. So accomplishment of the task can be organized as follows:

1. first write down all the natural numbers up to 90
2. eliminate 1 (which for well-known (?) reasons is not to be counted among the primes)
3. add the smallest non-eliminated number to the list of primes
4. eliminate all multiples of this same number
5. repeat steps 3 and 4 as often as necessary (what is the exact stopping rule?).

When asked to accomplish such a task, many people might have the tendency to display the original list of natural numbers in ten columns (at least if working in base ten):

1	2	3	4	5	6	7	8	9	10
11	12	13	14	15	16	17	18	19	20
21	22	23	24	25	26	27	28	29	30
31	32	33	...						
						...	88	89	90

But there are clearly no deep reasons for such a disposition of the numbers. Any more or less systematic display would also work. What about the following one:

2	3	4	5	6	7
8	9	10	11	12	13
14	15	16	17	18	19
20	21	22	23	24	25
26	27	28	29	30	31

32	33	34	35	36	37
38	39	40	41	42	43
44	45	46	47	48	49
50	51	52	53	54	55
56	57	58	59	60	61
62	63	64	65	66	67
68	69	70	71	72	73
74	75	76	77	78	79
80	81	82	83	84	85
86	87	88	89	90	

Search for the multiples of 2 eliminates the first, the third and the fifth columns; also search for the multiples of 3 eliminates the second column (the fifth having already been eliminated). So all other primes to be found will be either in column four or in column six. The following result is thus transparent, just from the way we have displayed the original list of numbers: Except for 2 and 3, all primes are of the form $6k \pm 1$.

It is worth noting also that elimination of multiples of other primes is greatly facilitated by the particular form of these primes. For instance, since $11 = 6 \times 2 - 1$, all its multiples are to be found on slant lines obtained by going down two rows and going left one column.

It is clear that the very idea of displaying the natural numbers on six columns comes from the prior knowledge of the result that primes are of the form $6k \pm 1$ (except for 2 and 3). So the original idea is motivated by some 'existing' knowledge. So in presenting such a display to, say a student, it would be important to allow her/him to discover the result for her/himself: this illustrates clearly how crucial the organization of information can be.

Suggestions for Further Discussion, for Research and for Development

In the writing of these chapters and in the surrounding discussions the authors were aware of the many questions which the subject raises for policy makers, teacher educators and teachers in training. We see our writing as only the start in addressing these questions and an important outcome of our work being in the further discussion, research and development which may allow. We list here the points for discussion and the suggestions for research and development identified in the preparation of the final draft of this publication.

Questions for Discussion

1. What is the basis of support for the proposition that the learning of mathematics and science has a common root and procedure?
2. Can a common approach to learning be supported at the same time as recognizing the ways in which subjects differ, for example in respect of evidence from the real world being the ultimate source of authority in science whilst the logic of reasoning having this role in mathematics?
3. Is this same constructivist approach to learning appropriate to other subjects?
4. What accommodations may need to be made where cultural expectations of children's behaviour conflict with the tenets of constructivist learning; where children's views and questions are not valued, for example?

5. To what extent is a constructivist approach to learning compatible with a detailed and highly structured curriculum or syllabus?
6. What are the limiting factors affecting the validity of the proposed model for teacher decision making? In particular how does the model apply where the teaching conditions are not to the teacher's choosing, for example in the matters of class size, availability of materials, a restricting curriculum?
7. To what extent is the rationale for the proposed model valid in different cultures and contexts?
8. What are the implications of the model and the approach to learning for the teaching of subject matter of mathematics and science in teacher education courses?
9. What can be done to help teachers in training resolve conflicting philosophies of education which may be implicit or explicit in different parts of their training courses?
10. To what extent can the workshop approach be applied in all aspects of teacher education?
11. What can be done to break into the vicious circle of society's generally negative attitudes to science and mathematics, which creates teachers with little confidence in these subjects who perpetuate the negative views in their pupils?
12. Does popularization of science and mathematics help the primary teacher? If so, what further efforts can be made towards this end?
13. Can mathematics 'fairs' be devised which serve the same purpose as school science fairs?
14. In the implementation of a unified approach to mathematics and science what steps need to be taken to avoid mathematics being treated as a toolkit for science?

15. What changes are needed in the assessment of children's learning in mathematics and science so that credit can be given for responses which may not be exact but which represent valuable steps in development of ideas and skills?
16. How can the encouragement of collaborative work and cooperative learning in the classroom be reconciled with the popular demand to assess pupils and students individually?
17. What are the implications for school and class organization of approaches to learning which encourage pupils to express, use and discuss their own ideas?
18. In the context of problem solving and activity in mathematics and science how is a teacher to deal with children's questions answerable only by reference to complex concepts which are not intellectually accessible to primary pupils?
19. How are different degrees of 'concreteness' and 'abstractness' in mathematics and science topics to be identified and communicated to teachers?
20. How can the teacher's role be presented as going beyond the provision of materials and including crucially the stimulation of pupils' reflection on their activity without seeming to support overly directive teaching?
21. What role is there in primary schools for specialists in primary mathematics and in primary science?
22. What are the implications for the secondary school curriculum of the need for primary teachers with a good background in science and mathematics?
23. How can students with a good interest and ability in science and mathematics be attracted to primary school teaching?

Proposals for Research

(i) An international survey along IEA lines of primary teacher education course content and methods.

(ii) The documentation by teachers of their experiences of attempting to apply a constructivist approach in order to feed back into teacher education information about the range of problems likely to be encountered.

(iii) A long-term follow up study of a cohort of newly qualified teachers with a view to relating training experiences to later experiences in teaching.

Areas for Development

(i) Materials to support workshop activities in teacher education which are designed to convey the commonalities of science and mathematics education at the primary level.

(ii) Cases studies to exemplify teacher education courses where there are joint science and mathematics components.

(iii) Classroom materials for teachers to use in a unified approach to learning mathematics and science such that the essential identity of the subjects are respected.

BIBLIOGRAPHY

Adey, P. and Harlen, W. A Piagetian analysis of process-skill test items. *Journal of Research in Science Teaching*, 23, 8, 1986, 707-726.

Describes the analysis in Piagetian terms of process-based test items used in the national surveys of 11 years olds' achievement in science. The level of cognitive demand was found to be a reliable predictor of the limiting difficulty of an item. Departures from this pattern revealed areas where further effort in teacher education and curriculum development would be profitable.

Bishop, A. *Mathematical Enculturation. A cultural perspective on mathematics education*. (Dordrecht: Kluwer Academic Press, 1988).

Learning Mathematics is seen as mathematical enculturation. Bishop presents *six basic fields* in which we can find the roots of mathematics (ethno-mathematics) in each of the following: counting, measurement, orientation, designing, playing and explaining.

Bishop, A. and Goffree, F. Classroom organization and dynamics. In *Perspectives on Mathematics Education*, Christiansen, B., Howson, A.G., and M. Otte (eds), pp. 309-365. (Dordrecht: Reidel 1986).

The message in this chapter is that mathematics teaching needs *communication, interaction and negotiation*. When starting mathematics education pupils have their own (intuitive and informal) concepts, knowledge and conceptions. Teachers should link this personal knowledge to formal mathematics by negotiating and sharing meanings.

Cavendish, S., Galton, M., Hargreasves, L. and Harlen, W. *Assessing Science in the Primary Classroom: Observing Activities* (London: Paul Chapman Publishing 1990). Examines the value of systematic observation in assessing pupil performance in science. Gives guidance for teachers in organising observation in their own classrooms.

Christiansen, B. and Walther, G. Task and activity. In *Perspectives on Mathematics Education*, Christiansen, B., Howson, A. G. and Otte, M. pp. 243-308 (Dordrecht: Reidel 1986).

The authors explain that in order to create learning by doing teachers and educational designers have to know about 'activity' and consider tasks and activities in mathematics from this perspective.

Elstgeest, J. *Ask the antlion*. African Primary Science Programme, 1967, E.D.C. Newton, Mass, USA, 1967 also in *New trends in Integrated Science*, value of a trend-setting Unit of Primary Science in Africa

The articles describes how good science can be done by children making use of an inset larva that is available almost everywhere.

Elstgeest, J. Children and Agriculture. In *Agriculture and Education* Rao, A.N. (ed.), pp. 15-21, (Oxford: Pergamon Press, 1988).

The ordinary "things of the land" provide children anywhere with rich scientific materials with which they can work and from which they can learn. Encounter is the base of elementary agricultural science as well as elementary agricultural practice.

Elastgeest, J. Children and their Health. In *Education and Health* Kelly, P. and Lewis, J. (eds), pp. 53-59. (Oxford: Pergamon Press, 1988).

How process based since education assists children to develop insight in and sound attitudes towards proper health care.

Elstgeest, J. Primary science is integrated science. In *New Trends in Integrated Science Teaching* Vol. VI, pp. 57-60. (Paris: UNESCO 1990).

Argues, through elaborate illustration of children working with soils, that primary science is built on two integrating factors: (1) children undergo their natural environment by encounter and dialogue; (2) children form concepts and forge their intellectual structure by encounter and dialogue.

Elstgeest, J. and Harlen, W. *Environmental Science in the Primary Curriculum* (London: Paul Chapman, 1990).

The theme of this book is the interaction of children with their own environment. In these 'encounters' children are encouraged to find answers through scientific investigation of the objects or events being studied. Ways of assessing scientific skills are included.

Elstgeest, J. Science and technology. In *Council of Europe Handbook of Primary Education in Europe*, Chapter 3.2, pp. 271-288 (London: David Fulton, 1991).

Illustrated by real classroom experiences the article describes the newer trends in process based primary school science, and traces the occurrence of such innovative science and technology curricula in various parts of Europe.

Fosnot, C.T. *Enquiring Teachers, Enquiring Learners: A Constructivist Approach for Teaching* (New York: Teachers College Press, 1989).

Focuses on empowering the learner to be an 'autonomous, inquisitive thinker'—one who questions, investigates and reasons; deals also with the educational empowerment of teachers; gives detailed illustrations using science and mathematics investigations;

includes investigations in language, psychology and in interdisciplinary settings.

Freudenthal, H. *Mathematics as an Educational Task* (Dordrecht: Reidel 1973).

An analysis of mathematics learning, particularly in relation to secondary education is presented. Interesting didactical concepts elaborated include *anti-didactic inversion*: the final product of mathematical thinking over a long period. A criticism of secondary school mathematics is that the process of mathematising is eliminated, poor structures are taught instead of creating rich contexts in which pupils can experience themselves what mankind did before (*guided reinvention*).

Freudenthal, H. *Mathematics Education Revisited* (Dordrecht: Kluwer Academic Press, 1991). Freudenthal present mathematics as a state of *common sense*. There are many levels of common sense. By doing mathematics in real life settings followed up by reflection, this level of common sense can be raised. Reflection is a key concept; it causes jumps in mathematical learning processes.

Gbamanja, S.P.T. *Modern Methods in Science Education in Africa* (Owerri, Nigeria: Totan Publishers, 1991).

This book discusses the nature of science and various promising inquiry-based science education programmes in Africa. It provides a broad discussion of resources for science instruction.

Gravemeijer, K., van den Heuvel, M. and Streefland, L. *Contexts, Free Productions and Geometry in Realistic Mathematics Education*. (Utrecht: OW&OC, 1990).

Makes a distinction between realistic mathematics education and mechanistic, structuralists and empiricist approaches. The distinction can be illuminated using '*contexts* and '*free productions*', the latter having proved to be useful in primary grades, where, for example, pupils are stimulated to create sums, tasks or test items for their classmates, to write a guide for a young student in order to use a pocket calculator etc.

Harlen, W. (ed.) *Taking the Plunge*. (London: Heinemann 1985).

How to encourage children to make a good start in science; what to do with children's questions; how to organize good since teaching.

Harlen, W. Education for equal opportunities in a scientifically literate society. In *International Journal of Science Education*, Vol. 11, No. 2, 1989, pp. 125-134.

Reviews the traditional gender linked differences which account for the masculine image of science as it is traditionally taught. Indicates how teaching science as an enterprise resulting in tentative knowledge many make it more attractive to females.

Harlen, W. Performance Testing and Science Education in England and Wales. In *Assessment in the Service of Instruction*. Champagne, A.B., Lovitts, B.E and Calinger, B.J. (eds), (Washington, D.C American Association for the Advancement of Science, 1990, pp. 181-206).

...also printed in *Assessing Thinking and Learning*, Kulm, G. and Malcolm, S. (eds) (Washington D.C. American Association for the Advancement of Science, 1991)

Describes the recent changes in the curriculum and in assessment in science in England and Wales and the practical and theoretical implications.

Harlen, W. Does content matter in primary science? *School Science Review*, Vol. 59, No. 209, June, 1978, 614-625.

Argues the pros and cons of a common curriculum which defines the content of primary science and proposes a form of statement which give guidance without restricting teachers' freedom to use their particular school environment as content.

Harlen, W. and Dahar, R.W. A scientific approach to the improvement of science teaching. *Journal of Curriculum Studies*. Vol. 5, No. 2, 1981, 113-120.

Argues the case for process-based science education particularly in developing countries and describes an extended workshop in Indonesia where the introduction of process skills was attempted.

Harlen, W. Basic concepts and the primary/secondary science interface. *European Journal of Science Education*. Vol. 5, No. 1, 1983, 25-34.

Suggests criteria for identifying science concepts for the primary curriculum; discusses implications for classroom practice and for the knowledge that primary teachers need.

Harlen, W. and Osborne, R. A model for learning and teaching applied to primary science. *Journal of Curriculum Studies*. Vol. 17, No. 2, 1985, 133-146.

Proposes a model of teaching as a set of procedures related consistently to a certain view of learning, The features of the model are discussed in general and with particular reference to a constructivist (generative) model of learning.

Harlen, W. Girls and primary-school science education: sexism, stereotypes and remedies. *Prospects*, Vol. XV, 4, 1985, 541-551.

Briefly reviewed the reasons put forward to explain the poorer participation of girls than boys in science and proposes positive action designed to remedy the situation. This is necessary not only to remove the disadvantage to girls but to provide a view of science which better services society as a whole.

Harlen, W. Process-based learning for pupils and teachers: the work of an international project in primary science. *Science Education International*, Vol 1. 4, 4-7, 1990.

Describes the activities of a group of science educators from different countries who have produced workshop materials for teacher education which take seriously the view that to improve learning opportunities in the classroom requires radical changes in teacher education methods.

Harlen, W. What can primary science contribute to ethics and social responsibility? In *Ethics and Social Responsibility in Science*. Frazer, M. J. and Kornhauser, A. (eds), Oxford, Pergamon, 1986, 149-154.

Discusses what is appropriate and possible at the primary level in terms of developing attitudes to science and the environment.

Harlen, W. Industry and Technology in Primary Schools: Some General Principles. In *Education, Industry and Technology*. Waddington, D.J. (ed), Oxford, Pergamon, 1987.

Discusses the benefits and limitations of linking science work at the primary level with industry. It suggests that most appropriate industries are small scale and provides examples of school projects linked with industry.

Harlen, W. (ed) *New Trends in Primary School Science Education*, Volume 1 (Paris: UNESCO, 1983).

A seminal collection of chapters by world-wide specialists covering the aims and constraints of primary science, curriculum materials, assessment and record keeping, equipment and teacher education.

Harlen, W. *Teaching and Learning Primary Science*. (London: Harper & Row, 1985) 240 pp.

Takes a clear view of the meaning of learning in science at the primary level and uses this as a basis for discussion of the content, methods, organization, resources and the teachers' role which promote this learning.

Harlen, W. and Jelly, S. *Developing Primary Science*. (Edinburgh: Oliver and Boyd, 1989) 72 pp.

A short book for the teacher or student who is starting out in primary science as well as for the experienced teacher.

Harlen W., Macro, C., Malvern, D., Reed, K. and Schilling, M. *Progress in Primary Science: Workshop Materials for Teacher Education* (London: Routledge 1990) 200 pp.

A series of modular topics for workshop use in in-service or initial teacher education courses. Contains course leader's notes and tasks for course participants. Linked to teaching the National Curriculum in England and Wales, but transferable to any other curriculum.

Harlen, W. *The Teaching of Science* (London: David Fulton Publishers, 1992).

A guide to the teaching of science in primary schools, addressing issues in planning, provision, assessment and evaluation of classroom learning experiences.

Harlen, W. and Elstgeest, J. *UNESCO Source Book for Primary Science Teacher Education* (Paris: UNESCO, 1992).

Discussion and activities for primary teachers which describe and embody an active approach to learning science. The content is designed to help teachers to develop children's understanding of science through their own mental and physical activity. Can be used for independent study although groups are preferable for some activities. Includes classroom activities which exemplify the approach.

Hawkins, D. Messing about in science. In *Science and Children*, Vol. 2, No. 5, 1965, pp 5-9.

How children's natural inclination to explore should be utilized in science education by: (a) allowing it, and (b) guiding it towards specific and effective inquiry.

Hawkins, D. I, thou, it. In *ESS Reader* (Newton, MA: Education Development Center, 1970).

Describes the triple interaction taking place between (1) subject matter, (2) the children, and (3) the teacher in good lessons, including science.

Hein, G. (ed) *The Assessment of Hands-on Elementary Science Programs* (Grand Forks, N.D: North Dakota Study Group on Evaluation, 1990).

A rich resource on assessment in science education; a collection of specially commissioned papers by outstanding science educators discussing assessment theory, large-scale assessments, assessment in science education research and development, and new approaches to assessment in science education. Each chapter begins with a thoughtful introduction by the editor.

Hilton, P. and Pederson, J. *Fear no more. An adult approach to mathematics* (Menlo Park: Addison-Wesley, 1983).

Two Fundamental faults of the 'Back to the Basics' movement are mentioned: authoritarianism and mystification (p. 5).

Howson, A. G., Keitel, C. and Kilpatrick J. *Curriculum Development in Mathematics.* (Cambridge University Press, 1981).

Chapter 1: '...producing new ideas and materials alone is not sufficient to change practice...'

Krabbendam, H. and de Vries, M. (eds.) Goals and methods. In *Science, Mathematics and Technology Education in the Netherlands.* (Enshede: SLO, 1990).

Report of a conference in the framework of the OECD project 'Science, Mathematics and Technology Education'.

Leitzel, J.R.C. (ed.) *A Call for Change: Recommendations for the Mathematical Preparation of Teachers of Mathematics* (Washington, D.C.: Mathematical Association of America, 1991).

Taking as a background the vision of school mathematics put forward in Curriculum and Evaluation Standards for School Mathematics of the National Council of Teachers of Mathematics (NCTM), this document describes the post-secondary mathematical experiences that a teacher must have encountered in order to meet this vision and the need for teachers to have a sound foundation in mathematics.

Morris, R. (ed.) *The Mathematical Education of Primary-School Teachers* Studies in Mathematics Education volume 3 (Paris: UNESCO, 1984).

A collection of papers by an international set of authors, addressing various aspects of the mathematical preparation of primary school teachers. Topics covered include the required background for teaching mathematics at the primary level, both with respect to mathematics itself and to the theory of learning; classroom activities; visualization and geometry; the influence of technology. It also presents reports about various teacher education experiments—both for prospective and practising teachers—in developing as well as in developed countries.

National Council of Teachers of Mathematics. *Curriculum and Evaluation Standards for School Mathematics* (Reston, VA: National Council of Teachers of Mathematics, 1989).

Focuses on the 'what' and 'how' of the teaching of mathematics and on various aspects of assessment of pupil progress and evaluation of mathematics programmes.

National Council of Teachers of Mathematics. *Professional Standards for Teaching Mathematics,* (Reston, VA National Council of Teachers of Mathematics, 1991).

Addresses the various dimensions of the preparation of teachers of mathematics. Provides guidance as to the learning environments appropriate to the mathematics education described in the earlier report (see above). It has sections on standards for teaching (concerning for instance the role of the teacher in the classroom in creating a stimulating learning environment), standards for the professional development of teachers (focusing on what teachers need to know about mathematics itself, about school mathematics, about how students learn mathematics and about assessment of student learning) as well as standards for the evaluation of the teaching of mathematics.

National Science Resources Center. *Science for Children: Resources for Teacher.* (Washington, D.C.: National Academy Press, 1988).

Especially useful in North America; it is a guide of carefully selected resources that 'provide outstanding support for carrying out effective hands-on, inquiry-based programmes'; covers curriculum materials, supplementary resources (e.g. magazines for children and teachers), and sources of information and assistance for teaching primary/elementary school science.

Nesher, P., and Kilpatrick, J. (eds.) *Mathematics and Cognition: A Research Synthesis* by the International Group for the Psychology of Mathematics Education. (Cambridge University Press (ICMI Studies Series), 1990.

Olsen, S. M. *The Politics of Mathematics Education,* (Dordrecht: Reidel, 1987).

Activity (with a capital A) is what students need in order to acquire mathematics as a personal tool. So teachers must try to find real life situations as starting points for mathematics teaching in which students feel the need to solve the problems.

Orwa, W.O. and Underwood, M. *Science Education*. (Nairobi: Kenyatta University Press, no date).

Although the book focuses mainly on primary education in Kenya, it provides some interesting discussions of hands-on science learning. It also has useful discussions on the child and the learning of science.

Polya, G. *How to solve it?*, (Princeton: Princeton University Press, 1945).

Chapter 1: Heuristics are (in a kind general) hints in order to help problem solvers finding a good direction for a solution. Opposite to algorithms, which are rules to solve specific problems without any delay.

Reigeluth, C.M. *Instructional Theories in Action. Lessons*, (Hillsdale, 1987). Illustrates selected theories and models.

This is the outcome of eight theoreticians in the field of educational design (including Gagne & Briggs, Merill, Scandura, Landa and Reigeluth himself) having been invited to design some lessons in optics. Their *background theories, approaches and annotated results* (lessons) are described.

Richmond, P. E. (ed) *New Trends in Integrated Science Teaching, Vol III: Education of Teachers* (Paris: UNESCO, 1973).

Papers and proceedings of the ICSU/CTS conference on "The Education of Teachers for Integrated Science", University of Maryland, USA, April 1973.

Russell, T. and Harlen, W. *Assessing Science in the Primary Classroom: Practical Tasks* (London: Paul Chapman Publishing 1990).

Describes the development and use of techniques to assess children's science investigations. The advantages and disadvantages of practical assessment are discussed and guidelines given for teachers to develop their own classroom-based practical assessment procedures.

Schilling, M., Hargreaves, L., Harlen, W. with Russel, T. *Assessing Science in the Primary Classroom: Written Tasks* (London: Paul Chapman Publishing 1990).

Discusses the limitations and opportunities provided by written tasks for the assessment of children's achievements in science. Particular attention is given to assessment of process skills. An extended example is provided of assessment within a theme, which could be adapted by teachers to assess process skills within their own topics.

Schmidt, H.G. Problem-based learning: rational and description, in *Medical Education*, 1982.

The author suggests that problem solving can be used as the stimulus to using prior knowledge, elaborating on it and creating new knowledge in line with it. The problems, in this case of medical education, are found in, for example, physics and the practice of medicine. In groups, students tackle the problems in seven steps, the learning process rather than the solution being seen as of crucial importance.

Schon, D. *The Reflective Practitioner: How Professionals Think*. (New York: Basic Books, 1983).

Gives arguments against the practice of insisting on one correct answer to issues; suggests that when we open up issues for reflection we shall see that there are no unreasonable answers. A later book, *Educating the Reflective Practitioner: Toward a New Design for Teaching and Learning in the Professions*. (San Fransisco: Jossey-Bass, 1987) builds on the notion that it is educationally sound to view each person as contributor, recognise the unusual and unique and look for positive aspects, much as a coach does.

Schwartz, J. The intellectual costs of secrecy in mathematics assessment. In *Expanding Student Assessment*, Perrone, V. (ed) (Washington, DC: Association for Supervision and Curriculum Development, 1991).

Criticises the prevalent practice in the United States of America of not publishing test questions after the test has been taken saying the practice precludes intellectual and scholarly scrutiny of the worth of the tests; provides a strong stand against multiple-choice types of testing in mathematics; gives interesting examples of what can be done.

Science Education Programme for Africa. *Handbook for Teachers of Science* (Accra, Ghana: Science Education Programme for Africa, 1978).

Gives illustrations of primary-school children doing science inquiry, teacher training college student learning science; also discusses children's learning of science and provides descriptions of specific science activities.

Skemp, R.R. Relational understanding instrumental understanding. In *Mathematics Teacher*, pp. (20-26), 1976.

Children can understand the mathematical relations, structure, procedures or they merely understand what to do (without knowing why)?

Steen, L.A. (ed.) *On the Shoulders of Gaints: New approaches to Numeracy.* (Washington, DC: National Academy Press, 1990).

This volume aims at stimulating creative approaches to mathematics curricula in next century. It contains five essays offering a rich vision of school mathematics under various strands: dimension, quantity, uncertainty, shape and change. The basic standpoint is that mathematics is the language and science of patterns, a living subject, and this must be reflected not only in the way it is practised, but also in way it is taught and the way it is learned. A recommended reading, providing a very refreshing view of mathematics.

Thier, H.D. The involvement of children in the science programme. *Science and Children*, Vol. 2, No. 5, 1965, pp 19-21.

Discuses hierarchical levels of involvement of children in science inquiry from lowest to highest: reading a book about science, classroom discussion about science, demonstration to illustrate some natural phenomena, direct interaction with systems of objects from the environment (the highest level); the highest level is discussed in detail with illustrations; these levels can be used in combination.

Thompson, A. G. The relationship of teachers' conceptions of mathematics and mathematics teaching to instructional practice. In *Educational Studies in Mathematics,* Vol. 15 No. 2, 1984, (105-128).

A relation between 'how teachers go about their work and their views on learning' is considered.

Treffers, A. *Three Dimensions. A Model of Gaol and Theory Description in Mathematics Instruction*—The Wiskobas Project, (Dordrecht: Reidal, 1987).

The document shows that mathematical process skills play an important role in mathematics education.

UNESCO *The Training of Primary Science Educators—A Workshop Approach.* Document 13 of the Science and Technology Education series. (Paris, UNESCO, 1985).

Indicates the necessity to train teachers by involving them in workshops in order to give them 1) confidence in their own learning and 2) experiences of process based science education.

Wagenschein, M. *Ursprunglisches Verstehen and Exactes Denken I,* Stuttgart 1965, Vol. II Stuttgart 1970.

Science and mathematics (secondary education) used to be presented via overloaded programmes in which the subject matter is exhaustively treated. Wagenshein has the courage to make a good selection and teach it in an exemplary way, stressing the essentials of discipline.

Watt, D., and Russell, T. The Science Process And Concept Exploration project: *'Sound'*, Research Report, (Liverpool University Press, 1990).

One of several reports of the Science Processes and Concept Exploration project describing collaboration research with teachers into children's scientific ideas. Describes ways of eliciting ideas and strategies for advancing them as well as illustrating the range of ideas held by 5-11 years old.

Young, B.L. *Teaching Primary Science*. (Harlow: Longman, 1979).

This book is one of earlier attempts to deal with science and mathematics as related subjects. It also gives a very good discussion of science processes as well as of how children learn. Also included is a discussion of commonly available materials for teaching hands-on science.

Part III

IN-SERVICE TEACHER EDUCATION IN SCIENCE TECHNOLOGY AND MATHEMATICS

Introduction

Rationale

The tremendous advances in scientific knowledge and rapid technological development have made education in many countries worldwide cognizant of the need to prepare science and mathematics teachers at the basic level for a new role: to equip students with the necessary knowledge, skills and values to live effectively in a world that is becoming increasingly scientific and technological.

From 7 to 12 December 1992, the UNESCO Principal Regional Office for Asia and the Pacific (UNESCO-PROAP), Bangkok and the University of the Philippines Institute for Science and Mathematics Education Development (UPISMED) convened a Regional Workshop on *"Improving the Quality of Science, Technology and Mathematics Education at the Basic Level"* focused on in-service education of teachers. The Workshop was held at the Science Teacher Training Centre, UPISMED, Diliman, Quezon City, Philippines.

Objectives

The objectives of the workshop were to:

- review innovative strategies (and possible initiatives and programmes) on improving the quality of in-service training of teachers;
- identify acceptable (satisfactory) "indicators" which will show enhanced quality in in-service teacher training;
- develop a workable strategy of accurately measuring/evaluating the extent to which the identified "indicators" are achieved; and

- propose recommendations for direct action for national implementation.

Participants

The workshop was participated in by 19 key science and mathematics educators and resource persons from Bangladesh, India, Indonesia, Lao P.D.R., Malaysia, Nepal, New Zealand, Pakistan, Philippines, Sri Lanka, Thailand, United Kingdom, the Socialist Republic of Vietnam, SEAMEO-RECSAM and UNESCO-PROAP Bangkok (see Annex A for the list of participants and resource persons).

Officer Bearers of the Workshop

The workshop elected the following officers:

Chairperson	Dr. Avelina T. Llagas (Philippines)
Vice-Chairpersons	Dr. A.K. Sharma (India)
	Dr. Malcom Carr (New Zealand)
Rapporteur-General	Dr. Siti Hawa Ahmad (Malaysia)

and the Officers of the Working Groups were as follows:

Group A:

Chairperson	Dr Malcom Carr (New Zealand)
Rapporteur	Mr. D.S. Mettananda (Sri Lanka)

Group B:

Chairperson	Dr. A.K. Sharma (India)
Rapporteur	Ms. Azian Tengku Sayed Abdullah (Malaysia)

Inauguration

The participants were welcomed by Prof. Porfirio P. Jesuitas, Director of UPISMED, Dr. Emerlinda R. Roman, Chancellor of the University of the Philippines Diliman Campus; and Dr. Lourdes R. Quisumbing, Secretary-General of the UNESCO National Commission of the Philippines. All three delivered short messages during the inauguration of the Workshop. Mrs. Lucille C. Gregorio of UNESCO-PROAP, Bangkok spoke on behalf of UNESCO.

In his welcome talk, Prof. Jesuitas remarked that the workshop was both timely and appropriate; timely because a new programme of the Philippines Department of Education, Culture and Sports (DECS) will focus on basic education especially at the elementary level; and appropriate because the objectives of the Workshop are closely aligned with UPISMED'S goals and concerns. UPISMED, he said, is aware that there is need to employ innovative and more effective schemes to improve science, technology and mathematics education in the in-service teacher training. He added that the demand in the Philippines for teacher training is ever growing and therefore results of the workshop will be awaited with much anticipation as these could be useful in assessing training programmes which are being done in the country.

After extending greetings for UNESCO and thanking the host country and the University of the Philippines for accepting UNESCO-PROAP's offer to host the Workshop, Mrs. Gregorio explained that the Workshop is within APEID's framework of education innovation for development. She also mentioned that the theme of the Workshop is within the central theme of the "World Conference on Education for All" held in Jomtien, Thailand in March 1990. She stressed that the Workshop has been organized to tackle the issue of how to effectively train teachers at the basic level to prepare them for the various aspects of science education. There is a need, she said, to review and develop different models and strategies of teacher education to cope with rapid developments in science and technology. The participants were also informed to two forthcoming conferences. The first, which will be held on January 3-8, 1993 in Israel, will focus on "Science Education in Developing Countries: Theory into Practice" and will serve as a feeder meeting to the International Forum of Project 2000+: Scientific and Technology Literacy for All. Project 2000+ which is a joint endeavour of UNESCO, UNDP and other partners, in collaboration with ICASE, the International Council of Associations for Science Education will deliberate on six focus areas, one of which is "Teacher Education and Leadership of Scientific and Technological Literacy for Year 2000+".

In her message, Dr. Roman stressed that with the rapid changes the world has been experiencing and witnessing, it is very important to develop our educational system not only in proportion of these changes but to achieve the purpose of aiding mankind to cope with the environment. She said that education must not only adapt to the changes but must in fact spur change and reform. She expressed that the strategies on improving the quality of in-service training of teachers formulated through the Workshop will support the University's thrust for innovations toward academic excellence.

Dr. Quisumbing mentioned that the teacher is the most important tool in any educational endeavour. But then, she continued, the teacher has to be helped because there is so much he or she has to catch up, and this is especially true for science teachers. Citing two priority programmes of UNESCO: "Education for All" following the Jomtien Declaration and "Environment and Sustainable Development" following the Earth Summit held in Brazil, Dr. Quisumbing revealed that UNESCO recognizes that the first key to basic education is 'functional literacy which includes scientific and technology literacy.

After the inauguration, the participants were toured around the Science Teachers Training Centre (STTC) to view its laboratory set-ups and acquaint them with the projects of the UPISMED.

The Methodology of the Workshop

The Workshop was divided into ten sessions, five of which were conducted in plenary and the rest, in two small groups where intensive deliberations were undertaken and from which this report was produced.

The country papers prepared by the participants were synthesized and shown in Chapter One of this report, while resource person's papers are in Annex B.

Adoption of the Report and Closing of the Workshop

The Workshop adopted the draft final report, with minor editing and modification during its last session.

During the Closing Ceremonies, brief remarks were delivered by the participants, the resource persons and the UNESCO-PROAP representative. A message of thanks was expressed by the Chairperson of the Workshop, and finally the Workshop was declared officially closed by the Director of UPISMED.

1

Synthesis of Country Reports: Emerging Trends and Issues

A. Synthesis of Country Reports

The country reports showed a variety of modalites for in-service teacher education in science and mathematics currently practiced. In-service training is undertaken for any one or more of these three functions:

1. To update teachers' knowledge and skills in science teaching;
2. To qualify untrained teachers who are already teaching;
3. To provide professional growth and further certification.

The following sections summarize the state-of-the-practice of in-service training of teachers in the member countries.

Bangladesh

In-service training of teachers uses the following modalities:

1. Refresher Training Course—organized by the Primary Training Institutes (PTI) at vacation time. The purpose of the course is to upgrade the knowledge, capabilities, skills and attitudes of primary school teachers.
2. Cluster Training—a needs-based and school-based training programme organized by the Assistant Thana

Education Officers (ATEO's) and Thana Education Officers (TEO's) with the help of the Directorate of Primary Education (DPE).

3. Training of Teachers on Competency-Based Primary School Curriculum.

   Some 53 Essential Learning Competencies (ELC) have been identified in the whole primary school curriculum. Before this curriculum was disseminated, the PTI Instructors, TEOs and ATEO's were trained. Later they acted as trainers to provide in service training to about 175,000 primary school teachers.

4. In-service training of secondary school teachers through the Secondary School Education Programme (SSEP).

   In-service training of secondary school teachers under the "Secondary School Development Project with Emphasis on Science Education" funded by the Asian Development Bank and the Government of Bangladesh was started in 1985. Through this project one national centre and eight regional centres known as the Secondary Education and Science Development Centres (SESDCs) have been established in the campuses of teacher training colleges. By December 1992, about 20,000 secondary school teachers have received 2-3 weeks training through the SESDCs. A group of teachers also received training from the UPISMED through this project.

Indicators of quality in-service training are:

1. Increase in the enrolment and increased retention of children at the primary school systems.
2. Improved teacher skills and efficiency in the teaching-learning class management and learning outcome assessment.
3. Better results in the Secondary School Certificate (SSC) examination of schools under the SESDCs.

In-service trainees are evaluated through pre-test and post-test to assess gains. School performance and students' performance in the public examination through the Zonal Project Officers under the SESDCs are also done.

INDIA

Introduction

The need for in-service training of teachers has received a sharp focus in the National Policy on Education (NPE) 1986 with modifications undertaken in 1992. The national scenario of planning and management of in-service teacher training is described in the next sections.

Strategies, Initiatives and Programmes

Some important initiatives and programmes towards in-service teacher training in Science, Technology and Mathematics Education (STME) are outlined below:

(a) Extension Services Centres in Teacher Training Institutions

The catchment of these Extension Services Centres is primary and secondary teachers drawn from within the jurisdiction of the Teacher Training Institutions.

(b) Summer Institutes in Science and Mathematics

During the early sixties a significant programme for the in-service teacher training was undertaken through Summer Institutes in Science and Mathematics. The responsibility for organization of the Summer Institutes was assigned to some universities. A large number of teachers were exposed to new ideas in curriculum development, methodology of teaching, organization of laboratory work and use of learning aids. The Summer Institutes are continuing as strategies of in-service training but on a much reduced scale.

(c) Summer School-cum-Correspondence

During the sixties there was a growing need to clear the backlog of untrained secondary school teachers in the country. This called for a crash programme of in-service teacher training. The strategy adopted was two months of actual contact in two summer vacations on either side of the academic session, sandwiching between them a correspondence programme. The course consisted of learning through print materials and by contact sessions. A large number of untrained teachers of Science and Mathematics were covered throughout the country.

(d) Seminar Readings for Innovations

Through this programme of in-service growth, teachers, and teacher educators are encouraged to write about their classroom experiences, action research undertaken and innovative approaches in instruction adopted by them. Selected papers are awarded and published for circulation.

(e) Establishment of Central and State Agencies

A major landmark in the organization of in-service training of the educational personnel concerned with primary and secondary education has been the establishment of the National Council of Educational Research and Training (NCERT) and its state level counterparts, the State Institutes of Education (SEIs)/ State Councils of Education Research and Training (SCERTs). These are now the prime agencies for planning, implementing and monitoring in-service training in the country.

(f) Correspondence-cum-Contract Courses (CcCC)

The programme, lunched in 1977, was designed to strengthen the competence of teachers in science subjects apart from the methodology of teaching and evaluation of these subjects.

(g) Centres of Continuing Education (CCEs)

As a part of the above strategy, initially about 100 CCEs were set up all over the country so that there was at least one such centre for three to four districts. As these centres were operating in a small area, it cut down cost on travel and board; at the same time resource material in the form of correspondence lessons could be used again and again in different centres. The cost of training was thus reduced.

Each centre undertook the following major activities:

- Tutorials for correspondence courses
- Contact programmes
- Consultancy for school teachers and primary teacher educators

- Self study facilities
- Continuing education facilities

(h) Programme of Mass Orientation of School Teachers (PMOST): A Cascade Model

In 1986, a National Scheme for In-Service Training of School Teachers was conceptualized to cover 500,000 teachers annually through in-service teacher training camps organized during vacation periods. The print materials used in this programme consisted of separate modules for primary/upper primary, and secondary teachers. These materials were in Hindi, and other regional languages. The non-print material comprised video films especially prepared to meet the programme objectives.

The training strategies included orientation of a Task Force of about 800 key persons and was based on materials, methods, and programme organization logistics. About 15 such courses were conducted in the different regions of the country. The key persons in turn organized a few cycles of orientation for resource persons at the states who in turn oriented batches of 50 teachers in teacher orientation camps.

(i) Institutionalization of In-Service Training

The whole scheme of in-service training is now institutionalized. This was necessary to ensure provision of in-service training to all teachers at periodic intervals. This has been done through a scheme of setting up District Institutes of Education and Training (DIETs) for elementary teachers, and strengthening Colleges of Teacher Education (CTEs)/Institute of Advance Studies in Education (IASEs) for in-service training of secondary teachers. The country is divided into 450 districts. To date 307 DIETs, 34 CTEs and 15 IASEs are on ground acting as nodal institutes for in-service teacher training.

(j) Distance Education for In-Service Training

This strategy has just been initiated and is likely to become the mainstay of in-service teacher training in the country. The course work is being designed on modular framework so that a system of credits could lead to earning a certificate/diploma/degree.

(k) Scheme of Science and Mathematics Education, and Environmental Orientation to Education

This programme envisages training in the concepts included in the new curriculum of Physics, Chemistry and Biology. The nodal responsibility for such a training rests with the NCERT and its Regional Colleges of Education (RCEs). To meet with the orientation and training of secondary school teachers in Science and Mathematics, the NCERT's role is limited to training of resource persons for the States. The areas covered are related to Integrated Science and development of experimental skills.

A related programme is concerned with training of teachers in environmental orientation to education involving the methodology of teacher about environment, through environment and for environment.

(l) Countryside Classroom

Programmes of a wide variety in the area of Science, Technology and Mathematics have been designed and developed by media research centres set up in the country and offered on the national television network twice a day in what is called "countryside classroom". The programmes are targeted to audiences covering teachers at different levels, students and given general public.

(m) Academic Staff Colleges

The 48 Academic Staff Colleges set up in different parts of the country offer core courses of educational pedagogies plus specialized programmes in different areas of Science and Mathematics at an advanced level. The institutions have to depute teachers to these courses.

Non-governmental agencies have also been actively involved for in-service teacher training.

INDONESIA

In-service training is intended to maintain and to improve the quality of teaching-learning and the quality of teachers' academic capabilities. To handle the task of providing training to the large number of teachers in the country, national in-service training centres which took care of upgrading subject area knowledge, have been established by the Ministry of Education. A provincial in-service training centre has been established in each province. There are at present 27 such centres. Their function is to provide in-service training for teachers at the primary and secondary levels.

There are nine national in-service teacher training centres whose functions are the following:

1. To provide in-service materials for subject area instructors.
2. To develop training materials to be used in provincial training centres.
3. To serve as clearinghouse for their respective fields of study.

The training in the centres is usually for 1 to 3 weeks full time. Otherwise, the teachers train for a shorter period and carry out assignments in their schools. A third type of training is one where the teachers train in the centres for 1 or 2 weeks, return to their respective schools for 2 to 3 weeks teaching practice and then come back to the centre for a week to further improve their skills through selected activities.

In-service training is also made possible through teachers meeting workshops where teachers share their ideas and experiences in the profession. To date, 247 such Teachers Meeting Workshops have been established.

The trainings provided are of three types:

1. Refresher—to update teachers' knowledge in science and technology.
2. Qualification training—to upgrade teacher qualifications through a certificate.
3. Promotion training—to improve administrator capability in educational management.

In-service training is done at the national, provincial, school and subject levels.

The effectiveness of training is based on these indicators:

1. attainment of the training objectives;
2. teacher's performance in their schools; and
3. student performance in school examinations.

School-based and subject area-based training will be complemented in every district. Leader schools are to function as innovation centres.

LAO (P.D.R.)

A 1990 national government survey showed that:

1. 35.6 per cent of primary level teachers are untrained, i.e., they have received only primary level education;
2. in-service teacher training is largely ad-hoc; and
3. the predominant teaching method used is the rote-memorization method.

Currently there are 59 centres which provide per-service training. To improve the quality of in-service training there is a plan to reduce these to 11 national centres by the year 1999 which will be used as in-service training centres.

Science teachers in the upper secondary schools were trained through 2-month training courses during annual school vacations. Thirty (30) teachers who attended the series of seminars on methods of teaching mathematics conducted by the Research Institute of Education have been serving as trainers at the regional level training centres.

For 1992-96, a major project, the "Educational Quality Improvement Project", supported by ADB and World Bank loans, will establish a National Teacher Development Centre which will carry out in-service teacher training and curriculum development.

A UNICEF-supported network for teacher upgrading has been set up to meet the needs for teacher trainees in rural areas and minority communities. Teachers remain at their teaching posts and attend training sessions at the upgrading center during school holidays. The training is for 24 weeks spread over a 2½-year period.

Teachers complete a series of carefully graded assignment modules through distance education. Mobile training teams monitor and evaluate the trainees' progress in their respective schools.

Indicators of effectiveness of the training are increased primary enrolment rate in the 6-10 age group, increased enrolment rates in mountain districts, increased survival rates and increased enrolment of girls. Feedback from mobile trainers constitute evaluation of the training.

MALAYSIA

In-service teacher training programmes in Malaysia are conducted for three main reasons, namely:

1. to upgrade the academic and professional knowledge as well as competencies to teachers in various subject disciplines;
2. to orientate teachers towards new developments in teaching methods, techniques and curricular programmes; and
3. to enhance the commitment and motivation of tenured teachers.

Courses conducted vary in length and may last from a week to a year. These courses are conducted by relevant Divisions in the Ministry of Education, State Education Departments and District Education Offices as well as the universities. The Regional Centre for Science and Mathematics Education (RECSAM) situated in Penang also conducts courses in mathematics and science teaching-learning.

The Teacher Education Division conducts in-service programmes for trained graduate and non-graduate teachers, that is, the Diploma and Specialist Programmes for 1 year, and courses of 14 weeks and one month duration. On the courses offered at various Teacher Training Colleges, not many are related to mathematics and science.

With the introduction of the new primary and secondary curriculum in 1983 and 1989, respectively, one week orientation courses were conducted by the Curriculum Development Centre for key personnel in various subject matter. These key personnel in turn conduct courses in their respective state for all the teachers. In order to minimize the 'dilution-effect' and cost incurred, an alternative method was developed called the 'Training Package' (Pukal Latihan) for the secondary school teachers.

The Training Package consists of printed documents and video tapes to be used during in-house training in schools. The Principal plays an important role in the in-house training as the training and curriculum manager.

In innovative strategy for in-service training which has been proposed is to develop a pool of resource persons or experts at the district level in both primary and secondary mathematics and science. Teachers in the various districts will meet at their respective Teacher Activity Centres to discuss and exchange knowledge and skills as well as produce teaching-learning materials with the help of the experts.

It is of great importance that in-service teacher training be a continuous process at the school level and the professional role of the Principal as an instructional leader be strengthened. Peer supervision should also be encouraged to enhance teaching-learning and the quality of in-service training in schools.

NEPAL

Because the demand for large numbers of teachers for the schools cannot be fully met by the Teacher Training Colleges, many teachers are hired even without pre-service training. These teachers get certified through in-service training.

In-service teacher training in science and mathematics are organized by the Primary Education Development Project (PEDP), the Basic Education Project (BEP) and the Science Education Development Centre (SEDC).

Basic education teacher training for those who are already teaching but do not have pre-service training, comprised 150 training hours. In-service teaching training in science and mathematics is carried out by 25 SEDC units each headed by a Science Master Teacher and assisted by some mobile teachers.

The Science Master Teachers go from school to school to train teachers, observe classroom teaching and inspect the school laboratory.

NEW ZEALAND

State of In-service Teaching Training

The Ministry of Education provides some funds centrally but now distributes the bulk of resources to individual schools. National courses are run and programmes to assist new developments are also provided at regional level. There is a new curriculum for mathematics and for science and a substantial process of regional courses is being funded. This process is currently experiencing difficulties as the teachers are refusing to implement the new curricula as a protest against new developments in the administration of schools. A major research contract at the University of Waikato has been investigating in-service work in science aimed at encouraging more interactive teaching.

Innovative Strategies

The paper "School and Teacher Development in New Zealand" printed in the second part of this Report lists a number of innovative strategies which have been used in New Zealand.

School-based and regional programmes in which teachers (at least 2 from a school) meet and interact with facilitators in a co-operative programme are showing interesting results. The process of change is being explored.

A number of major programmes are being provided, though internal disputes are hampering them. The impact of research on these programmes can be seen in that they are not one-day 'quick fix' efforts. Even so, there is understandable doubt about the best manner to support innovation when there are many unresolved features of the programmes (such as how long a period is need for the particular aims, how to encourage wide implementation, how to support change as it is tried, etc.).

Indicators of Enhanced Quality

The research mentioned above has been looking for indicators of teaching which engages with learners' ideas. This has proved to be a difficult area, and the current view is that exploration of the detailed talk between teacher and learners is necessary before useful information is obtained.

Improving the quality in mathematics science and technology at the basic level through in-service teacher training requires careful reflection on:

1. the needs of the particular society in terms of knowledge and skills;
2. matching curricula to the local needs as well as to international expectations;
3. starting from the best practice of local teachers;
4. accepting the change to be a difficult process, and exploring these difficulties in the particular society.

PAKISTAN

Curriculum, being a dynamic process, changes and results in developing the society. These changes demand that the teacher should be kept aware of the on-going changes because these can come into practice only by the teacher. This originates the idea of In-Service Training Programmes.

The State of In-service Training

The pre-service training which is proposed for prospective teachers is also given to untrained teachers after they are hired. Many untrained teachers are hired because more teachers are required for the increasing school-going population.

However, in-service training programmes are carried out at the national level by the National Bureau and in the provinces by the Provincial Bureau. The Provincial Bureau carries out curriculum development and extensions programmes.

In-service Training Past and Present

In the late 60s the school curriculum in Pakistan was revised and modernized. Teachers were trained through crash programmes. A teacher's kit was made and a teacher's handbook and guides were printed.

Population education, narcotics and drug prevention, environmental educational, etc. are the domains of INSET nowadays. Regular INSET programmes are carried out by the extension units. Some NGOs are also helping in shouldering the responsibility.

The duration of different inset programmes differ according to need.

Pakistan is striving for the universalization of primary education. Some significant projects which are working toward the target are the Integrated Curriculum and Primary Education Curriculum Reform Project.

The MOSQUE school programme can be introduced only when all the teachers are prepared. INSET helps in putting forth such programmes in action.

Indicators used to assess the outputs of INSET are:

- Pre- and Post-tests;
- Assignments;
- Performance in practicum sessions; and
- Post Workshop Survey.

Follow-up of training programmes and their monitoring will generate useful information if these can be done.

For an affective INSET programme, a strong follow-up of trainees is suggested. There is a need for a separate programme for each subject.

A continuous programme of training should be sustained through adequate financial support. There is also a need to do research on the INSET programme.

PHILIPPINES

The national report focuses on: (a) the training component of the recently concluded Secondary Education Development Programme (SEDP) and a complementary programme entitled Philippine Australian Science and Mathematics Education Project (PASMEP); (b) present and future in-service training programmes in science and mathematics that relate to the established training network or infrastructure to ensure continuous upgrading of the competencies of teachers.

The SEDP was a major educational reform subsequent to the massive project geared towards the improvement of elementary education. The SEDP reform package consisted of the following components: curriculum development, staff development, physical facilities development, technical assistance, and special studies and research. The teacher training component included content, strategies, and evaluation of learning outcomes.

The operationalization of PASMEP gave a big boost to science and mathematics education. The project operated within SEDP and supported that latter through the training of trainers, teachers, and administrators, equipment, and consumables supply, and preparation of supplementary teaching/learning materials.

With the institutionalization of an infrastructure for in-service teacher training at the national level, regional level at regional leader schools, divisional level at divisional leader schools, and school level at secondary schools, a strategy for continuing training of teachers has been provided.

The teacher training component of SEDP and PASMEP was conducted with the assistance of the University of the Philippines Institute for Science and Mathematics Education Development (UP-ISMED). Present and future projects at UP-ISMED will address different levels of the established infrastructure as follows:

1. DECS-Integrated Scholarship Programme for classroom teachers to strengthen the teaching of existing curricula;
2. Training courses for teacher educators from Regional Science Teaching Centres (RSTC) of the Department of Science and Technology (DOST);
3. Training programmes for teachers coming from the node schools of the Science and Technology Co-ordinating Council of DOST-SEI;
4. Philippine-Japan Science Education Manpower Development Project;

5. Mobile laboratory to reach out to teachers in far-flung areas; and
6. Short-term course offerings that enable the Institute to immediately respond to the needs of practitioners in the field.

Some innovative features of the in-service training programmes are the following:

1. Co-operation and co-ordination between different agencies and organizations involved in science and mathematics education;
2. Integration of content and strategies, theory and practice, in the delivery of instruction;
3. Use of several approaches and strategies to stimulate participation;
4. Up-to-dateness; incorporation of contemporary issues;
5. Output-orientation; and
6. Tailor-suited to the needs of the clientele.

Evaluation of the training programmes include questionnaires surveys, classroom observations and interviews, diagnostic tests addressed to trainees-trainers/administrators. An impact study of SEDP is being conducted. An impact study of UPISMED courses is also being planned to find out the effect of training courses on student learning. Indicators shall be adopted which are compatible with the courses objectives.

SRI LANKA

The training of teachers and other education personnel comes within the purview of the Ministry of Education and Higher Education (MOEHE) and is implemented through different departments of the National Institute of Education (NIE) and Network of Colleges of Education and Teachers Colleges. Short-term in-service training courses are conducted by different departments of the NIE and MOEHE in collaboration with provincial departments or divisional offices of education.

In-service training is provided through:

1. Hands-on practical activities

   In the 5-day Initial Life Skills Teacher Training Programme, 70 per cent of the training time is devoted to hands-on practical activities.

2. On-site training

   Practical training for teachers is given in premises/ workshops of governmental and non-governmental agencies.

3. Distance Education

   Courses for new recruits of trainee-teachers make use of print modules.

4. Provincial trainer teams

   These are organized through MOEHE-NIE-University collaboration.

5. Non-government Organization (NGO) supported seminars for teachers and science camps for pupils.

6. One-day orientation sessions for principals on life skills.

Indicators of Effectiveness of Training:

1. Performance of trainees at examination and in assignments, projects and teaching practice.
2. Pupil achievement (Performance at National Examinations).
3. Cohort Student flow at different levels.
4. Measures of teacher competencies in subject matter mastery, professional skills and attitudes.
5. Self-evaluations based on oral and written responses at the end of the training session.
6. Professional attitudes about teaching, students and the community, based on validated attitude scales.

THAILAND

It was once a tradition in Thailand to recruit science and mathematics teachers for secondary schools from two sources: one from universities which train subject specialists in basic sciences, i.e., Mathematics, Physics, Chemistry, Biology and General Sciences; another from teacher training schools which ran three-year or five-year teacher training for Grade 10 students. The system had worked reasonably well until the later 50's. Because of the pressure to provide more primary and secondary schools to more children, coupled with the situation that young students chose to go in for engineering and medicine training rather than in basic science, a large number of untrained teachers had to be employed. To help untrained teachers develop confidence and efficiency in their teaching and also qualify for promotion, a correspondence programme in teacher education, backed up by special laboratory courses held during the summer vacation, was systematized.

With the establishment of 36 modern teachers' colleges (with an average of 3,000 enrollees per teacher college) granting a bachelor's degree in science and mathematics education and others, there is no longer any need to recruit untrained and unqualified teachers. Hence, there seems to be no need for the correspondence programme with its highly questionable relevance to the work of the teachers.

Teachers who do not have a bachelor's degree are encouraged to enrol in the evening classes of teachers colleges in their locality or to take a correspondence course offered by the only open university in Thailand. In either case, they should have a bachelor's degree within a reasonable time. Teachers who already have a bachelor's degree have the right to ask for a study leave in order to pursue a master's degree at any university of their choice. Teachers in primary and secondary schools with either a bachelor or master's degree may upgrade their rank (Rank I, II, and III, or Specialist) through satisfactory performance as teachers and by submitting creative and original works such as research work, instructional materials, textbooks, and teachers's guides to referees appointed by the Office of Teachers Commission. Rank-upgrading is commensurate with the salary scales. The salary ceiling goes up with the rank. Rank

III teachers and specialists are on par with assistant and associate professors of universities, respectively, and in terms of salaries.

Teachers are encouraged to attend short training courses organized by various organizations—governmental as well as private. Registration fees, travel costs and living allowances are often covered by the schools. Although there are no immediate incentives for attending these courses, teachers may use the materials from the courses to do independent work for rank-upgrading application.

VIETNAM

State of In-service Teacher Training

Realizing the importance of in-service training programmes for enabling teachers to keep pace with developments of education in Vietnam, policy guidelines have emerged to link promotion with participation in in-service education programme.

Since 1981 there have been changes in the textbooks in the whole education system. In the present educational reform, in-service teacher training programmes have been implemented in two main forms:

1. Standardization training for teachers who have not earned a diploma from the teacher training colleges; and
2. Frequent school-based training sessions for all teachers.

Many teachers have taken part in in-service training programmes. Innovative strategies on improving the quality of in-service training of teachers have been considered.

The training programmes are carried out for all teachers at all levels in the whole country. These are implemented in various forms (continuous, discontinuous, distance-training, etc.). The training programmes aim to:

1. Upgrade the skills of teachers and school administrators who are graduates of teacher training colleges or high schools;
2. Enable teachers without pre-service training to get certified;

3. Enable teachers to teach subjects which they did not study in college; and
4. Equip teachers with instructional theory and practice.

The Ministry of Education and Training, some teacher training colleges and local education offices share responsibilities in planning and organizing in-service teacher training courses.

Evaluating Results of the Programme

Teachers taking part in in-service training courses are assessed in knowledge and the qualification they have achieved. This is done through interviews, actual classroom teaching, examinations after each course and at the end of the entire training to merit a certificate.

Recommendations

In order to improve the quality of in-service teacher training programme in Vietnam:

1. There should be a reform in teacher training colleges so that their graduates have better knowledge and qualification to meet the needs of education and schools; and
2. The contents and implementation of in-service training should be carefully considered to ensure high quality training.

B. Trends and Issues Emerging from the Country Papers

1. General

The national report for In-service Education of Teachers (INSET) Workshop on Improving the Quality of Science, Technology, and Mathematics Education at the Basic Level brought out several trends of development. All countries obviously rely on the instrumentality of education for socio-economic-cultural development. The role of science, technology, and mathematics is highlighted in the national policy statement of each country; these subjects are now an integral part of school curriculum. Whereas technology as a subject has become reflected in the school curriculum of some countries, a majority of them have yet to incorporate this component in their school curriculum and eventually in the teacher training curriculum.

The educational structures of the countries have, in general, common features of 11-12 years of schooling (10 years for the Philippines) except in the distribution of time/class periods within the school system.

The structure of pre-service teacher training for secondary teachers is fairly well established but a similar emphasis on primary teacher training is not well articulated in the national presentations. The in-service teacher training is at various stages of design and development; some countries are even moving towards institutionalizing it on long term basis. There is also a trend towards decentralization of the educational apparatus to ensure that the benefits of training teacher the intended levels.

2. *Curriculum Design*

Over the recent past there are evidence of the countries' attempts to update the curricula in science and mathematics. The curriculum objectives are stated to reflect the real concerns of science and mathematics teaching. However, in the context of "Education for All" (EFA), the concept of "Science, Technology and Mathematics for All" to ensure scientific technological and mathematical literacy for all requires some re-orientation in the curricula presently being followed in the teacher training programmes in the countries. There are concerns to make science and mathematics curriculum more relevant to the learners by decentralizing the process of curriculum development to local levels. Interesting points emerged regarding influence of multicultural settings on the design and transaction of curriculum in science and mathematics.

3. *Curriculum Transaction*

Whereas the countries have successfully designed new curricula in science and mathematics and in most cases it can be said to be up-to-date and commensurate with respective national concerns, its actual transaction in the classroom is not presented to be uniformly satisfactory in most countries. The curricular objectives take courage to question. Objectivity, creativity, problem solving, decision making, etc. are the expected outcomes of learning science and mathematics, but the transactional strategies being followed are generally not found appropriate to the development of skills and values vital for development of societies with scientific temper. Such inadequacies reflected in the presentations have implications for both pre-service and in-service teacher training.

4. *Teacher Training*

Both pre-service and in-service teacher training programmes are highlighted in the presentations. The ambiguity of meaning attached to pre-service and in-service persists in the contexts in which the terms are used in different countries. The structure of pre-service teacher education is broadly common. Longer duration of 3-4 years' teacher training integrated programmes are followed in most countries but the one-year model is also prevalent after the first university degree in arts or science. Though teacher training programmes are generally based on a school experience of 12 years, it appeared that in one country the baseline entry to the teaching profession is drawn after 10 years of basic schooling.

The in-service training in science and mathematics is offered to provide for enhancement of professional qualification leading to a diploma or degree, but generally the in-service training programmes are meant for professional updating in content and pedagogy, methodology, and evaluation of learning. There is a general consideration to have the programmes relevant to the needs of the teachers, although programmes determined relevant by educational authorities are also offered.

In-service teacher training is mainly confined to science and mathematics; incorporation of technology as a concrete component is not adequately reflected except in a few programmes offered by one country.

Considering the importance of institutionalizing in-service teacher training, most countries have created infrastructures which act as nodal centres for this activity at national, state and district levels. There are indications of possible networking for the optimum output from these setups.

5. *Strategies Adopted*

The participating countries have conducted in-service training programmes in science and mathematics to meet the specific needs generated by national policy imperatives and new curriculum development efforts. However, the appropriateness of the approaches followed, and the effectiveness of the training provided and its impact on the achievement of learners have not received the needed focus.

Various strategies adopted by the participating countries include one or more of the following:

- Distance Education (print, non-print, audio, video support materials development);
- Cascading strategy involving various tiers of training;
- Attachment programmes with centres of higher learning (for specialized areas in science and mathematics, in-service training);
- Mobile training teams;
- Site visits by supervisors;
- Training packages for teachers;
- Development of leader schools and school complexes;
- Setting up of Teacher Resource Centres;
- School-based In-service Training, 'In-house' Training, Setting up of Learning Action Cells;
- Professional Associations of Teachers, Teacher Support Group;
- Encouraging support on Non-Governmental Organizations; and
- Institutionalization of in-service training on a continuing basis.

6. Evaluation

There are efforts reported in several countries to undertake evaluation of their in-service training programmes. In terms of the objectives laid down and parameters connected therewith, a detailed analysis of the quality "indicators" has not surfaced in the presentations. Not much research is done in the countries into the evaluation of indicators. There is also a concern that unwise choice of evaluation procedures may also go against the spirit of evaluation.

7. Major Issues

Based on the presentations, several issues have emerged. A few of them are listed for deliberations towards possible recommendations:

- Mechanism of assessment of needs for in-service training in science and mathematic;
- Concerns relating to technology as a component for in-service teacher training;
- Importance of the role of principals, head teachers;
- Networking of technical support for in-service teacher training by universities and related systems involved in the organization of teacher training;
- Improving the learning environment in schools;
- Resource support needed for distance education for in-service teacher training.
- In-service teacher training in areas of special needs (gifted, slow learners, ethnic group, children with handicaps, girls, etc.);
- In-service training for teachers working in difficult locations (mountains, hilly terrains, islands);
- Cycle of periodicity of teacher training, duration, etc.;
- Lack of women teachers in science and mathematics;
- Need for programmes to enhance supervisory skills;
- Need for institutionalization of science and mathematics in-service training;
- Motivation aspects for INSET;
- Incentives; and
- Research into in-service teacher training.

2

In-service Teacher Education in Science, Technology and Mathematics at Basic Level: Strategies and Evaluation

A. In-service Training (INSET) Defined

In-service training includes all training activities which address the differentiated needs of teachers in schools (including teachers without pre-service training) to improve their knowledge, skills and attitudes for better instruction.

B. Rational for In-service Training

1. In some countries in the region, there are many teachers already in the service who had not received pre-service training. They were hired because the large demand for education and the inadequate supply of trained teachers. These untrained teachers need teaching skills before they can be certified as teachers.

2. The skills and competencies of many teachers who have received pre-service training is inadequate.

3. Pre-service teacher training in some teacher education institutions is of low standard. Thus the teachers turned out by these institutions are not equipped with adequate skills for teaching.

4. Teachers have to be agents of change for improving the life of the community. However, many trained teachers do not have enough competencies and confidence to carry out their role beyond the classroom.

5. Teachers have not kept pace with the rapid growth of knowledge, particularly in science, technology and mathematics. Their knowledge and skill in these subjects need to be upgraded.

6. Educational development programmes in some countries (e.g. Philippines and Thailand) have resulted in new curricula. These new curricula bring about a need for teacher retraining.

In sum, teacher in-service training in science, technology and mathematics (STM) is needed for anyone of these purposes:

1. To upgrade teaching competencies and skills in STM;
2. To update teachers' knowledge in these subjects;
3. To enable teachers to implement new curricula; and
4. To familiarize teachers with new methods and approaches to teaching STM.

C. Some Guiding Principles for INSET

1. A national policy for INSET needs to be developed and implemented. The policy should articulate pre-service and in-service training.

2. INSET should directly address the needs of teachers and the community.

3. There should be an efficient process for disseminating successful INSET courses to the whole region.

4. INSET should encourage independent learning and a desire for continuing professional development amongst the participants.

5. There should be continuous feedback and communication within the system.

6. INSET should draw on and benefit from the findings of research. Similarly, research should be built into INSET.

D. Policy on INSET

1. To improve education particularly in science, technology and mathematics at the basic education level, and to ensure the implementation of "Education for All" (EEA), in-service education should be provided to teachers and other educational personnel.

2. There should be a comprehensive INSET programme which will:

(a) provide training based on the differentiated needs of teachers, principals, supervisors and other education personnel.

(b) establish the infrastructure needed for carrying out INSET.

(c) emphasize the use of available technology and resources in the locality.

(d) motivate teachers and other educational personnel (either intrinsically or extrinsically) to grow in their profession.

(e) address gender and ethnic issues as well as special needs of learners.

(f) narrow the gap between the intended curriculum and the curriculum actually implemented in the schools.

(g) encouraged independent learning by participants (including the ability to undertake action research in the classrooms) as one of the long-term INSET objectives.

(h) INSET should address the needs of its target clients. As such, the trainees should be involved in the planning of INSET activities to make these relevant to those who will undergo the training.

(i) Adequate funding and material support should be given to INSET to ensure the implementation of quality education for all.

(j) Research and evaluation on various aspects and at different levels of INSET should be the basis for policy formulation and programme planning.

E. Issues Requiring Consideration

The Workshop recognized the following issues as possible source of difficulties in ensuring that INSET courses will assist in improving education at the basic level:

1. Support

Unless key personnel in the system (principals, inspectors and others) are aware of, and support changes thought through INSET, success will be unlikely to occur.

2. Motivation

Matching INSET courses to the needs of the participants will be necessary to help overcome lack of motivation caused by negative attitudes towards, and low perception of the value of these courses.

3. Time

There is tension between the need to contain costs by reducing the length of INSET courses and the need to build in time for trial of new ideas and for reflection. This may mean that local delivery or carefully supported Distance Education modalities will be important strategies to consider.

4. Approach

INSET courses need to be interactive and provide participants with opportunities to model new techniques.

5. Evaluation

INSET courses should have clearly specified aims and evaluation should match these aims. This means that some aims involving considerable change to teaching/learning approaches will require complex evaluation methods. Trainers may require assistance in developing and implementing these.

F. Conditions for Effective INSET Programmes

Certain conditions have to be met in order to ensure that an INSET programme is of high quality and effective in helping teachers improve their performance. The conditions identified are listed below:

1. *Needs Assessment*

An assessment of training needs of teachers must be undertaken. Assessment can be done by the teachers themselves, their head teachers, supervisors, or their students. Based on the differentiated needs, the teachers can be grouped accordingly and the appropriate training provided can be utilized to identify teachers' weaknesses.

2. *Setting Objectives*

A set of objectives has to be formulated and explicitly stated incorporating the needs of the teachers. These will guide the organizers and trainers to do their jobs effectively.

3. *Congruence of Programme with Teachers' Needs*

A training programme should be designed so as to ensure that the needs of the teachers are met, in terms of: the subject content to be covered, the methodology to be used, and the values/attitudes to be inculcated. Selected teachers who would be participants in the training can be invited to help in designing the programme.

4. *Identification of Trainers/Resource Persons/Facilitators*

Trainers who are knowledgeable in the subject area and committed to the task should be identified. They should be competent in communication skills and in operationalizing the principles of andragogy.

5. *Development of Quality Materials*

Materials (print and non-print) should be developed. Competent teachers and trainers can be involved in the preparation. As far as possible the materials should be tried-out before use. Attention was to be paid to the format, presentation and language used in the materials so that teachers would be inclined to make use of them.

6. *Appropriate Length of Training*

The duration of training should be adequate to cover all the objectives specified, while aiming to minimize the number of days so as reduce cost and conveniences.

7. *Suitable Training Centres.*

Training centres can be set up at various places such as leader schools, teacher training colleges, universities or other institutions. But each centre needs to ensure availability of basic amenities as well as the necessary facilities and equipment for the training.

8. *Participatory/Interactive Training Activities*

The activities during the training planned to enable all participants to be actively involved, to interact among themselves and with the trainers, to undertake hands-on activities, and to model some of the practices to be used in the classroom. Time should also be provided for participants to reflect on what they have learned.

9. *Developing the Capacity for Independent Learning*

Within the training activities, provision should be made to provide participants with the knowledge, skills and motivation to undertake independent learning. This ability would enable participants to grow professionally on their own initiative.

10. *Continuous Feedback and Corrective Measures*

A mechanism for monitoring the conduct of the training should be provided for, so that feedback is available at all times. Such feedback is to be used to improve the training on a day-to-day basis.

11. *Follow-up and Support Activities*

Teachers attend attachment programmes to local or foreign institutions to upgrade their competencies. Upon their return from such programmes, they become trainers.

G. Strategies for In-service Education and Training in the Region

Participating countries have come up with various strategies to meet different needs. A brief description of each strategy and examples of how some countries of the region have used the strategy are given below:

1. Distance Education

Distance education has been tried and carried out successfully in some countries of the region. The strategy has been used in India and is likely to become the ministry of in-service education in that country.

It is important that a good communication network be put up and that new self-learning materials and audio visual support be developed to ensure success of this strategy.

2. Cascading Modality

Selected groups of teachers are trained at the central level to become trainers at the provincial/state/district levels. The modality has been used in the Philippines in the training of teachers for the Secondary Educational Development Programme (SEDP) and in Malaysia on the training of its key personnel for the New Primary School Curriculum (KBSR) and the Integrated Curriculum for Secondary Schools (KBSM).

This strategy is most appropriate for crash orientation programmes where large number of teachers are involved and the time frame is limited. To ensure effectiveness, the levels should be minimized and standardized materials should be developed and disseminated to all the levels.

3. Use of Resource Centres and Teacher Activity Centres

This involves the setting up to ensource centres or teacher activity centres in every province or district. These centres are venues for conducting INSET. Teachers hold regular meetings at the centres to discuss and produce teaching learning materials. For this purposes, the centres need to be equipped with reference and audio visual materials.

Some resource centres are based in universities and teacher training institutions. INSET are conducted by the university/ institutions, faculty and academic personnel.

Malaysia has about 350 teacher activity centres throughout the country. Other countries in the region have also started establishing resource/activity centres for teachers.

4. Identification of Leader Schools

Leader schools are provided with facilities and equipment to be shared by neighbouring schools in the cluster. These are selected for having shown consistently good performance and have done innovative projects. Teachers from the leader schools are trained to serve as trainers of the teachers in the cluster.

Leader schools are found in the Philippines and Thailand.

5. In-house/School-Based Training Modality

In this modality, INSET programmes are carried out at the school level and conducted by the school principal, headmaster or senior subject teachers. Experts from other institutions may be invited to the schools to conduct the training. This modality calls for principals' or headmasters' management skills. They too need to be trained to become good curriculum leaders and managers as well.

In-house training should be continuous process and need to be incorporated in the school system. This modality not only reduces the dilution affect of the cascading modality, it is also found to be cost effective.

6. Establishing a Pool of Experts

A pool of science and mathematics experts is selected from among experienced teachers who are then sent for training at the national level. Upon their return from training, they serve as resource persons at the resource centres or teacher activity centres. Upon their returr they meet regularly with teachers from the district to discuss the teacher's teaching-learning problems and innovative strategies for overcoming these problems.

Several strategies have also been identified. These are:

1. Setting up and Strengthening of Teachers Professional Organizations

Teachers' professional organizations such as Science and Mathematics Teachers Association have to be set up and strengthened to help improve teacher education. These organizations conduct courses and training programmes for members and non-members.

2. Setting up of Database on Experts in Various Educational Fields

To ensure the effectiveness of the in-house training or training at the national level, a database on experts in various educational fields can be set up by a national or state institution which also serve as cleaninghouses for the dissemination of educational information.

3. Subscription to Journals and Periodicals

To update teachers on recent trends and developments, schools are encouraged to subscribe to educational journals. This is also done to promote teachers' reading habits. Subscriptions are offered at specially discounted rates or sent free of charge.

4. Attachment Programmes for Teachers

Teachers attend attachment programmes to local or foreign institutions to upgrade their competencies. Upon their return from such programmes, they become trainers.

H. Evaluation

In the context of training programmes, evaluation can be defined as the process of collecting information which can be used as basis for making judgements about the programme, which judgements can in turn be used for making decisions.

Evaluation can be done before, during and after the training. The evaluation done before the programme can take the form of needs assessment, pre-training or base line data. It gives information on some input factors.

Evaluation which is carried out during the training is formative in intent. It is meant to provide basis for action toward further improving the programme, or taking corrective measures, or maximizing the attainment of the programme objectives. Such evaluation focuses on the process component.

Evaluation at the end of the training, or even some time after the training is concerned with getting information which will be used as basis for forming judgements and the effects, outputs or outcomes of the programme.

Two key evaluation criteria will be treated: effectiveness and efficiency. Effectiveness is the extent to which a training programme attains its objectives. Efficiency is the effectiveness of the programme in relation to its cost. As an example, between two in-service training, modalities which are equally effective, the criterion to consider is efficiency, i.e., which one entails less cost in terms of time, efforts and money.

I. Indicators of Quality In-service Training

In a systems framework, evaluation of the quality of a training programme entails making judgements about the inputs, the processes and the outputs. For each of these three components there is a need to identify indicators.

Some of categorized indicators are listed below:

Inputs	Process	Outputs/Outcomes
Trainee characteristics	Management of the programme	
Trainer characteristics	Methods and techniques used	(Knowledge (Skills (Attitudes (Practice)
Programme characteristics	Inter-personal communication	

The indicators of quality inputs are:

1. Trainees who meet the specifications about who should be trained; appropriateness of the level of their educational background; willingness to be trained;
2. Trainers who have the expertise, experience and skills to conduct the training;
3. Programme objectives which are clearly understood by the organizers, the trainers and the trainees;
4. Materials which are relevant, appropriate and adequate for the trainer;
5. Capable resource persons; and
6. A well planned (well sequenced) programme.

The Quality Process Indicators are:

1. Active involvement of the trainee participants;
2. Time management during the training;
3. Verbal interaction between trainees and trainers and among the trainees;
4. Trainee involvement in the planning and conduct of the training activities;
5. Ideas generated from the trainees;
6. Communication between trainers and INSET administrators/supervisors;
7. Readiness/Willingness of trainees to participate;
8. Attention span of the trainers;
9. Self-learning and trainee-generated activities; and
10. Use of materials and resources; improvisation of equipments.

The output indicators are:

1. Gains in knowledge;
2. Changes in behaviour, attitudes and values;
3. Willingness to apply learnings in regard to methods and materials and techniques used in the training;
4. Positive attitude and perceptions toward the training programme;
5. Readiness to continue/attend other INSET courses; and
6. Improved achievement of the trainees' pupils.

The methods and Techniques for Evaluating INSET are:

1. Self-reports using questionnaires, checklists, rating scales, etc. by trainees;
2. Paper-and-pencil tests given as pre-post tests to the trainees;
3. Opinion surveys of participants (trainees, trainers, administrators);

4. Peer evaluations;
5. Individual or group interviews of participants;
6. Participant-observation;
7. Guided observations;
8. Focused-discussion groups;
9. Diaries and journal entries by trainees;
10. Performance Tests (e.g., teaching demonstrations); and
11. Testing pupils of the trainees.

Below is a set of questions, the answers to which will give indications of how well a training programme meets the requisites of quality (effective) INSET.

This instrument can serve as a checklist for assessing the training programme.

Question: Does the INSET course

- have as its primary aim improved lending by students in the classroom?

Does it

- address teacher needs?
- involve participants in all stages of planning?
- address community requirements?
- address student requirements?
- take place over an appropriate time frame?
- have support from principals and other change agents?
- provide motivation:
  - intrinsically, by addressing needs?
  - extrinsically, by providing incentives?
- involve modelling of classroom activities?
- value interaction with participants?
- assist teachers to bring their practice closer to the intended curriculum?

- increase teacher confidence/knowledge/skills/attitude?
- encourage independent learning?
- address gender and ethnic issues?
- incorporate environmental concerns?
- address community values?
- take advantage of new and available technologies?
- encourage community involvement?
- provide appropriate opportunities for evaluation by participants?
- have a research component?

3

Recommendations and National Plans of Action

A. General Recommendations

In the context of the Workshop the participants recommended that:

1. Clear cut national policy for INSET be developed and implemented and the necessary political WILL be solicited to ensure success of implementation.
2. Programmes in pre-service and INSET complement and supplement each other.
3. INSET be research-based so that outcomes can be the basis for review and development.
4. INSET be synchronized and harmonized with national and regional educational programmes.
5. Issues on gender, ethnic groups and learners with special needs be important focus areas in the implementation of INSET.
6. Mechanisms assessing for in-service training in science and mathematics be looked into at the national level.
7. Technology education be made a component for all INSET.
8. The roles of principals, head teachers and supervisors be given importance in organizing INSET.

9. Networking mechanisms be developed in order to encourage technical support for INSET by universities and related systems involved in the organization of INSET.
10. Resource support needed for implementing distance education programmes for INSET be identified.
11. Regional/National Workshops organized on developing of instruments for evaluation quality INSET.

B. Proposed National Plans of Action

BANGLADESH

I. Title of the Project

National Training Workshop on "Improving the Quality of Science and Mathematics Teachers at the Basic Level"

II. Objectives

The objectives of workshops are:

1. To acquaint the teacher educators and other concerned personnel with the output of the 'Regional Workshop on Improving the Quality of Science, Technology and Mathematics Education at the Basic Level', held in UP-ISMED, Quezon City, Philippines, 7-12 December 1992.
2. To identify possible ways to implement the guiding principles for INSET identified in the Regional Workshop in the context of Bangladesh.
3. To suggest initiatives to be taken to enhance the quality of INSET Science and Mathematics.
4. To implement the indicators and strategies identified in the Regional Workshop for evaluating INSET in the context of the country.

III. Project Description

a. Participants

About 30 Science and Mathematics teacher educators, curriculum designers and educational planners from the following agencies/institutions will be invited to the workshop:

Teachers Training Colleges and PTI	15
SESDCs	10
NCTB	2
NAPE	1
Directorate of Secondary Education	1
Directorate of Primary Education	1

b. Resource Persons

Four to five professional science and mathematics teacher educators who have also up-to-date knowledge and information about INSET at how and abroad will be invited to serve as resource persons in the workshop. Each will also be invited to present a paper based on the workshop objectives.

c. Workshop Procedures

There will be a short inaugural session in the workshop. After the inaugural session the workshop papers will be presented in the general plenary session. After each presentation the participant will discuss about the theme and after modification, if any, the workshop paper will be incorporated in the workshop report.

After the presentation of the workshop papers, the participants will be divided into four groups having one chairman and one rapporteur in each group. The group will be performing activities to identify the guiding principles, issues and problems a list of initiatives to be taken, prepare; and suggest strategies for evaluating INSET. If necessary actual INSET that are going on in the country will also be evaluated.

The outputs of group deliberations will be discussed in plenary.

d. Staff and Agencies to be Involved

The venue of the workshop is the Teacher Training College, Dhaka. The Dhaka TTC Staff and its facilities will be utilized to hold the workshop. If necessary the National SESDC staff and facilities will be used as both are located in the same campus.

e. Time Frame

The workshop will be organized for 7 to 10 days duration.

f. Workshop Output

A report of the workshops output and proceedings will be published.

g. Significance

In order to improve the learning of students in the classroom specially in science and mathematics, holding of such workshop is of great importance and significance.

h. Budget

To hold the above workshop and to publish the report workshop proceedings, the amount of US$5,000 will be necessary.

i. Co-operating Agencies

- UNESCO Principal Regional Office for Asia and the Pacific, Bangkok;
- Bangladesh National Commission for UNESCO (BNCV);
- Ministry of Education, Government of Bangladesh.

INDIA

I. Title of the Project

Design and Development of Exemplar Distance Education Materials for In-Service Training of Key Teacher Educators in Science, Technology and Mathematics

II. Project Description

There is a big movement towards institutionalization of in-service training of education personnel including those involved in teacher training in Science and Mathematics. Institutional infrastructure like nodal institution and District Institutes of Education and Training (DIETs) have been put in place. There are great expectations from the Staff recruited to these institutions to demonstrate that through a decentralized system of the DIETs, it is possible to universalize and ensure qualitative improvement of elementary education. There are 400 DIETs and their Staff (23 per DIET) have to be given induction training so that they perform at the same high level of expectation.

There is a Memorandum of Understanding signed by the NCERT with Indira Gandhi National Open University (IGNOU), New Delhi, under which a Distance Education programme for training of key teacher educators in science and mathematics as a collaborative effort of the IGNOU and the technical academic support by the NCERT.

III. Objectives

1. Identification of core areas of training in science, technology and mathematics education.
2. Development of modules for training.
3. Development of audio and video support materials. (The NCERT has its own infrastructure through its Central Institute of Educational Technology (CIET) to undertake this task).

These objectives will be accomplished using the resources of the NCERT and involving experts from the University and related systems.

IV. Time Frame

The work can be completed within one year of commencement of the project.

V. Expected Output/Results

Exemplar distance education materials for training in science, technology and mathematics education.

VI. Significance of the Project

The exemplar distance education modules will serve as models for other teacher training materials which can be developed by the states in the context of science, technology and mathematics education.

VII. Funding/Budget

The expenditure to be incurred will be for calling the workshop to develop the materials (print and non-print) and to reproduce a suitable number of copies of the modules developed. The NCERT has its own resources to be ploughed into it but financial support to this project from UNESCO to whatever extent possible will be a help.

INDONESIA

I. Title Project

Workshop on *Improving the Quality of In-Service Training (INSET) for STM Teachers.*

II. Objectives of the Project

1. To set up a programme in the context of the improvement of the quality of INSET.
2. To develop evaluation instruments to assess the effectiveness of the programme.
3. To encourage trainers to conduct research on the effectiveness of INSET.

III. Project Description

1. Preparation of the Workshop

(a) 3-day meeting of 5 experts to design the draft of the INSET programme based on the strategies adopted at the UNESCO Regional Workshop.

(b) 2-day meeting of 8 key administrators to discuss the strategy of the workshop and to formulate the objectives of the workshop.

2. Workshop Participants

(a) Heads of the Provincial INSET Centres for 10 Provinces (10 participants).

(b) Selected trainers from 10 concerned Province (10 participants).

(c) Staff and Agencies to be involved:

i. Directorate of Primary Education

ii. Directorate of Secondary General Education

iii. Directorate of Teachers Education and Technical Staff

iv. Experts on basic science/mathematics education

v. National Science Teachers Upgrading Centre

vi. Selected trainers

4. Staffing of the Project

(a) Co-ordination	1
(b) Technical staff	2
(c) Administration staff	3

5. Activities

(a) Experts meeting

(b) Key administrators meeting

(c) Workshop

IV. Expected Outcomes

1. Standard INSET programme to be used in the INSET Centres all over Indonesia.
2. Model of evaluation programme instruments.
3. Increase the awareness that the research should be conducted to ensure effectiveness of the INSET programme.

V. Approximate Budgetary Requirements US$6,500.000

1. Preparation of the Workshop

   (a) 3-day meeting of 5 experts

   (accommodation/transportation)

   (b) 2-day meeting of 8 key administration

   (accommodation/transportation)

2. Workshop

   5-day workshop

   20 participants from 10 provinces

   (accommodation/transportation)

   5 resource persons/experts

   (accommodattion/transportation)

3. Project Staff

   (transportation/incentive)

   10 working days

VI. Co-operative Agencies

1. National Science Teacher Upgrading Centre
2. UNESCO National Commission Indonesia
3. UNESCO PROAP-Bangkok
4. Other EFA Partners

LAO P.D.R.

I. Title of the Project

Training of a *Writing Team to Develop Self-Learning Modules in Mathematics for Primary School Teachers*

II. Objectives

1. To train personnel to develop training materials to improve the quality of teaching-learning Mathematics at Primary School.
2. To help teachers to improve their performance in teaching mathematics at Primary School.
3. To introduce new methods of teaching mathematics at Primary School.

III. Description

1. To hold a Workshop to:

(a) Identify felt needs of the Teachers in teaching mathematics at Primary School.

(b) Train trainers how to develop the self-learning modules which meet the needs of the teachers.

2. Participants

(a) Mathematics Teachers from Primary Teacher Training Institutions.

(b) Administrators from the Ministry of Education.

(c) Teachers from Primary School.

IV. Staff Involved

1. Director of Commission for UNESCO Lao P.D.R.
2. Director of General Education Department

4. Director of Research Institute of Education and Science
5. Directors of Educational Authorities

   (provincial and district levels)

V. Duration

1. 3. days for preparation
2. 3 days for identification of felt needs of teachers and selection of Writing Teams.
3. 7 days for training the writing team.

VI. Expected Output

1. Listing of set needs for Training of Writing Teams.
2. Development of self-learning Modules.

VII. Significance of the Project

The difficulty of teaching mathematics is the urgent and immediate problem of the teachers in the primary schools. Teachers need to be trained on how to produced teaching materials which are relevant to their own environment.

VIII. Co-operating Agencies

1. UNESCO PROAP Bangkok
2. UNESCO National Commission LAO P.D.R.
3. EFA Partners

IX. Approximate Budget US$3,500

MALAYSIA

I. Title of the Project

Upgrading Primary Science Education

II. Objectives

1. To train selected key primary school teachers in the content of science and the methodology of teaching science.

2. To transform these teachers to play the roles of teacher trainers, facilitators and agents of change in primary science education in their respective districts.

III. Project Description

Science is not taught as a single subject in the Malaysian Primary Schools, but as a component of the subject called **"Alam dan Manusia"** (Man and the Environment) starting from grade 4 to grade 6. Prior to this level, a modicum of **"science education"** is integrated wherever possible in other subjects such as Bahasa Malaysia and English in the form of comprehension passages. In as much as teachers in the primary schools are regarded as general purpose teachers, many of them lack the knowledge and competencies in science and its methodology of teaching. These hinder the successful implementation of **"Alam dan Munusia"**. However, pupils in the primary schools need to be exposed to a good science education in order to prepare them to live in a world which depends more and more on science and technology. Hence the upgrading of tenured teachers' knowledge and competencies in science is sine-qua-non. Massive retraining of these teachers through the usual cascading modality would be costly and inefficient. INSET through the use of the local Resource Personnel in primary science will be employed instead on a trial basis in selected school districts. If this modality proves to be successful the project can be expanded to other districts gradually. Apart from conducting the course, they can also help the teachers in the districts to produce their own instructional materials. Regular and continuous INSET can be carried out either at the Teacher Activity Centre (TAC) or in the schools.

At the outset, key teachers have to be selected carefully to ensure successful and sustainable implementation of the project. Experience, commitment, self motivation, qualification, willingness to work after school hours are some of the characteristics to look for. For the start, only school districts in the northern states of the Peninsula will be involved (20 key teachers will be selected).

They will be trained at RECSAM (probably one month duration). The course content, materials and methodology of training will be discussed and developed later. After the training, those resource personnel will go back to their respective districts and begin playing their roles. In order to initiate and to give impetus to the whole project at the district level, first INSET will be carried out at TAC with the help of the Curriculum Development Centre (CDC) and the State Education District Education Office.

CDC and State Education Office will monitor the implementation of this project. At regular intervals, the Resource Personnel would be given further input by CDC or other institutions to further enhance capabilities, motivation and commitment. Evaluation on the project will be carried out from time to time.

The procedure of the project is as follows:

1. Getting approval from the authority
2. (Government of Malaysia, UNESCO)
3. Selection of resource personnel
4. Needs Assessment
5. Production of course materials
6. Training at RECSAM
7. Orientation to Work
8. First INSET at district level
9. INSET in other districts
10. Evaluation of project
11. Decision on the project

    (to continue? to expand?)

The success of the project depends on many factors i.e.; Resource Personnel, Headmaster, Teachers. The final indicator is the performance of pupils themselves.

IV. Approximate Budgetary Requirements US$ 7,700.00

1. Workshop to deliberate on the Project and production of materials.

2. Training of Key Personnel at RECSAM (US$ 20 per head).
3. Travelling Expenses
4. Production of Course Materials
5. INSET at district levels.

NEPAL

I. Title of the Project

In-Service Science Teacher Training

II. Rationale and Objectives

From observations during our supervision work we come to know that some teachers have no clear concepts of some lessons like Magnet, Matter, Gas, etc. There is also a lack of instructional materials in the school. The teachers teach the science lesson not differently with the other subjects thus the need to train them on science teaching methodology. At least one week training is needed for these teachers. The training is based on textbook using local resources. The training centre is either within walking distance to the teachers school or to the leader secondary schools or Science Education Development Project (SEDP) in the District Headquarter.

At the end of the one week in-service teacher training the teachers must be able to:

1. use a variety of science teaching methodologies
2. use different strategies of teaching
3. use locally available materials and other teaching aids in teaching
4. acquired skills in preparing good lessons plans.

III. Co-operating Agencies to be Involved

1. Science Master Teachers from SEDEC
2. Local District Officers
3. Science Education Development Centre, Nepal

IV. Time Frame

Training Schedule:

1.	Registration	1 hour
2.	Teaching lesson with demonstration	25 hours
3.	Instructional material making	25 hours
4.	Microteaching	19 hours
5.	Evaluation	2 hours
		72 hours

V. Expected Output/Research

The teachers are expected to teach their lessons more effectively and come to realize the need to use teaching/learning aids. They will feel that the teaching of science in the school is facilitated by teaching aids.

VI. Significance of the Project

This type of in-service training is not so costly. The Training Centre is mostly within walking distance. The most significant is that teaching becomes very easy. They get satisfaction for their teaching.

VII. Approximate Budgetary Requirements $ 3,000.00

PAKISTAN

I. Title of the Project

National Workshop to Design a Model INSET Programme for Science, Technology and Mathematics Education (STME) at the Primary Level

II. Objectives of the Project

1. To develop a model of INSET programme in STME.
2. To develop support materials (AV aids, write ups, activities) to be used in INSET Training Programmes at the grassroots levels.
3. To train key persons and resource persons to handle the task.

4. To bring about a qualitative improvement in STME at the primary level.

III. Project Description

A 10-day National Workshop will be organized at Islamabad having 5 key persons from each of the four provincial Bureaus. The workshop will develop materials for future training programmes, find ways and means to make STME effective, frame worksheets for the children of classes I-V, and work out strategies to ensure the success of programmes.

This workshop will have discussion sessions, practicum sessions and the responsibility to produce instructional materials as an objective of the workshop.

IV. Co-operating Agencies

Key persons (about 2-4) from the local agencies involved in curriculum development and teacher education and at least one resource person from UNESCO.

V. Time Frame

Any time during summer vacation (i.e. 1 June to 15 July).

VI. Expected Output/Result

1. They key persons will train 20 resource persons in their respective provinces.
2. The 20 resource persons will conduct the workshop to train teachers in handling STME in their provinces.
3. The output will become the basis for national programmes in the future.

VII. Significance of the Project

Though INSET programmes are being organized for primary schools they generally cater to the general syllabus of primary level. In the present situation STME is not given due treatment. This National Workshop will seek to train key persons from each province to try out an effective model of INSET in STME.

VIII. Approximate Budgetary Required $ 3,000.00

PHILIPPINES

I. Title of Project

Development of Instruments for INSET Quality Indicators

II. Objectives

1. To identify indicators of quality INSET.
2. To develop, try out and revise the instruments.

III. Project Description

Within the Secondary Education Development Project is a staff development programme which includes:

1. Training of Pilot Teachers
2. Regional Trainers' Training
3. Mass Training of Teachers
4. Short Term Fellowships (local & foreign)
5. Long Term Fellowships (local & foreign)

An assessment of these different in-service training programme followed using instruments designed specifically for each programme.

Through the years, the need to improve the training programme has always been the concern of educational planners and curriculum workers. At the UNESCO Regional Workshop on quality INSET, the delegates from the Asia-Pacific region tried to identify some indicators of quality INSET. The Philippine delegates saw fit to prepare as a national action the development of instruments for quality INSET. The instruments to be developed are envisioned to rise the quality of INSET conducted in the country.

IV. Activities and Tasks

- Conduct a live-in workshop to develop the instruments
  (a) identification of indicators
  (b) definition of identified factors

(c) determination of the type of instrument to be developed

(d) preparation of instruments

(e) validation

(f) revision

(g) finalization

V. Co-operating Agencies: UNESCO, DECS

VI. Time Frame: One month

VII. Expected Output

1. Final Forms of the Instruments
2. Manual for Users of the Instruments
3. Workshop Report

VIII. Significance of the Project

The instruments to be developed shall be used in planning and evaluation INSET programmes and eventually in policy formulation regarding INSET.

IX. Approximate Budgetary Requirements for:

- Board and lodging
- Supplies and materials
- Consultant's fees
- Contingency

****

I. Title of Project

Development of Support/Enrichment Materials on Environmental Education

II. Objectives

1. To identify topics and issues on Environmental Education where enrichment and support materials are needed.
2. To prepare, validate and revise materials developed.

III. Project Description

Environmental issues today have become the concern of all, young or old, in-school or out-of-school. Thus, the school system, in order to be relevant as well as responsive to the needs of society, needs to continually update its curriculum.

Although environmental concepts are included in the course content, there are certain issues which need to be studied in-depth and issues which need to be dealt with objectively. The project is thus geared towards the development of support materials in the study of environmental education at the secondary school level.

IV. Activities and Issues

1. Identification of Topics/Issues
2. Writing the Materials
3. Tryout/Validation
4. Revision
5. Finalization of Materials

V. Co-operating Agencies: UNESCO, BSE-DECS, UPISMED

VI. Time Frame: 11 months

VII. Expected Outputs

1. Support and Enrichment Materials
2. Workshop Report

VIII. Significance of the Project

Enrichment and support materials will be useful to students and teachers in increasing their awareness of environmental issues and possibly their role in improving the environment.

IX. Approximate Budgetary Requirement: $6,000.00

SRI LANKA

I. Title of Project

Development of proposals for suitably restructuring/modifying school-based Life Skills (LS) and Junior Technical Certificate (JTC)

Programmes to meet entry level requirements for Tertiary Level (TL) vocational/technical training courses.

II. Need

In Sri Lanka, a large number of vocational/technical training courses are conducted at the Tertiary Level (TL) by government and non-government agencies. These courses lead to a certificate or diploma which would enable the participants, mostly school leavers with 7-9 year of schooling, to enter into a vocation, or seek employment.

Year 7-8 Life Skills (LS) and Year 9 Junior Technical Certificate (JTC) courses are school-based courses which are expected to provide a foundation for vocational/technical training and a preparation for the world of work and employment. However, a school leaver at the respective levels cannot use such school-based courses as an entry level qualification for TL training. There is a strong-felt need to make LS and JTC courses an entry level requirement for Tertiary Level Training (TLT) programmes. Such a step would pave the way for the building up of a technical ladder with provision for vertical and horizontal movements and make school-based LS and JTC courses more relevant and related to the TL vocational/technical training needs. This relationship could be established by suitably restructuring/modifying LS and JTC courses on the basis of a detailed content analysis.

III. Objectives

1. Analyse and match content of LS, JTC and TLT courses.
2. Make proposals to restructure/modify LS and JTC courses to make them entry requirements for TLT courses.

IV. Project Description

A representative sample of TLT courses will be selected in consultation with the Tertiary and Vocational Education Commission and, subjected to a content analysis, to identify the knowledge, skills, techniques and processes needed for such training. LS and JTC courses will also be subjected to a similar analysis to identify same providing a basis for vocational/

teaching training. The contents are matched to see the extent to which LS and JTC courses form the base for TLT courses. On the basis of an identification of areas of LS and JTC courses which need to be strengthened or filled up to make them a better foundation for TLT courses, proposals will be made for suitable restructuring/modification of TLT courses.

V. Activities/Tasks

1. Analyze content of LS and JTC courses to identify knowledge, skills, techniques and processes providing a basis for vocational/technical training.
2. Analyze content of a representative sample of tertiary level vocational/technical training (TLT) courses to identify knowledge, skills, techniques and processes involved in such training.
3. Match content of LS and JTC courses with those of TLT courses.
4. Identify areas of LS and JTC courses which need strengthening or filling up in order to make them a better foundation for TLT courses.
5. Make proposal for restructuring/modifying LS and JTC courses in order to make them entry level requirements for TLT courses.

VI. Staff and Agencies Involved

1. Director General and staff of the Tertiary and Vocational Education Commission (in consultancy capacity).
2. Selected members of Life Skills and Technical Education, Agriculture branches of the Ministry of Education and Higher Education.
3. Selected members of the Technical and Vocational Education Department of the National Institute of Education.
4. Trainers of LS, JTC and TLT courses.
5. Practising teachers of LS and JTC courses.

VII. Time Frame

12 months (1993)

VIII. Expected Output/Outcome

Guidelines for restructuring/modifying 50 LS Learning events and 53 JTC courses to make them an entry requirement for TLT courses.

IX. Significance of the Project

This will lay the foundation for a graded system of technical education in Sri Lanka and build up a technical ladder connecting the school-based technical courses to vocational/ technical training courses available for school leavers, with provision for vertical as well as horizontal movements.

X. Approximate Budgetary Requirement: US$3,000.00

THAILAND

I. Title of Project

An In-Service Training Programme for Primary School Science Teachers of the Hilltribes in Thailand

II. Project Description

There are about 300,000 to 500,000 hilltribes in Thailand. Most establish their homes on hillsides 3,000 feet above the sea level. Most of these locations are remote and do not have easy accessibility from the nearest town centre. The children of the hilltribes are required to attend government-run schools until Grade 6. This is in line with the long-term goal which calls for participation from all citizens. Towards this end, science, mathematics and technology education has a role to play in helping the hilltribes children to function as members of their society in the context of their cultural settings.

III. Project Activities

A hilltribes village such as Baan Musir, 25 km west of Tak City will be chosen as a venue for main activities. Twenty-five trainees will be drawn from the hilltribe primary schools in the

Northern part of Thailand. A team of trainees consisting of 4 IPST staff members, 2 each from Pitsanulok and Kampaengpet Teacher Colleges will be formed.

A survey will be conducted on the contemporary life of the hilltribes village, focusing on technologies that are already existing in the village, e.g.

- method of producing, processing and preserving food;
- method of obtaining drinking water and water for other purposes;
- common disease and sanitation;
- shelters for protection against rain and cold;
- energy sources.

Trainers and trainees are to meet in a workshop to discuss and analyse the result for the survey. Objectives will be drawn, and activities for lessons to be taught to the hilltribe children will be designed and developed.

Trainers will demonstrate how teaching may be conducted. At the end of each lesson, trainers and trainees will meet to evaluate the teaching and give suggestions to improve the lesson.

IV. Time Frame

The project will be completed in six months and may start in early February 1993.

V. Expected Outcome

A comprehensive report of project activities beginning with project planning, implementation and evaluation will be produced. A set of slides for coloured photographs will be included in the report.

VI. Project Impact

The procedures adopted by the project will be disseminated among the teachers of the hilltribe schools, and will form the basis for designing future training programmes funded by the Government.

VII. Approximate Budgetary Requirement

Request is hereby submitted to UNESCO for funding in the amount of US$3,000. A counterpart fund of about US$4,000 will be sought from private donor.

VIET NAM

1. Title of the Project

Planning for In-service Teacher Training In Vietnam

II. Objectives of the Project

1. Upgrade teachers at the basic level in the whole country on new knowledge and skills which encourage thinking and problem solving among trainees.
2. Set up agencies related to the programmes, which share responsibilities for the programmes in order to improve the quality of the in-service teacher training.
3. Develop necessary curricula and necessary materials for the programme.

III. Project Description

1. Activities

(a) Teacher training could be carried out through short-term programmes such as workshops, seminars, demonstration classes and through consulting services.

(b) For long-term programmes teachers could be given scholarships to obtain advanced degrees or certification in the special needs identified. These can be provided by colleges and universities.

Programmes should also have a balance of theory and practice to cover new teaching strategies, to update knowledge in the subject areas.

(a) Continuing education programmes for teachers could be provided by schools through co-operative efforts with universities, schools administrators and teachers. Strategies for training may include use of radio and TV, distance learning, correspondence learning, etc.

(b) Evaluation of programmes will be carried out before and after the courses.

2. *Co-operating Agencies*

- Universities;
- National Institute for Education and Training, Hanoi, Vietnam;
- Teacher Training Colleges;
- Teacher Training Centres at Provincial and District Levels;
- Publishing House, Hanoi, Vietnam;
- Mass media, including radio and TV.

IV. Time Frame

The 1st cycle: 1992-1996.

V. Expected Output:

1. 60 per cent of teachers at the basic level in the whole country should be trained in cycle (1992-1996).
2. Necessary curriculum materials (textbooks, handbooks, booklets, etc.)

VI. Approximate Budgetary Requirement including Government Counterpart: US$ 8,000.00

For Orientation Workshops

Developing Curricula and some materials

SEAMEO, RECSAM

I. Title of the Project

Training Workshop for Mathematics, Science and Technology Education Trainers from National Science Education Centres

II. Proponents

SEAMEO, RECSAM, Penang, Malaysia

III. Objectives of Project

1. To foster exchange of ideas and to share experiences among key trainers of mathematics, science and

technology on latest issues, approaches and thoughts about training in the areas of mathematics, science and technology in the SEAMEO member countries.

2. To develop appropriate INSET strategies for mathematics, science and technology trainers in the SEAMEO member countries.

3. To learn new ideas, knowledge and methodologies of INSET.

IV. Project Description

1. One key trainer for each subject area from each of the SEAMEO member countries and RECSAM will be invited to attend this six-day training workshop. The selected trainers will come from the country's National Science, Mathematics and Technology Education Centres. The total number of participants for each of these training workshops will be ten.

2. RECSAM will coordinate the training workshops and will host one of them. The other two will be hosted by centres in the member countries. This is to broaden exposure and enrich the experiences to each country participants.

3. The participants are expected to share with their colleagues the knowledge gained from these training workshops and also to train other trainers in the country.

V. Expected Outcome

The expected outcome of this project are:

1. A wider experience and knowledge in the area of training conducted by other countries in this area/region.

2. Increase the skill and confidence of the trainers to conduct the course in their respective countries.

VI. Significance of the Project

This project will generate better approaches, techniques, and methodologies in INSET among SEAMEO member countries. It will also help bring greater understanding among national level trainers about training being conducted in SEAMEO member countries. These can increase the trainers' confidence to conduct the training in their respective countries.

This project also can help to train key/master trainers in the country.

VII. Approximate Budgetary Requirements for the three workshops: US$30,000.00

ANNEX I

Resource Persons' Papers

1. Innovative Strategies (And Possible/Initiatives And Programmes) For Improving the Quality of In-service Teacher Training *(by A.K. Sharma, NCERT, India)*

Introduction

In view of rapid changes in science, technology and mathematics education, teachers of these subjects need periodic renewal and continued education throughout their professional career. This need becomes all the more pronounced for teachers due to their role in shaping the destiny of the younger generation. Pre-service teacher training is only an initiation into the teaching profession; the real guidance and professional support is needed when the teacher actually interacts with the reality of the classroom. Research has supported positive contribution of in-service training and its vital role in improving the quality of education. Most of the teachers in service, received their pre-service education some time ago. The knowledge and skills to be learnt today require their constant professional development.

In the context of the present paper, in-service training generally implies those activities engaged in by primary and secondary school teachers, following their initial training, and intended primarily or exclusively to improve their professional knowledge, skills and attitudes in order that they can educate their pupils more effectively. In-service training may also be conceived as meeting the needs of children through meeting corresponding needs of teachers.

Objectives

The objectives of in-service training may be broadly summed up as follows:

1. To help continuous professional improvement of teachers in terms of knowledge, attitude, values and work ethos.
2. To improve effectiveness of user agencies and institutions such as schools, Departments of Education, Teacher Training Institutions, supervisory staff, etc.
3. To help teachers upgrade their qualifications leading to the acquisition of certificates, diplomas and degrees in general, academic and professional areas.
4. To fill gaps between preparation through pre-service education and the requirements of classroom practices. (The new teacher needs a great deal of support in the first year of his/her work in school.)

Rationale

In most countries curriculum revision is an on-going exercise and incorporation of new areas of learning consequent upon revalidating their educational policies and programmes require an appropriate orientation of teachers. The inputs may include new content in science and mathematics and also new pedagogical strategies. In some countries there is a shift from subjectwise orientation to the teaching of Science as Physics, Chemistry, Biology, etc. to teaching Integrated Science. In respect of biology, there is a shift towards Life Science. Obviously the teachers in-service will have to be reoriented to enable them to handle the new concerns and approaches.

There is also an expression of new thrust to teaching of Science which may not be reflected in the practices actually followed. For example, Science Education is to develop in the child well defined abilities and values such as: spirit of inquiry, creativity, objectivity, courage to question, aesthetic sensibility, problem solving skills, decision making skills discovering the relationship of Science with Health, Agriculture, Industry and other aspects of daily life. There may yet be another over riding concern to develop *"Science for All"*.

Science might be currently taught in the school system in a traditional information transmission modality. It is required to be taught in a more interactive mode by generating activity-based and learner-centred programmes.

There is also an area of development of experimental skills which in most educational systems has received a back seat. The in-service training programmes must provide the correct strategy so that the teachers who are already in the system are in no way handicapped in discharging their commitments effectively.

Likewise Mathematics should be visualized as the vehicle to train a child to think, reason, analyze and to articulate logically. Apart from being a specific subject, it should be treated as a concomitant to any subject involving analysis and reasoning. With the recent introduction of computers in schools, educational computing and the emergence of learning through the understanding of cause-effect relationships and the interplay of variables, the teaching of mathematics will be suitably redesigned to bring it in line with modern technological devices, these thrusts to the teaching of mathematics will make it imperative to redesign in-service teacher training programmes.

The basic premise underlying in-service training arises out of several factors such as teachers' personal motivation for professional upliftment and to be knowledgeable about the current trends in his/her subject. However, what will motivate a teacher to update himself/herself professionally? Teaching, by its very enterprise is generally a repetitive activity and if the knick-knacks of the 'trade' are acquired once, most teachers may not feel the need of in-service teacher training unless the educational system has imposed it on them. The need for acquiring new knowledge may also express itself if the areas of inadequacies of the teacher are identified by him or her through his/her classroom interaction. Unless an in-service training is linked with real needs of the teaching community, it is likely to miss the kind of impact it is expected to make.

How is need identification to be done? At the back of this is creation of a climate of autonomy both for the teacher and the learner. The biggest source of motivation for professional development of teachers are their young pupils whose innocent yet penetrating question on their environment can pose a lot of challenge to the teacher. There has to be, therefore, a conscious effort on the part of the teacher to constantly draw upon this source and to make conscious efforts not to allow his/her students to become passive listeners. Perhaps in-service teachers training and development of this professional trend in the teachers is very relevant.

There are thus three broad guiding principles which determine the organization of in-service teacher training:

1. Introduction of curricula based on new policy thrusts and training of teachers on the new demands.
2. The felt needs of the teachers.
3. Dissemination of innovations that have been found effective in the field situation.

Development of in-service training is also linked with creation of appropriate infrastructures and provision of learning materials and financial resources. How are these concerns related in the educational programmes of the countries? Such parameters are generally ignored and the theoretical dimensions of in-service teacher training generally receive greater attention thus creating shortfalls in the realization of the stated objectives.

Innovative Strategies, Initiatives and Programmes

Several strategies, initiatives and programmes are being attempted in India and they have been outlined in a separate paper. Those along with some suggested in this section are relevant for discussion.

1. Distance Education for In-service Training

The role of Distance Education for in-service teacher training needs serious consideration for its effective exploitation. This is more so when the number of teachers required to be covered in certain countries is large and the time available for training all of them limited. The open learning systems are now becoming quite important with reference to training of teachers in Science, Technology and Mathematics. This, however, requires many additional inputs to be simultaneously designed and developed. For example:

(a) Development of self learning modules on conceptual aspects, content enrichment and pedagogy in the concerned subjects.

(b) Development of audio visual learning support.

(c) Provision of face to face contact sessions preferably in institutions which can provide technical support for learning of experimental skills and other related laboratory work.

(d) Design and development of appropriate kits to obviate the necessity of making available laboratory space and simultaneously provide facility of doing substantial parts of experimental work in Science and Technology even at the homes of the teachers.

(e) Catering to the needs of teachers working in far-flung areas, difficult terrains and disadvantaged locations.

Distance Education programmes can be offered in terms of earning of credits. This can be a great incentive to the teacher if he/she completes courses at his/her own pace and accumulates credits towards the requirements of a certificate, diploma or degree. Such a strategy can pay a lot of dividends in improving the professional level of teachers. The national systems of school education could think of providing the necessary subsidies and support to the teacher in this regard.

2. Audio/Video Cassettes

With the advent of electronic technology, the print matter is now receiving a lot of support from audio visual inputs. This needs to be exploited for the in-service training of teachers in Science and Mathematics. Lectures/demonstrations of eminent teachers could be prepared and made available for libraries, and individual purchase for use at the convenience of the teacher. The whole strategy will require a conscious effort for development of such materials and making them accessible to institutions and teachers at reasonable cost. This will offer an opportunity of getting to interact with the best of learning materials for professional upliftment.

3. Interactive Video

Most countries are now experimenting on the use of this media especially for training professionals. Teacher training needs to focus its attention of using this modality as well.

4. Interactive Learning with Computers

Face to face contact programmes have their own limitations, though they are important in the realization of certain objectives in affective and psychometry domains. Use of computer as an interactive mode of learning offers a promise of great value. Development of appropriate hardware and software is perhaps required to benefit from this modality of great potential.

5. Teachers' Resource Centres

Teachers' resource centres could be set up within reasonable negotiating distances of institutions and basic equipment made available in them, both in terms of learning materials and experimental work. A core faculty could be provided in such centres. This faculty could be such that they have the necessary capability of acting as resource support for those who come to be centre for professional guidance. The main focus of the centres should be to offer services to Science and Mathematics teachers to go there according to their convenience and to discuss their clarificatory points and to come back enriched. Such centres could work on weekends, holidays and vacation period so that they can be optimally utilized by the teachers for their in-service need.

6. Attachment Programmes

In every country there are centres of advanced learning in Science and Mathematics located at the district or the national level where professionals are engaged in creation of new knowledge in their respective disciplines. A strategy of attachment of teachers for varying periods of time to work in these centres, to interact with the Scientists and Mathematicians and to work on some identified project related to their work and produce some innovative report worthy of sharing with other professionals could be worth a trial. Such attachment or apprenticeship can lay the foundation of a new culture of in-service orientation.

7. School Complexes

It should be possible to identify a particular school amongst the different schools in an area to be developed as a lead school. Whereas resources may not permit enhancing the facilities of each school in terms of reading materials, learning materials like films, film strips, models, etc., if should be possible to equip one of the schools chosen as a lead school and make that as the centre for periodic in-service training of teachers working within the complex. This idea can be useful in cutting down costs. The resource available in a lead school can also be shared by all other schools in the region and thus a large number of involvement of in-service teachers can be expected.

8. Learning Materials

It is a stark reality that most teachers do not go beyond reading the same books which have been prescribed for their students. This itself narrows their vision in that subject and also comes in the way of their handling the innate curiosity of their students. There has to be a provision of making available to teachers some professional materials even at subsidized rates. It is a common experience that good reading materials in the hands of the teacher is in itself a great in-service education for him/her. In every country there are subject based journals, magazines which could be identified. In India, for example, the country has seen bloom of excellent journals in science brought out within the country. They can possibly be exploited as a means of in-service training.

9. Teachers' Associations

The role played by subject teacher associations could, as a matter of fact, be a very powerful influence on curriculum planners but in practice one finds that such associations have been reduced in many countries to remain away from academic programmes. Teachers' associations could themselves evolve programmes for the in-service education of their members by periodically inviting experts to speak to their members and also by organizing discussion on areas of topical interests in the emerging scenario of each country.

"Indicators" of Enhanced Quality in In-service Teacher Training

Any in-service teacher training to be relevant, effective, appropriate to the needs of teachers has to conform to some expected norms. The quality parameters will be related to the objectives that have been identified for a specific in-service programme. Some such broad indicators could be the following:

- Whether the training relates to the identified needs of teachers;
- Whether it is related to the requirements of new science and mathematics curriculum;
- Whether it incorporates new teaching-learning strategies for curriculum transaction;
- Whether the new technologies used in the training are practiced by the teachers in their classroom;
- Whether it has enhanced the confidence level of the teacher; and
- Whether it has produced better learning in the children.

In-service training programmes fail to achieve their purpose unless these are characterized by quality and relevance. Very often it is observed that the in-service training clientele has an unpredictable, variance in regard to age, educational qualifications, entry level knowledge, professional experience, level of motivation. The situation is further complicated by the heterogeneity of provisions in the training programmes as inputs both human and material and capabilities of resource faculties assigned to interact with practising teachers. The educational development, cultural and ethnographic characteristics, the socio-economic activities in different places relevant to explaining and elucidation from local environment. In view of it, questions arise as to what should be the indicator of a quality in-service education programme. Here are some **"indicators"**:

1. *Effectiveness of the inputs* (materials, print and non-print) for teachers at the training programme level.

2. *Benefits derived by the participating teachers in terms of:*
   - degree of awareness created;
   - perception of the expected roles;
   - degree of motivation generated;
   - degree of positive attitudes towards continuing education of teachers; and
   - competence acquired for enhancing pupils' achievement in curricular and co-curricular areas.
3. *Change in the perception of teachers with regard to:*
   - learner-centred approach;
   - continuous and comprehensive evaluation; and
   - use of Educational Technology in classroom situations.
4. *Perception of effectiveness* of the programme in the eyes of educational administrators.
5. *Appropriateness of the:*
   - selection of training sites and equipments for training; and
   - availability of basic facilities in the training programmes.
6. *Orientation of the resource faculty* to the objectives, content, methodology and evaluation aspects of the programme.
7. *Adequacy of the financial resource* provided to the organization of the programme.

The above issues and questions have their relevance to the planning of the in-service education programme. But the ultimate agenda of any quality programme has naturally to be reflected in the betterment of the learning capability of the children. Because they are the ultimate beneficiaries of the whole in-service training of the teachers and the impact of any in-service programme is to be assessed through the children. This is, of course, a long term goal of any intervention in education. There will be intermediate and mid-term goals which would be equally important, e.g. if a new technique was introduced in the in-service training, if this technique is reflected in the classroom, it will be a satisfactory situation irrespective of what effective it has produced on the learning attainment of children.

Evaluating Indicators of Achievement of Quality

There can be several measures to evaluate the effectiveness of in-service education programmes. These are:

Indicator	Suggested Evaluation
1. Awareness level objectives	Group discussions, open book assignments
2. Skill based objectives	Pre-test Post-test Demonstrative teaching
3. Affective level objectives	Follow up in the behaviours with pupils classroom situations
4. Content upgradation	General test at the end of the course
5. Motivational and attitudinal aspects	Opinionaires, questionnaires and scales
6. Methodological aspects and use of teaching learning aids	Follow up in classroom situations and demonstrative teaching exercises

In the NCERT, we adopted the modular approach to material development wherein the key information was put in boxes with a three step exercise as:

- Collect
- Collate
- Discuss

This helped in involving individual teachers in participative learning.

Parameters of Improving Quality

In-service training has come to be accepted as an important instrument to bring about qualitative improvement in teachers and school education. Some infrastructure has taken shape in most of the states to look after this activity. However, there are a few shortcomings such as the following:

- Inadequate understanding of the importance of in-service teacher training;
- Lack of attention to methodology of in-service training;
- Unsystematic selection of participants and resource persons;
- Ineffective follow-up;
- Absence of a national system of in-service training;
- Poor co-ordination and monitoring of in-service training programmes. Adhocism both in planning and implementation;
- Limited opportunities for training of in-service training personnel;
- Absence of research base for making in-service training education more effective;
- Inadequate infrastructures for in-service training at appropriate levels.

Research in In-service Training

There is a need to carefully study researches at Ph.D. and project level conducted by different institutions in the area of in-service teacher training. The areas of research could broadly conform to the following categories:

- Planning;
- Incentives and motivation;
- Methods and techniques of in-service education;
- Impact;
- Other collateral research not directly related to in-service training but the findings of which influence the organization in the programmes of in-service teacher training.

Incentives

Proper environment for participation by teachers in in-service training activities is significant for the success of the system. Incentives will include both extrinsic and intrinsic motivation. Though extrinsic motivation as in terms of external awards is criticized by some for having only short-time effect leading to unhealthy competition and petty rivalries among participants' aspirations, its immediate utility in providing the momentum and stimulus for action cannot be ignored. Intrinsic motivation arising out of a feeling of satisfaction and the sense of commitment is most desirable. The significance of planning and organization of in-service cannot be underrated. It includes appropriate planning strategies, ensuring proper arrangements, employment of right resource persons, provision of needed materials, availability of physical facilities, support of technological aids and follow-up and training of the in-service educators.

Suggested Programmes

1. Successful completion of formal structured credit courses of at least about a semester every five years should be obligatory for all teachers. Besides the usual short term adhoc programmes, provision should be made for such formal or structured programmes which may be offered in a distance education mode supported by contact programmes for interaction and practical work.

2. The non-credit programmes aim at refreshing or updating of the teacher through a variety of techniques such as refresher and orientation courses, seminars, symposia and workshops and even short-term activities like an extension lecture, exhibition, or demonstration, etc. These inputs are made by external agencies and are not related to be specific needs of schools.

3. School-based in-service training is specifically significant in order to universalize the provision of in-service training. It is a strategy of teacher development from the grassroots. Individual work undertaken by school or individual teacher is a source of this training.

4. Teacher based in-service training has also significance of its own not only in terms of providing necessary

motivation but also in improving efficiency of in-service training programmes at all levels. Self education by teachers may include independent reading, article writing, self-evaluation and action research.

Implementing Agencies

Individual countries may have to identify Central State and District level agencies to determine the broad areas of in-service teacher education. Agencies at different level, need to undertake exercises at their respective levels to determine in-service needs.

Some of the implementing agencies for in-service training could be the following:

- Universities;
- Teacher Education Institutions;
- Research Institutions;
- Supervisory Staff;
- State Education Departments;
- Corporation or Municipal Boards;
- Teachers' Association;
- Community Groups;
- Commercial agencies like publishers;
- Mass media including radio and television;
- School complexes

2. Innovative Strategies (and Possible Initiatives and Programmes) on Improving the Quality of In-service Teacher Training *(by Malcolm Carr, SMER Centre, University of Waikato, New Zealand)*

Acknowledgements

This paper has been prepared by Dr. Malcom Carr for presentation to the Workshop. The assistance of the University for travel, and the New Zealand National Commission for UNESCO for accommodation is gratefully acknowledged.

2.1 School and Teacher Development in New Zealand

Overview

A recent development in the administration of New Zealand education has been to give much of the responsibility for teacher development to schools through their Boards of Trustees.

An emphasis on whole school development through action research processes has been a major thrust in work and writing on teacher development in New Zealand over the past few years. Research noted the need for in-service provisions to become more systematic and regularized, aimed at the needs of teachers, and to provide time for reflection.

The acknowledgement of the importance of schools culture has also influenced the type of professional development programmes which identify the needs of the school as a whole, then focus on the needs of the individual who make up the whole.

Model Encouraged by the Ministry of Education

In addition to funding through Boards of Trustees, the Ministry sets aside a budget annually to fund a range of teacher professional development programmes to support national curriculum objectives. These funds are used to provide teacher professional development programmes, based on current research philosophies, which might become models for others to follow.

None of the contracts led by the Ministry is for the traditional "one-off" course, rather they consists of a series of sessions, giving participants opportunity to try out ideas in the classroom before meeting again with colleagues and a courses director. Often during the period between sessions courses participants may be visited by a facilitator who provides valuable onsite support and assistance.

Essential Elements

Although the processes and strategies used by contractors vary greatly, there are a number of features which the teacher development programmes share, which are important if programmes are to have long term effects on what teachers do in their classrooms.

In order to be effective in changing what teachers do, teacher development programmes must:

- be appropriate to the needs of the teachers;
- be "owned" by the teachers involved;
- involve a mixture of practice and theory;
- take place over an extended period of time;
- involving support and guidance as well as professional "input" session;
- fit within the context of the school culture; and
- have the support of the principal.

Some Innovative Strategies

Within the context of the above essential elements, a wide range of delivery mechanisms exist.

For example:

- many programmes have groups of teachers meeting together, usually with a facilitator, to share ideas and collectively solve problems;
- the teacher development contract to support there education syllabus making use of a comprehensive video package which was developed to train teachers, particularly in the new aspects of the syllabus;
- one of the Curriculum Leadership (Principals' Training) contractors is using an electronic bulletin board/mail service to provide on-going support for a small group of rural principals who are too far from other schools to make regular meetings feasible. All principals in the programme have access to the electronic bulletin board/ mail service and use it to communicate reports of their progress, reviews of literature they have read, and other ideas;
- in many programmes, teachers are given specific task to try out within their own classrooms, and are expected to report back on their experiences at a meeting with other teachers;

- facilitators in a science contract have used a video camera to record a colleague teaching, and used the recording to provide feedback to the teacher concerned, as well as to demonstrate good teaching ideas to a group of teachers involved in the programme;
- facilitators in a widely spread geographic region have used teleconferencing for their own training and reporting of progress to an external evaluator;
- in many instances provision is made for teachers to taks time out to read appropriate papers and reflect on their own practice, so that they can gain for having some time and space to think about their own programmes.

Research has provided evidence of the combination of variable which is needed to effect teacher change. No one delivery mechanism is the answer. Rather, it is the combination of a range of different elements and the use of styles best suited to the particular group of teachers, which gives any programme the flexibility needed to meet the needs of the teachers involved.

Teachers' Refresher Course Committee

New Zealand Ministry of Education also funds the above organization which organizes suitably qualified people to direct courses. The courses are usually run in vacation time, a typical list of offerings are those for August/September 1993:

Physics/chemistry/biology (senior science).

Typing/word processing/keyboarding/text processing.

Social studies/history and geography (two courses to be hold at the same venue).

Te Reo Maori.

School/industry links.

Junior art.

Assessment—methods (primary/secondary).

and January 1994

English-J 1 to Form 7.

Teaching approaches at enhance learning (co-operative learning).

Home economics/clothi[illegible] nd textiles.

Establishing technology in primary education.

School management.

Art and natural world (early childhood).

The Teachers' Refresher Course committee will provide participants air travel between cities and a course venue that is further that 200 kms or reimburse an equivalent bus fare for all other travel.

Other Provisions for Teacher Development

A number or organisations provide opportunities for professional development through courses and programmes. Colleges of Education and Universities are particularly active in this area. The University of Waikato, for example, provides Diploma courses in science and mathematics education, and offer Advanced Studies for Teaching Unit courses which are relevant to the theme of this Workshop.

2.2 Teacher Professional Development to Support Mathematics and Science in the National Curriculum

Background

Mathematics and science have been a focus of recent curriculum development activities. The draft curriculum statements, "Mathematics in the National Curriculum" and "Science in the National Curriculum" have both been published and circulated to all schools for comment. Feedback from schools and the commercial sector on the mathematics statement has resulted in revised curriculum statement. Responses to the draft science statement have been affected by a teacher moratorium.

The provision of a curriculum statement is seen to be only the first step in the implementation of a new curriculum. Teachers need time, support and information to assist them to identify and make changes to their teaching practice.

The Ministry of Education has investigated new and existing resources to provide the maximum number of teachers with help in implementing the mathematics and science curriculum statements. A range of teacher professional development opportunities has been identified.

Major Teacher Development Programmes

During each of the next three years, a number of contract teacher development programmes will run throughout the country. These programmes will support mathematics and science in 1993, and technology as new curriculum statements are completed.

The programmes will run for a minimum of six weeks. They will continue meetings, workshop and in-school support. They will provide for professional input and reflection, and time for teachers to try out some strategies or ideas within their classrooms. Because the importance of peer support in effective teacher professional development is recognized, the programmes have been structured to ensure that no fewer that two teachers from each school (other than sole charge schools) will normally be involved at any one time. A greater number of teachers from larger schools will be able to be involve together. This will enable mutual support and the sharing of ideas and experiences.

Other Ministry-Funded Teacher Development Programmes

Teachers in some areas will be able to participate in longer term programmes as part of the teacher development opportunities provided through contracts. Along with the professional leaders, in many cases some provision for teacher realise is also made. However, all programmes also rely on a commitment of time, and/or resources from the teachers and schools involved.

Teacher Support Services

All schools have the support of advisers through their local teachers support services. The Ministry has reached an agreement with the Colleges of Education to co-ordinate the teacher professional development opportunities available for the implementation of the new curricula. During 1993 some advisers may be involved in working closely with schools which are not involved in the programmes described above. They may be also have a role in providing on-going support for teachers who have previously participated in the major programme.

Advisers will have an overview of all programmes within

area and as they have worked with Ministry of Education staff during the development of the statement, are likely to be involved in the training of the facilitators of the major programme.

Teacher Refresher Course Committee Programmes

Courses in science and mathematics will be provided as indicated above.

School-Based Initiatives

Schools may find ways of meeting teacher development needs by using a combination of the above opportunities, and/ or other sources of assistance. For example a school might involve two teachers in the major programme, and request the services of an adviser to work with those teacher in a series of school might also support a staff member who enrols in an assessment courses at a tertiary institution, or provide an opportunities for staff members to visit a neighbouring school to observe a good mathematics programme in practice.

2.3 The Research Base for Teacher Development

The Science and Mathematics Education Research Centre of which I am the Director has a major programme of research into Teacher Development directed by Dr. Beverly Bell, and with Mr. John Pearson as project officer. In addition Mr. Andy Begg is researching mathematics teacher in-service for his D. Phil. The paper now reflects on the lessons learnt in this research and the application of these lessons to the Workshop. Much more detailed accounts are to be found in various publications from the Centre.

Major current concerns in science and mathematics education in the perspective of this Workshop

First it is important to say where the paper stands with respect to current issues in science and mathematics education. The significance points which informed our research were:

- the science, mathematics and technology education should be accessible to all students.

- that learning which is centred on existing knowledge and skills will engaged all students and provide a rich basis for learning (this implies finding local contexts for learning).
- that learning involves the construction of new knowledge from existing knowledge rather than a passive acceptance of transmitted data.
- that in-service training needs to start from the experiences and concerns of teachers, using their best practice as a guide.
- that interactive approaches, which build from the existing knowledge and skills of teacher in a co-operative manner, provide the best basis for setting up courses.
- That it is vital to describe the goals of in-service work carefully, so as to match the programme to these goals. The acquisition of some new knowledge may be provided in a short course because the goal is straightforward. When the goal is a different way of interacting with students in the classroom a much longer time frame will be necessary.
- the most of the changes required to improve the quality of science, mathematics and technology education at the basic level provide major challenges to existing practice. To assist major change there must be a recognition of the difficulty of change, and of the need for continuing support throughout a change process which may be long and demanding.

The workshop therefore, needs to look at procedures described in the Draft Report on a Planning Meeting held in London for the "Project on Improving the Quality of Science and Mathematics at the Basic Level: the Role of Higher Education". The strategy is there described as:

1. start from where the teachers actually are;
2. be interactive and participatory;
3. be in context.

That is an acknowledgement that INSET designed to encourage teachers to teach in a more open and interactive way must itself be conducted in that way: the INSET process should model the approach sought in the classroom. This meeting repeatedly affirmed that:

- the process of change requiring a shift in personal philosophy and attitude is extremely challenging; and
- change needs to be open and sustained over long periods. Change of this kind cannot take place without continuing support.

The basis for the above strategy acknowledges that most teachers are challenged to change their implicit theories of students, schools, how students learn, the nature of knowing and knowledge, and the implications of these for teaching.

Findings from the first year of LISP (Teacher Development) on the content of courses which promoted changing beliefs and attitudes on teaching and learning indicated that course components which the teachers found important were:

1. *Feeling* and experiencing the new teaching approach as a student when the course facilitator role-modelled the approach.
2. *Knowing* about the nature of the new teaching approach and the findings of previous research project about learning in science.
3. *Doing:* using and evaluating the approach with students.
4. *Developing* a unit of work based on the new teaching approach.
5. *Reflecting* on aspects of using the approach with respect to teaching and learning, assessment, the role of the teacher, curriculum development, the nature of science, gender issues, establishing a supportive atmosphere in the classroom.

Aspects of the course which teachers found helpful for the above were:

- role-modelling;
- information on different parts of the approach;
- readings on aspects of science education;
- sample resource units from previous research project;
- sharing sessions of ideas, feelings and experiences;
- keeping journal or diaries;
- the facilitator;
- support of course colleagues and in their schools;
- flexibility in the course design;
- sharing ideas with other sectors of the school structure (primary with secondary); and
- time between sessions for trial and reflection.

2.4 Evaluation of Inset

The Workshop is also required to identify "indicators" of enhanced quality and to suggest a strategy to identify the extent of achievement of these indicators. This is an area which, to my mind, requires extreme caution. The Workshop will need to carefully consider the match or mismatch between the goals of in-service work in assessment of success. The amount of new knowledge of their discipline acquired by teachers at in-service courses is probably easy to measure, but may not be a good indicator of better quality teaching and learning. Developing indicators of the success of teaching which engages more with context that interest the learners, and which helps learners to construct knowledge, is much more difficult. The New Zealand research has found it very difficult to establish indicators of better interactive teaching.

3. Innovative Strategies and Possible Initiatives and Programmes *(by M.D. Ibe, College of Education, University of the Philippines)*

In-service training includes all activities engaged in or provided to school teachers, principals, and school supervisors after initial formal professional education certification to improve their professional knowledge, skills and attitudes to better deliver instruction. In-service training usually aims to stimulate staff development, improve school practices and implement educational policy.

In-service education for science, technology and mathematics teachers is generally aimed at: (a) upgrading teacher skills and competencies, (b) updating their knowledge in these subjects, (c) enabling them to implement new curricula, and (d) providing professional growth by updating their knowledge of psychological, sociological and pedagogical theories.

In-service Training Modes

In-service training for science and mathematics comes in different modalities. These include the following:

1. Mass training at multi-levels: e.g., national, provincial, district, and school-level training programme. At the national level, key personnel are trained, who in turn give training at the regional level: the trainees at this level give training at the next level.
2. Summer Institutes: These are 4-6 week programmes focused on particular subject matter and skills.
3. Subject or level-based training: Teachers of a school conduct in-service training sessions for science only or math only or grade grouping, e.g., for Primary 1-4 teachers only, or for mathematics teachers of Primary 5 to 6 only.
4. Single-school based: All teachers in a school attend training sessions carried out during regularly designated times (e.g., during teachers' meetings).
5. Cluster-school in-service training: Teachers of the same grades or same subjects from schools belonging to a cluster meet regularly for in-service training sessions. Inter-school visits could complement, or actually be a part of the cluster-school in-service training mode. Visits to different schools enable the teachers to see the innovations carried out in other schools.
6. Mobile individual/team trainer: This too could be tied

up with the cluster school concept, where a human resource (e.g., a technician or teacher trainer) goes to each of the schools in the cluster. However, such a human resource could be working also with others hence could be servicing a wider area.

7. Mini-courses (either for formal academic credit or continuing education credits) conducted by a college accessible to teachers in a region or province, or by a professional organization (e.g., the Math society, Biology Teachers Association, etc.).
8. Distance-education or open-university education through print modules, audio and video tapes. There are courses for which teachers can get academic credits for their participation in Distance Education courses.
9. Science, Technology and Mathematics workshops and symposia conducted by science related agencies, professional organizations, and the Ministry of Education.
10. Post-graduate and advanced courses in university. These, however, are availed of only by a few teachers, particularly those interested in earning additional qualifications.
11. A school adopted by a college or attached to a university, the latter making regular contacts with the school to provide in-service training.
12. Action research in schools. Such research provides in-service training for teachers.

Most of these in-service training modalities are already being done in different countries in the region. What perhaps needs to be emphasized is the efficiency with which they are being carried out, and imbuing teachers with a deeper commitment to improve and upgrade themselves.

Effective In-service Training

Evaluation studies (e.g., Yonge, 1982; Bolam, 1987) of teacher in-service programmes have identified the following as characteristics of effective in-service training:

1. Trainees participated in identifying goals and activities.
2. Trainees were involved in the planning of the programme.
3. Trainee participants shared ideas and materials during the training.
4. Programmes where ideas were generated by the trainees and materials constructed by them were more successful than those where these tasks were centrally directed.
5. Training which provided opportunities for self-instruction.
6. Short and inter-related courses which were part of a long-term staff development programmes rather than one short course.
7. In-service training which were school-based, rather than regionally- or nationally-based.
8. Training which clearly focused on participants' current and future needs.
9. Training which included a follow-up, i.e., on-the-job assistance and supervision.

Bolam (1987) in his synthesis of British studies on in-service training found that careful briefing for participants weeks before the training and debriefing after the training, sustained support characterized some of the more effective training programmes in his review.

Some Initiatives and New Programmes

A number of characteristics identified in successful in-service training programmes point to a personalistic and affective dimension. Participation and involvement in planning and managing in-service training seems to be a common thread in many of the characteristics identified.

When large numbers of teachers need to be trained, within a set period (as in the case of national educational development programmes), there are few alternatives to mass training using the multi-level or echo training approaches.

Some individual and small group initiatives for non-formal teacher upgrading are the following:

1. A materials exchange and cleaning house. This is feasible when a school is designated as a learning resource centre where teachers and students can go, see, touch, and manipulate science/math materials and instructional devices.
2. Field trips and visits to science centres and display venues (e.g., Science Centrum, Science Teacher Training Centre, Science Museums, commercial science laboratories, etc.).
3. Radio and TV science-related programmes: TV contents in science and mathematics.
4. Popular science magazines and other print media which maintain columns for science and mathematics.
5. Linkages with extension workers in science and technology-related agencies, for them to give lectures and extension education demonstrations in schools similar to those they give in communities.
6. Science-oriented resource persons from the community as speakers in school forums.
7. Science club activities which are instruction related (e.g., science/math quiz, science fairs, science bazaars).
8. Science awareness community campaigns and forums jointly organized by the school and the community on issues like environmental pollution, forest denudation; phenomena like red tide, earthquakes, acid rain, global warming, etc.
9. Weekly science and science-fiction film presentations for students and teachers. Many foreign embassies have films which lend out resources to schools.
10. Involvement of science club officers/members as teacher-auxiliaries.

4. Quality Indicators for In-service Teacher Training *(by M.D. Ibe, College of Education, University of the Philippines)*

The title of this paper connotes evaluation or judgement of in-service teacher training. Before we go into the discussion of indicators, there is a need to set up a framework by which indicators can be logically treated in a programme.

On such framework is the systems approach which considers inputs, process and outputs. These are basic to the rest of the discussions that will follow:

Inputs: These are the resources which are antecedents necessary to get an educational programme or intervention going. They are there, or are put there deliberately. For example: the pupils and their traits, the teacher's characteristics and capabilities, the physical plant, etc.

Outputs: These are the direct and immediate effects of educational programmes. Examples are the knowledges acquired by the students, and skills and attitudes they learn, the beliefs and values they develop, etc.

Process: Refers to what is done to the inputs, or the interactions and operations among them, so that they will lead to the expected outputs.

I would like to define the term indicator as a sign or manifestation of something; a quality indicator is a trait or description of worthwhileness (e.g. how good, how well). An indicator is an evidence of the presence or absence of as trait we are seeking to establish.

In educational evaluation, we seek evidence of validity and reliability of techniques, methods, materials, etc. We evaluate educational interventions, for example, in regard to evidence on whether or not the objective is reached in terms of:

- Quantity How much?
- Quality How well?
- Time (by) When? Within what time frame?
- Target clients Of/For whom?

Indicators of the quality of a teacher in-service training programme could include signs as regards its **effectiveness, efficiency, acceptability, external validity, replicability**, etc.

Effectiveness: refers to how well or to what extent the desired objectives or outputs are achieved. Objectives are statements of the desired/target outputs.

For example, if one of the objectives of a training programme is to increase the subject matter knowledge of training programme participants, then the programme is effective if there is a significant increase in their knowledge of the subject matter covered after the training. The logical indicator therefore is a positive change or gain in knowledge attributable to the programme. Hence, indicators of effectiveness include all those signs and manifestations that the programme objectives are met.

Efficiency: pertains to effectiveness relative to cost. For example, between two programmes which are able to produce similar outcomes, the question with regard to efficiency is: For the same outcome which programme has minimum cost in time, effort and money? Efficiency is concerned with maximizing a desired mix of outputs (effectiveness) for a given level of inputs (cost), or minimizing inputs for a desired output.

A programme is effective if it attains its objectives. It is efficient if it achieves the same level of effectiveness as another programme but for a lesser cost.

Acceptability: pertains to the clients' and pertinent agencies' receptions of the programme, their degree of identification with it, their readiness or predisposition to receive it. For example, in-service training programmes which entail teachers' having to put in extra hours to avail of the training tend to be low on acceptability. In-service training programmes which are scheduled on weekdays take the teachers away from their classes, hence tend to be unacceptable from the point of view of administrators, students, parents and the community served by the school.

External Validity: refers to the generalizability of the finding of the effectiveness of a training programme to other situations and contexts. For example, the findings on the effectiveness of the cluster-school scheme for in-service staff development has low generalizability for schools which are miles apart geographically. The cluster school concept has not worked in some regions of the

Philippines because the teachers have to take long rides and spend much for transportation to avail of the training given to the teachers from the schools in the cluster. Here, low acceptability of the programme is also demonstrated.

Replicability: This pertains to the extent to which a training programme can be repeated or done again in exactly the same way. Some training programmes are successful in certain contexts because of other factors which are present. Examples of such factors are: the sense of oneness of a group, the facilitative skills of the leader, the "chemistry" between the facilitators and the trainees. These may not be present in a "copy" or repetition of the same training programme, hence we say that it has low replicability.

Indicators of Quality Inputs

Inputs to teacher in-service training programmes include:

1. Teacher/trainee characteristics (e.g. age, sex, educational background, etc.);
2. Trainer characteristics (e.g. age, personal competence, knowledge, etc.);
3. Trainer and trainee attitudes and values; and
4. Planning and management inputs (e.g. preparation, materials, equipment, venue, delegation of responsibility).

Age is an indicator used as a proxy for emotional maturity, receptivity to training, readiness, etc., when these cannot be measured directly. In the mass training of teachers in the Philippines, trainees beyond 60 years were excluded because it was contended that such teachers are close to retirement, hence will likely not be sufficiently motivated to make use of the training. The young trainees in the mass training of 4th year math/science teachers were found to have gained more from the training than those who were past 45 years (Ibe, 1992). Civil status did not significantly correlate with knowledge gains in the training.

Teacher and trainee characteristics are taken as indicators of quality inputs because the expected output is viewed dependent on these characteristics. They are basic to the effectiveness of the training programme in that the training is perceived needed most by the clients who possess those characteristics. If for example an in-science training programme designed to compensate for inadequate subject matter knowledge of science/math teachers attracts those who are already majors in science/maths, then the programme is less effective and lower on efficiency because it is not reaching the primary target clients—the non-majors. Such a programme will be no more than just a review programme for the trainees, hence is an inefficient use of funds.

Trainer characteristics are also quality indicators of input. In many cultures, the age of a trainer is an important determinant of the authority and respect that will be accorded to him/her by trainees and administrators. The subject specialization and professional background of the trainer are also determinants of the quality and level of in-service training.

One of the key indicators of the quality of the mass training of science and math teachers in the Secondary Education Development Programme in the Philippines (IBE, 1992) was the fact that all the trainers were trained at the national level at the Institute for Science and Mathematics Education Development (ISMED), University of the Philippines. At least 20 per cent of them trained also in Australia as PASMEP scholars. In the evaluation of trainees in all subjects, the math trainers, followed by the science trainers, were rated highest by the trainees. Trainer specialization is therefore a quality input indicator.

Trainee perceptions and attitudes toward in-service training could be taken as both an input and output indicator of quality. Positive perceptions and attitudes make for successful programmes. If measured before or at the beginning of a training programme, then they can be quality indicators of input. Measured at the end of the training, they could be indicators of output or effects of the programme. The difference between post training and pre-training scores is definitely an indicator of outcome of the training.

In the 1992 mass training of secondary school teachers in the Philippines, the specific trainer-characteristics on which each science/math trainer was rated by peers, supervisors and the trainees are the following skills/abilities:

1. Communicates personal enthusiasm;
2. Communities ideas clearly;
3. Delivers topic with confidence;
4. Organizes resources for training;
5. Adapts activities to the needs of the trainees;
6. Assesses trainees' progress; and
7. Employs appropriate strategies for integration of learning.

Three indicators relate directly to desired characteristics of trainers. They are: (a) subject mastery, (b) verbal ability, and (c) attitudes and values.

Another instrument by which the trainers were rated by the trainees is one which assessed them in regard to: (1) Mastery of the subject matter, (2) Motivational skills, (3) Evaluation skills, and (4) Personal attributes.

The same two evaluation instruments were used on trainers of other school subjects. In both instruments, the science and mathematics trainers came out scoring higher than trainers of teachers of other school subjects.

Trainer availability can be used as an input indicator. It could refer to the number of trainers available relative to other units of input. For example: trainee-trainer ratio, trainer per region and trainee hours per day (per week or per month). The trainer per group measure helps identify those situations when over- or under-utilization of trainers can occur because of an inability to match trainer with trainee groups. The data on trainer-trainee ratios from different regions could lead to indicators of efficiency because they give indications of relative cost of training across regions.

Another measure of trainer availability is expressed in the number of hours of training or instructional time spent per day or per week. This availability measure can be bed on official "**expectations**" or observed behaviour.

The other input indicators comprise characteristics of facilities, equipment, training materials and administrative capacity. The facility characteristics pertain to quantity, availability and utilization. The same indices can be applied to equipment and instructional materials.

The most common measure to indicate administrative competence is the educational attainment of the administrator. Sometimes this measure is refined to reflect specific exposure of the administrator to training, and management and planning skills.

Process Indicators

The analysis of an in-service training process is the study of the interaction that takes place among the inputs under different forms of classroom technologies or instructional systems. Focus is made on: (a) trainee behaviour, (b) trainer behaviour, and (c) administrative behaviour.

Process indicators are signs of the quality of interactions, tasks and activities which take place during the in-service training programme, and which are designed to result in the desired outputs. They include:

1. Interactions between the trainees and the trainer;
2. The methods and techniques used in the training; their variety, quality and appropriateness;
3. The communication and interaction between trainers and administrators; openness of communication;
4. Linkages with, participation and involvement of related agencies;
5. Activities undertaken; assignments given to the trainees;
6. Elicitation and use of ideas from participants; encouragement of creativity;
7. Participatory and co-operative learning tasks;
8. Scheduling and pacing of activities;
9. Balance between:
   (a) cognitive and affective dimensions of learning, and
   (b) scholarship and values; and
10. Emergent leadership; investigative and inquiring stances.

More than in other subjects, the trainees in science, technology and mathematics should see a modelling of the above indicators so that they can do the same in their teaching of these subjects.

One type of process data on administrative behaviour relates to incidence and form of administrative monitoring, e.g. the frequency, length and purpose of visits by school supervisors to the training sessions. Another set of indicators are those that measure the school administrator's interaction with the trainers, trainees and resource persons.

Trainer activities could be divided into instruction/training tasks, administrative tasks and monitoring and evaluation tasks. The measurement of the time distribution among these activity categories provides a useful indicator of the trainer's role in the training programme. The greatest proportion of time should be given to the instructional/training activity.

Time allocation data on trainees are not direct indicators of effectiveness or efficiency, but they provide bases for more informed judgement about whether the training process is using resources properly.

The trainee time-on-task matrix below given an idea of some activities, interaction types and resource-use which take place in an in-service training setting.

A Hypothetical Matrix of Trainee-Time Allocation

Trainee Interaction	Form of Material Use				
	No. Materials	Textbooks	Support Materials	A/V Equipment	Total
Full Group	50%	10%	8%	2%	70%
Small Group with Trainer	2%	2%	1%	0%	5%
Small Group without Trainer	1%	6%	3%	0%	10%
Tutorial	0%	0%	0%	0%	0%
Trainee Alone	0%	10%	5%	0%	15%
Total	53%	28%	17%	2%	100%

Indicators of Outputs and Outcomes

The effectiveness of an in-service training programme can be viewed in terms of what is produced. Three categories will be dealt with here, namely:

1. Attainment effects,
2. Achievement effects, and
3. Attitudinal/Behaviour effects.

Attainment effects are provided by statistics on numbers trained, which would allow comparisons over time or across groupings (e.g. by subject area, region, sector). The attainment measures give indications of how many (and/or what per cent of the target number) are trained. For achievement effects, the most commonly used output measures are absolute test scores and pretest-posttest gains.

A measure of achievement can be a test or the result of observational judgement. The measures of achievement can be interpreted in effectiveness terms in any of the following ways:

1. Absolute level of achievement: as represented by a test score or assigned grade.
2. Average level of distribution of achievement: individual scores can be compared to the group's achievement.
3. Group achievement relative to the larger group: sub-groups can be compared to the whole group.
4. "Mastery" level of achievement: a criterion is set for what constitutes mastery.
5. Achievement gain: change or difference between posttest and pretest.
6. Effect size: this is the difference between the average scores of an experimental group and a control group, divided by the standard deviation of the control group.

Attitudinal and behaviour effects of in-service training include such items as effort, motivation, value for the training, and commitment; there is a need to devise instruments to obtain such measures.

Outcomes are the result of the interaction of outputs with a great variety of external influences. An outcome of in-service training could be upgrading and accreditation of teachers for promotion purposes, stricter recruitment and retention policies for teachers, etc.

The matrix below shows the interrelationships of the inputs and processes with outputs and outcomes.

Figure 1. Major Factors in the Education Production Function for In-service Training

Deeterminants		Effects	
Inputs	Process	Outputs	Outcomes
Trainee Characteristics	Forms of Instructional Organizations (e.g. grouping)	Achievement; Learning and Attitudes	Upgrading; Promotions
Trainer Characteristics	Alternative methods and techniques	Improved training skills	Wider involvement
Programme Characteristics	Planning, Management and Evaluation	Attitudinal changes; Values	Attitudinal changes; Expansion of expertise
Instructional/ Training Materials	Use; construction and validation	Behavioural changes	Skills; Behavioural changes

Indicators become meaningful and useful if they can be measured and/or operationalized. For the indicator to be useful, criteria have to be set up for the signs or manifestations.

Based on the earlier discussions, here are sample indicators and corresponding criteria.

Inputs

Indicators		Criteria
Trainer Characteristics	Age:	within specified range
	Readiness:	high
	Attitude:	favourable to training
Programme Characteristics	Relevance: Efficiency	
Materials/Equipment	Adequacy:	Appropriateness

Process

Interaction and Communication:	High Trainee Involvement
Activities	Participativeness of Trainees; Co-operative problem solving

Output

- Achievement: Positive change

Outcomes

- Improved skills
- Integration of non-cognitive skills in lessons
- Usefulness: Actual use of skills learned

The indicators which an evaluator should identify are those which are directly relevant to judging the quality of the in-service training programme. When one speaks of quality indicators of a training programme, one needs to look into signs of quality in inputs, process, outputs and/or outcomes of the programme.

5. A Review of Inset From England and Wales *(by Mary Harris, Institute of Education, University of London)*

This review has been prepared by Mary Harris, Visiting Fellow at the Department of Mathematics Statistics and Computing, University of London Institute of Education, 20 Bedford Way, London WC1H OAL.

Introduction

The term 'basic' (the first nine years of schooling), covers the primary phases (ages 5-11) and the first three years of secondary schooling.

The concept of INSET has recently undergone radical change. Up to and including the 1980s, INSET was increasingly people-centred, being concerned with the professional development of teachers in their classrooms. This model supplanted and effectively discredited earlier models which and concentrated chiefly on information transmission and specific teaching skills. The past two years have seen educational reform including the introduction of the National Curriculum and its attendant assumption that educational change is a technical problem. INSET has become mainly concerned with the transmission of information about the new subject materials, the structure of the curriculum, teacher assessment and the training of dissemination skills: it has become systems-oriented. However, as the results of teacher appraisal (also introduced by the reforms) begin to reveal the needs for professional development, and as evaluation of some of the new INSET is beginning to show, the focus will need to change towards professional development again. At this stage it can draw on handling the innovations of the people-oriented developments of the 1980s and before. This review will the therefore attempt to summarize positive lessons from INSET both in the previous and current periods.

A brief note on the structure of the national Curriculum is given in the Appendix (Section 4) Mathematics and Science are in the 'core'. Technology is included in the **'foundation'** subject and like the core, must be taught form ages 5 to 16. Technology is a new subject in which it has been attempted to combine the **'old'** subjects of craft, design and technology with home economics and textiles and with information technology; its definition, content, delivery and assessment are under continuing debate.

Currently, twenty day INSET courses in science and mathematics for primary teachers are being run by the Department for Education (DFE), at various institutions of Higher Education often working co-operatively with Local Education Authority Advisory. In October 1992 the Government announced proposals for further course for 'enhancing primary teachers' subject knowledge' for 1993-94. These courses will include technology.

The current situation is one of frequent, rapid and confusing change. Any brief review of INSET in England and Wales is necessarily superficial and will be out of date within months if not weeks of its publication. This review is dated November 1992.

The experience of the writer of this review in Mathematics education with a cross-curricular and cross-phase focus, suggest that projects concerned with the interactions of science, technology and mathematics need to be clear about their view of mathematics. Mathematics had become a particular case because of its historical inability to reconcile its academic, service and pre-vocational roles. Concentration on the service aspect runs the risk of offering pupils a limited version of mathematics, of obscuring access to some of its more profound aspects and of not utilizing results of research in learning mathematics that could affect practice in science and technology.

INSET Initiatives. Some Lessons from the 1980s

It is impossible to summarize briefly the range of INSET activities that took place during this very active period. The decade saw the publication of a major inquiry in mathematics teaching (the Cockcroft Report 1982), the beginning of a substantial industry-education movement including some large research project, the introduction of new technology (particularly computers and calculators), an initiative in technical and vocation education in schools funded by government money unrelated to the Department for Education, the publication of some major research in mathematics and science education (including for example, Hart, 1981) and the introduction of a new secondary school leaving examination where mathematics included investigations and course work. There was thus a wide range of implication for INSET. Initiatives included the introduction of Advisory Teachers, supported by new Local Education Authority funding and working mainly in schools (for example the Primary Mathematics Consultancy Scheme of the Inner London Education Authority); research based in Higher Education but with a strong INSET focus, for example the Microworlds project at the University of London Institute of Education (Hoyles et. al. 1991) and the Calculator Aware Number (CAN) project based at Homerton College Cambridge (Shuard, et. al. 1991); research and materials development projects at the school-work interface such as Maths in Works (Harris, 1991); and government funded projects such as LAMP (Low Attainers in Mathematics Project: Ahmed, 1987) based at West Sussex Institute of Higher Education and working with six Local Education Authorities.

General lessons from much of this INSET in mathematics, including principles of good practice are summarized by Woodrow (1991), a brief account of which follows. Two main lessons are expressed as 'descriptive slogans' which embody the paramount convictions of experience:

- curriculum development follows teachers development; and
- teacher confidence leads to pupil confidence.

Woodrow also derives five principles:

1. **Localization.** The introduction of Advisory Teachers working in the classroom, demonstrated clearly the effectiveness of locating INSET at the teachers' workplace. This innovation was soon taken up in science and information technology INSET. Moves to localization also came form course mounted by Local Education Authorities and Higher Education institutions in various mechanisms for accrediting prior learning (for examples teachers' journals or class-based research) and current moves towards modular awards. The assumption underlying these developments is that:

professional development is more likely when supported by professional practice.

2. **Personalization.** Teacher development must start from the teacher's perspective and teacher's context. Theory is the responsibility of both teacher and INSET provider and the focus of INSET must be on creating and justifying theory in the classroom rather that on merely importing it; the provision of a packet of information and ready-made theory is on longer appropriate. This point leads to the next, that of,

3. **Collaboration Practice.** Teachers working together are in the position to contrast interpretations and extrapolations from the same situation.

> *Shared decisions are more often professional decisions* than personal decisions. A variety of INSET provisions (activities, workshops, lectures, discussions) can approach objectives simultaneously to enrich the symbolic relationship between teacher knowledge and teacher practice.

4. **Training Trainers**. A problem identified by Advisory Teachers was the conflict between scale and depth of development. Its resolution was through placing emphasis on the role of school-based curriculum specialists as trainers for action, rather than as information and resource providers. Such a development can be self-enhancing since

giving responsibility leads to the taking of responsibility.

5. **Whole School Policies**. Whole school policies on INSET have proved to particularly effective in primary schools where subject co-ordinators do not have a direct management role.

A longitudinal study and evaluation of the impact of INSET in Primary Science, made by Kinder and Harland (1991) derives a typology for conceptualizing outcomes and therefore effectiveness of INSET. The INSET conducted by Advisory Teachers, took place in five primary schools in the Local Education Authority of Caderdale, before the introduction of the National Curriculum. The evaluation was made in such a way that a generalizable conceptual framework or model of INSET outcomes may be tentatively formulated and general lessons learned about the nature of effective INSET may be gleaned (op. cit., pp. 2-3). In a field where there is little empirical work, Kinder and Harland,

1. attempted to study some of the internal methodological difficulties in studying the effects of INSET;
2. offered an exploratory and provisional framework for conceptualizing INSET outcomes;
3. portrayed some of the opportunities and problems entailed in trying to bring about changes in teachers' classroom practices through INSET.

The materials being used by the teachers were those of the Initiatives in Primary Science published by the Association of Science Education which use the Joyce and Shower (1980) typology. The typology describes INSET outcomes under four categories:

- general awareness of new skills;
- organized knowledge of underlying concepts and theory;

- learning of new skills; and
- application on-the-job.

This typology ignores motivation and value-orientation and is limited to individuals. Kinder and Harland's analysis of the accounts of teachers, head teachers and advisory teachers suggested that the outcomes were more complex and had significant consequences for the analysis of the relationship between INSET inputs on classroom practice. Motivation and value orientation can highly influence outcomes with crucial influence on teachers' subsequent practice. As a result Kinder and Harland set up an alternative technology for which process they stress a number of points:

1. they focused on outcomes, paying little attention to inputs or processes of delivery;
2. they concentrated on outcomes whether intended or not, that is their analysis was not goal-oriented, they not match outcomes against specific criteria;
3. their typology of outcomes was developed specifically from primary teachers' classroom practice in science and one scheme in particular; and
4. the analysis also included negative effects.

The analysis yield nine categories in contrast to the four of Joyce and Showers. The following is a very brief summary of the nine categories. A copy of Kinder and Harland's own summary is available at this workshop.

1. Material and Provisionary Outcomes
    - the procurement of physical resource and services as a result of participation in in-service activities.
2. Informational Outcomes
    - the state of being or cognisant of the background of facts and news about curriculum and management and their implications, as distinct from outcomes relating to deeper understanding of underlying curriculum principles.

3. News Awareness

- Perceptual shifts were related to some of all of the following: science, so to speak, had 'entered' their curriculum consciousness, the boundaries and substance of science as a curriculum area had altered, the teacher's way of working in primary science was clarified, distinctive kind of pupil learning behaviour and attitude was apparent in science.

4. Value Congruence Outcomes

    - the personalized versions of curriculum and classroom management informs a primary practitioner's teaching, and how far they come to coincide with INSET messages about good practice. The scheme used, noted three aspects of practice which seemed pivotal to value congruence, pedagogical style, i.e. the organization and delivery of children's learning experiences. Given that discrepant teaching style are after unaddressed at school level, an INSET programme which exposes value discongruence may prove a valuable opportunity for tackling its resolution—curriculum content, i.e. the kind of activities offered to children. If teachers' preferences as classroom managers ultimately determine the learning experience of pupils, then achieving value congruence on the former perhaps emerges as one of the greatest imperatives of any curriculum innovation.
    - curriculum design i.e. the way the whole curriculum is planned and the proportionate importance attached to different subject areas.

Overall, value congruence emerge as a major factor in subsequent classroom practice, not always positively. Leaving teachers with the encouraging message 'you're already doing it' can be a positive strategy in removing anxiety but can result in inertia.

5. Affective Outcomes

   - also can be positive and negative. There is a difference between short-term reassurance and long-term confidence. Universal strategies impact very differently on different course members.

6. Motivation and Attitudinal Outcomes

   This is one of the strongest and most significant outcomes and is crucial to any professional development exercise. However heightened enthusiasm and deeper understanding are not synonymous and pursuing the former does not necessarily deliver the latter.

7. Knowledge and Skills

   Merely raising awareness had minimal direct impact on practice; affective outcomes could be short-lived; development in scientific knowledge and skills are necessary to many.

8. Institutional-Strategic Outcomes

   INSET can have an important collective impact on groups of teachers. This finding was consistent with other INSET workers who have noted that:

   - INSET provision is likely to be more effective if it is related to current organizational changes and developments in school; and
   - than individual teachers' attempts to innovate following an INSET programme have a greater chance of succeeding if they are shared with sympathetic knowledge and supportive colleagues and supervisors. Continuing professional development seemed to depend on the whole school taking responsibility for it.

9. Impact on Classroom Practice

   This outcome represented the goal of the other outcome types as well as a type in its own right. Aspects of practice which Kinder and Harland felt to be important were:

Frequency: all teachers were doing science more regularly and/ or more frequently. This included those who realized that they were already doing it though disentangling it from language and number work was problematic.

Planning: Encouraging teachers to become critical, selective 'plagiarists' of teacher materials seemed a more helpful strategy and emphasis than the above. Variations if teachers intended learning outcomes testify to markedly different ways of interpreting and internalising INSET messages.

Organization and Management: Good practice advocated by Advisory Teachers remained an unresolved dilemma, most teachers agreed that science could only be delivered in group situations but for some, was neither acceptable nor feasible.

Teacher-pupil Interaction: Though teachers' perceptions and/or rhetoric indicated the elevation and integration of science into their curriculum design, their practice seemed to testify to a reliance on existing pedagogical skills and curriculum predilections unless further INSET was a feature of their recent professional experience; the identification and implementation of process skills was underplayed.

As implied in the above summary, a hierarchical relationship between some of the outcomes can be perceived. Some of the first eight outcomes rank as being more contiguous with the final one than others. Kinder and Harland attempt to frame the outcomes in an order of significance for changing practice, stressing again that their model is tentative, specific to their particular context and descriptive, not prescriptive. It is assumed that the goal of INSET is to change practice and noted that the significance of certain outcomes may be affected by existing practices and values of individuals.

INSET suggests three order outcomes as follows: (Typology on INSET Outcomes from Kinder and Harland (1991) p. 163)

3rd Order: Provisionary: Information: New Awareness

2nd Order: Motivation: affective: Institutional

1st Order: Value Congruence: Knowledge and Skills

Evidence suggest that:

- INSET that focuses on 3rd order outcomes are least likely to impact on a teacher's practice unless higher order incomes are also achieved or already exist.

- 1st order outcomes are equally dependent on lower order outcomes, especially motivation.

The model highlights the complexity and inter-dependency in a way that Joyce and Showers does not. The order may be different form other goals of INSET. Other INSET designers and recipients may find these orderings inconsistent with their conclusions. Kinder and Harland used their model to plot the impact of routes' as indicators for future INSET needs.

Evaluation Design

Kinder and Harland (1991) proposed an evaluation design which was organized around five main phases:

1. Study of the general background to the scheme and its mode of working followed by research in three schools (the retrospective case-study schools) which had experienced the school-based input in the first year the scheme was operative.
2. A study of the expectations and existing provision for science in two schools (the 'prospective' case study schools) due to participate in the school-based input.
3. Observation of the school-based input in the two prospective case-study schools.
4. Follow-up research in all five case-study schools.
5. Follow-up research at a later date in all five case-study schools.

INSET Initiatives. Some Lessons from 1990 and 1991

In association with the introduction of the National Curriculum, Government defined primary teachers' INSET needs in science and mathematics in terms of enhancement of knowledge and skills. Grant support was provided for 20 day courses of INSET involving Higher Education Institutions, in a shift of policy from providing support to Local Education Authority Advisory Teacher Schemes. Draft criteria and frameworks for courses were devised in consultation with some Higher Education institutions, Advisory Teachers, subject associations and the Governments National Curriculum Council and Schools Examinations and Assessment Council. Higher

Education institutions were then invited to submit proposals to meet the criteria and seek funding. Copies of these criteria are available at this workshop. A programme of one of these courses undertaken at the University of London Institute of Education with Hackney and Islington Local Education Authorities is also available.

The courses were evaluated by Her Majesty's Inspectors (HMI 1992) and by the National Foundation for Education Research (Harland and Kinder 1992). From these evaluation, the Departments For Education identified a number of features common to effective courses (DES 1992).

1. a pattern of attendance in which short blocks of full-time study were integrated with school and classroom assignments. The most effective inputs, seen by participants as one model of good practice, consisted of short expositions, followed by focused questioning and extended opportunities for learning from experience.
2. staffing characterized by a small course team with complementary interest, where tutors demonstrated subject expertise, a familiarity with primary practice, and skill and experience in teaching extended courses.
3. a strong LEA/HE partners in setting up a course, establishing clear criteria for selecting participants, identifying those who would most benefit and ensuring that provision was designed to meet participants' needs. In some instance, teachers were selected so that they could represent school cluster within an LEA area. This made to effective case of AT support and offered a potential structure for further training through mutual assistance such as self-help groups.
4. teachers most able to affect the work of their colleagues were in schools where course attendance was synchronized with whole school development work, characterized by:

(a) headteachers who were actively supportive of the training and were involved in the recruitment process;

(b) some non-contact time to work other staff and the expectation that they would do so;

(c) follow-up in school provided by the course tutors or AT's;

(d) a venue readily accessible to both teachers and tutors, offering appropriate resources and accommodation, with an ambience conducive to improving knowledge as well as developing skills.

The Department goes on the emphasize that it will be looking for clear evidence of these characteristics when scrutinizing proposals for technology INSET.

In their evaluation (HMI 1992) the Inspectors note that strategies for dissemination were not well developed and had less impact on the work of other teachers than had been anticipated. The impact of any future courses of this kind would be increased of all courses include time for school-based work and over training in dissemination. On the other hand, given the amount to be covered in the time, dissemination training should not deflect attention from other important aspects. Schools too can improve dissemination. They might well consider further the concept of a coordinator. The role needs to be widened, beyond having a responsibility for organizing resource and drawing up curriculum plans, to include working alongside other teachers and helping in the planning of their lessons. Only a little can be done assist teachers who have not attended courses unless non-contact time is increased for those who have, in order for them to carry out these task (op. cit. paras. 65 and 66).

Appendix: The National Curriculum

The National Curriculum covers 10 Foundation Subjects, the first three of which constitute the Core. Core subjects which must be studied by every child from 5 to 16 are English, Mathematics and Science. Foundation subjects are Art, Music Geography, History, A Modern Language, Physics Education and Technology. Art and Music are compulsory to 14 but optional after that time; History and Geography are compulsory to 14 after which pupils may drop one; a Modern Language is compulsory from 11 to 16; PE and Technology are compulsory from 5 to 16.

Each subject is broken into Attainment Targets, Attainment Targets into Strands and each strand into 10 levels, identified by Statements of Attainment. Programmes of Study describe fields of learning which children should cover at various levels.

The Levels of the National Curriculum are grouped into Key Stages.

- Key Stage 1 covers Levels 1-2
- Key Stage 2 covers Levels 2-6
- Key Stage 3 covers Levels 3-8
- Key Stage 4 covers Levels 4-10.

Children are tested in every National Curriculum subject at the end of each Key Stage at 7, 11, 14 and 16. The tests are aimed to place children at particular levels. At 16 the current examination is the General Certificate in Secondary Education (GCSE) of which there are a number of syllabi in each subject published by a number of Examination Boards. GCSE was introduced before the National Curriculum and its relationship to it is very far from simple. Nevertheless from 1994 GCSE will be graded according to National Curriculum levels.

Addendum: One Curriculum and Materials Project in Mathematics

I attach a brief note on my own work, some of which is presented during this meting in the form of an exhibition of mathematics in the context of daily life and work, and in the form of a workshop that I shall be conducting in relation to it. The background to the work is in curriculum development in mathematics up to the first-school leaver level (age 16) conducted by a project called Maths in Work. This project aimed to make closer links between the mathematics of schools and the mathematics that takes place outside the formal (paid) and later, informal (unpaid, for example domestic) work. During its research phase the project switched its focus from the school mathematics syllabus to the activities of workplaces, which proved to be a much richer resource for mathematics. The project produced packs of learning material for mathematics that presented it in the context of familiar, practical and cross-curricular activities. The learning exhibition which grew out of one of the packs of materials has been redesigned by the British Council for touring. The workshop will give a brief theoretical introduction, followed by a practical session and discussion. Maths in Work materials will also be available for viewing and photocopying but not for sale. Both the exhibition has been seen in Norway, Denmark, Turkey, Nigeria, Cameroom, Uganda, Kenya, Malawi, Zimbabwe, Sri Lanka, Thailand, Malaysia, Singapore, Australia, Philippines. Countries to be visited include Botswana, Lesotho, Swaziland, Tanzania, Hong Kong and New Zealand.

REFERENCES

1. Ahmed, Afzal, (ed), 1997. *Better Mathematics*. A Curriculum Development Study based on the Low Attainers in Mathematics Project. London, Her Majesty's Stationery Office.
2. Cockcroft, W.H. (ed), 1982. *Mathematics Counts*. Reports of the Committee of Inquiry in the Teaching of Mathematics in Schools under the chairmanship of Dr. W.H. Cockroft. London, Her Majesty's Stationery Office.
3. Department of Education, 1992. *Grants for Education Support and Training: 1992-1993 Programme*. DFE Circular 10/92. London. Department of Education.
4. Hardland, John and Kinder, K. 1992. *Mathematics and Science Courses for Primary Teachers: Lessons for the Future*. National Foundation for Educational Research, The Mere, Upton Park, Slough, Berkshire, SL1 2DQ. ISBN 07005 13116. Also obtainable if an educationalist in the UK from Martin Wimpress, Teachers Branch B, Department for Education and Science, Sanctuary Buildings, Great Smith Street, London SW1P 3BT.
5. Harris, Mary. (ed), *Schools, Mathematics and Work*. Basingtoke, Falmer Press.
6. Hart, K.M. (ed) 1981. *Children's Understanding of Mathematics 11-16*. London, John Murray.
7. HMI, 1992. *Designated Courses in Mathematics and Science for Primary Teachers*. April 1990-April 1991. A Report by HMI. Reference 2/29/NS. London, Department of Education and Science.
8. Hoyles, C. et. al. 1991. *Final Report on the Microworlds Project 1986-1989*. London, Institute of Education.
9. Joyce, B. and Showers, B. 1980. *Improving In-service Training: The Messages of Research*. Educational Leadership. Vol. 37, No 5, pp. 379-385.

10. Kinder Kay and Harland John. 1991. *The Impact of INSET: The Case of Primary Science*. National Foundation for Educational Research, The Mere, Upton Park, Slough, Bershire, SL1 2 DQ. ISBN 0 7005 1311 6

11. Schools Examinations and Assessment Council, 1992. *Technology Standard Assessment Tasks for Seven Year Olds*. Briefing Note No. 3. January 1992. London, School Examination and Assessment Council.

12. Shuasrd, H et. al. 1991. *Calculators, Children and Mathematics*. London, Simon and Schuster.

13. Smithers Allan and Robinson Pamela. 1992. *Technology in the National Curriculum: Getting it Right*. London, Engineering Council.

14. Woodrow Derek. 1991. *Losing the Thread: How In-service Training Council Learn from Experience*. Education Today, Vol. 41, No. 4.

Part IV

TRAINING OF TRAINERS IN SCIENCE AND TECHNOLOGY EDUCATION

Preface

Many developing countries are striving to provide quality science, technology and mathematics education (STME) as part of basic education in a context of limited resources. The Commonwealth Secretariat's work in STME is in four main areas: training of trainers; scientific and technological literacy for all; measures to enhance the participation of girls and women in science and technology; and training of laboratory technicians.

Efforts to improve STME through better quality pre-service and in-service teacher education have often neglected the needs of those who are providing training at universities and colleges of education. In order to address this issue the Commonwealth Secretariat organized in the UK a planning meeting of science, technology and mathematics educators from Commonwealth countries. The participants at this meeting recommended the development of monographs to assist teacher educators in the delivery of science, technology and mathematics teacher education programmes. The basic framework of the monographs was also developed in this meeting.

The draft monographs were produced by practising African science educators in a workshop organized in Nigeria, and were reviewed in an international conference in Botswana organized by the Commonwealth Association of Science Technology and Mathematics Educators (CASTME). They were then revised, on the basis of the comments received from the reviewers, by a team of African science educators in a workshop held in South Africa.

On behalf of the Commonwealth Secretariat, I wish to express gratitude to all the participants who have contributed to the development of these monographs. I am also thankful to CASTME for arranging the review of these monographs during their Botswana International Conference. I also wish to express my sincere gratitude to the Rockefeller Foundation and Primary Science Programme, South Africa, for co-sponsoring the workshops in Nigeria and South Africa respectively. Last but not the least I wish to thank my ex-colleague, Professor Sam Bajah, who initiated this project and the development of the drafts, and Dr Ved Goel who accomplished the revision of the monographs and their editing into their present form.

We are fully cognizant of the fact that these monographs have not been tested in the field prior to printing. I therefore sincerely request the science and technology educators in Africa to try out the monographs and send us their evaluations and suggestions for further improvement.

Introduction

An important aspect of science education reform in the world today is the implementation of science and technology education. Technology bridges science and society, brings relevance to science teaching, and unifies different subjects. It provides approaches to problem solving, relates different subjects to life and helps to link theory and practice. The science teacher educators in many developing countries are finding it difficult to prepare science teachers for this kind of science education. They recommended in a Commonwealth Secretariat meeting that monographs be developed which could guide science teacher educators in their attempt to prepare science teachers for science and technology education. These monographs have been developed to meet that felt need of science and technology teacher educators.

Science graduate programmes in the Universities have long been organized in terms of separate subjects namely botany, chemistry, physics, zoology etc. Consequently the scope of science knowledge of most science teacher educators is limited—they are familiar with one or two science subjects. However, science and technology education usually involves inter-subject teaching. This requires teacher educators to have a broad base of science knowledge. In Chapter 1 **'Training needs of science and technology educators'**, it has therefore been highlighted that while recruiting teacher educators, candidates what broad-base knowledge of science subjects be preferred. Selected candidates and existing teacher educators who lack breadth in their science knowledge be provided opportunities to acquire the perceived deficiencies through in-service courses or attachments with science departments in universities/colleges.

It has also been recognized that most science teacher have tended to stress science while neglecting technology in their classes because of lack of training in linking technology with science. The priority task is therefore to improve the pedagogical skills of science teacher educators themselves such that they could relate science and technology using examples of local technology. This also requires that teachers educators' will be able to help teacher trainees to think in many different ways, including the selection of methods and the use of different materials and tools. Science teacher educators must provide this kind of experience to the teacher trainees during the course they conduct for science teachers. In Chapter 2 **'Teaching practice for science and technology'**, a two-tier approach to the training of science teachers has been suggested whereby the science teacher educator first demonstrates the use of a pedagogy followed up with practice by the prospective teachers. Considerable emphasis had therefore been laid on practice teaching and its supervision.

Effective science and technology education requires the use of variety of resources. Lack of availability of material resources specially the science equipment has been regarded as an impediment in providing quality science and technology education. Many science teacher educators fail to recognize the use of locally available and improvised materials as an opportunity to provide relevant and life related science and technology education. The reason for this cynicism partly lies in the lack of their ability to identify, use and improvise suitable locally available materials. Chapter 3 **'Resources in science and technology education'** has therefore been written to help teacher educators' first in the identification and use of locally available material and how they can go about improvising such materials in their own teaching. Secondly, it helps them to provide guidelines to teacher trainees in the use of such resources.

An important feature of the monographs is that they not only provide guidelines to the teacher educators to improve their own teaching but also provide strategies which could be used by them with their trainees to make them better science and technology teachers. Another common thread throughout the monographs is the emphasis on the regular use of those methods, materials and approaches by the teacher educators in their own teaching which they expect teachers to use. It is based on the understanding that when the trainees observe a skill in action, and get the opportunity to practice that after observation, the chances of transfer of skill improve.

Science teacher educators require tools and techniques to assess teacher trainees both at the formative and summative levels. They also have to provide training to the prospective teachers in evaluation to enable them to evaluate their students. Chapter 4, **'Evaluation'** precisely does this by discussing purposes, uses and techniques of different kinds of evaluation.

To improve the training of science and technology teachers in the teacher training institutions, and the delivery of science and technology education in schools requires coordination at all levels. Chapter 5, **'Coordination in science and technology education'**, discusses the important interactive relationships within and across teacher training institutions, schools and external institutions and provides guidelines on achieving such a relationship. Chapter 6, **'Participating in science and technology education research'** has been written to stimulate action research amongst teacher educators and domonstrates how they could generate such research among teachers.

1

The Training Needs of Science and Technology Teacher Educators

1.1 Overview

In most developing countries the provision of a good basic education is a matter of great concern. High quality science and technology education depends on effective and efficient training of teachers. This in turn depends on the quality of the teacher educators. At present, there is little comprehensive information available about the academic and professional qualifications of science and technology teacher educators, or about their responsibilities and training needs. The best intentions for improving teacher education will fail unless attention is paid to improving the quality of science and technology teacher educators.

1.2 Objectives

The objectives of this monograph to help policy makers and administrators, responsible for the recruitment and training of science and technology teacher educators, by:

- identifying the professional and academic qualifications and training needs of science and technology teacher educators;
- considering ways of improving the qualifications of science and technology teacher educators and of enabling them to keep abreast of developments in their fields.

1.3 Recruitment and Training

The recruitment process normally involves some form of advertisement seeking applications, followed by short-listing of candidates against established criteria, and selection based on performance in oral interviews.

The ideal candidate for a science and technology teacher educator post would usually need to meet the following criteria:

- Possession of an appropriate professional qualification, such as B.Ed. or a Post-Graduate Certificate in Education (preferably directed at primary or basic education), and ideally, an M.Ed. qualification. Relevant teaching experience at the appropriate level would be a specific advantage. (A candidate with secondary experience would need to show evidence of some clear interest, involvement or willingness to gain direct experience of work at the primary level of science and technology education.) Three to five years of primary teaching experience is the usual basic requirement.
- Academic qualifications indicating a broad basic grounding in science and technology, including ideally, a first degree in a science-related area or equivalent qualifications in technology. Candidates who lack breadth in their academic qualifications would need to indicate a willingness to remedy such shortcomings within a given time.
- Evidence of involvement with, and active participation (including extra-mural activities) in, a relevant professional organization, such as the following, would be an advantage:
    - Science Teachers' Association of Nigeria (STAN)
    - Ghana Association of Science Teachers (GAST)
    - Southern Africa Association for the Advancement and Research in Maths and Science Education (SAARMSE)
    - Namibian Association of Science Teachers (NAST).

- Possibly some indication of research interests, or evidence of a capacity for, or commitment to, research in science and technology education through academic, professional or popular writing.
- Reliable testimonials and confidential referees' reports.

At the short-listing stage, due consideration needs to be given to gender equality. In many countries, science and technology education departments in colleges and universities are dominated by men. These countries should make deliberate attempts to identify suitable women candidates. Women science and technology teacher educators not only bring a different perspective to the training of teachers, but can provide teachers with strategies for promoting participation by girls in science and technology.

At interview stage, the extent to which short-listed candidates meet the following criteria can be assessed:

- Positive attitude towards science and technology education, including the gender perspective, and keeping abreast of current developments in science and technology education.
- Potential ability to adapt to, and understand, the contextual needs of the specific institution and the community it serves.

The teaching ability of candidates might be compared by requiring them to present a prepared lesson, lecture or practical class to students. This emphasizes that practical teaching ability is as important as paper qualifications and skilful interview technique.

Unless a country is already well supplied with candidates meeting these criteria for science and technology teacher educator posts, appropriate training will need to be provided to make up the short-fall. The selection process involved in recruitment will indicate clearly what the general and individual training needs are and how they might be met through in-service training courses.

1.4 Career Paths

Criteria for promotion of science and technology teacher educators, as for other academic staff, usually include:

- A satisfactory period of service—normally two to three years after appointment.
- Evidence of a research interest in science and technology education, through the presentation of case study or research papers to peers, or through publications.
- Evidence of administrative capability and leadership skills.
- Satisfactory Head of Department's assessment report and recommendation.
- Evidence of involvement, with local and regional science and technology teachers, in ongoing professional support and development, as well as a commitment to professional development of colleagues.

1.5 Academic and Professional Needs and Responsibilities

In order to improve the quality of science and technology education at the basic level we need to meet the academic and professional needs and responsibilities of science and technology teacher educators. The quality of science and the technology teachers depends on the availability of science and technology teacher educators with sufficient grasp of the challenge and complexity of introducing young learners to the basics of these disciplines in a holistic and integrated way.

Currently, there are no courses that specifically train such teacher educators. In the short term, quality In-Service Education and Training (INSET) for science and technology teacher educators will be required. In the long term, a clear route will need to be developed to enable potential science and technology teacher educators to gain the academic and professional qualifications they need. Their academic needs may include updating on knowledge of subject matter and content. Their professional needs include an understanding of and confidence in the use of subject-specific pedagogical skills, together with an understanding of appropriate methods for science and technology education research.

These specific requirements exist within the wider context which will include gender issues, ethical and humanistic issues in science and technology, cultural awareness, communication skills and liberal and African studies. The academic and professional needs interact with one another as well as with the context, as shown in Figure 1.

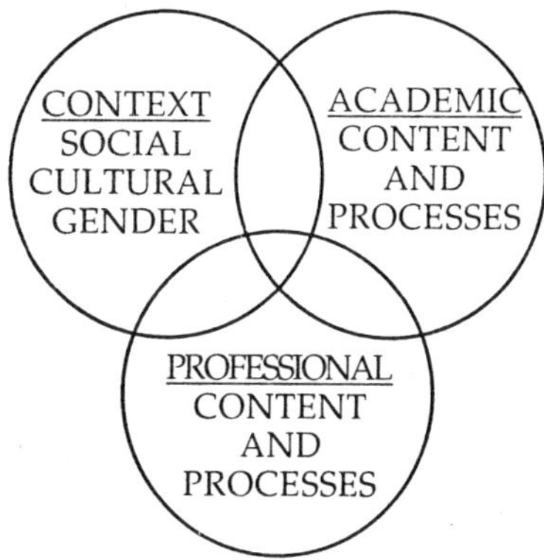

Figure 1: The interactive nature of the areas of training

Table 1 summarizes the broad training needs of science and technology teacher educators and indicates where subsequent training might be required for individuals with identified professional or academic shortcomings.

Table 1: Academic and professional needs of science and technology teacher educators

Academic		Professional		Context	
Science and technology subject knowledge	Science processes	Education studies	Subject-specific pedagogical skills	Curriculum studies	Manpower development studies
	Observation. Classification. Experimentation etc.	Educational psychology. Philosophy of education. Sociology of education.	Teaching methods. Micro-teaching. Teaching practice.	Science and technology education research. Materials development.	General liberal studies. Cultural/ community awareness. Communication (language skills, etc).

Science and technology teacher educators will have to develop competence in their trainees across the whole breadth of science (biology, chemistry, physics, earth science) and technology, including coverage of all the areas that the teacher will have to teach. They need to:

- be able to demonstrate the investigative and problem-solving approach to science and technology;
- be able to present examples of open-ended investigations and how to report them scientifically;
- encourage trainee teachers to generate their own investigations and follow them through, so that they in turn learn how to support and encourage their pupils in the same processes at their own levels;
- be able to demonstrate the significance of classroom skills in relation to real-life problems;
- be up-to-date with current learning theory, such as the recognition that different children build up knowledge in different ways.

1.5.1 Academic Responsibilities

Science and technology teacher educators usually have the following responsibilities:

- **Teaching.** To organize, implement, and critically evaluate the content of science and technology curricula and appropriate teaching methods.
- **Practice teaching.** To support student teachers in teaching practice (see Chapter 2).
- **Research.** To design, plan, conduct, and publish research.
- **Evaluation.** To carry out continuous review of existing programmes and the diagnostic and formative assessment of student's academic attainment and progress.
- **Record keeping.** To keep accurage records of examination results, nominal rolls, laboratory stock, workshop materials, etc.

It is important for science and technology teacher educators to be academically well prepared and equipped to meet the demands made of them. They should be familiar with the subject matter and content of the curriculum. They should understand how science and technology, their philosophical foundations and sociological aspects, are interrelated. This is important, because problems in science and technological tend to require skills and knowledge that are cross-disciplinary in nature and best handled by team-teaching. Science and technology teacher educators also need to have a basic knowledge of everyday applications of science and technology, their social implications and how the concepts and processes are used in industry and commerce.

Administrators can encourage teacher educators to take up research by:

- making research opportunities available;
- offering grants;
- facilitating attendance at conferences;
- organising in-service training in research methods and report-writing and providing professional support at different levels of research;
- communicating research findings through newsletters of journals.

1.5.2 Professional Responsibilities

The science and technology teacher educators needs to possess pedagogical knowledge, both of concepts and procedures, and to able to pass this on to pre-service students and in-service teachers to improve their general effectiveness in the classroom. They therefore need to develop competence in the following areas:

- *Pedagogical Skills.* These are the conceptual knowledge and procedural skills needed to enable teacher educators and teachers to bring about effective learning. They include selection and use of appropriate teaching strategies for particular objectives, class sizes, available materials, learning environments, etc. They also include the ability to guide students in reflecting on their teaching and to encourage their involvement in the teaching-learning process.

- *Supervisory, guidance and counselling techniques.* The science and technology teacher educator needs to develop skills in classroom observation, guidance and counselling of students on academic and professional matters, including supervision of teaching practise or during 'micro-teaching' sessions.
- *Social and psychological considerations.* Understanding the social and psychological characteristics of prospective science and technology teachers and pupils at basic education level, and providing guidance to prospective teachers on how to deal with them. Understanding gender issues in science and technology education and the strategies to deal with them.
- *Curriculum development.* Construction curriculum materials and teaching-learning aids.
- *Research.* Carrying out 'action research' and other types of research in education, which can contribute to understanding the needs of the pupils, the classroom and the school in general.

There is currently an imbalance in the practice of these academic and professional responsibilities. Science and technology teacher educators need to put themselves in the place of teachers, attend seminars and spend time actually working in schools. This will make their own teaching much more realistic and effective, because it will be based on real classroom experience.

1.6 Strategies for Ongoing Professional Development

Science and technology teacher educators needs support, throughout their teaching careers, to develop both academically and professionally. In the *Final Report of the International Forum on Scientific and Technological Literacy for All* (UNESCO, 1993), it was stated that such support should include:

- partnerships between the world of production and the community, which would allow teacher educators to be exposed to the latest technology and also increase society's commitment to science and technology teacher education programmes;

- updating appropriate teaching/learning instructional materials, facilities and equipment;
- updating of teaching skills, knowledge of learners and content;
- induction programmes for beginning teacher educators;
- assistance in developing leadership skills;
- adequate reward for teacher educators for those activities which are related to maintenance of their continued involvement with teacher as a dynamic profession.

These measures can be realized through:

- in-service education programmes organized by universities, colleges of education, subject associations and employing authorities (i.e. Ministries and Departments of Education);
- formal links, including visits and attachments, with industry;
- teaching at the school level and carrying out action research with science and technology teachers;
- provision of resources by governments, including improved salary conditions;
- joining professional organizations;
- corresponding with other professional science and technology teacher educators.

1.6.1 Types of INSET Programmes

In-Service Education and Training (INSET) is essential for updating the knowledge and improving the professional competence of science and technology teacher educators and teachers. At present, there are no regular INSET programmes specifically designed for science and technology teacher educators. Provision should focus on development needs, current issues and policy matters, as well as training and certification needs. The following are suggestions for types of INSET programmes.

Issue-based INSET

- *Workshops*. Hands-on activities designed to cater for specific professional development in terms of knowledge and skills.
- *Seminars*. Discussion—usually of short duration—of academic and/or professional issues and problems. They normally consist of talks or presentations followed by discussion, often in small groups. There should also be opportunity for plenary, summary discussion.

Certification-based INSET

- *Sandwich courses*. These can be organized by colleges of education, universities and polytechnics during long vacations to upgrade science and technology teacher educators professionally. Periods of normal teaching are alternated with short periods of full-time attendance at local colleges. Sandwich courses can be supplemented by distance-learning modules or specific practical projects or tasks (action research). Follow-up field visits by course co-ordinators contribute to the effectiveness of sandwich courses.
- *Study courses*. Science and technology teacher educators are granted full-time study leave in order to attend courses leading to a qualification. Such courses are INSET in the sense that a serving teacher educator breaks service to study. This is a means by which underqualified teacher educators can obtain qualifications and qualified teacher educators can upgrade qualifications.
- *Distance-learning course*. Structured learning modules are made available to students through a variety of media. There is minimal contact with tutors, and the student does not need to obtain study leave to be able to participate. Professional elements such as teaching practice are assessed by specially designated local personnel.

Institution-based INSET

- *In-College activities and meetings.* Organized by college departments, these enable science and technology teacher educators to exchange ideas and experiences and thus improve the quality of their teaching.
- *Conferences.* These may be local or international. They usually involve presen-tations, by science and technology teacher educators, of innovative methods and examples of good practice in schools. They provide teacher educators with the opportunity to update themselves on the latest equipment and published materials for science and technology education. Such conferences are a very valuable resource for sharing problems and new ideas.

School-based INSET

It is important for science and technology teacher educators who have been in a post for some years, to be officially released for a period to update their teaching experience at the level for which they are training students. This given them a better understanding of the needs, characteristics and aspirations of the teachers and pupils in schools, and encourages the teacher educators to see themselves first and foremost as educators rather than as subject specialists.

Peer-group INSET

Science and technology teacher educators meet together as equals to share their problems and success stories. They can develop learning materials during such meetings. These can be at least as effective as the traditional 'course' led by an 'expert'.

Visits

Science and technology teacher educators should be encouraged to visit industries and other science and technology-based establishments such as science museums to acquaint themselves with the applications of science and technology principles in daily life. Visits may be for a day or involve extended periods of attachment to an establishment.

1.6.2. Content of INSET Programmes

INSET programmes for science and technology teacher educators should include consideration of:

- the needs of the community in which the teacher educators are likely to work and of ways of orienting science and technology towards community problems;
- the content and objectives of science and technology education at different levels;
- problem-solving techniques;
- gender issues and show they can be addressed;
- the use and maintenance of science equipment and a laboratory;
- learning science and technology in a second language;
- management, co-ordination and use of resources;
- hands-on activities which integrate science and technology;
- the cultures of scientific and technological enterprises; their values, attitudes, assumptions, organizational structures and limitations.

Table 2: Examples of INSET programmes for science and technology teacher educators

TYPE	ORGANISER	LENGTH	ACTIVITIES	OUTCOME
Issue-based				
Workshop	Professional association, educational agency, private organization, Ministry of Education, college of education, polytechnic, university	Varies	Lectures, demonstrations, discussions, practicals	Improvement in professional and academic competence
Seminar	As in Workshop	1-3 days	Lectures, demonstrations, discussions	As in Workshop
Certification-based				
Sandwich courses	College of education, polytechnic, university	2-10 long vacations of about 10 weeks each	Practicals, lectures, demonstrations	Undergraduate diploma
Study courses (vacation courses)	College of education polytechnic, university	1-2 academic years	Lecturers, demonstrations, practicals	Undergraduate diploma
Distance learning	University	1-3 years	Self-instructional modules, with follow-up contact for lectures, demonstrations, discussions	Undergraduate diploma
Institution-based				
In college activities and meetings	college of education	Usually not more than a day	Discussions, demonstrations	Exchange of ideas, update of professional and academic knowledge
Conferences	Professional association, educational agency, university	1-5 days	Lectures, demonstrations, discussions, practicals	Exchange of ideas, update of professional and academic knowledge

2

Teaching Practice for Science and Technology Education

2.1 Overview

The quality of science and technology education in schools depends on the training of teachers which in turn depends upon the quality of teacher educators. However good the curriculum, its aims cannot be achieved if, through inadequate training, teachers lack the confidence to implement it. Practical teaching experience in the classroom is a vital part of teacher training.

Frequently, insufficient attention is paid to this aspect of teacher education. Teaching practice is often given low priority and only the minimum requirements met. For instance: Have the students carried out the required number of lessons? Have the supervision requirements been met? Have the statutory weeks of teaching practice been complied with? The net result is that teaching practice is seen merely as a set of regulations to be complied with rather than the most critical aspect of teacher education, where theory and academic content merge into practice.

In many instances, primary teacher education students avoid teaching science and technology lessons and fulfil the teaching practice requirements with what they perceive to be 'easier' or 'safer' options. Science and technology topics tend to be seen as difficult and complicated by students who lack confidence or background in the subjects. On the other hand, confident students sometimes teach topics in a mechanical way that does not always ensure real understanding.

Technology is most often ignored in teaching practice. Teacher educators must make a conscious effort to provide opportunities where technology can feature more prominently than is presently the case. Links between science and technology should be emphasized in conventional subject teaching, and where possible the technical applications of science should be incorporated. Technologies in the local environment should be considered as possible starting points for science and technology teaching.

2.2 Objectives

The main aim of this monograph is to provide guidelines for teacher educators in science and technology to enable them to:

- plan and implement practical teaching experience;
- design programmes for retraining/updating through in-service teacher education (INSET);
- devise strategies for teaching large classes in science and technology;
- effectively manage classrooms in science and technology;
- implement appropriate strategies for supervision.

2.3 Pre-service Training of Teachers

Many factors have to be taken into account when planning and implementing a pre-service teacher education programme for science and technology teachers.

2.3.1 Students' Science Background

The entry requirements and length of training for primary science teachers vary from country to country. In some, A-level GCE, or its equivalent, is the qualification required for admission to a primary teacher training college which gives one to three years of training. In other countries a first university degree is the minimum qualification for admission to a one-year teacher training course. A formal qualification in science is not usually required for admission to a primary teacher training course, in spite of the fact that most primary teachers are expected to teach all subjects including science. This has implications for teacher training programmes.

Teachers' lack of confidence in the subject matter results in them being unable to:

- understand the logical flow of ideas and translate them into meaningful classroom learning activities;
- ask questions which promote thinking and are based on the existing ideas of students;
- respond to students' questions.

Pre-service training courses, especially those of only one year's duration, may not be able to make up for trainees' deficiency in knowledge of subject matter. But such courses may help trainees to identify areas or topics in which they do feel confident, and to translate this subject matter into a logical sequence of learning activities including thought-provoking questions. They can then try these out in the classroom under the guidance of the teacher trainers or an experience teacher. This helps to build up their confidence. Future in-service training programmes can help to fill gaps in subject-matter knowledge.

To overcome trainees' lack of confidence in teaching science, it should be compulsory for every trainee to teach a certain number of science lessons during their teaching practice. These need to be supervised either by science and technology teacher educators themselves or by very experienced advisory or science teachers.

2.3.2 Resources

In many developing countries, lack of material resources is considered to be the main reason for the poor quality of science and technology education. It is true that there is a lack of suitable printed learning materials in the local language, based on the local cultural and physical environment, and this handicaps both teachers and learners. But a lack of scientific equipment in primary schools is not as great a problem as is often claimed. This does not imply that no scientific equipment is necessary to teach or learn primary science.

For primary science teaching, the immediate local environment provides a wealth of resource materials, with plants, animals, food, housing, clothing, tools, transport, soaps and detergents, gardens and ponds offering a rich variety. In addition, empty bottles, cans, bottletops, plastic and paper bags, and low-cast materials such as nails, moulding clay, balloons, pipes, straw and string, can all be used to improvise materials for teaching science.

Teachers will need specific guidance on identifying and using locally available materials, and on procuring, storing and maintaining science materials. Science and technology teacher educators must ensure that during their own teaching they:

- increasingly use material from the local environment;
- use improvised items made from local materials;
- give enough practice to the trainees in the identification and use of local materials;
- encourage all trainees to improvise;
- give tasks to teachers in which they learn to use simple mechanical tools;
- show enthusiasm in using local materials to help to develop a positive attitude among trainees towards use of local materials;
- make use of audio-visual materials and train teachers in the use and maintenance of materials available in schools.

2.3.3 Working Environment

Another important consideration is the environment in which teaching and learning will take place. Teachers may work in remote rural areas, in hilly areas, in schools with large classes, in single-teacher schools and in schools without enough classrooms and storage space for science equipment. The training must take into account the prevailing conditions and the implications for teaching and learning.

The motivation of teachers depends to a large extent on their working environment. A teacher working in an urban school may have lots of material resources but may face the problem of overcrowded classes. On the other hand, a teacher in a rural school may have fewer students to a class but be the only teacher in the school, and have to teach all grades.

Many teacher training institutions are insensitive to the range of environments in which teachers work. Training tends to be geared to an 'ideal' school environment. As a result, many teachers do not find the training very helpful. Science and technology teacher educators should therefore:

- Familiarize themselves with the variety of school situations in which teachers will work after their training.
- Discuss and demonstrate a variety of teaching methods which can be employed in different situations. Trainees then need to practice these methods in real school situations. They need to learn classroom management techniques, involving management of the curriculum, human and material resources in different working environments. Some management strategies which have been found useful in dealing with large classes and multi-grade situations are:
- the use of class monitors;
- senior students supervising the work of juniors;
- group work;
- use of printed learning materials such as work cards and supplementary readers;
- the activity method.

2.3.4 Curriculum

The nature of the science and technology curriculum and the associated philosophy of teaching is another important area to be considered in planning a teacher training programme. While one curriculum may emphasize science content, others may encourage problem-solving and thinking on the part of learners or lead to a recitation of facts from textbooks.

The pre-service training of science and technology teachers cannot be limited to the curriculum currently being followed in a country or a state. Pre-service training has to be much broader and must consider a variety of methods which could be employed in science and technology teaching. The teacher educators must develop the following skills and competencies amongst the trainees:

- Relating methods, materials and teaching aids to the defined objectives. An activity approach may be too time-consuming if the objective is to pass on knowledge. Similarly, if the objective is to teach science processes, the lecture method is inappropriate.
- Asking questions which can be answered by using the materials at hand.
- Integrating subject matter and skills into a teaching-learning strategy.
- Use of process skills and understanding how they may be developed in children.
- Building on children's existing ideas and thought processes to develop scientific ideas and ways of thinking.
- Being aware of, and using scientific knowledge to correct, the many false beliefs and superstitions which children often bring with them to class.
- Relating science and technology to agriculture, health, industry, nutrition and other aspects of real life.
- Using real-life learning experiences from the local environment to develop scientific ideas.
- Using lock technologies to build scientific ideas and skills.
- Developing formative and summative evaluation skills.

The trainees need to be introduced to the large number of methods and techniques which can be used to achieve teaching goals. Science and technology teacher educators must explain that a particular method may be suitable for one teacher in a particular situation but not in another, and provide opportunities for the trainees to practise these methods and techniques during their training.

2.3.5 *Language*

Language presents a particular problem in science teaching. In many countries science is taught in English in spite of the fact that it is not the first or even the second language of the students, while many other objects, such as social studies and moral science, are taught in the local language. Even in countries where science is taught in the local language, there are sometimes no local words for particular scientific ideas and terms. This problem needs to be considered during the training of teachers.

A Namibian primary school head teacher, who is also a science teacher, recently said: "*My biggest problem with science teaching is the language. We have the policy of teaching science in English. Children do not have a good command over the English language because it is not even the local language, let alone the mother tongue. Most of my time in science class is spent in teaching English*'. He added that the situation is worse with teachers who themselves do not have a good command over English language.

In countries where this is a real problem, science and technology teacher educators should advise teachers to explain scientific ideas in the local language or the language most familiar to students. Teachers should be trained to speak slowly in simple sentences, to use a variety of ways of communicating ideas, such as graphs, drawings and modelling, and to wait longer for students to respond to their questions. This requires patience and practice.

2.4 Teaching Practice for Retraining and Updating

2.4.1 *Need for INSET in Science and Technology*

Many practising teachers with responsibilities for science and technology do not have recognized science and technology qualifications or experience. They require some form of in-service support and assistance if they are to be held accountable for the quality of science and technology education in their classrooms. Other teachers have thought aspects of science and technology is isolated subjects or have only been exposed to outdated methods of teaching it. They will not be able to make the links and appreciate the connections between science and technology components. Thus the In-Service Education and Training (INSET) programmes in science and technology are organized for:

- meeting the subject-matter deficiencies of teachers;
- introducing active-learning approaches;
- helping the teachers gain qualifications;
- implementing a new curriculum which requires additional skills related to methodology, classroom management and assessment;
- the professional advancement of teachers.

2.4.2 INSET Strategies

Direct experience of teaching practice should be the focus of teacher development programmes. Practical experience of formulating tasks, accessing and mastering content, planning, preparing and then testing out science and technology teaching approaches in realistic settings is the only sure means to ensure that teachers will develop the confidence to adopt, adapt, implement and appraise new ideas or approaches. It is essential that science and technology teacher educators responsible for INSET provision are sensitive to and committed to such experience/practice-led approaches.

The approach suggested here is that during the pre-service and in-service training, teachers experience the kind of science and technology teaching which they will be expected to practise themselves in schools. This implies that teacher educators must create situations in which teachers experience at their own level problems which they have to investigate. Teacher educators should respond to the questions of teachers as though they were teachers responding to the questions of pupils in schools, and help them solve problems in a similar way. This approach should enable teachers to achieve a better understanding of the joys and frustrations of children in the classroom.

Having experienced problem-solving at their own level, teachers should then be helped to formulate curriculum-based questions and problems for the students to try out with children in schools. It is essential that science and technology teacher educators responsible for INSET are committed to this two-tier empirical approach.

INSET programmes should respond to the 'felt needs' of teachers regarding their specific roles and responsibilities. It is therefore important for teacher educators to appraise the needs of teachers through discussion. Analysis of a new curriculum to find out the skills and competencies required to implement it may be useful. If teachers request help with a specific area of content, then this should be given in a practical way. The content falls into place for the teacher and is clarified when they carefully think through how in can be taught. It is important for the science and technology teacher educators to realize that one of the aspects of training where teachers need most help is in the skill of translating content into teaching/learning activities. This is achieved during teaching practice, and, if properly supervised by teacher educators, can avoid many of the problems of inappropriate science and technology teaching. INSET programmes are more productive when they focus on a practical approach that draws on theory and academic content.

In an INSET course teachers often expect teacher educators to do more than simply tell them what is required of them. They actually want to see how to do things. This may be achieved by means of a demonstration lesson or a video lesson. In either case, it should be followed up by practice session in real classroom settings, with feedback from the teacher educator.

One of the problems which teachers face is the lack of in-service support after initial training. Without encouragement and assistance when new approaches are being introduced, change is unlikely to be sustained. For this to happen, headteachers, school inspectors, education officers and subject specialists all need to be included in training programmes, and their skills in classroom observation and providing feedback based on this observation also need to be enhanced.

Example of a pattern of INSET workshops—a South African NGO

> At Primary Science Programme (PSP) Western Cape INSET workshops, we try to provide cultural sensitive and contextually responsive support and encouragement in an interactive and

practical way. Teachers identify topics of concern at a mass planning meeting at the beginning of any year. Rotating panels of teachers participate in the specific planning of each cycle of workshops on a topic. Some teachers with special interests or abilities are invited to join in the presentation of the workshops.

In the workshops we review science content and draw together related background knowledge (usually based on a mind-mapping process). Collectively, we consider a range of different potential methodologies and approaches, with an emphasis on teaching science in a practical and relevant way. We try to ensure that the ideas co-developed in the workshops are tested in the reality of a classroom setting with as many as 60 or 70 pupils. Then we spend time collectively reflecting on the apparent outcomes that we observe. At the end of a cycle of workshops a booklet is produced that accurately documents the workshop process and these support materials are distributed to the workshop participants.

The content and ideas in a workshop report are not seen as final. Rather they are a record of a developing process which can always be improved upon, and often is, in that teachers tend to request a repetition of topics over a period of a year. Revisiting and refining topics is now seen to be a critical element of ongoing support.

2.5 Methods of Teaching

2.5.1 Whole-class Teaching

Whole-class teaching in a large class can be a stimulating and entertaining learning method, if it is carried out in an interesting manner by a teacher with good verbal and presentation skills. However, overuse with little feedback from students should be discouraged. Students lose concentration quickly, and a lesson should rarely be taught to be whole class for more than 30 minutes and even less for younger or less able students. Teacher educators should appreciate this and not often resort to whole-class teaching with their trainees.

Short spells of whole-class teaching may be useful for conveying instructions, for introducing a lesson, for passing on simple content and for summarising.

Whole-class teaching can be made interesting by introducing demonstrations. The teacher educator should explain that demonstrations can be used for a variety of purposes, such as illustrating process skills, safety procedures and sequencing, or reinforcing a concept that has been taught. Whenever demonstrations are used, teacher educators should encourage students to be involved in using the equipment, thereby ensuring better interactive learning. The teacher educator should also discuss where the teacher should stand during demonstrations, especially if they involve the use of apparatus. It may seem logical for the teacher to stand behind the apparatus and the students in front, but this can present the teacher with problems. For example:

- the apparatus is back to front for the teacher, with stands, clamps, etc., on the teacher's side, making handling more difficult;
- meters and other instruments that need to be read will be pointing towards the students.

Whilst the trainee teachers are likely to be quick to point out disadvantages associated with the teacher standing on the same side of the demonstration as the students, the teacher educator should discuss possible advantages of this method. The teacher can:

- see the apparatus from the same viewpoint as the students, who are at a distance from the demonstration, allowing a better overall view;
- move around easily;
- hold up part of the demonstration, or take it nearer to the students if they need a close-up view;
- have the same view as the class when guiding students in assisting with the demonstration.

Demonstrations can be very effective methods of learning, especially if participants are helped to focus on exactly what should be observed.

2.5.2 Problem-solving Approach

In the problem-solving inquiry method, teachers facilitate learning rather than teaching directly, through:

- indentifying phenomena and selecting materials that are rich in learning possibilities, and motivate students to pursue their own investigations;
- capitalising on students' curiosity;
- providing suitable materials that pose problems;
- asking challenging questions;
- using good judgement about when to interact with students and when or when not to hold whole-class discussion (not all students may have sufficient experience of the phenomena to contribute).

Use of the problem-solving inquiry method requires a good mastery of the subject matter by the teacher, who should at the same time be open to problems as they arise and be willing to learning long with the students. Much time needs to be spent after such activities on reviewing and evaluation the students' experiences in terms of the knowledge, process skills, attitudes and values acquired. Problem-solving inquiry methods of teaching should be given priority in science and technology education, even though they may be difficult to introduce with large classes. In such situations, classes can be broken up into groups and practical work arranged in the form of a 'circus' for the groups to move around. The groups can also be assigned investigative project work. Parents or assistant teachers could prove very helpful in supervising these groups.

An example of the problem-solving inquiry approach

Project to determine the best buy of fruit drink in terms of citric acid content

Basic information for students: All fruit drinks contain citric acid.

Whole-class session: Students brainstorm different ways to determine the citric acid content in fruit drinks.

Agree method: Titration with a base, e.g. NaOH solution.

Practical work: Students find out for themselves.

Pupils are given a problem to solve which is related to their own experience. For example, if you have to buy a piece of cloth to mop the kitchen tables which of the three given samples would you choose? Initially, all groups can do the same problem.

Later, different groups can be involved in different problems at the same time, with parents or assistant teachers monitoring the groups.

It is important in the problem-solving inquiry approach that the teacher educator provides a situation where the learners are made to think, plan, execute using science processes and draw conclusions. Teacher trainees should be given many problems to solve at their own level, so that they come to appreciate fully the value of this approach. They should be helped to identify lots of problems which they can use with children.

2.5.3 Other Valuable Techniques

Many scientific ideas can be introduced with the help of games, toys, stories and models. Their appeal to children should be fully, but not excessively, exploited. For example, the game of push and pull can be used to introduce ideas related to force: which is easier to push or pull, the greater or smaller force? Similarly, children could be given different boxes with one object in each and asked to predict what the objects are and what they are made of. An element of competition can also be introduced, but games must be simple and safe. There must be rulers to be followed, with penalties for breaking them, and a clear learning objective for each game.

Toys are not teaching methods but are an invaluable resource to help develop scientific ideas. A simple bow and arrow can be used to develop ideas of elasticity, force, action and reaction, etc. Teachers should be encouraged to ask children to bring own toys to school for possible use in learning situations.

Children like listening to stories: they stimulate interest and will often hold their attention. Stories should be short and have relevant content which provides the focus of the lesson.

Models are specially useful in science and technology science they put concepts which may be difficult for children to grasp into concrete form. They can also be used to demonstrate various working principles in a practical way.

2.6 Micro-teaching to Develop Teaching Skills

Micro-teaching provides the opportunity for student teachers to practise specific teaching skills that they will need to become effective classroom teachers. It has the following characteristics:

- **Nature.** Micro-teaching is a teaching method in which the normal complexities of the classroom are reduced to that the teacher of can practise the teaching of one specific skill at a time until it has been mastered. A number of separate experiences or skills are identified, isolated and practised.
- **Skill development.** Micro-teaching can be designed to help student teachers develop skills in areas such as: introducing a lesson, using questions, providing reinforcement, use of instructional materials, explaining concepts, giving directions, varying stimuli, class control and lesson closure.
- **Duration.** Each micro-teaching session should be between 5 and 10 minutes per student depending on the number of student teachers.

2.7 Classroom Management

Instruction in classroom management in science and technology teaching should be about the effective and efficient utilization of both the curriculum and the available human and material resources. This entials planning, organising, co-ordinating, delegating, monitoring and controlling the teaching/ learning situation.

A considerable amount of time should be spend by the science and technology teacher educator on planning classroom activities (schemes of work, lesson plans and so on). Relevant resources should be organized for putting these plans into practice. For example, the apparatus or materials to be used need to be assembled, enough seating accommodations needs to be provided for all the groups, and decision made on how groups are to be formed and who will be the group leaders. This should be practised in different working environments.

Close monitoring and control of the teaching/learning situation is essential. It is important for the science and technology teacher educator to move about the groups to ensure that everyone participates and to help resolve any problems which may arise. Delegation could include identifying group leaders/monitors (in schools this might include parents or assistant teachers) to supervise the work of the groups.

A strategy to overcome the burden of big classes was implemented by an innovative mathematics teacher in a Zimbabwean school

The teacher realized that pupils who experienced difficulty in mathematics were in need of individual help. Science it was not possible for the teacher to provide individual attention for all these children, the teacher appointed 10 pupils, who scored the highest marks in maths, as 'tutors'. The rest of the class was then evenly divided into 10 groups of more or less equal ability. The groups of pupils sat in circles with their tutors. The teacher introduced a topic and the pupils carried out problem-solving exercises. The tutors helped members of their groups with any difficulties.

This proved to be very effective:

- pupils in smaller groups were more inclined to ask questions, mention their problems, etc.;
- pupils who experienced difficulties with maths benefited from individual attention;
- tutors were themselves stimulated and enriched;
- the teacher's burden was lightened;
- the tutors eventually competed with each other, comparing 'their' groups' performances.

An approach well worth exploring.

Many teachers are unable to use active learning techniques because they lack classroom management skills. Science and technology teacher educators should therefore ensure that they provide enough opportunities for their trainees to practise these skills. Time needs to be spent on reviewing and evaluating the trainees' experiences to ensure that they have acquired the necessary classroom management skills, in different working environments.

2.8 Supervision of Teaching Practice in Science and Technology

2.8.1 Aims of Supervision

Supervision of student teaching practice by science and technology teacher educators has two broad aims:

- To assess and evaluate the level at which the student teachers are able to apply science and technology teaching methods and procedures. In this context, supervision of teaching practice is an evaluative process.
- To provide both the teacher educators and the student teachers (pre-service and in-service) with opportunity to evaluate and reflect upon class teaching procedures and practice, to maximize learning in the situations prevailing in particular schools.

The supervisor and the student teacher should work out appropriate supervisory strategies for alternative procedures in the classroom. Thus, the supervision of student teaching practice becomes a reflective experiences for both teacher educators and student teachers. It becomes and information-gathering process (a research process, if you like) which enhances and promotes growth in the competencies of all the participants.

2.8.2 Different Strategies or Models for Supervision

Reflective Collaborative Supervision

This model emphasizes close, reflective growth between supervisor and the student teacher, and involves four stages of development:

- **Pre-observation conferences.** The supervisor and the student meet before the beginning of the lesson, to discuss the objectives of the lesson and other aspects of teaching procedures to be followed. The student teacher describes his/her proposed classroom procedures and the supervisor gives his/her reaction to them until agreement is reached. The supervisor's observations are not predetermined but are based on the student teacher's suggested procedures.

- **Observation and teaching.** The supervisor observes the student teacher in action, following the agreed-upon teaching procedures, and records his/her observations with comments for further discussion during the post-observation conference.
- **Post-observation conferencing.** The teacher educator and the student exchange views on the observations, feelings, strengths and weaknesses of the procedures followed during the lesson. They then agree on alternative strategies/procedures.

  The guiding principle in this phase is reflective evaluation of both the classroom procedures of the student teacher and the supervisory practice of the supervisor. For this purpose the supervisor needs to be accurate in recording his/her observations, highlighting only those procedures dealing with specific science and technology content and their methodological treatment as agreed upon during the pre-observation conference phase. A suitable pro-forma may be developed to record the observations.
- **Establishing alternative classroom procedures.** The supervisor and the student teacher draw up alternative classroom procedures as agreed upon during the post-observation conference. These are not prescriptions of 'good' procedures from the supervisor, but alternatives which should be tried out by the practising student teacher for subsequent observation. While these alternatives may be entirely new, they may have been tried out in different contexts elsewhere. In this instance, the student teacher and the supervisor would be adding the 'new' alternatives to their repertoire of science and technology teaching procedures for reflective evaluation in subsequent lessons.

This method of supervision gets the student teachers into the habit of seeking out new teaching procedures and promotes in supervisors the desire for reflective supervisory practices.

Possible Constraints of the Reflective Collaborative Supervision Model

One inherent constraint of reflective collaborative supervision of student teaching is time. While the approach may work effectively in on-campus teaching practice settings, time constraints could prevent teacher educators from using this model in its entirety when teaching practice takes place in schools remote from teacher training institutions.

Instead, the following strategies could be tried:

- use of co-operating teachers us supervisors in the teaching practice schools (apprenticeship model);
- peer supervision;
- involvement of headteachers, education officers or subject specialists.

Using Co-operating Teacher Supervisors (The Apprenticeship Model)

In this model, the teacher whose classes the student teacher takes over becomes the co-operating teacher supervisor, with the student teacher becoming his or her 'understudy'. The co-operating teacher sits in on all the lessons taught by the student teacher, following the procedure set out above for reflective collaborative consultation. The teacher educator supervises the student teacher on only a few occasions.

Practising teachers have to undergo a short period of training before they are certified as co-operating teacher supervisors. This system of supervision makes the schools partners in the initial training of the teachers and therefore makes them feel responsible for training the kind of science and technology teachers they would like to employ in their schools.

In order for this system to work the teachers' interest and enthusiasm in co-operating with the teacher educators must be sustained. This could be done by providing incentives for the co-operating teachers, such as:

- certificates as tokens of appreciation which could be considered for promotion purposes, earning exemptions for enrolling in teacher education programmes, etc.;
- recognition as teacher leaders in the running of INSET workshops, seminars, etc.;
- participation in the assessment and evaluation of science and technology education programmes;
- recognition as 'resource persons', visiting lecturers, etc.

Peer Supervision

In peer supervision, with the agreement of the student teacher, his or her peers sit in during the lesson. If four or five student peers comment on and discuss the lesson presented, the learning process would be in line with the latest views on the 'socio-constructivist' learning approach. A variation on this is 'buddy-teaching', also used in teaching practice, when two students are coupled for a period of time over the three week practice teaching period. While one presents the lessons the other supervises, and vice versa.

3

Resources for Science and Technology Teaching and Teacher Training

3.1 Overview

A wide range of resources is available that science and technology teacher educators can use and introduce to their trainees to assist with the teaching and learning process. These include conventional things like tools, equipments and consumable supplies, printed materials and human resources. They also include locally available materials and technologies, thus linking what is being learnt in school with everyday life, and bringing relevance to the teaching of science and technology.

The science and technology teacher educator has two main responsibilities with regard to resource materials:

- to identify the resources needed for science and technology in the teacher education programme;
- to be fully conversant with the human and material resources which schools can utilize and the skills required by teachers to develop and use them effectively.

It is also important that the science and technology teacher educators use resources during training that are similar to those available in the schools or environments where their students are or will be teaching.

3.2 Objectives

The objectives of this monograph are:

- to identify resources that science and technology teacher educators might use;
- to outline strategies for making use of resources, especially those locally available, for teaching science and technology;
- to discuss issues relating to the use of resources in science and technology education.

3.3 General Considerations in Identification, Selection and Use of Resources

Several factors must be considered when deciding what resources will be needed for teacher training. Decisions are guided by answers to questions such as:

- What investigations are anticipated?
- How will students be grouped?
- What resources may be needed to investigate problems and questions raised by student teachers?

The following are general criteria for the identification, selection and evaluation or resources:

- **Appropriateness.** Are the resources appropriate to the age group, to the teaching objectives, and in their subject content? Are printed materials at the appropriate reading and comprehension level?
- **Accuracy.** Is the content of the material accurate? Are there errors, biases, including gender biases, unwarranted conclusions?
- **Cost.** Does the outcome of use justify the cost in terms of money, time and effort?
- **Demand.** Does the material engage the thinking skills of learners? Does it demand creativity, problem-solving and a high degree of participation on the part of the student? Will the resource hold students' attention for a reasonable amount of time?

- **Comprehensiveness.** Does the material explore concepts etc. in enough depth and breadth? Does it allow learners to organize information as well as gather information? Do textbooks contain questions, advance organizers, illustrations, summaries, glossaries?
- **Relevance.** Are the contents appropriate to the students' needs, interests and abilities?
- **Validity.** Will the resource bring about the learning outcomes hoped for? What evidence is there of this?
- **Usability.** Can the resource be used by students and science educators? Is equipment simple to use and reliable? Is it flexible?
- **Variety.** Does the resource provide experiences which are not otherwise possible?

3.4 Manufactured Materials

These consist of equipment and chemicals, needed specifically for teaching science and technology education, and general hardware items used in the teaching of all subjects. A list of useful manufactured resource materials for science and technology is given as Table 1.

Table 1: Useful manufactured items for science and technology education

Magnifying lens	Potassium permanganate
Measuring cylinder	Formalin
Clinical thermometer	Alcohol
Laboratory thermometer	Ammonia
Torch cell	Dilute acids
Insulated wire	Chisel
Fuse	Steel plane
Electric switch	Hammer
Ball bearing	Pliers
Pulley	Clamp
Standard weights	Calliper

Spring balance	Screw driver
Plastic tubing	Hand drill and bits
Meter rule	Assorted tiles
Funnel (plastic)	Spanner
Bar magnet	Wire cutter
Banking soda	Tin cutter
Iodine	Iron saw

Teacher educators should be familiar with materials in manufacturers' catalogues and their availability for use in schools. They should liaise closely with the Ministry of Department of Education in selecting 'good' resource materials to ensure that a common message is being given to teachers and pre-service trainees. In many countries, science kits are being supplied to schools. Teacher educators need to be aware of the contents of such kits and able to demonstrate their use to teachers and trainees.

Teacher educators need to be sensitive to the fact that resources they have in their training institution may not be available in schools. For example, teacher training colleges may have overhead projectors, whereas schools may not. While teacher educators may wish to use such resources for teaching students, they should not train the student teachers in their use unless they are available in the schools.

3.4.1 Procurement of Materials

Policies for procuring manufactured resources for schools vary, and science and technology teacher educators need to liaise with schools about administrative aspects. They need to be fully aware of the existing policies and to ensure that their students understand the procedures to be followed. Such procedures might include:

- award of contract or tender by the institution or a central tender board;
- order against a budget, where schools are provided with a budget for this purpose;
- order from a resource centre—as in Nigeria.

3.4.2 Storage and Maintenance

It is also important for science and technology teacher educators to teach their trainees about the proper storage and maintenance of manufactured resources. Many primary schools do not have science laboratories. The teacher educators need to look out for examples of good practice with regard to storage in schools, and discuss these with the trainees. For schools without laboratories, materials should be stored as close to the user as possible so that the chances of their being used are increased. Also, if materials are stored in glass-fronted coupboards students may see them and want to use them, thus reducing the possibility of teachers forgetting to use them.

Manufactured materials must be properly maintained to ensure their efficient operation and long-term use. Science and technology teacher educators should learn how to maintain every manufactured item used in schools and pass on this knowledge to their trainees. Poor maintenance of science equipment is a serious problem in many countries, and science and technology teacher educators have a big responsibility to correct this situation by providing proper training in maintenance to teachers.

3.4.3 Safety

Teaching about the proper and safe use of manufactured resources is another responsibility of the science and technology teacher educator. Teachers need to be shown how to use equipment so that they do not damage the equipment or injure themselves. Teacher trainers also need to ensure that their trainees are fully aware of possible dangers from chemicals they may use.

3.4.4 Equipment Pools and Lending Systems

Many schools do not have the manufactured science equipment they need because of lack of funds. To overcome this problem, alternative means of supporting schools have been developed. In some countries schools are grouped into 'clusters', which share human and material resources. Other countries have established 'science centres' or 'teachers' resource centres' at the district or sub-district level, which store equipment and make it available to schools on request. For such a system to be effective, procedures need to be in place for the quick supply of equipment to schools or for the teachers to be able to come to the centre to collect the equipment.

3.5 Locally Available Materials and Technologies

3.5.1 Local Materials

The use of locally available materials should not be viewed as a poor alternative to using manufactured 'bought-in' science equipment. It makes teaching more relevant to students by relating it to their real everyday lives.

Locally available materials are those available either free or cheaply from the immediate environment. They include: wood, clay, iron filings from the blacksmith, pith, soil, grains, plants, empty bottles and bottletops, comb, wax, nails, sawdust, coal, common salt and limestone and locally produced manufactured items such as magnets, balloons, paper clips, plastic bowls and candles. Many of the items generally available in children's homes, such as bulbs, knives, clothes pegs, razor blades, pieces of fabric, are also valuable resources.

Teacher educators should be aware of different kinds of locally available materials and their various uses in science and technology education. They should ask the trainees to collect such items and in turn advise the trainees to ask children to collect. However, enthusiastic children may collect too many things, so teachers should be advised not to ask every child to bring the same thinks. Asking children to volunteer to bring different items, will improve their motivation and interest in learning about things in their environment.

Teacher educators should mount exhibitions of locally available materials used in their institution for the training of science and technology teachers and encourage teacher trainees to mount similar exhibitions in their schools. Sessions should be set aside for per-service teachers to gain practice in adapting locally available materials for teaching situations and illustrating their use in making teaching more meaningful.

3.5.2 Local technologies

Local technologies are as important a resource as locally available materials. Young learners bring with them to school, experiences of science and technology which they have observed within their homes and the wider community. Science and technology teacher educators should use these experiences during training and help their trainees to utilize similar experiences. It should be emphasized to them that local technologies have the potential to make learning more relevant and meaningful for the children by linking their real-life experiences with what they learn in school. The use of community resources for teaching science and technology also provides an excellent opportunity of introducing students to social concerns which need to be addressed. Such interaction can allow students to gain useful insight into the purposes served by technology, how technologies influence individual people's lives as well as their interaction with each other and with their environment. Moreover, parents also start taking interest in the education of their children as they feel children are learning useful things. The following panels given some examples of local technologies with relevance to science and technology education.

Production of 'Akpeteshie', a local gin in Ghana

Palam wine, a sugary sap tapped from the palm three, is allowed to undergo fermentation by being left to stand in metals drums for at least three days. During these three days, the sugar in the plam wine is converted to alcohol by the action of yeast that is present in the plan wine as a result of its being exposed to the air.

The drum containing the plam win is connected from the top by means of small-diameter metal tubing which either passes through another drum filled with water or passes through a pond or slow moving stream to a smaller metal or glass receptacle.

When heat is applied to the drum containing the plam wine, the alcohol evaporates, passes through the tube, and is condensed by the cooling effect of the water in the pond, stream or drum and collects in the receptacle.

The 'strength' of the resulting alcohol is tested by applying a lighted matchstick to a small portion of the product. If the alcohol is 'strong' it inflames; if it is 'weak' it does not.

Repelling Mosquitoes

In Swaziland a plant called 'unsutane' is used by some communities to repel mosquitoes. The insects are repelled by its scent. It is rubbed on the body or the leaves placed in strategic parts of the huts overnight.

Jelly pan 'photocopies'

This technique was extensively used when photocopy machines were not available, and is still being used in rural schools in South Africa. It works very well for drawings, graphs, sketches and printing large-letters.

You need:

500 ml glycerine

75 ml gelatine

450 ml water

80 g sugar

2 flat baking trays (about the size of A4 paper)

1 sheet of spirit carbon paper

The spirit carbon paper is not ordinary carbon paper, and must therefore be ordered by your institution from an office supplies dealer. The advantage of using it, however, is that with this method, a school can produce hundreds of copies with a single sheet of spirit carbon paper.

Method

1. Presentation of jelly pan

Dissolve gelatine in a tin of hot water. Add sugar. Boil the mixture. Add glycerine. Now boil mixture gently for another 15 minutes.

Stir continuously with a bread-knife or flat spatula. The mixture should have no bubbles and must be dissolved properly. Pour gently into the two baking trays, spreading it evenly.

Smooth any little bubbles to the sides. Leave for 24 hours. Now your jelly pan is ready to be used.

2. Making a master copy

Arrange the paper from which you want to copy, the carbon paper and the paper on which you want to make the master copy as follows:

Top: Paper with design, drawing, graph etc. (face up)

Middle: Spirit carbon paper (can be used to make hundreds of master copies), carbon side (face down) on the white paper

Bottom: Clean white paper (will be the master copy: can be used to make imprints on a number of jelly pans)

Take a drawing or big letters which you want to copy. Arrange the plain paper, the carbon paper and your drawing on a hard surface such as a table. Make sure the face of the carbon is on the clean white paper. Now trace the boundary of the drawing or each letter so that it leaves an imprint on the white paper.

Now take the white sheet with the imprint on it and place it on to the jelly so that the imprint side of the paper faces the jelly. Press the paper gently over the jelly. You will find the imprint on the jelly. Now use this jelly plan as a master. Place paper sheets over it and press gently by hand to obtain hundreds of copies.

3. Making copies in pupils' exercise books

It is not necessary to tear a page out of a pupil's exercise book. Simply, put a clean page face down on to the jelly pan, smooth over the page, and drawing is in the pupil's pool! You will be able to make more than a hundred copies with one tray before it goes 'dull'. You can use the same jelly once again, just cook it for a while and repeat the process.

A method that is well worth trying out!

In many schools in South Africa mathematics is taught in an interesting way using a calendar

Choose any month and play a game of numbers and addition as follows:

M	T	W	T	F	S	S
1						
2	3	4	5	6	7	8
9	10	11	12	13	14	15
16	17	18	19	20	21	22
23	24	25	26	27	28	29
30	31					

Select any two consecutive dates and add diagonally across from each as follows:

Suppose we select 2 and 3. The number diagonally across from 2 is 10; 2 + 10 = 12. The second number is 3 and the number diagonally across is 9; 3 + 19 = 12. The sum is the same. Try this with any other two numbers. What is your conclusion?

1. 2 + 10 = 12

9 + 3 = 12

2. In the same way, add three numbers diagonally across:

3 + 11 + 19 = 33

17 + 11 + 5 = 33

The sum is always the same. Try with any other three numbers diagonally across.

3. Add numbers making up a 'Z' shape:

e.g. 5 + 6 + 7 + 13 + 19 + 20 + 21 = 91

You have added seven numbers. The middle number is 13. The multiplication of these two numbers (7 and 13) will give 91. Do more of these with this month or any other month.

4. Choose a rectangle of nine numbers and add them together:

e.g. 6 + 7 + 8 + 13 + 14 + 15 + 20 + 21 + 22 = 126

The total is 9 times (the total of numbers added) the middle number (14).

Hint: Always check your middle term and compare it with your answer. Is there a quicker way to get to the answer?

Simple technologies are used in water filtration

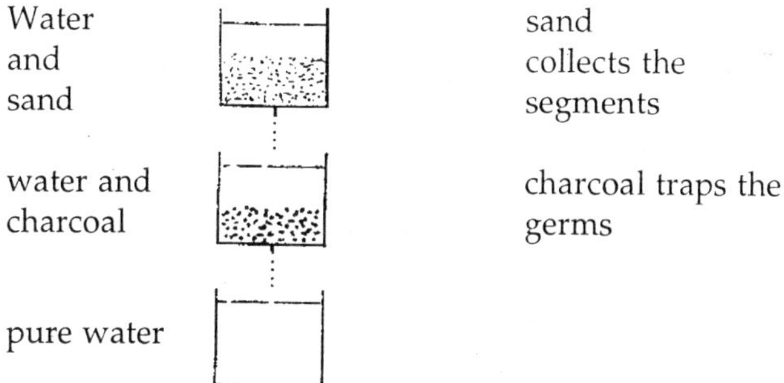

Making clay pots

In Malawi, village potters have been making clay pots for many years. They have learned to choose suitable soils and oils, and to control the drying and banking processes to reduce cracking.

Despite the acquisition of technological skills, one elderly woman potter still attributed her successes to a superstition:

'Since I started using my granddaughter to light the fire', she said, 'no pot has broken'.

She was referring to the backing of the pots she made. Perhaps the reason why the pots never cracked during baking was due to her mastery of the technology of pot-making.

3.5.3 Other Local Resources

Teacher educators also need to be aware of, and to encourage teachers to use, other local out-of-school resources. This might include:

- Visits to different construction sites to study the methods, materials and tools used. Children must be encouraged to put 'why?' and 'what?' types of questions to the people doing different jobs.
- visits to a furniture-making factory or a carpenter's workshop to study measurement tools, materials and techniques used for joints, techniques used to strengthen furniture, different shapes and their relationship to strength and design of the furniture.

- A local blacksmith or potter's workshop are also useful resources for learning about tools, skills and techniques.
- In the local market place children may observe and learn about different types of foods and the popular food choices, transportation used, how different items are measured and sold, methods of preserving food, materials used to pack food, hygiene and sanitation aspects of food, etc.
- Visits to a local hospital, health centre, doctor, restaurant, garden, plant shop, railway station, etc., can be very rewarding as a means of linking real-life experiences with school science and technology.

All of these will help to integrate what the children learn in school with real life in the communities.

3.6 Improvization of Scientific Equipment

Improvization is an important aspect of science and technology education. It involves scientific processes such as problem solving, planning, decision making, designing and evaluating, which are all important for living in the modern world. Improvization not only helps to overcome the shortage of equipment, but, equally importantly, it helps to develop teachers' scientific process skills, technological skills and a positive attitude towards improvization and science and technology. Many of the 'bought-in' manufactured items used in science and technology education could be improvized from locally available materials. Books are available which give guidance on preparing improvised materials.

Some examples of items which can be improvized include:

- balances;
- measuring cylinders from discarded feeding bottles;
- measuring cylinders on air pressure pumps from discarded syringes;
- corks from bamboo pith/raffia palm;
- gum from mixing discarded stayrofoam packing material and petrol;

- concave and convex mirrors from bottoms of tins;
- indicator dye from leaf extracts;
- rulers from graduated sticks;
- acid from the juice of unripe fruit;
- formalin (perspective) from the local gin;
- funnels from the top parts of discarded plastic bottles;
- weather instruments—wind vanes and water gauges.

Science and technology teacher educators may suggest over items which could be improvized and are suitable for particular situations. They should encourage teachers to put forward their own lists of items which could be improvized, and, more importantly, demonstrate the use of improvized materials during the normal teaching situation. The teacher trainees should actually produce a few improvized items during their training.

As well as learning how to improvize, pre-service teachers should consider who might be able to help, for instance fellow teachers, local artisans or craftsmen, and the pupils themselves. Improvization by pupils can present a valuable learning experience if handled appropriately. Science and technology educators should advise teacher trainees on how they might go about creating a learning situation that involves pupils in improvizing materials. A common approach is through problem-solving exercise or projects.

3.6.1 How to go About Improvization

An important aspect of improvization is having the initial idea: some have been listed above. Teachers will need advice on the procedures to be followed for improvization. A suggested procedure might be:

- examine lesson contents and specific objectives;
- identify the need for use of equipment/materials;
- write procedures for assembling improvized materials;
- assemble materials;
- try improvized materials out before final use.

Improvization ideas should be disseminated in magazines or newsletters, such as the newsletter of a local science teachers' association.

3.6.2 Basic Equipment Required for Improvization

Improvizing materials will sometimes require use of tools. Training insititutions should have simple mechanical tools such as wooden compasses, callipers, tape measure, screw driver, punch, wood saw, metal saw, pliers, chisel, steel plane, hammer, hand drill, clamping and holding tools, spanners etc. Science and technology teacher educators should be conversant with the use of these tools and be able to guide trainees in handling them in a safe and purposeful manner. Provision should be made in pre-service and in-service training courses for teachers to handle many of these tools.

3.6.3. Attitude to improvization

Many teacher educators and teachers do not have a positive attitude towards improvization. They regard improvization as an activity forced upon them by shortage of funds, and considered improvized items as inferior. It is important for them to appreciate the positive advantages of improvization and the common disadvantages of bought-in manufactured materials:

- Many manufactured items or kits are supplied to schools without funds or a policy for replacement. They get looked into the stores or head teachers' office for fear that, if the items get destroyed or broken, either the teacher will have a pay or they may not be replaced for a long time.
- There are educational advantages in using familiar materials which can stimulate investigations and can be replaced fairly quickly and cheaply.
- Improvized materials can be available in larger quantities, possibly for handling by each student, which may not be possible with sophisticated and costly manufactured items.
- Improvization leads to development of problem-solving skills amongst teacher educators and teachers which may be passed on to students.

3.7 Resources Centres

Teachers' resource centres have been found to be very useful in some countries in promoting the development and use of locally available materials. At these centres, teachers and teacher educators meet frequently to share and develop teaching and learning materials using locally available materials. These centres can be established in such a way that 25–30 teachers work together for a whole day once in every month or two. Such a centre could be located in one school for a year or two and then perhaps rooted amongst the other participating schools. This requires some initial funding by Ministries of Education or non-governmental organizations for buying consumable and non-consumable materials.

Such resource centres, if they are to serve the purpose, must be established within easy reach of the teachers whom they serve. Science and technology teacher educators and teachers should be able to go to the resource centres to work in groups to develop teaching and learning resources, share resources, and discuss problems and successes experienced in promoting science and technology education. These centres can also display examples of good improvized materials and other work.

Since teachers may not have time during regular school hours to improvize materials, the teachers' resource centres may provide an appropriate forum where teachers can pool their efforts and skills to generate improvized materials. Every time teachers meet at these centres were should be time earmarked for improvization.

Science and technology teacher educators must develop skills amongst teachers to use the resources efficiently. School timetables may have to be arranged in such a way that there is no competition for materials. For example, in a school with science teachers the timetable could be arranged in such a way that not more than one or two science classes take place at the same time.

4

Evaluation in Science and Technology Education

4.1 Overview

Evaluation is an integral part of the teaching-learning process. Through systematic evaluation procedures science and technology teacher educators can measure the progress of pre-service and in-service teacher trainees in attaining the objectives of teaching programmes. Evaluation also enables teacher educators to measure the effectiveness of their own teaching strategies and methods. Similarly, trainee teachers need to develop skills and competence in evaluation techniques which they can then apply in their own teaching in schools. Evaluation results can also play a part in an accountability system for ensuring that institutions, teacher educators and teachers deliver good quality science and technology education.

It is important that the objectives of a lesson or course should be clear, so that science and technology teacher educators can select appropriate learning experiences, teaching methods and information-gathering techniques in order to achieve the objectives.

4.2 Objectives

This monograph aims at helping science and technology teacher educators to:

- acquire the necessary knowledge and skills to evaluate trainees;
- acquire the skills of evaluating their own teaching;
- become aware of the problems associated with evaluation;
- become aware of the need for and methods of record keeping;
- develop the necessary understanding and skills of evaluation amongst trainee teachers.

4.3 The Purpose of Evaluation

Evaluation is carried out for the following purposes:

- to measure progress;
- for accreditation and certification;
- to determine whether objectives of a teaching programme have been achieved;
- to rank learners;
- to identify gaps in the knowledge and skills of learners;
- to provide information on progress to parents, teachers, teacher educators and decision makers.

The teacher educator should emphasize to the teacher trainees that the purpose of evaluation is not only to let the learner and parents know about the progress of the learner. It is also of vital importance to teachers because it informs them about the success of their own teaching. Information from evaluation can be used by teachers to plan their lessons. This should be demonstrated by the teacher educator.

4.4 Types of Evaluation

The purpose of evaluation determines its type. Informal evaluation techniques may be used to collect information needed for decision-making. Evaluation may be carried out to collect a variety of information about teacher trainees, such as academic performance, performance in the classroom, ability to handle classroom material, presentation and communication skills and ability to plan and execute practical work. Similarly, teacher educators may evaluate trainees with regard to their knowledge and skills in planning and administering evaluation in school.

It is the use of the information collected which determines the nature of evaluation. If the information is used to diagnose the cause of a particular problem faced by a trainee, the evaluation is called diagnostic. If information gathered is used to monitor teachers' progress during pre-service or in-service programmes and to take corrective measures whenever required, evaluation is called formative. This type of evaluation is carried out periodically and is therefore also called continuous evaluation. Evaluation which is carried out at the end of a course or session is called summative evaluation.

4.4.1 Formative Evaluation

Formative evaluation is carried out to provide the teacher, as well as the learner, with feedback that can be used in taking corrective measures at different stages in the teaching—learning process. Objectives of formative evaluation are:

- to determine the progress being made by the learners and the difficulties they may be experiencing;
- to guide the learning process;
- to decide which students need further help and the nature of activities and strategies that might help them;
- to pace the learning process and make the learner more alert to his or her performance.

Formative evaluation is conducted mainly to improve learning. This does not mean that tests used for formative evaluation cannot be graded. However, the grading is done to find strengths and weaknesses in that teaching–learning process. Formative evaluation, therefore, provides both teachers and learners with feedback on the achievement of the objectives. Teacher educators should model how this can be done in their own teaching.

4.4.2 Continuous Evaluation

As the term implies, continuous evaluation is carried out periodically during the teaching-learning process. It has two main purposes:

- for formative evaluation;
- to supplement summative evaluation.

This means that the final grade a learner receives in a course is not based on a single final examination, but takes into account the results of the continuous evaluation.

Characteristics of Continuous Evaluation

- **Systematic.** It is systematic in that measurements to be made of the teacher's performance at different time internals have to be planned.
- **Comprehensive.** It is comprehensive in that it makes use of many different techniques to collect information over the range of abilities. Information about cognitive, affective and psychomotor skills may be collected through tests, projects, assignments, observations, interviews and questionnaires. This holistic evaluation provides valuable information on the teachers.
- **Guidance-oriented.** Continuous evaluation is oriented towards providing guidance in that the information obtained is used to guide the teacher trainees' future professional development.

It is important that teacher educators demonstrate these characteristics of continuous evaluation in the evaluation of the teacher trainees and them enable the teacher trainees to use the strategies with their students during teaching practice. This will help the trainees to develop appropriate skills.

Problems Associated with Continuous Evaluation

Teacher educators should be aware of the problems outlined below, discuss them with pre-service trainees, offer suggestions and allay fears.

- **Workload of the teacher.** There can be no denying that continuous evaluation makes demands on the teacher. Weather this work is above and beyond that which the teacher can reasonably be expected to undertake as part of teaching depends on particular situations. As was stressed above, evaluation and feedback are essential in teaching. Where continuous evaluation is used to provide feedback, it is reasonable to expect teachers to integrate this into their normal workload.

The problem with continuous evaluation arises, however, when the outcomes need to be recorded for use by other teachers and outside bodies. This usually has to be done in a standard format that involves the teachers in additional clerical work and in carrying out evaluations at stipulated periods for record keeping rather than at times most appropriate to the teaching situation.

- **Teacher-student relationship.** Some teachers are concerned that formally evaluating students will interfere with teacher-student relationships and with the role of the teacher in providing feedback and counselling. The perception is that students will be afraid to give ideas and opinions because they may be penalized during evaluation.

  Teacher educators must realize that evaluation and feedback are one and the same and that evaluation, of any form, needs to be an integral part of teaching. When students understand this and are able to establish and accept the need for evaluation and feedback, the teacher-student relationship can be enhanced. It appears that the fear of teacher trainees is associated with an inability to link evaluation with teaching.

4.4.3 Summative Evaluation

Evaluation which is carried out at the end of a course with the sole purpose of grading, promotion or selection is termed summative evaluation. Results of summative evaluation are also used for accountability purposes of individual teacher educators or teachers or of their institutions. Summative evaluation also informs policy makers about the standards of education and the efficacy of the curriculum.

Summative evaluation is normally carried out using paper and pencil tests and/or practical tests administered towards the end of a term or academic year. Such tests may be conducted by the institution itself or by an external examining agency.

In some countries, teacher trainees' success or failure at the end of a teacher education programme is mainly determined by an external examination body. It has been advocated that teacher educators should have some input in determining the final grades of their teacher trainees.

For a valid evaluation of the student teacher, the results of continuous evaluation should be used to supplement summative evaluation.

4.5 Methodology of Evaluation

Harlen (1983) has suggested that evaluation begins by asking a few questions. She suggests the following sequence of questions:

- What is the purpose of evaluation?
- What information is required to serve the purpose?
- What methods are appropriate to gathering this information?
- What form of record is suitable for accumulating the information?
- What interpretation and use are to be made of the information?
- Does this use serve the initial purpose?

The first four questions must be asked before the evaluation takes place and the last two after the information has been collected through informal means such as observation or formal means such as tests. Thus the purpose of evaluation and the information required for making judgements determine the tools and techniques to be used to collect the information.

Teacher educators should ask themselves these questions when planning evaluation of trainees. After the evaluation exercise has been completed the teacher educators should discuss the basis of decisions on each question with the trainees. This will help the trainees to see evaluation in action and identify appropriate method(s) for collecting a particular kind of information, and the most suitable method of recording it. The trainees may then be given appropriate assignments to practise these skills. They may be asked to decide the kind of information to be collected, the tools and techniques to be used to collect the information and the form of record to be kept. A common mistake which occurs is to set a task or question designed to evaluate a particular objectives or criterion which does not provide opportunity for the learner to demonstrate the achievement of that objective. This must be avoided.

In order to give practice in the interpretation and use of information collected, trainees may either be given some hypothetical information to interpret or asked to collect formation themselves and interpret and use it. It is important for teacher educators and the trainees to know that the purpose of evaluation and the type of information collected could inform vital decisions. These decisions may be regarding the achievement of each learner or the class as a whole, difficulties being faced by individual learners and the class, the efficacy of the teaching–learning strategy utilized, and remedial activities that may be necessary.

Nature of Information Required for Evaluation

The nature of information to be collected for different purposes depends upon the objectives being evaluated. In most countries the objectives relate to the cognitive, psychomotor (including processes) and affective domains, but emphasis placed on each varies, as the following examples illustrate. In some countries there is heavy emphasis on content while in others the emphasis is on the development of psychomotor skills. The development of scientific attitude, interest and values is emphasized by all to varying degrees.

In Namibia, the syllabus given the aims of the science course as:

- to acquire sufficient understanding and knowledge to become citizens of a confident world;
- to take or develop an informed interests in matters of scientific importance;

- to recognize the usefulness and limitations of scientific processes and appreciate their applicability in other disciplines and in everyday life;

In the **Kenya** Syllabus for Primary Schools Science, the objectives for standards 1-3 emphasize the development of attitudes, skills and acquiring information about the immediate surroundings through first-hand observation.

In **Nigeria** the objectives of science teaching are the acquisition of basic scientific skills: observing, manipulating, classifying, communicating, inferring, hypothesising, interpreting data and formulating models.

In **Uganda** the objectives of science teaching are to develop in children skills of observation, experimentation and evaluation.

Thus, the objectives of science and technology education about which information will have to be collected are in the areas of:

- knowledge and understanding of scientific facts, principles, methods and materials;
- process skills such as observation, classification, communicating, inferring, hypothesizing, experimenting, designing and problem solving;
- attitudes, interests, curiosity, critical thinking, perserverance, openness.

4.6 Information-gathering Techniques

A variety of techniques can be employed to collect information about learners' progress. These techniques may be classified as:

Formal

- written tests;
- practical tasks carried out by individuals or groups;
- questionnaires;
- scheduled interviews;
- rating scales;
- check lists.

Informal

- observation during normal activities;
- written records of work produced including drawings;
- listening to oral explanations.

4.6.1 Evaluation of Problem Solving

To solve a given problem, a learner has to use certain ideas and skills. From the point of view of evaluation, it is vital that these are carefully identified and documented, so that the extent to which they have been used successfully can be evaluated. For the purposes of grading and assessing progress, a series of statements in terms of what learners will or will not be able to do at stage should is needed. Each stage can be assigned a mark. The panel shows how this approach is being followed by the INSTANT project in Namibia.

Possible investigative skills to be assessed and development stages

SKILL 1: Using and organising techniques, apparatus and materials

Stage 1: Can follow written, oral or diagrammatic instruction to carry out one operation; needs help to do more; uses familiar apparatus adequately, but needs showing how to use unfamiliar apparatus; rather thoughtless over safety points.

Stage 2: Can follow written, oral or diagrammatic instruction to carry out an operation involving a series of steps and uses familiar apparatus adequately and safety; needs demonstration of how to use unfamiliar apparatus.

Stage 3: Can follow written, oral or diagrammatic instruction to carry out an operation involving a series of steps and is able to modify the instructions to improve the operation of the equipment; uses familiar apparatus adequately and safely; can make a fair attempt at using unfamiliar apparatus.

SKILL 2: **Observing, measuring and recording**

Stage 1: Can follow detailed instructions to make observations; can make simple measurements using a simple measuring device; records results in an appropriate way when shown how to do so.

Stage 2: Makes measurements, given a brief outline of how to do it; can use some more complex measuring devices such as those having a scale where 1 division is equal to 0.1 of a unit or 2 units; reads most devices but may not do so what complete accuracy; records results in an appropriate way given an outline format.

Stage 3: Makes relevant observations that are as accurate as possible; can read any scale correctly; records results correctly without being given a format.

SKILL 3: Handling experimental observations and data

Stage 1: Can process results adequately given detailed instructions on how to do it; can draw one obvious conclusion from the results.

Stage 2: Can process results adequately given outline instructions on how to do it; can recognize results that might have experimental errors; can draw conclusions from the data.

Stage 3: Can process results adequately without help, recognizes experimental errors and knows how to deal with them; can identify possible reasons for the error; can draw conclusions; and also makes general deductions from data.

SKILL 4: Planning and investigating

Stage 1: Can suggest a simple experiment to investigate a practical problem, although this may not work; can attempt modifying the experiment if it does not work.

Stage 2: Can list a series of steps to carry out an investigation; can modify the steps that do not work well; can recognize the need to control variables though may not be very clear about how to do it systematically.

Stage 3: Can list a series of logical steps to carry out an investigation that is likely to work in practice; modifies the steps that do not work well; recognizes the need to control variables in a systematic way.

4.6.2 Evaluation Through Observation During Normal Activities

Observation (as a technique to collect information) provides qualitative information about the objectives being evaluated.

Through observation, skills, attitudes and acquisition of concepts can be evaluated over an extended period of time. Since the learners are being evaluated through observation of their normal activities, they are not under stress; also, there is no loss of teaching-learning time. All the learners need not be evaluated at the same time through one activity. To aid observation, actual classroom activities could be video-recorded. These recordings could also be used by trainees to develop and practise observation skills.

Observation is a very powerful information-gathering technique since it can be used to collect information about a wide range of behaviours spread over several objectives. However, the teacher educators and the teachers need to recognise that observation goes beyond simply looking at what students are doing. For the technique to be used successfully, the activities to be observed and the particular stages within them, must be clearly identified. The emphasis is not on observing whether or not the learner is doing the right things but on what the learner can or cannot do.

In addition, criteria have to be established, against which observations can be measured and recorded. The criteria are generally derived from the learning objectives and the stage of development of the trainee. This aids proper interpretation of the observations and in establishing the learner's progress, information which is very useful for the teacher educators and teachers in planning future activities for the learners.

One disadvantage of collecting evaluation information through observation is the element of subjectivity. The observer has to be skilled in the technique: an unskilled observer may miss certain important factors that should be noted.

4.6.3 Using Written Tests for Gathering Information

- Written tests may contain a variety of questions such as:
    - short-answer;
    - essay-type;
    - multiple-choice;
    - fill in the blanks.

Written tests are used mainly for collecting information about students' cognitive abilities and some drawing skills. They cannot be used for testing a wide range of psychomotor skills. They can, however, be used for both formative and summative evaluation. Most written tests include essay-type and multiple-choice questions, and some characteristics of these are listed below.

Essay-type Questions

These questions require more extended written answers and the ability to integrate and express ideas involving:

- description, explanation and prediction of processes and structures;
- description of instruments, apparatus, etc.;
- factual knowledge;
- presentation of theoretical knowledge;
- interpretation of experimental and numerical data;
- discussion of results of experiments and solutions of problems.

Advantages

- They reduce guesswork in answers;
- They reduce the possibility of cheating.
- They provide freedom of response.

Disadvantages

- In marking essays, the teacher tends to carry impressions from one paper to another.
- Essays cannot be used effectively with learners with low levels of language development.

Evaluation through essays at primary school level should be limited to short paragraphs only.

Multiple-choice Type Questions

Multiple-choice questions can be useful in covering a range of curricular objectives. A multiple choice questions usually consists of a questions or statement, called the 'stem', followed by four or five choices of answers or 'options'. The stem may also be a partial statement that is completed by one of the choices. Only one of the options is the correct answer to the question or ending to the statement. The other options are called 'distracters'.

Other forms of multiple-choice questions include:

- **True/false questions.** These are not particularly useful since there is a 50 per cent chance of guessing the right answer.
- **Fill-in-the blank questions.** Here possible responses are supplied to the learner, only one of which is correct.
- **Matching questions.** These are presented in the form of two lists of statements. For each statement in one list there is one correct statement in the other list and the learners have to match them. The primary cognitive skill tested by matching exercises is recall.

Teacher education programmes should include practice in the construction and review of different types of questions and written tests. The review should include analysis of each item of the test.

4.6.4 Evaluation of Individuals in Group Work

Most evaluation in science and technology education is carried out by teacher educators, but student teachers can be good evaluators of each other specially when they work as a group on an activity. An example of how this works is drawn from South Africa.

In innovative teacher in a school, at St Stithians, South Africa, came up with an interesting approach to evaluating group work

An overall point (percentage) is awarded for the activity or assignment of the group as a whole. The members of the group then decide how the marks should be distributed amongst themselves, according to the contribution each made to the work. The total marks for individuals must, in the end, equal the mark the teacher gave to the group. If they feel they all contributed equally, they can each earn the same percentage. According to the teacher, this strategy works very well. Within a group, each individual knows very well who did the work or who was just sitting around!

4.7 Recording Keeping

There are many different ways to keep records of learners' achievements and progress. The nature of the record depends to a large extent upon the technique used to collect information. For example, the record of an observation tends to be descriptive, giving information on the absence or presence of the trait being observed. Similarly, the record of a written test tends to be numerical. The type of record to be maintained also depends upon the purpose or use of the record. In general, a numerical record is not useful if one wants to know what learners can or cannot do. But if the purpose is grading the learners then a numerical record is more useful than a descriptive record.

During formative evaluation, most of the information gathered is interpreted and used immediately for taking corrective measures in the learning activities of individuals and for planning future activities. A record of the stages of development reached by the learner can be very useful in deciding long-term activities.

A common practice is to prepare a list of activities and tick them off as individuals complete them. This kind of record is not very helpful since it does not tell the reader what the learner can or cannot do. To improve the usefulness of such a list, a column can be added where the skills observed/achieved could written. Alternatively, a list of possible skills to be assessed could be drawn up, and for each learner the particular skills observed/ achieved ticked off.

Activity no.	Skill 1	Skill 2	Skill 3	Skill 4	etc.
Name 1					
Name 2					
etc.					

4.8 Profiles

A profile is method of building up a picture of attainment that allows separate grades, scores, marks and other measures to be recorded for each student. The picture can be broadened by including factors such as attitudes, health data, punctuality, absenteeism and self-esteem. These additional attributes can be judged on, say, a 3-or 5-point scale.

Profiles can be of two types:

- An extension of the conventional evaluation data, in the sense that student performance is reported on a larger number of dimensions.
- Information presented as a record of the student's abilities, skills and attitudes, which are explicitly states and which describe the student's characteristics and attributes on a criterion-referenced basis.

In the first type of profile, the data obtained from examinations is put forward as a kind of report. The data are presented in greater detail in the sense that greater numbers of subdivisions are included. But the data themselves are still either the percentage scores, or the percentages related to a 3- or -point scale, which may be numerical or labelled, for example, above average, below average. When the middle grade is labelled as average (average for the student population), the profile is said to be based on norm-referenced evaluation.

4.8.1 Developing Criterion-related Profiles

If adequate information is given about the learners, the profile system mentioned above can be meaningful. But in the absence of such data (which is often the case), more meaning is attached to the profile by including the specific criteria against which measurements are taken. There is however a tendency for the profiles to be based on criteria and be related to criterion-referenced evaluation.

In a criterion-referenced profile, the numbers represent a 5-point range, with 5 being a high proficiency and 1 a low proficiency rating. The numbers could be easily substituted by grades or use could be made of other systems. For example the ability to use a scientific instrument could be graded as:

5 = can use a scientific instrument accurately and safely;

4 = can use a scientific instrument, with guidance, and is aware of safety aspects;

3 = can use a scientific instrument, with guidance, but is not aware of safety aspects;

2 = cannot use a scientific instrument, even after guidance, but is aware of need for safe practice;

1 = cannot use a scientific instrument, even after guidance, and does not consider safety aspects.

4.8.2 Extending the Profile

Profiles can extend beyond characteristics that relate to cognitive ability or practical skills. The example below shows part of a profile covering aspects of attitude. Again, a criterion-referenced format is being followed.

Relationship with fellow students

4 A leader/dominant personality

3 Accepted member of student groups

2 Likes to join with other students, a follower

1 Independent, quite isolated; tends to be on his/her own

Ability to work with others

4 Works well as the leader of a team

3 Works well as a member of a team

2 Prefers to work on his/her own

1 Does not fit in well as a member of a team

Punctuality in the last year of school

3 Excellent

2 Some lateness

1 Poor

Discipline

4 Self-discipline—able to relate to a normal adult/child, teacher/student situation

2 Accepts a specified pattern of behaviour and rules

2 Accepts an imposed pattern of behaviour and rules where there is a degree of supervision

1 Does not always accept a pattern of behaviour required by the student group

4.8.3 Problems with Profiling

Three are three main issues associated with the profiles as a method of record keeping:

- the time it takes to develop and maintain the profile;
- the type of profile to be designed and the qualities to be described in them;
- the technical respects of the educational measurement on which the profile is to be based, including validity and reliability.

The type of profile developed depends on the needs of the end-user.

Profiles are usually developed to show what a student can achieve. It is a record of achievement and attitudes. The technical aspects of the profile are to do with the development of levels that show gradations in academic achievement or attitudinal development. The acceptability or validity of the profile depends on how meaningful the statements being made are to the end-user.

5

Co-ordinating Science and Technology Education

5.1 Overview

The current trend towards the provision of a broader general education in schools implies the need for a more cross-curricular approach to education at all levels. In science and technology education, calls for curricula which will produce socially responsible, technologically and scientifically literate citizens, also point in the direction of an interdisciplinary approach.

Such an approach can best be achieved in the context of co-ordination between all levels of education, and between educational institutions and all those external bodies which have an impact on them.

The usual structure of university degree programmes makes it unlikely that there would be many teacher educators with competent in both science and technology. However, the contents of these disciplines lend themselves ideally to cross-curricular links. Additionally, many organizations external to, but which impact on teacher education, are involved in activities that are relevant to both these subjects.

Co-ordination is considered here at three levels:

- Between institutions of teacher education and those agencies and organizations which influence them, either directly through the making of policy, or through the professional development of teacher educators; or less directly through their influence on the social, economic or cultural climate in which teacher education takes place.

- Within and between teacher education institutions themselves.
- Within and between schools.

This view of co-ordination envisages a set of mutually interactive relationships occurring within and across all three levels (see Figure 1).

LEVELS OF CO-ORDINATION IN SCIENCE AND TECHNOLOGY EDUCATION

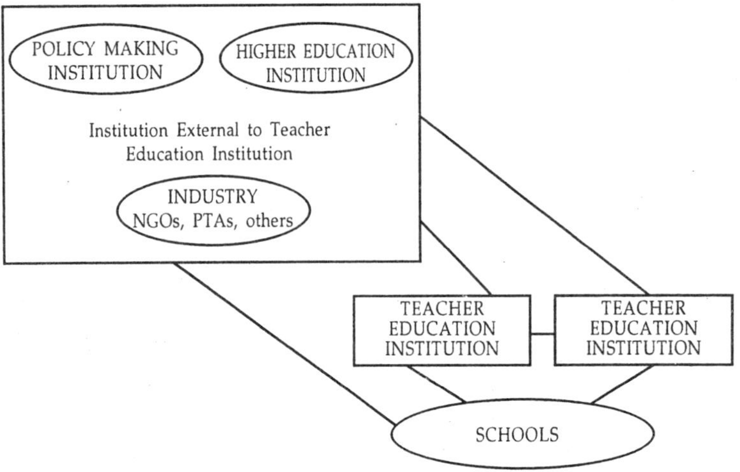

5.2 Objectives

The objectives of this monograph are:

- to inform science and technology teacher educators about those organizations, their policies and practices which must be considered in the education of teachers;
- to enable science and technology teacher educators to identify those agencies which can influence science and technology in their own contexts;

- to provide guidance on how science and technology teacher educators can influence co-ordination at all levels.

5.3 Co-ordination with Institutions and Organizations External to Teacher Education Institutions

Some of these are concerned with policy, others with professional training and/or academic growth, and still others with providing support for teacher education.

5.3.1 Organizations and Institutions Concerned with Policy

Ministries of Education

The Ministry of Education decides on the national priorities and policies for education. Science and technology teacher educators should be aware of relevant policies. These may be contained in a general policy document of the Ministry of Education with a section on science and technology or there may be a separate policy document. This is likely to include policy statements and guidance on:

- the type of science and technology to be taught in schools;
- the general methodology to be followed in delivering science and technology to children;
- the assessment procedures to be followed;
- any in-service training which will be provided to teacher and others.

The Ministry of Education usually manages the appointment and placement of teachers, provides material resources to schools, supervises schools, and advises on textbooks and other learning materials. Science and technology teacher educators should be aware of their Ministry's policies and placement practices, of the kind of physical resources provided to schools for science and technology, and the policy with regard to their maintenance and replenishment. Teacher educators should have an input into the formulation of these policies and practices. Ministries of Education also decide on staff development policies, another area with which the teacher educator must be familiar.

Practices with regard to school supervision and inspection, such as its frequency, procedures and nature, are also determined by the Ministry of Education. Teacher educators can help to allay teachers' understandable apprehension about the content and method of inspection by making student teachers aware of inspection procedures.

Curriculum Development Units

The importance of a well developed and managed curriculum is well recognized. The responsibility for this task resides with a curriculum development unit, which usually comes under the aegis of the Ministry of Education. Tuition given by the science and technology teacher educator is more likely to be relevant and contextual if curriculum development is a collaborative effort involving teacher educators.

Science and technology education can benefit from a cross-curricular approach. The curriculum guidelines provided by the development unit should encourage such an approach and facilitate its implementation.

5.3.2 Organization and Institutions Concerned with Professional Training and/or Academic Growth

Higher Institutions

For their own professional and academic growth, science and technology teacher educators should co-ordinate with higher education institutions concerned with science and technology content and pedagogy. They should attempt to attend meetings, workshops, seminars and short courses organized by these institutions in areas which are of interest to them.

In order to facilitate a cross-curricular approach in science and technology, teacher educators should press these institutions of higher learning to provide:

- Short courses which allow teacher educators to upgrade their knowledge as required. For example, technologically oriented courses, ideally enhanced by using resource personnel from industry.
- Broad-based degree programmes to allow students the opportunity to pursue integrated degrees.

Within teacher education institutions, opportunities for participation in these seminars, workshops and courses, need to be planned for a enable all members of the science and technology staff to participate.

INSET Agencies

In-Service Education and Training (INSET) is usually conducted by the Ministries of Education, whereas pre-service teacher training is organized in colleges and universities. Where both are avenues to gaining the same teacher qualifications, it is important that the philosophy underlying them is similar. Both sets of agencies should be in constant communication, so that those completing their courses will have equal opportunities in the workplace.

5.3.3 Support Organizations and Institutions

Examination and Assessment Agencies

If teachers have been taught to follow a teaching approach which emphasizes processes and problem-solving in science and technology, but the examinations test only recall of knowledge, teachers will abandon or modify their approach and adopt a didactic approach more suitable for memorizing the knowledge needed for passing the examination.

At the college level, within land across colleges, teacher educators in all subject areas should coordinate their efforts to ensure that examinations reflect the teaching approaches used.

At the school level, the problem calls for co-ordination between the curriculum unit and the examining agency. If there is no co-ordination, teachers will tend to follow the approach most suited to getting pupils through the examination. Differences between examination and curriculum policies and practices clearly have implications for the education of teachers.

Problems may also be cause if the examination system does not take account of pupils' performance in continuous assessment in the award of the final grade. It will need to be made clear to student teachers, that continuous assessment in the classroom provides valuable feedback for the improvement of learning and teaching, even if it is not required for formal examination.

Professional Organizations

Science and technology teacher educators will find it helpful to be involved with relevant professional organizations, to know of their current activities and understand the issues that concern them. Such professional contacts will help the science and technology teacher educators to make pre-service teachers aware of current issues and work with them so that they themselves can contribute to current debate and appropriate activities when they become teachers.

Local Industry

To ensure that science and technology is relevant and realistic, particularly in its technology aspects, teacher educators will want to draw examples from local, traditional and modern industry. Local industry is an excellent resource since it provides real contexts and genuine problems. Teacher educators should co-ordinate with local industry so that they may draw on their human and material resources. This should be a two-way flow of information and skills. If possible, science and technology teacher educators should visit various industrial plants for short periods, so as to familiarize themselves with the demands of these industries. Similarly, persons from industry might visit teacher education institutions for lectures, discussions or demonstrations or firms might provide teaching materials or equipment.

Such co-ordination will not only help science and technology teacher educators develop realistic activities, but help industry to understand how science and technology are taught in school, and thus develop confidence in their local teaching institutions. Science and technology educators will also gain an understanding of the requirements of industry, and the kind of curriculum which will meet these requirements.

Schools

Co-ordination with schools is needed for the purpose of:

- practice teaching;
- action research;
- providing professional support;

- understanding the working environment;
- acquiring first-hand experience of working with children.

To keep up to date with current practice in schools, it is important for science and technology teacher educators to devote regular period of time to working in the primary school, alongside science and technology teachers. Such time, is invaluable in helping teacher educators to keep their own teaching realistic.

Teacher educators might also promote science and technology in the primary school by encouraging principals to adopt flexible time tabling arrangements, for example, block time tables, which allow class teachers flexibility across subject areas.

5.4 Co-ordination Within and Between Teacher Education Institutions

Co-ordination and collaboration between the colleges of education will provide an revenue through which teacher educators can foster their own professional growth, promote some uniformity in the quality of experiences provided for teacher trainees, and develop across-curricular links and interdisciplinary approaches. These may be achieved through:

- Developing professional organizations for science and technology educators. These may relate to the two disciplines separately, or in any combinations as the specific circumstances of different countries dictate.
- Promoting regional co-ordination between such national professional organizations.
- Mounting workshops, seminars or conferences for sharing ideas on teaching approaches and resource materials, and for engaging in discussion on current issues and trends in science and technology education.
- Preparing position papers representing the consensus views of teacher educators as a means of influencing policies and decision-making with respect to teacher education.

- Making proposals for new directions in teacher education in response to prevailing social, economic or cultural influences.
- Fostering collaborative approaches to teaching, such as team teaching and team planning.
- Developing theme and project approaches to teacher education. As well as improving the delivery of the science and technology teacher education, curriculum, such approaches will benefit teacher trainees by providing them with models for across-curricular approaches in their own classrooms.
- Exchanging human and material resources within and between colleges and both nationally and regionally.

5.5 Co-ordination of In-school Activities

Teaching science and technology in schools involves the organization of a number of activities. These may be broadly classified as:

- those directed towards the professional growth of teachers;
- activities directed towards effective teaching and learning;
- co-curricular activities leading to promotion of science and technology amongst students and the community.

5.5.1 The Science and Technology Co-ordinator

For effective implementation of science and technology education programmes, a staff member needs to be designated as an science and technology co-ordinator. It could be the head-teacher, or an enthusiastic class teacher in the school with an interest in developing science and technology. Their teaching load may have to be marginally reduced to make room for the demands of co-ordination.

5.5.2 Co-ordination of Activities for the Professional Growth of Teachers

Activities which promote the professional growth of teachers normally take the form of participation by teachers in meetings, seminars, workshops and INSET courses. Such activities are usually organized by the Ministry of Education, colleges of education and teacher associations. Activities are also organized in schools by those teachers who have had the benefit of attending INSET programmes.

Ministries of Education organize INSET courses for a variety of reasons:

- to introduce a new curriculum;
- to introduce a new teaching methodology;
- for upgrading content;
- for certification of untrained teachers;
- for introducing a new assessment of supervision system.

Depending on the nature of the INSET course, the Ministry of Education may specify the number of teacher from each school who will attend the course. If the course is for a limited number of teachers from a school, the co-ordinator will be responsible for selecting those teachers who would benefit most from a course. If it is a course for content upgrading, for example, it would be inappropriate for a new science graduate to attend. On the other hand, a course leading to teaching certification would be most suitable for an uncertified teacher. To facilitate selection, the co-ordinator will need to maintain the following record for each teacher in the schools:

- educational qualification;
- teaching experience and results produced;
- participation in science and technology education workshops, seminars and so on, with dates;
- strengths and weaknesses.

The science and technology education co-ordinator must ensure that the teacher who attends an external INSET course organizes a meeting of all the school's science and technology teachers and briefs them on the course attended. This feedback will serve three purposes:

- it will help the teacher to consolidate what he or she learned on the course;

- the teacher will have to be a more attentive when on the course, knowing that he or she will have to present it themselves when they return to school;
- other teachers will benefit from the course.

Thus one course can benefit more than one teacher in a school. In addition, the course providers can benefit from the teacher's report on his or her feedback to school, so that the course itself may be improved.

The focus of the teacher's feedback briefing to school should be:

- implications for teaching and learning within the school;
- changes which could be made within the school in relation to these implications, which would make the science and technology and teaching more effective.

5.5.3 School-based INSET for Professional Growth and Effective Teaching and Learning

In the busy school schedule, teachers rarely have time to sit together and share experiences. In a large school, teachers may be facing some common problems which could be resolved through sharing experiences and discussion. Similarly, some teachers may have success stories and unique classroom experiences which may benefit other teachers. It is therefore always useful if the co-ordinator can arrange for the teachers in a school to meet, possibly after school or at a weekend, for, say, half a day each month. The object of this meeting would be pre-determined through mutual consent, and known to all teachers concerned beforehand, so that everybody comes prepared. It is important for the co-ordinator to plan the meeting, draw up a timetable, and assign responsibilities. Teachers should be encouraged to volunteer to take up responsibilities rather than be coerced.

School-based INSET programmes, though generally short, can be useful in:

- preparing teaching-learning materials by sharing ideas;
- improving materials;

- resolving conflicts arising out of the use of resources;
- disseminating action research findings and generating idea for action research;
- developing collaborative work amongst teachers.

A major advantage of a school-based INSET programme is that the innovations can be sustainable. Science new ideas are being generated and tried out amongst colleagues, and chances of successful innovation are greater. A new idea coming from a colleague is much more likely to be accepted than one imposed from an outside source. Thus, school-based INSET programmes are not only useful for the professional growth of teachers, but contribute to improved teaching and learning. Alternatives to school-based programmes may be needed for smaller schools and for those where teachers are not willing to try new ideas.

5.5.4 Co-ordination of Resources

This is another important role of the co-ordinator. In primary schools, the resources supplied by the Ministry of Education are generally limited. Most of the materials required for science and technology education will be drawn from the immediate environment. The co-ordinator will need to ensure that while the materials are safely stored, they are also easily accessible to the users. This means discussing this with the relevant teachers and identifying a place suitable for all of them. Over a period of time students and teachers of senior classes may develop teaching and learning materials which could be useful in junior classes. Such products should be identified, displayed and stored, and teachers encouraged to use them.

5.5.5 Co-ordination of Extra-curricular Activities

The science and technology co-ordinator can encourage activities such as those listed below, aimed at developing the interests of children in science and technology. These will also need proper co-ordination.

- **Debates and quizzes.** Science, technology and mathematics-related issues can be debated by pupils. Quizzes taking the form of question and answer can be devised. As part of an INSET programme, teachers could build up a bank of topics for debate and questions for quizzes. Careful selection of topics for debate and quiz questions within the school setting can arouse interest and encourage children to explore the relevance of science and technology to the out-of-school environment. Topics which encourage girls to participate in science and technology should be given preference. Inter-school competitions allow teachers to exchange ideas about more effective ways they may have developed for teaching science and technology concepts and skills. Students could also gain from sharing ideas with their peers in other schools.

- **Fairs, exhibitions and museums**. Periodic school fairs and exhibitions of science and technology materials made by pupils and teachers can be arranged. Exhibits can form the basis for a more permanent school museums that can become a resource for future generations of students. Labels showing the names of students and dates should be attached to exhibits to boost the moral of their creators. The items exhibited could be projects carried out by the pupils. Exhibits that show links between science and technology in schools and community activities can be particularly encouraged. Schools should also be encouraged to participate in exhibitions organized by other schools and agencies.

- **Science and technology clubs**. Science and technology co-ordinators should discuss the formation of a science and technology club within a school and how this might function. Ideas from the teachers and students can be shared and a report complied with recommendations for teachers to implement. Science and technology clubs can be a useful way of encouraging the exchange of ideas and promoting excellence in science and technology. In such clubs students can pursue science-related hobbies and extend the concepts that they have learned in class. It could be a junior engineers' club, a technicians' club, flying club, photographic club, maths club or general scientific club. The clubs could be named after well-known scientists or engineers, or a local traditional industrialist whose skills are widely respected. Every effort should be made to name some clubs after women how have achieved prominent positions.

- **Weekend rallies**. Teachers can encourage informal learning by organising weekend rallies. In a relaxed atmosphere, pupils can exchange ideas and work on science and technology activities. These rallies can be used to attract and encourage girls to study science and technology and to pursue related careers. They could take the form of science and technology 'clinics' where girls could meet and talk to role models and mentors. Girls could be encouraged to visit science and technology based institutions and industries and engage in hands-on activities. These rallies serve to stimulate pupils' interest and popularise science and technology in the community.

- **Science and technology news and bulletins**. A bulletin board on which children's and teachers' work can be displayed, along with relevant news items, can be a very effective means of stimulating interest in science and technology. The content should reflect children's activities and teachers' accomplishments. Children can be asked to write short descriptions of their science and technology class activities for display on the board. They should also be encouraged to read the news or bulletins during school assembly. Any science and technology-related news from the newspapers should be read and explained for the benefit of everybody.

- **Science and technology awards and souvenirs.** Awards and souvenirs for outstanding pupil performance can also stimulate interest in science and technology. To promote science and technology amongst girls there could be awards exclusively for girls. Award winners can be identified and presentations made to them by pupils or by well-known figures from the community. Similarly, awards can be given to teachers for effective teaching and innovations in science and technology education. The community must be encouraged to promote such awards: involving the community in the choice of award winners will develop an active interest on science and technology in the school amongst the community.

6

Participating in Science and Technology Education Research

6.1 Overview

Educational research is the only should basis for effecting improvements to the educational system. Its practitioners—teacher educators and teachers—are the most important resource in science and technology education. With them lies our best hope of finding solutions to the problems of science and technology education at the primary level in our schools. They are the agents of change. They know the problems, the subject matter and the demands of the relevant disciplines. They know their pupils' changing needs, interests and aspirations. They are aware of existing conditions in their classrooms and local environments. As part of the local community, they are conscious of what parents expect of schools. No one is better placed to recognize the first indications of success or failure in implementing curricula, and to effect the necessary improvements and changes in the classroom.

It is therefore vital that teacher educators participate in research and are able to guide and steer teachers towards developing a positive attitude to research in their classrooms.

Science and technology education research belongs to the classroom. Improvements to science and technology education at the primary level can be realized through teacher educators' and teachers' participation in research, both as researchers and as users of research findings.

6.2 Objectives

This monograph aims to:

- stimulate the interest of teacher educators in science and technology education research by outlining the advantages of participation in research;
- encourage teacher educators to develop their research skills;
- assist teacher educators in developing the action research skills of teachers.

6.3 What is Science and Technology Education Research?

Science and technology education research can be broadly characterized as activities that:

- through problem identification, information-gathering and analysis of data, lead to a better understanding of problems in science and technology education;
- produce findings which lead to improved classroom practices, programme planning and implementation, and more informed policy decisions at the school or college level.

An example of research leading to improved practice

Matthew is a teacher in a well-endowed urban primary school situated near a teacher training institution in Ghana. He become anxious about his pupils' difficulties in understanding the particulate nature of matter. After consulting Ian, a science teacher educator at the teacher training institution, they decided that Ian should observe Matthew's classroom as he taught the topic 'particles in nature' to his class the following year.

Ian's study of Matthew's class involved observation, audio-taping, examination of the textbook, and interviews with Matthew and some of the pupils in the class.

Three issues became clear from the information Ian collected:

- Matthew's teaching in class was text-bound;
- he worked on the assumption that the particulate ideas were simple enough for pupils to understand;

- pupils were unable to apply the particulate ideas. They thought that particles expand, melt, reduce in size, break up on application of heat, and that in a solution of water sugar particles remain particulate while the water is continuous.

Matthew, with Ian's help, then developed five lessons plans on the particulate nature of matter, which utilized the constructivist approach. The development of these plans took Matthew out of his classroom once a week for six weeks. Part of this time was used in trying out the activities with Ian's help. Matthew taught the new lessons while Ian observed and recorded. After each lesson, which required pupils to carry out activities that challenged their prior ideas about particles, Ian interviewed Mathew on some of his actions. Pupils were also interviewed, using questions prepared jointly by Ian and Matthew.

The findings indicated a marked change in the initial ideas of almost all the students in the class. Matthew commented on the confidence he had gained in using the constructivist approach and was determined to use it in teaching other topics.

Research can be carried out using interview, observation and audio-video recording to collect in-depth information on a problem such as teachers' and students' use of curricular materials, and teaching particular science and technology topics. When narrative information is collected and used to give a detailed account of the problem under investigation, the approach to research is described as **qualitative**. In this approach to research, the emphasis is not on drawing generalizations but on describing a situation in detail.

In the **quantitative** approach to research, a problem is analysed by collecting numerical data through the use of questionnaires, tests, attitude scales and observations. In quantitative research the emphasis generally is on drawing generalizations. Qualitative research can support quantitative research and vice versa.

Example 1: Quantitative research

Research done by Parker and Rochford (School of Education, University of Cap Town) was directed towards young scientists' perceptions of the nature and method of science.

The 1993 modified 'Aikenhead scales' were employed to measure the perceptions of the nature and method of science held by:

(a) 82 keen young scientists and mathematicians who had entered the annual Science Talent Quest (EXPO) competition at the University of Cape Town;

(b) 391 of their non-specialist mainstream classroom counterparts in the more general senior science years of five representative high schools in Cap Town.

A statistical analysis of the responses of the two samples to 26 items on the three scales, disclosed significant differences with respect to the relative importance attached by the two groups to:

- finding cures for diseases and helping the environment;
- exploration of the unknown and discovery of something new;
- finding and solving puzzles;
- formulating theories to explain things;
- careful recording of results;
- questioning, hypothesising, collecting data and forming conclusions.

Possible implications of these findings are suggested for the identification and fostering of budding young scientists.

Example 2: Qualitative research

A piece of qualitative research was done by R. Paulson (Johannesburg College of Education) on the use of diagrams in fraction work at primary level.

Part of the research involved interviewing pupils. These interviews revealed a wide range of understanding and methods, not always evident from the written responses. Some children who had the correct answer for computational tasks, were found to hold basic misconceptions about the underlying procedures. They interviews were most instructive and personal eye-opener to the researcher. From the study it was evident that it is the way in which diagrams are being used that makes the differences in pupils' understanding of fractions.

6.4 Relevance of Science and Technology Education Research

Primary science, integrated and environmental science, and technology are some of the more recent innovations at the primary level of education. Teachers at this level are expected to put into practice the intentions of curriculum developers as specified in the various curriculum documents. In reality, observations of pupils' and teachers' activities in science and technology classrooms reveal that the intentions of curriculum developers are often reinterpreted by teachers to suit particular classroom contexts. Teachers face problems in putting curriculum specifications into action, and in making the far-reaching decisions expected of them in carrying out managerial responsibilities in the classroom. Teachers need opportunities to familiarize themselves with information on new curricula and on curriculum-related issues. This suggests the need for modification in policy as well as in classroom practice, and of providing a focus for reflection to enable all parties to take appropriate decisions.

This is where knowledge of research findings and action research become relevant. Very often research findings have not been widely applied in classrooms because teachers have limited access to them. This limited access may also be the result of a lack of awareness on the part of science and technology teacher educators and research findings, or difficulty in understanding the findings and interpreting them for classroom application.

By taking advantage of relevant research findings, teachers educators can improve their own classroom practices and help teachers to improve theirs. This could ultimately lead to informed and improved policy decisions and better classroom practices.

In sum, what research has to say to science and technology teacher educators may be defined in terms of **feedback** providing a focus for further reflection and action. Cases Study 1 illustrates this point.

CASE STUDY 1

In a recent study (Okeke and Inomesia, 1986), an investigation was carried out into primary science teachers' perceptions of the teaching of primary science in two states of Nigeria. It was found that:

- 37 per cent of primary science teachers surveyed in the study were unable to state any meaningful objectives of Nigeria's Primary Science Core Curriculum.
- 59 per cent considered teacher-centred activities indicated good science teaching.

This research raises issues for the pre-service and in-service training of teachers. The implications for teacher educators could be extended to similar research in teacher preparation in integrated science, mathematics and technology.

6.5 The Science and Technology Teacher Educators as Researcher

Science and technology teacher educators, as researchers, are mainly concerned with gaining a better understanding of their own classrooms, so as to enable them to make informed decisions before, during and after teaching/learning transactions. Such improved understanding will lead to improved quality in science and technology teacher education. It is not sufficient for teacher educators' work to be studied solely by outsiders: they need to study their works themselves. As insiders, science and technology teachers educators have a more intimate knowledge of the setting, even though they see it in their own way. An outsider, who may be a colleague or research expert, is best used in a collaborative pact with the teacher educator, bringing specialists skills of 'seeing' and thinking about events.

The science and technology teacher educator as a researcher can collaborate with science and technology teachers at the primary level in order to understand and clarify aspects of the classroom situation at that level. The aim is to use the findings to improve science and technology teaching was well as teacher education. In such a research partnership, the roles and responsibilities of each partner could be as shown in Table 1. The teacher's role as researcher is rooted in their everyday practice in the classroom.

Table 1: Relationships and responsibilities in a teacher-development research partnership

Phases of research *Key actors*	*Planning and preparation for research*	*Data-collection techniques*	*Analysis and interpretation*	*Report writing and use*
Science and technology teacher educator	Primary responsibility for articulation of purpose, co-ordination of research and negotiation of activities	Identification and negotiation of possible strategies; primary responsibility for gathering mutually agreed information	Preparation and presentation of preliminary analysis; mutual interpretation of preliminary analysis leading to final analysis	Primary responsibility for writing account; responsive to teacher's editorial comments; perceived mutual benefit
Teacher	Negotiated participation in terms of perceived benefit, commitment and procedure	Identification of information sources and negotiation of appropriate strategies	Responsive to preliminary analysis; mutual interpretation leading to final analysis	Negotiated representation in report writing and editing of personal accounts; perceived mutual benefit

Source: Adapted from Cole, A.L.. & Knowles, J.G. (1993) Teacher development partnership research: a focus on methods and issues. *American Educational Research Journal, 30(3), 473–495.*

When teacher educators are researchers, they are learners too. As learners, in their daily classroom activities, science and technology teacher educators have a responsibility to listen to their students' ideas and language, to assess their own teaching approach, to observe their students and to reflect on classroom transactions in an attempt to make changes that will improve learning.

Thus, science and technology teacher educators are, at least informally, carrying out **action research**—using classroom data to clarify curriculum and learning problems. As researchers, teacher educators develop problem-solving skills and a questioning attitude. This questioning attitude can further refine their data-gathering methods and analysis techniques and so improve the quality of teaching and learning.

6.6 Action Research

Action research has been defined as 'research carried out by practitioners with a view to improving their professional practice and understanding it better'. It is a form of inquiry centred on relevance and context to bring about change in practice. Action research involves trying out ideas in practice as a means of increasing knowledge about and/or improving curriculum teaching and learning. Collaborative action research with science and technology teachers helps to eliminate the isolation that has long characterized teaching, as it promotes professional dialogue leading to the creation of a professional culture in schools. Collaborative action research can also assist teachers doing research for the first time.

There are a number of models for action research. Problem-solving projects are common forms of this type of research. Action research models usually involve a cycle of reflecting, planning, collecting data, trying out strategies, obtaining and analysing feedback, modifying plans in the light of feedback, and continuing on the cycle as summarized in Figure 1.

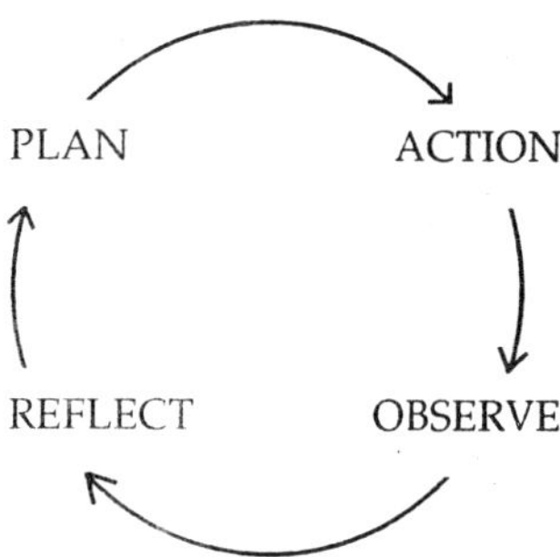

Figure 1

6.6.1 Characteristics of Action Research

Action research, like other types of research, seeks to increase knowledge and understanding of a phenomenon or event. However it differs from more formal research methods in a number of ways:

- Action research does not require extensive training in research methods. Teacher educators can carry it out on their own, in collaboration with another teacher educator, a research specialist or a teacher.
- The goal of action research is to obtain knowledge that can be applied directly to the situation being studied.

It also helps to improve the teacher educators' performance.

- Problems investigated in action research are ones that teacher educators view as interfering with their efficiency or that of their colleagues.
- Action research does not require the rigorous literature review expected in more formal research. A literature review using secondary sources is usually adequate to being with.
- Action research can use the students, with whom the teacher educators work, as subjects.
- Action research is flexible: immediate changes can be made to plans in response to the particular conditions of a situation.
- The tools used to not need to be tested in separate trials and reliability and validity established.
- Analysis of most action research data involves use of simple descriptive statistics instead of inferential procedures. The subjective opinion of the researcher is given prominence. The focus is on practical significance of the results rather than statistical significance.
- In contrast to formal research, where research findings are reported in terms of their theoretical importance, action research findings are reported to portray the impact of the findings on the science and technology teacher educator's work. They are also reported to inform other science and technology teacher educators about the implications of the research for professional development.

6.6.2 Focus Areas for Action Research in Science and Technology Education

Since action research is geared towards helping practitioners to study their own practice in order solve their problems, the content of the research should be relevant to the teaching activities of the teacher educators and teachers.

CASE STUDY 2

Attracted to science: A close look at a primary science lesson

A single science lesson was video-taped in Guguletu for an action-research module of the B.Ed. course at the University of Cape Town (UCT), by the Primary Science Programme, Western Cape (South Africa).

Teaching in large classes (1:55) through a second (or third) language as a medium of instruction (English), with insufficient science equipment, is common in the majority of primary schools. Hope for immediate meaningful change therefore depends on teachers taking responsibility for improvement.

In this case study, a series of group practical activities on the topics of magnetism, and measuring volume was conducted, giving pupils the opportunity to observe the features and properties of magnets and the measurement of volumes of liquids, so that they could develop a clearer understanding.

Amongst other things, the following featured very strongly:

- pupils used a vernacular (Xhosa) during the practical activity to argue/explain/discuss the topic with each other;
- pupil activities served as a basis for thought and problem solving;
- the powerful role of the teacher as a mediator of learning.

This case study focused on a specific aspect of shifting the ownership of learning to the pupils. It resulted in the teacher shifting from his role as dispenser of information to a facilitator of pupils' own leaning.

Research based on the activities carried out by science and technology educators and teachers can be classified into the following broad areas:

- **Students' Learning.** This may involve using strategies to explore students' ideas about science and technology or identifying the problem-solving strategies of students. Areas such as pupils' misconceptions; questioning; designing and making; scientific vocabulary and 'second-language-science-learning' could be investigated.

- **Teaching Strategies.** This may include trying out different approaches to teaching science and technology topics. For example, the teacher may be interested in finding out how he or she can help pupils to have a better understanding of the particulate nature of matter. The teacher educator may also be interested in finding out how a teacher or trainee teacher uses a teaching technique to which he or she has been introduced.

EXAMPLE

Does an alternative strategy to traditional practical work in schools, which is more cost-effective, achieve similar objectives?

Will participation in 'hands-on' activities help pupils to develop:

- a more positive attitude towards science practicals?
- an increased understanding of certain basic scientific concepts?
- designing and making skills?

• **Attitude.** This will include developing ways of increasing pupils' interests in science and technology and counteracting negative attitudes. It may also involve developing ways of increasing the involvement of girls in science and technology. For example: Is there a gender difference in pupils' enjoyment of practical work? What kinds of 'hands-on' activities increase the motivation of girls to study science and technology?

• **Assessment and Evaluation.** Assessment and evaluation are integral parts of the educational process because they provide vital feedback about the extent to which the objectives of science and technology education are being achieved. The information obtained through assessment and evaluation can be used to take corrective measures. Teacher educators and teachers can conduct research on issues and problems related to assessment and evaluation, such as:

- god assessment practices for the measurement and evaluation of students' behaviour, ethics and values;

- techniques for assessing the skills of acquiring, organising and using information.

6.7 Promoting Science and Technology Education Research

As stated earlier, science and technology teacher educators are expected to conduct research for their own professional development, on their own, in collaboration with colleagues, teachers and with other researchers. Relevant research findings can have beneficial effects on their competence, on the content of the curriculum, and on the learning environment. They need to know how to initiate, execute and use research.

Science and technology teacher educators may obtain problems or ideas for research by:

- observing and listening to students and teachers in the classroom;
- obtaining feedback from research findings which may motivate them to initiate action research;
- reflecting on their own teaching procedure;
- observing and examining classroom teaching practice of trainee teachers;
- developing a habit of questioning and testing the ideas of other practitioners in the field;
- critically examining assessment results and assignments;
- critically reviewing research studies conducted by others.

This list is by no means exhaustive. However, for science and technology teacher educators to take a research approach to their teaching, they should be willing to examine their own practice critically and systematically, be able to identify discrepancies between the reality (in their classrooms) and what is considered 'good practice'. Such an approach requires open-mindedness on the part of teacher educators.

6.7.1 Why a Research Proposal?

Once a research idea has been conceived, or a problem identified for research, it is good practice to write it up as a research proposal.

Apart from possibly being needed for an application for funding or a proposal for studying a higher degree, writing a formal research proposal can also serve to focus attention on:

- classifying and stating the problem;
- clarifying the objectives of the research;
- identifying the population, sample and procedure for collecting and analysing data;
- specifying the individual activities in the study and when to perform them;
- identifying the materials required for the study;
- estimating the cost of the various aspects of the study.

A written research proposal also allows the researcher to receive feedback from colleagues on the clarity with which the problem is presented, the procedures to be used in the study, and on the relevant literature available.

6.7.2 Writing a Research Proposal

Science and technology teacher educators need to develop the skill of writing research proposals, as part of their professional responsibilities and development. A research proposal is a systematic description of the researcher's whole plan of action designed to collect the data intended, resolve the problem, provide an answer or demonstrate a need for further research.

The basis elements o' research proposal are:

- **The title.**
- **An introduction and background to the study.**
- **Identification of the problem** to be investigated—a precise statement of the problem or purpose is needed.
- **Identification of research questions or objectives** arising from the problem statement, and the hypothesis, if any, be tested.
- **Details of the research design and procedure,** describing the activities the would lead to the attainment of the objectives—answering the research

questions or testing the hypothesis. These should include: identification of target population and sample, and instruments/materials to be used; phases of the activities, their components, methods or procedures for collecting data and techniques for data analysis.

- **The time schedule.** This should give an indication of the starting date for the research, when it will end and the timetable for the different phases.
- **A budget.** This gives an indication of how much the research will cost. If should be detailed and comprehensive and should include all items of expenditure and the total amount required.

6.7.3 Writing a Research Report

One of the most important aspects of a research study is communicating the results to others. Research reports are means of documenting and disseminating research information. Science and technology teacher educators and their students need to be conversant with the skills of writing research reports.

There are many formats for writing reports but there is general agreement on the format detailed below.

- **The title.** The report must start with a title. The title must clearly indicate the subject of the research to the reader.
- **The abstract.** After the title comes the abstract, which contains the important ideas and main steps of the study. It is a brief summary of the whole study and should include a statement of its purpose, the type of subjects used, brief statement of design, data and analysis techniques, results and findings. The whole should be on longer than three-quarters of a side of A4 paper.
- **Statement of the problem.** The statement introduces the reader to the problem which should be clearly described. If research hypothesis were formulated, these should also be included in this sections of the report.
- **Literature review.** This summarises the researcher's critical appraisal of relevant published material, which

highlights the need for the study. It also provides a theoretical framework for the study.

- **Design and procedure**. In this section the researcher should clearly explain the following aspects:
  - the nature of the design including the sample: whether it is a descriptive survey, correlational or experimental design; the characteristics of the samples, including number, sex, age-range, class or form, and sampling procedure.
  - the instruments, such as questionnaires, rating scales, tests, etc., which served as the main tools for obtaining data, including the name of the instrument, complete details of its source, and psychometric characteristics such as reliability and validity information;
  - the procedure followed to conduct the study: a detailed step-by-step description of how it was carried out.
- **Results.** There are many ways of presenting results depending on what they are, how they are collected and what they are intended to show. Tables, graphs, lists or figures should be used where possible to help present results clearly, and referred to in the account of the results. All tables, charts, graphs and terminology used should be clearly explained so that they help the reader to understand the report. Where statistical tests of significance have been indicated, it is useful to include all formulations that led to the rejection or acceptance of the stated hypotheses. In qualitative research, a detailed description of observations made, including some of key statements made by the source of data, should be included.
- **Discussion of results.** In this section the results should be carefully explained (of course within the limitations of the study), question by question or hypothesis by hypothesis. Part of the discussion should include explanations of the results within the context of existing knowledge of the problem. Do the results contradict or

corroborate other findings? Or do the results stand out clearly on their own? Are there unexpected results?—Why? Here the researcher should explain, argue and possibly make predictions based on his or her findings. This is the section for the researcher to propound his of her views.

- **Bibliography and references.** The bibliography is a list of the publications studied by the researcher. Quotations or particular references to other work in the report are listed under 'References'. If the report is intended for publication in a journal, the author should refer to that publication and follow their style for setting out the references or bibliography.

As well as teaching their students the skills of writing research reports, science and technology teacher educators themselves should put these skills into practice.

6.8 Recommendations in Support of Research in Science and Technology Education

- **Research data banks.** To promote research in science and technology it would be immensely helpful if data banks were created where research data could be stored and made available to researchers to support action research. The data bank could also provide researchers' and teachers' research findings for use in their research/teaching. The Commonwealth Secretariat may like to support the establishment of such banks and their networks.

- **Workshops in action research.** Many science and technology teacher educators working at the primary level do not have enough experience of research. They do not lack knowledge of research problems and issues but they lack competence and experience in research methodology. It would be very useful if workshops could be organized for teachers and teacher educators to develop their skills of research methodology. This would help promote action research. The Commonwealth Secretariat may like to support such training programmes or conduct workshops in member countries.

- **Private sector involvement.** Education authorities, industry, public and private sectors should be called upon to encourage and support research.
- **Regional cleaning houses.** Science and technology research materials, such as research reports and evaluation instruments published in the local language, should be collected in regional centres. Many educational institutions cannot subscribe to journals. Ways should be found to make formulas available to educational institutions doing research.
- **Networking.** Networks of researchers and institutions conducting research in science and technology should be established.
- **Dissemination**. Mechanisms should be set up for the dissemination of research information, particular at the local level.
- **Support mechanism for novice researchers.** Teacher educators of primary teachers generally lack research skills. To promote research, teacher educators need training in research methodology. They also need support at different stages of research through the establishment of suitable mechanisms. The establishment of research advisory committees could be one way forward.

Part V

TRAINING OF TRAINERS IN SCIENCE, TECHNOLOGY AND MATHEMATICS EDUCATION: REGIONAL WORKSHOP REPORT

1

Executive Summary

1. The regional workshop was held in Kaduna, Nigeria from 30 May to 11 June 1993. Three organizations sponsored the workshop with varying inputs. The Commonwealth Secretariat provided seed money for the workshop and the Rockefeller Foundation sponsored the non-Nigerian consultants. The Nigerian National Commission for Colleges of Education (NCCE) hosted the workshop.
2. The NCCE was selected as host for the workshop because of its parastatal status. The Commission was set up by the Nigerian Government of administer all colleges of education in the country. The Commission also provides to the colleges guidance and support in academic and professional growth.
3. The workshop agenda was organized around seven key questions that relate to education of staff for colleges of education:

   Issue 1: Who needs to be trained and why?

   Issue 2: Where should the training take place?

   Issue 3: How many people need to be trained?

   Issue 4: How long should the training be?

   Issue 5: What should be taught and how?

Issue 6: Who should do the training?

Issue 7: Who should pay for the training?

4. Right from the beginning of the workshop, it was made clear that paper presentation would be reduced to a minimum—this was a workshop, instead of a talkshop. Consultants, therefore, presented their papers during the first two days and these were later used as background material for group discussions.

5. A special feature of the workshop was a classroom interaction with teachers in a college of education. The consultants, led by Mr Mike Savage, held very useful discussions on how to use the Candle Experiment to generate questions. Principles which involved scientific, technological and mathematical skills were discussed. Novel activities with the burning candle were derived. Mr. Savage continually stressed the need to use the activity method in teaching science.

6. Participants were divided into three groups for the workshop sessions. Each group developed two monographs. The monographs, still in draft form, were discussed in plenary sessions and were modified by groups according to comments from plenary sessions. The six draft monographs have been bound separately and will be distributed as a separate volume.

7. Participants made a number of recommendations during the evaluation session that was held at the end of the workshop. They included:

(i) Regular INSET programmes should be organized for both academic and non-academic staff of colleges of education.

(ii) There should be a national/regional forum for academic staff of the colleges of education to meet and discuss topical issues in the teaching of STM.

(iii) As the computer has become a versatile equipment in education, plans should be made to have special workshop on use of computers in colleges of education.

(iv) Participants strongly recommended follow-up workshops for all of them who attended the workshop, and stressed the importance of the distance education.

(v) The importance of distance education as a contribution to INSET programmes was stressed.

(vi) Participants recommended that the Commonwealth Secretariat should include their names on the Secretariat's regular mailing lists for receipt of future Comsec publications.

2

Introduction

The initiatives which created the forum for this workshop were provided by the Education Programme (EDP) of the Commonwealth Secretariat. This followed the mandate given by the Eleventh Commonwealth Conference of Education Ministers in Barbados 1990 (11CCEM) and the Commonwealth Heads of Government Meeting in Harare in 1991, to pursue programmes that will improve the quality of basic education. Resulting from this, attention was focused on the role of Higher Education in Science, Technology and Mathematics Education in improving the quality of STME.

Based on the above information, a national/regional Training of Trainers workshop was jointly organized by the Commonwealth Secretariat in London and the National Commission for Colleges of Education, Kaduna, Nigeria, to review the strategies of training STM teachers for the primary and secondary school level of Education in Nigeria and other Commonwealth countries. The workshop was scheduled to last 12 working days.

I. Scope and Objectives

The workshop specifically focused on:

(i) trends in the recruitment of STME staff lecturers in colleges of education;

(ii) suitability of academic and professional staff in colleges of education;

(iii) minimum level of academic and professional qualifications of lecturers;

(iv) initial training needs of STME teaching staff in colleges of education; and

(v) evolving suitable in-service programmes for STME teaching staff in Colleges of Education.

II. Participants

A total of 20 participants from colleges of education were selected to represent the disciplines of science, technology and mathematics. However, the workshop attracted well over 36 participants—16 more participants outside the initial plans (see appendix IV).

Six resources person were drawn from Ghana, Malawi, Zimbabwe, Kenya, Tanzania and Nigeria.

III. Opening Ceremony

The workshop was declared open by the Deputy Governor of Kaduna State, Mr James Bawa Magaji, who was accompanied by the Honourable Commissioner for Education. In his brief address, he drew attention to the importance of science and technology in the development of any country. He particularly underscored the role which teachers could play in science, technology and mathematics education. Kaduna State, he said, was particularly grateful to the Commonwealth Secretariat for initiating and supporting the workshop. He concluded by pledging support for the planned activities during the entire workshop.

The chairman of the occasion, the Executive Secretary of the National Commission for Colleges of Education (NCCE), Professor P.N. Lassa read his address in which the remained the audience of the role of the NCCE. This workshop, he said, is one of the activities which has received the support of the Commission. He welcomed the participants especially the consultants from outside Nigeria.

The goodwill message from the Director of the Education Department of the Commonwealth Secretariat, Mr Peter

Williams was read by Professor S. T. Bajah, Chief Project Officer for Science, Technology and Mathematics Education (STME), Commonwealth Secretariat, London. The role of the Secretariat in improving the quality of basic education in member countries was highlighted.

IV. Plenary Sessions

The first plenary session, Setting the Pace, was presented by Prof. S.T. Bajah and introduced the framework for the workshop. The highlight of his paper touched on the scope and objectives of the workshop, context, strategy adopted, expected outcome of the workshop and follow up. Prof. Bajah emphasized that the essence of the workshop is an attempt to improve the quality of STME where the pupils are actors. Prof. Bajah explained clearly that the workshop was a writing one and not a conference.

At the end of the first day, participants were clear in their minds as to what their tasks and their expectations were going to be.

Activities of the second day was led by Mike Savage of the Rockefeller Foundations. He proposed that science teachers should endeavour to:

(i) teach science as an investigation,

(ii) conduct research, and

(iii) use resource materials from local environment.

The main events of the day were devoted to the presentation of papers by the six consultants and development of a framework for the monographs. During these presentations there were video shows to back up the areas of focus. The video films provided the basis and opportunity for discussions.

One of the exciting highlights of the workshop was the demonstration lesson at the Federal College of Education, Zaria. This activity was led and conducted by Mike Savage. The simple classical candle experiment generated a very interesting scientific discussion.

V. Group Sessions

For the remaining days of the workshop, efforts were concentrated on group work on development of the monographs. The workshop broke into three groups, based on the titles of the monographs. Each of the consultants served as facilitator to each group.

Group 1 - Monographs 1 and 6

Group 2 - Monographs 2 and 4

Group 3 - Monographs 3 and 5

The five objectives (identified above) for the workshop were carefully developed into the main focus areas. These focus areas provided the basis on which the monographs were produced. The six draft monographs and some of the highlights are as follows:

Monograph One—Training Needs of STM Tutors

- general overview/purpose
- recruitment of STME tutors
- selection procedure for STME tutors
- promotion prospects
- academic and professional needs
- professional responsibilities
- INSET programme
- recommendations

Monograph Two—Mobilising Material Resources for STME Training

- identification/acquisition of manufactured items
- identification/acquisition of locally available items
- improvization of items
- making of transparencies as teachers' aids
- proper use of OHP
- making/using video tapes for teacher education
- recommendations

Monograph Three—Co-ordinating Science, Technology and Mathematics in Schools

- orientation workshop/implementation of objectives
- managing school resources
- organizing in-school workshop and activities
- organizing out-of-school STM activities
- teaching STM to large classes
- summary

Monograph Four—Teaching Practice for STM

- organising/co-ordinating teaching practise
- duration of teaching practice
- supervision of teaching practice
- specialist supervision
- generalist supervision
- record keeping in teaching practice
- student-teacher placement record sheet
- assessment sheet
- attendance sheet
- micro-teaching
- summary

Monograph Five—Measurement, Assessment and Evaluation in STM

- need for accountability
- evaluation in STM programme
- make of accountability/monitoring system
- communicating quantitative/qualitative information
- formative/summative evaluation
- continuous assessment in STM

- evaluation in STM
- evaluation records

Monograph Six—Participating in Research

- purpose/what is STME research?
- what research says to STME tutors
- STME tutor as a researcher
- initiating research
- writing research proposal
- writing research report
- strategies for encouraging action-research

The aims and objectives of the workshop were achieved. All the monographs were completed in draft form at the end of the workshop. The workshop was rounded up with a closing ceremony. The Honourable Commissioner for Education, Kaduna State declared the workshop closed.

VI. Summary of Activities

Eight background papers were presented as follows:

1. **Trainers of Trainers in STME: Framework for Discussion**—Background paper by Professor S. T. Bajah, Chief Project Officer, Commonwealth Secretariat;
2. **Training Needs for STM Tutors** by Bryan Wilson—presented on his behalf by Prof. S. T. Bajah;
3. **Do We Practice What We Preach or Should We Change?** by Mike Savage, Rockefeller Foundation;
4. **Interactive Teaching** by Dr. R. A. Hodzi, Department of Science and Mathematics Education, University of Zimbabwe;
5. **Science and Technology Education and Society: Bridging the Gap** by Dr. J. Anamuah-Mensah, Department of Science Education, University of Cape Coast, Ghana;

6. **Video and Teacher Education: Primary School Science Video Teacher Education in Malawi** by Harold F. Gonthi, Malawi Institute of Education;

7. **Participating in Science Education Research—Supporting Teacher Change** by Dr. Gilbert O. M. Onwu, Department of Teacher Education, University of Ibadan, Nigeria;

8. **Science Camps for Children: A Model for Curriculum Renewal and Change** by S. S. Mohammed, Educational Research and Curriculum Development, Penba—Zanzibar, Tanzania.

3

Training of Trainers in Science, Technology and Mathematics Education (STME): Framework For Discussion

Professor S. T. Bajah

I. Introduction

Following the Commonwealth Conference of Education Ministers (CCEM) in Barbados (October 1990) and the recent meeting of Commonwealth Heads of Government in Harare (October 1991), the Education Programme (EDP) of the Commonwealth Secretariat was given a mandate to pursue programmes that will improve the quality of basic education. With respect to Science, Technology and Mathematics Education (STME), attention was focussed on the role which higher education institutions can play in improving the quality of STME. The Trainer of Trainers (TOT), i.e., academic/professional staff in Colleges of Education responsible for the training of STM teachers became a target group. This programme therefore is meant to raise the quality of TOTs so that their products, the teachers who go into basic education to teach will deliver STM in a stimulating way relevant to the needs of the children in schools.

II. Scope and Objectives

The National/Regional workshop should provide an opportunity for lecturers of STM in Colleges of Education to review their strategies for training STM teachers who are being propared to teach in both the primary and secondary school cycle of education in Nigeria and other Commonwealth countries. Innovative practices in the training of STM teachers will be identified and reviewed.

Focusing specifically on STME, the workshop would:

(a) identify the trend in the recruitment of STME staff for Colleges of Education;

(b) assess the suitability of the academic and professional staff in Colleges of Education;

(c) specify the minimum level of academic and professional qualification most suitable for STME lecturers in Colleges of Education;

(d) make suggestions for initial training of the STME teaching staff in Colleges of Education;

(e) evolve suitable in-service programmes for STME teaching staff in Colleges of Education;

Seven key issues/questions were derived from the above aims, with special emphasis on STME teachers in Colleges of Education:

Issue 1: Who needs to be trained and why?
Issue 2: Where should the training take place?
Issue 3: How many people need to be trained?
Issue 4: How long should the training be?
Issue 5: What should be taught, and how?
Issue 6: Who should do the training?
Issue 7: Who pays for the training?

III. Content

The training workshop is scheduled to last 12 working days:

Days 1-3 (3 days)	Orientation and developing plan of action
Days 4-8 (5 days)	Group discussion and exchange of experiences; writing of draft training materials;
Days 9-10 (2 days)	Plenary discussion and critique sessions;

Days 11-12 (2 days) Production of final versions of training materials.

The orientation will involve real classroom experience with STM teachers in an identified College of Education. Participants will be challenged and expected to participate in tackling the question-

"DO WE PRACTICE WHAT WE PREACH?"

A suggested list of monographs is attached.

IV. Participants

Three Groups of participants have been selected for this workshop:

(a) A total of 20 local participants were judgementally selected from Colleges of Education to represent the three disciplines of **science, technology and mathematics education.** The criteria for selection among others included ability to play leadership role in the training of other STM education lecturers in Colleges of Education. Out of this pool of 20 the group which will act as facilitators in similar regional workshops will be selected.

(b) A total of seven researchers were selected to present and discuss aspects of their work which is relevant to the training of STM tutors.

(c) A small core of consultants will be selected to act as group leaders in relevant aspects of training STM tutors.

V. Strategy Adopted

After every intensive discussion in-house here in the Education Programme, specific objectives were identified and a set of modalities purposed. A planning meeting of consultants was organized in May 1992 and a series of recommendation were made. One which is relevant to the above project relates to "a structure of continuing, school-focussed, and inter-related in-service education (INSET) for teachers and teacher educators involving the concept of key teachers and a Cascade Strategy". To that effect, a series of regional workshops followed by national workshops have been suggested. (This workshop in Nigeria is therefore the first in the series of national-regional workshops).

VI. Venue

This workshop is being hosted by the National Commission for Colleges of Education (NCCE), Kaduna. NCCE has completed arrangements to use the facilities available at the National Teachers' Institute (NTI), Kaduna for the workshop.

Accommodation in Kaduna will be in Durbar Hotel.

VII. Resource Persons (Consultants)

Resource persons have been identified and invited to the workshop. Three out of the five resource persons participated in the planning meeting in Hertford, the report of which is included in the folders. The resource persons, all experienced teachers trainers will in essence act as facilitators during the workshop.

VIII. Outcome

At the end of the training workshop, draft training monographs would be produced. The monographs will address the various issues raised and based on the advice of the consultants, the monographs will be combined into volumes. (See the attached list of suggested monographs).

IX. Sponsors

This regional workshop is being sponsored by three organizations:

(a) The Commonwealth Secretariat, London (COMSEC)

(b) The National Commission for Colleges of Education, Kaduna (NCCE)

(c) The Rockefeller Foundation, Nairobi (The African Forum for Children's Literacy in Science and Technology).

It is hoped that other interested international agencies who have been invited to this workshop as observers will fully participate in subsequent workshops.

X. Follow-Up

The focus of this workshop will be kept alive. Using our cascade model, a series of national regional workshops will follow, organized the run by participants who have attended this workshop. Two regional workshops have earmarked to take place before April 1994:

(a) Regional Workshop in Zimbabwe to cater for East and Southern Africa.

(b) Regional Workshop in Suva to cater for the Pacific and Small Island States.

Project 2000+-Science and Technology Education for All

These series of workshops in STM for the Trainer of Trainers have a direct link with the Phase 3 of the UNESCO/ ICASE/COMSEC initiative of **"Science and Technology Education for All"**.

Details of Project 2000+ have been provided in the documents made available to participants at this workshop in Kaduna.

IMPROVING THE QUALITY OF SCIENCE, TECHNOLOGY AND MATHEMATICS EDUCATION

Some Suggested Focus Areas for Preparation of Monographs

Monograph One

Training Needs of STM Tutors

- Survey of present trent in recruitment
- Academic and professional responsibilities
- Academic needs and qualifications
- Professional needs and qualifications
- INSET programmes for turots

Monograph Two

Mobilising Material Resources for STME Training

- Identification and acquisition of manufactured items
- Identification and acquisition of locally available items
- Making transparencies as teaching aids
- Proper use of OHP
- Making and using video tapes for teacher education

Monograph Three

Co-ordinating STM in Schools

- Selection and training of head teachers for STM
- Managing school resources for STM
- Organising in-school workshops
- Budgeting for STM in schools
- Organising out-of-school STM activities
- Teaching STM to large classes

Monograph Four

Teaching Practice for STM

- Organising and co-ordinating teaching practice
- Record keeping in teaching practice
- Micro-teaching

Monograph Five

Measurement Assessment and Evaluation in STM

- Need for accountability
- Communicating quantitative information
- Continuous assessment
- Record keeping

Monograph Six

Precipitating in STME Research

- What does research say to the STM teacher
- Initiating research
- Writing research proposals and reports
- Bridging school science and technology

Monograph Seven

STME For All

- Project 2000+

Monographs Eight—Ten

- Any suggestions?

4

Training Needs of STM Tutors

Bryan Wilson

Purpose

This paper is concerned with the proposed Monograph 1 at the Commonwealth Secretariat National-Regional Workshop, 1993. It attempts to provide a framework within which participants can develop a draft of the Monograph.

Introduction

The Commonwealth Secretariat Project has as its ultimate purpose the raising of the quality of STME at the Basic Education level in countries across the Commonwealth. The Project recognizes that STM tutors in institutions of higher education, including Colleges of Education, are the group of people who hold the key to this.

Traditionally, however, such tutors are recruited largely on academic criteria and qualifications, with comparatively little attention being paid to their school teaching experience, classroom effectiveness, commitment to children or appreciation of broader curriculum issues in schools.

The situation is made worse by the lack of training programmes, either initial or in-service, specifically designed for STM Tutors. It seems to be assumed that, if they have done well in their own academic studies, they are thereby capable of training teachers to teach that subject effectively to children.

This project aims to develop a set of Monographs which will both point to the need for serious INSET training for STM Tutors, and provide resources for such training. No. 1 in the series, "Training Needs of STM Tutors", will survey the present situation in terms of the recruitment, qualifications and responsibilities of STM Tutors, and outline principles for the development of INSET programmes for them.

Sections of Monograph

The following main sections are suggested:

- Recruitment of STM Tutors
- Academic responsibilities of STM Tutors
- Academic qualifications and needs of STM Tutors
- Professional responsibilities of STM Tutors
- Professional qualifications and needs of STM Tutors
- Content of INSET Programmes for STM Tutors

Participants should contribute views and information from their own countries/regions/institutions to help include answers to the following questions in the Monograph:

Recruitment of STM Tutors

What weight is given to formal academic qualifications—Doctorate/Masters/Diploma/Other—in the appointment of STM Tutors?

What weight is given to school teaching experience in the appointment of STM Tutors?

Is it possible for a person to be appointed as a STM Tutor who has never taught in a school at the level for which his/her students are being trained? If so, is this acceptable?

Is there evidence that present recruitment criteria for STM Tutors results in effective professional training for their students?

Who selects STM Tutors? How can they be influenced to adopt more appropriate criteria?

Academic Responsibilities of STM Tutors

What academic levels are aimed at in training STM teachers for the Basic Education cycle?

What academic examinations are incorporated into their courses? Are these examinations explicitly designed for teachers in training?

Are these academic levels and examinations appropriate for trainee teachers for the Basic Education cycle?

It is considered that the academic levels currently demanded are not appropriate, who has the power to change them, and how can they be influenced to do so?

Academic Needs and Qualifications of STM Tutors

Are the present academic qualifications required for appointment as a STM Tutor actually necessary for the fulfilment of his/her future academic responsibilities, or are they used simply to cut down the field of likely applicants?

It there any provision for the academic updating of STM Tutors? Does there need to be?

Professional Responsibilities of STM Tutors

Is the professional training of STM teachers left entirely to a 'Professional' Department? Or does every STM Tutor see his/her role in professional as well as in academic terms?

List the 'professional' responsibilities of STM Tutors.

Do all Tutors recognize all these professional responsibilities?

Is the academic professional balance of responsibility satisfactory? If not, how can it be changed?

In teaching their subject, do STM Tutors deliberately adopt methodologies that will help their students to see how the subject-matter can be taught in school?

Or do they just 'lecture'?

How can Tutors be influenced to use methods of teaching themselves that refinforce their students' professional training, and model the methods that they will be encouraged to use in schools?

Professional Needs and Qualifications of STM Tutors

In the light of the information thrown up in the previous sections, participants should consider some major recommendations under this heading, which is the main thrust of this Monograph. For example:

(a) Teacher education needs to be seen as a profession in its own right, separate from that of e.g. 'mathematician' or 'scientist' or 'researcher' or 'university lecturer' or 'academic'. See Mary Harris (1992), para. 31.

(b) There needs to be a major shift from the 'academic' to the 'professional' in the selection and training of STM Tutors.

(c) No STM Tutor should be appointed without successful school classroom experience, preferably for a minimum of five years.

(d) All newly-appointed STM Tutors should undergo a training programme to prepare them for their new responsibilities.

(e) INSET programmes should be available for all STM Tutors. It is for consideration whether regular participation in INSET should be a condition for continuing in post.

INSET Programmes for STM Tutors

Do any INSET programmes, specifically designed for STM Tutors, exist? If so, list them. Are they primarily academic or professional?

What form do they take? Are they in-college? Day-courses? Week-end courses? Vacation courses? Self study courses? Correspondence courses? In-school courses?

What provision is there for STM Tutors who have been in post for some years to update their own teaching experience at the level for which they are training their students to teach?

This project proposes a 'Cascade Strategy' of INSET provision; see Mary Harris (1992), paras 20-22 and 32-37. The strategy would involve both STM Tutors and STM teachers in schools. This Monograph should summarise this strategy, and explain that other Monographs in the series will deal more with the content of such INSET courses.

The basic principles on which such INSET courses could be based include:

- academic and professional INSET cannot be separated;
- tutors have varying needs at different career stages; see Mary Harris (1992), para 29;
- Key teachers should be involved in INSET for Tutors;
- courses should not be narrowly subject-focussed, but should be constructed against a background of broad curriculum issues and inter-disciplinary approaches. An excellent exemplar of such approach is Gibbs and Mutunga (1991), which develops the teaching of mathematics at Basic Level in a way which integrates it with health education. Two others in this series are due for publication by Longman in 1994: 'Health into Social Studies' (July 1994) and 'Health into Science' (September 1994);
- the professional associations for science, technology and mathematics education, e.g., STAN, MAN, MAG, GAST, should be fully involved in the development of national strategies for INSET for STM Tutors.

REFERENCES

Gibbs and Mutunga (1991), *Health into Mathematics*. Longman, Harlow, UK

Mary Haris (1992) *Improving the Quality of Science and Mathematics Education—the Role of Higher Education*. Commonwealth Secretariat, London, UK.

5

Do We Practice What We Preach? or Should We Change Our Practice or Our Sermon

Mr Mike Savage

Where Do We Stand?

Oxygen is necessary for burning. It is one-fifth of the air around. Things expand when they are heated. These facts are part of every educated person's culture, wherever she or he may live.

Over ninety per cent of teachers demonstrate the truth of these facts, or at least make pupils copy the appropriate diagram from the chalk-board. They do so by placing a glass or similar container over a burning candle that stands in a dish of water. The candle goes out, water rises in the glass. If the experiment is done properly and good measurements made, the water rise is one-fifth of the volume of the glass. If it is not, the experiment hasn't worked properly. Try again until it does or blame the faulty, locally made apparatus.

Many people call this science. Many people would call the demonstration that I have described, good teaching. Unformately both the science and the teaching are mostly rubbish. More unfortunately, much of what goes on in our schools in the name of science teaching is mostly rubbish and I'm not restricting my comments to Africa. Since my background is science, I have focussed my paper of science. Perhaps what I say is also true of technology and mathematics.

As leading science educators, we should be honest and admit when we are promulgating rubbish, or try to do something about it.

What is Science?

Why is what I've described not science and mostly rubbish? Do the experiment and actually observe what happens. Try using two or more candles; doing so shouldn't effect the result. But does it?

Part of the problem is that so few of us, whether we are university professors or primary school teachers have ever done most of what we lecture about, expect perhaps when we were being taught ourselves. When we find ourselves lecturing too much we say our teaching is becoming too "theoretical" and try to introduce some "practicals". Unfortunately both our "theory" and our "practice" too often has little to do with the scientist's use of these words as Shaaban S. Mohammed points out in his paper, "Science Camps for Children: A Model for Curriculum Renewal and Change". To scientists, theory, means an active intellectual search for meaning that uses experimentation (practicals) in an integrated fashion to better understand their world. To most science educators, theory means passing on the fruits of others' learning, and practical work means that students should follow instructions to establish the one so-called correct answer. To continue to do what we have been doing may be acceptable in the circumstances of our schools in Africa, but we must be aware of the fundamental misrepresentations we promulgate. Perhaps we should not call what goes on in our schools science.

To me, science is what we do to try to understand the burning candle. As Jos Elsgeest once put it, science lies between the question and the answer. The search may entail using all those scientific process we know so well. It may entail heated debate with others. It may entail a critical reading of books and articles. But whatever, I claim that science is the search. (Have you figured out what's going on with the burning candle? Can you convince me?)

Why Should Students Learn Science Anyway?

That the teacher, syllabus and so on says so are too arrival answers. So are answers such as to pass examinations, get a good job, or to earn lots of money. Examples of more sophisticated answers are to train citizens that can make rational decisions, contribute to national development, and so on. Every policy statements have such justifications.

In think we should all try to answer the questions about ourselves. I hated science and learned it at secondary school and university only because I was expected to follow the family tradition and become a doctor. Neither I nor my family were in any way interested in the content. We were only interested in the results. Had the syllabus been restricted to anatomy of nematode worms, that would have been fine with us as long as the universities and society recognized the examination certificate. I often ask myself whether the science I learned is of any use in my daily life and frankly, I cannot remember using any in the last six months, except of course when I'm teaching. I suspect that most people's answers would be similar to my own.

I learned some subjects at school because I enjoyed them and was good at them. Those subjects captured my mind; they entertained me as much as going to the movies or the disco, Fortunately, science leaving university I have come to enjoy learning science in the same sort of way. I am fortunate that the skills I have developed as a result of this enjoyment earn we good money in a well paid, and respected job.

I claim that children should learn science, indeed any subject, because it stretches their minds, in the way that learning some subjects stretched my own. Students learning should stimulate their creativity and give them maximum excitement. When I read policy statements that science contributes to economic and national development, I smile as I think of the boom economies of the Far East based upon the nimble fingers of uneducated, adolescent girls.

"Science is Doing the Damnest with one's Mind; on Holds Barred."

Peter Medewar, Noble Laureate

How Do We Learn Science

If we believe that science is remembering other's theories together with recipes for performing specified practicals, then probably rote memorization is a fine way to learn the subject; that is if one has a good memory. Rote learning probably works even if one already has conflicting conceptual structures developed as a result of living in one's particular cultural environment. Everybody acts schizophrenically at moments and we all have our own experience of this. For example, I still smoke cigarettes. But even if we believe science is only a matter of applying others theories is a new situation, or trying to experiment to find out something we don't already know, rote learning becomes problematic **(Have you solved the candle problem yet?).** If we do, maybe we have to considered teaching/ learning approaches based on constructivist learning theories.

Analysing the way I learn myself, I know that often it takes me some time to even see the problem **(Have you noticed yet what happens if you use more than one candle? Does this nose problems applying your hypothesis?).** As the constructivists say, I have to use my own conceptual frameworks to try to explain new phenomena that I observe (My theory that the water rises to take the place of the oxygen consumed is not adequate to explain what I observe when I use more than one candle. But then again, I do live in a country with amazing distance runners. Perhaps Kenyan air is richer in oxygen).

Personally, I don't think that even constructivist learning theories, and classroom practice derived from them is enough to encourage scientific creativity. Again being personal since I know myself better than I know anybody else, I confess that I have to be highly motivated to learn; I have to be trapped by a problem if I'm really going to stubbornly work at it to my satisfaction,—rather than to the satisfaction of the teacher or the syllabus. But probably more important, it has taken me long time of exposure to investigating puzzles such as the candle burning to become addicted to behaving scientifically. I have become better at seeing problems, puzzles and marvels all around me. Since I've used shorthand throughout this paper, let me use the phrase inquiring learning to communicate what I think is necessary to nurture this frame of mind.

What Should Teachers Know to Teach Inquiry Science

Nobody who has never engaged in inquiry science should teach it (I once spent six weeks, many hours each day, burning candles and thinking about it). You have to experience the excitement, the frustrain of one's hypotheses being inadequate, the boring repetitive work, one's own apparent stupidity and limitations, the need to become systematic, measures accurately, predict and design experiments to test the predictions, the appreciation of others' elegant solutions, the self confidence to continue. I would call this content and Shaaban S. Mohammed's paper has more to say about learning content. I would not call content adding yet more information to the information students have that has already proved inadequate to make them good teachers. Why add to what has already demonstrably failed? But I do not rule out consolidating what students know by having them apply their knowledge in problem solving situations, or to add to it as their expanding conceptual frameworks demand.

Secondly, nobody should teach inquiry science who has not reflected about learning. For a start, I think that students should be reflective and analytical about they themselves learn. I think that students should work with children to learn more at first hand about how they learn (Part of the six weeks I spent burning candles was with a couple of children in their fourth year of primary school and I now know something of how kids of that age think about phenomenon. This was in the days of Piaget. In the era of constructivism, I should have done this work in classrooms). I would call this educational psychology and Richard Hodzi and Anamuah-Mensah have more to say about educational psychology. I do not mean the standard educational psychology courses,—the tour of Piaget, Vygotsky, Driver et al. Again, I would not rule not study about them, but only after students have developed their own groping understandings of how children learn.

Thirdly, nobody should teach inquiry science without serving an apprenticeship in classrooms. (I spent my hours working with another researcher in a Standard IV class learning how to teach about burning candles). Students have to learn how to trap kids into work on phenomena. They too learn how to ask the right question and when not to interact. Students have to learn how to manage forty children busily at work. They have to learn when most of the class are ready to benefit from a classroom discussion, scientists theories of the problem and so on. Teaching is a craft, like carpentry, that can best be learned by practice, hopefully in the company of crafts people. I would call this pedagogy or teaching methods and Mohammed, Hodzi, Gonthi and Anumuah-Mensah have more to say about pedagogy. I do not regard pedagogy is best learned directly by working in schools and indirectly by being taught in a style that the teacher is advocating.

Educating student teachers the way that I advocate raises problems of time, of access to children, and of access to classrooms and experienced teachers to act as mentors. Problems of time relate to the syllabuses and examinations which can be changed. I have never found access to children or classrooms a problem in Africa, nor have I found changing syllabuses and examinations an insurmountable task. Perhaps the problem is one of will.

How Should Teachers Learn How to Teach Inquiry Science?

I have more or less discussed this issue in the preceding paragraphs. Teachers should learn the science content by being asked themselves to engage in inquiry. They should learn the necessary learning theory by working with children and the pedagogy by reflective, experimental teaching in classrooms. Teachers' education should empower them to make good classroom judgements.

What to do About Teachers Already in The Schools?

Practising teachers already know a lot. They know their children, their home culture, their environment, their interests and so on. More important, they know in their bones how lifeless, boring and unsatisfying teaching can be. More so that students, practising teachers respond positively when they see their pupils interested and actively engaged with their own learning. I have been practising teachers become excited over, and over again in every English speaking country in Africa, except the Gambia and Sough Africa where I have not worked. Certainly, teachers also always complain about syllabuses, inspectors, examinations and so on but those are our problems as policy makers and not theirs. Having tested inquiry learning and teaching, in my experience, teachers become strongly motivated.

Any in-service teachers education programme that ignores what teachers know, does so at its peril. Top-down models of in-service education,—where "experts' run training workshops for "ingnorant, unqualified teachers" have failed everywhere in the world where they have been tried. "Experts" increasingly frenzied efforts to pack more into courses, develop more streamlined methods and use modern media to impart their "expertise" have also failed. However effectively we communicate our message, unless teachers are motivated to change and are given some investment in doing so, in our absence they will do what they have always done when they return to their classrooms.

Such motivation and investment can be given if those of us involved in in-service teacher education realize that teachers are our colleagues and in some respects our professional superiors. We should strive for a collegiate relationship. We know more about some things than they do, but they know more about other things than we do. Practising teachers must also be exposed to learning about aspects of their environment through inquiry; to finding out first hand how children think about certain topics; and have the luxury of experimenting with a variety of teaching methods and reflecting on what they do. Clusters of practising teachers need support structure, where they can meet regularly. Teachers need access to others with more specialized skills, to relevant literature, even sometimes to technologies such as typewriters and word processors that will enable them to produce their own teaching/learning materials. Teachers need liberating from limiting syllabuses, examinations and tradition bound inspectors.

Shaaban S. Mohammed is involved with a group this in Zanzibar; Richard Hodzi in Zimbabwe, soon Anamuah-Mensah will be in Ghana. They are not alone.

To end on a more sombre note. In Africa today, when increasingly salaries buy less and less, I find it heartening that teachers are prepared to make any personal investment whatsoever in their professional growth.

6

Interactive Teaching in Primary Science

Dr. R. A. Hodzi

Abstract

Primary science is not just a matter of knowing and making sense of the world; there is an equally emphatic goal of helping children to behave as scientists in the world. While both aspects are important and relevant to science in the primary school, the distinction between conceptual understanding and procedural knowledge is a fundamental and useful one. Conceptual understanding is concerned with the ideas of science; concepts such as what is a plant and what distinguishes plants from animals. What is sound, how it is generated, how it travels, how the human ear receives sound energy.

Scientific concepts are more than insulated 'facts' in the sense that they may be ideas about quite complex relationship between things. On the other hand, science processes describe the ways of behaving scientifically. We might describe most of our daily behaviour as "common-sensical". . . with judgements made for "here and now"; scientific judgements attempt to embody greater generality. This paper presents with no claim completeness—some ideas about learning and teaching science at primary level that enable children to make sense of their world.

Introduction

Children have to construct their own meaning regardless of how clearly teachers or books tell them things, mostly, a child does this by connecting new information and concepts to what he or she already believes. Concept—the essential limits of human thought that do not have multiple links with how a child thinks about the world are not likely to remembered. Concepts are learned best when they are encountered in a variety of contexts and expressed in a variety of ways, for that ensures that there are more opportunities for them to become embedded in a child's knowledge system.

Effective learning often requires more than just making multiple connections of new ideas to old ones; it sometimes requires that children restructure their thinking radically. That is, to incorporate some new ideas, learners must change the connections among the things they already know, or even discard some long-held belief about the world. The alternatives to the necessary restructuring are to distort the new information to fit their old ideas or to reject the new information entirely. Children come to school with their own ideas, some current and some not, about almost every topic they are likely to encounter. If their intuition and misconceptions are ignored or dismissed out of hand, their original beliefs are likely to win out in the long run, even though they may give the test answers their teachers want. More centralization is not sufficient. Children must be encouraged to develop new views by seeing how such views help them make better sense of the world.

It needs to be kept in mind that the purpose of science education at any level is to help children make better sense of their world. Unfortunately, this does not always happen.

The question children are to consider, and the investigations they are to carry out, are usually selected by the teacher or teacher guided material, but not always with a clear understanding of the ideas children bring to the classroom. Even though a range of experience may have been provided, when children's ideas are ignored the children frequently do not discover what it is expected they will discover or change their present ideas in anticipated ways. Some teachers are inclined to say, "well, obviously they are not ready for the ideas" or "we will have to tell them the scientists' view because it is something they need". In my view neither:

(i) the selection of questions and investigations by teachers and curriculum developers without a real awareness of children's questions and ideas; nor

(ii) the extreme views quoted about what is the teacher's role once children have been given an activity;

does justice to the potential abilities of either children or their teachers.

Cognitive research is revealing that even with what is taken to be good instruction, many students including academically talented ones, understand less than we think they do. With determination, students taking an examination are commonly able to identify what they have been told or what they have read; careful probing, however, often shows that their understanding is limited or distorted, if not altogether wrong. This finding suggests that parsimony is essential in setting out educational goals. In planning instruction teachers draw on a growing body of research knowledge about the nature of learning and on craft knowledge about teaching that has stood the test of time. Typically they consider the special characteristics of the material to be learned, the background of their pupils, and the conditions under which the which the teaching and learning are to take place. In order for teaching to the successful there are central needs to be considered and these include:

Activities

Children need to have many and varied opportunities for collecting, sorting and cataloguing, observing, note taking, sketching, interviewing, polling and surveying. Classroom activities must take into account children's ideas and questions. Children need to get acquainted with the things around them including devices, organisms, materials, shapes and numbers and to observe them, collect them, handle them, describe them, become puzzled by them, ask questions about them, argue about them, and then to try to find answers to their questions.

Collection and Use of Evidence

Children should be given problems and at least appropriate to their maturity—that require them to decide what evidence is relevant and to offer their own interpretations of what the evidence mean. This puts a premium, just as science does, on careful observation and thoughful analysis. Children need guidance, encouragement, and practice in collecting, sorting and analyzing evidence and in building arguments based on it.

Conclusion

In making conclusions there is need to ensure that children are neither left to their own devices to form their own conclusions, nor forced to accept "scientific" conclusions that are often formed in technical language and cannot be related to the child's personal experience within or outside the classroom.

Research has shown that attempts have been made in exploring ways that would make children makes sense of their ways. The one that appeals to me is interactive teaching. Interactive teaching is based upon the following:

1. from a young age, children try to make sense of their world and not infrequently already hold ideas about a topic which a teacher intends to introduce;
2. the ideas which children hold about a topic are not necessarily those held by experts, but to the children they can be sensible and useful. When children are typing to understand a topic children will draw on their ideas about the topic, or on other ideas which they think might help them, and such ideas can influence their learning in significant ways;
3. scientific knowledge based on our history and culture is something which is neither simply transmitted from teacher to pupil, nor naturally developed from experience alone. Pupils and teacher must interact and discuss ideas derived from common experiences, investigations, reading books, and asking experts. It is in these ways that children construct more complete, effective and useful ideas than the ones they currently hold;
4. various skills (intellectual processes), particularly those relating to questioning and investigation, are important means by which children can make better sense of their world but children usually need help to develop such skills. Help will be most effective if given at the time when children see the need for specific skills.

5. children can begin to take responsibility for their own learning but this requires an atmosphere where both teachers and pupils genuinely care about and respect each other's ideas, an atmosphere which encourages the children to freely and responsibly express their personal views. It also requires that the teachers help the children separate their ideas from themselves so that questioning of ideas is no longer felt by the children to be a threat to self worth.

What Interactive Approach Tries to do

In my view interactive teaching is based on a interchange to talk among people who respect each other's ideas. From a teacher's point of view this begins with a genuine desire to know what a child thinks and why. The main purposes, therefore, of interactive approach to teaching include:

(a) to identify children's present ideas and questions;

(b) to provide children with stimulating experiences either to confront and explore those ideas or as a basis for developing ideas; in either case the experiences should help children raise questions;

(c) to help children develop, clarify, modify, and extend their ideas through seeking answers to questions they are interested (or can be interested) in or through checking proposed answers;

(d) to encourage children to reflect on how they came by an idea and whether it is a sensible and useful one;

(e) to assist children develop the skills they need to ask better questions, plan and carry out investigation, and construct and communicate ideas;

(f) to help children realize the explanations of why things behave the way they do are frequently not 'right' or 'wrong' but are rather consistent with the evidence or inconsistent, useful or less useful, plausible or not plausible, intelligible or not intelligible; and

(g) to convey to children an awareness that their genuine ideas and valued.

Major Component of an Interactive Teaching Approach

An interactive teaching approach is more than a sensitive way of interacting with children during a series of science lessons. It also involves structuring a study in a way that enables teachers to interact positively with children and at the same time enables children to begin to take responsibility for their own learning. In practice the interactive teaching involves the following:

1.	Invitation:	Observe one's surroundings for points of curiosity Ask questions Consider possible responses to questions Note unexpected phenomena Identify situations where student's perceptions vary
2.	Exploration:	Engage in focussed play Brain-storm possible alternatives Look for information Experiment with materials Observe specific phenomena Design a model Collect and organise data Employ problem-solving strategies Select appropriate resources Discuss solutions with others Design and conduct experiments Evaluate choices Identify risks and consequences Define parameters of an investigation Analyze data
3.	Proposing Explanations and solutions	Communicate information and ideas Construct and explain a model Construct a new explanation Review and critique solutions Utilize peer evaluation Assemble multiple answers/solutions

		Determine appropriate closure Integrate a solution with existing know-l edge and experiences
4.	Taking Action:	Make decisions Apply knowledge and skills Share information and ideas Ask new questions Develop products and promote ideas Use models and ideas to illicit discussion and acceptance by others Approach decisions makers in society urging them to act in specific ways
5.	Reflection:	In addition to conveying to children the feeling that their ideas are valued and that the teacher is not the source of all knowledge, the intention during this phase is to have the children reflect critically on their findings, to open their minds to further possible explanations and investigations, and to consider alternative ways of communicating findings to others.
6.	Evaluation:	Both teacher and children need to be able to assess the value of the investigations. This means asking the question "How valuable was this set of lessons"?

When using interactive teaching, the teacher no longer plays central role but the child. The teacher, however, still has several effective roles which he can adopt in the course of interactive teaching and these include:

Facilitator of Learning

In this role the teacher tries to bring children and relevant resources together. The teacher can do this by directing children to a particular book or equipment.

Resource Person

At times the teacher may have information that a child is seeking. In that ask the teacher can act as a resource person in the same way as a knowledgeable parent, expert or other member of the community.

Naive Fellow Investigator

In this role the teacher expresses ignorance of an explanation or situation. In a sense, the more genuine the ignorance and the more willing the teacher is to learn from the children the better.

Challenger of Ideas

Here the teacher deliberately but sensitively challenges those ideas expressed by the child which are inconsistent with evidence, not useful, not clear and so on. The challenges the teacher poses have the effect of revealing the children's commitment to their present views and perhaps help the children to clarify or reconsider their views. As a challenge of children's ideas a teacher should not always take children's responses at face value but should sensitively explore what they have in mind.

Conclusion

It is now widely recognized that the most effective and relevant science learning takes place through the process of solving problems that occur in, or are immediately 'connectable' to the life of the learner, rather than in contrived situations in a classroom. Learning in science must be based on the pupils' own knowledge and experience so that he/she can achieve real understanding. This means beginning with familiar objects and phenomena encountered in his/her world.

At primary level, it is quite possible, even with minimal apparatus, to embark on a programme of active enquiry, investigation and problem solving which provides experience of ways of handling evidence. Children can be encouraged to observe, raise questions for further enquiry, generate hypotheses, plan their investigations, record and present results, interpret data and so on. It is useful, whenever possible, for these activities to take place outside the classroom. Such an approach can promote the development of thinking pupils, who will become thinking citizens.

REFERENCES

Association for Science Education, University of Leeds (1990) *Children's Learning in Science Project.*

Biddup, F. and Osborne, R. (1984) *Making Sense of Our World.* Centre for Science and Mathematics Education Research, University of Waikato, New Zealand.

IBE-UNESCO 1987 *Science and Technology in the Primary School of Tomorrow.*

Liverpool University Press (1990) *Primary SPACE Project Reports.*

UNESCO 1983 *New Trends in Primary School Science Education*, Vol. I.

UNESCO 1985 *The Training of Primary Science Educators—A Workshop Approach.* Science and Technology Education Series, No. 13.

UNESCO, 1986. *The Teaching of Science and Technology in an Interdisciplinary Context.* Science and Technology Education Series, No. 19.

7

Science and Technology Education and Society: Bridging the Gap

Dr. J. Anamuah-Mensah

Abstract

Science and Technology have for a long time worked to alter societal values, economic progress and political systems. It is also recognized that pressing problems and issues affecting developing countries are related to the interfacing of science, technology and society. In addition, industries provide jobs for a substantial number of school leavers. There is also the recognition that scientific and technological literacy should form part of the basic education for all citizens in a democratic society where decisions have to be taken on issues bordering on science and technology.

Despite these, science and technology education have followed different pathways. Science education has not responded to the needs of the learners and the society. There has been a complete disregard for the many activities in the cultural environment. To bridge the gap two major approaches—'institutional link arrangement' and curriculum materials development—have been used. The STAG project uses the curriculum development approach to develop resource materials for teachers and students. This project involves industry in the write up of industrial accounts which then go through workshops, trailing and publication.

After initial concerns and reservations some industries provided write ups. It is hoped that the project would empower industries to develop materials not only for the formal school system but also for public education purposes.

Introduction

Over the years, the two enterprises, science and technology have worked to reshape societal values, beliefs and concerns, influenced economic development and altered political systems. They have become powerful agents of social and economic change.

Despite this collective influence, science education and technology education have historical followed different pathways and remained as strange bed fellows; convergence has been the exception rather than the rule. Science education as the separate disciplines of physics, chemistry and biology have been offered in most cases to a particular group of students while technical education has been reserved for the generally less academically oriented group of students. Even where students have the opportunity to take both science and technology courses the interconnectedness or science and technology have not been made visible.

Nature of Science and Technology

Science has been defined in different ways by different people.

It has been viewed as a way of seeking information and also as accumulated knowledge resulting from this search. In general science is thought of as being concerned with the generation of new knowledge and understanding (Gardner, 1993). Technology, on the other hand, has been seen to be concerned with the production and improvement of artefacts, systems and procedures to meet human needs and desires (Gardner, 1993) and not simply as a collection of artefacts, however sophisticated and complex they may be.

Another view of technology suggests that 'technology can be characterized as that form of cultural activity devoted to the production or transformation of material objects, or to the creation of procedural systems, in order to expand the realm of human possibility (Hannay and McGinn, 1980).

(Gardner, 1993) argues that the view that technology is the application of scientific knowledge (although supported by historical developments) should be seen as one of four philosophical positions concerned with the relationship between science and technology; and that "no one position provides an account of science-technology relationships which holds true for all cases over all historical periods". The other philosophical positions are: science and technology as distinct fields, technology as precursor of science and the interaction view of science and technology.

For many people today, there is little distinction between science and technology. The two have become closely knitted together such that they are inseparable.

Technologists have tended to use scientific methods of research to develop and improve their products thus making it difficult to determine where science ends and technology begins. Thus, in situations where, for example, parasitic proteins are analysed with the ultimate aim of preparing a sheep vaccine or grafting qualities of certain plants are investigated for the purpose of producing fast growing cassava species, there is obviously a problem of divisibility of the two enterprises.

However, in the school curriculum, we manage to separate them in such a way that they lose their interconnectendness leaving science education to be devoid of relevance for the student and his community.

The Social Context of Science—Technology Education

There is a growing concern that science education programmes have for a long time not been seen as responding to the needs of the learners and the society at large. This concern for qualitative improvement began about three decades ago and has now reached a crisis dimension (Yager, 1992; Gaskell, 1982).

In Ghana and Africa in general, the science taught in school has been closely linked to outmoded examination syllabuses which emphasize memorization of facts and principles (Towse and Anamuah-Mensah, 1991). The "chalk and talk" method has become the most widely used method of teaching science. Textbooks and other written materials such as model answer books and past questions continue to wield excessive power over both teachers and students. In United States, Yagar 1992, reports that 90 per cent of all science teachers use a textbook in excess of 90 per cent of the time while Goldstein 1978 points out that students use textbooks for up to 75 per cent of the time they spend in class and up to 90 per cent of the time they work at home. In Ghanaian schools where written materials are highly valued, the percentage will be much higher.

Another concern is that science education has been pursued with a no regard to the rich cultural environment with its many activities and practices. Science is thus regarded to be culture-free. Students Graduate from science education programmes without being able to change fuses; connect wires to plugs or carry out other such activities.

A way out of this crisis for science education to be responsive to personal goals of learners and the changing needs and values of society has been found in the science-technology and society framework. The current reforms in the Ghanaian educational system including the science syllabuses, place emphasis on science, technology and society issues.

The Need for Science-Technology-Society in Science Curriculum

The choice of science, technology and society framework in the science curriculum has been rationalized in many ways. Some of these are as follows:

Science and technology influence economic development and bring about new social values and arrangements. They therefore have a great impact on society. On the other hand, the activities of scientists and technologists are also influenced to a large extent by society. For example, society's unwillingness to fund research and development activities in certain areas is more than likely to curtail work in these areas.

Most of the pressing problems and issues affecting countries like Ghana are problems related to the interaction of science, technology and society. Some of the problems and issues of social value and population, health, nutrition, energy and environmental degradation which require literacy in science and technology.

Industries in Ghana provide work of a substantial percentage of school levers who always get thrown into the industrial arena with very little knowledge about how the scientific concepts they have learnt in school can be used in the industry (Layton, 1989).

Currently, there is a world-wide recognition that scientific and technological literacy should form part of the foundation of basic education for all citizens. That means that in addition to reading, writing and numeracy, science and technology should be seen as basic to the survival of the human race. It should be seen to cut across all subject domains to provide people with the capacity to be responsive to a wide range of situations that confront them in their daily life. The world needs liberally educated people who can make informed decisions about science-technology-society issues. Studies have shown that the degree of scientific and technological literacy among high school graduates is very high (about 90 per cent) and seems to be growing (Miller, 1989, quoted in Yager, 1993). This tendency needs to be arrested. There is also the realization that scientific and technological illiteracy exist among scientists and science and technology educators because of the high level of academic subject matter specialization granted by the educational system (Yager, 1993).

The democratic wind of change sweeping across many nations such as Ghana these days require the involvement of individuals in decision-making. Participation in democracy dictates that the general public be informed about science and technology (McConnel, 1982). This would enable them to participate in the making of appropriate choices and decisions. This is put more succinctly as follows:

> 'the very structure of a democratic society depends upon the existence of an enlightened citizenary. The political and social behaviour of this citizenry in voting, in influencing elective and appointive officials, and in engaging in political and social

activism will be more constructive for society if it is informed by solid scientific understanding' (Trachtman, 1981).

The question of relevance is another issue which has been debated in educational circles for a long time. Relevance can be viewed as how useful the content of learning is to the individual himself as well as to the nation. The learning should be such it can be applied to solving problems in the everyday life of the individual.

The gap that exist between science taught in schools and that encountered in the 'real' world outside especially in industry has been of major concern to many science educators and governments.

Bridging the Gap

In many countries in the world, attempts have been made to close the yawning communication gap that characterizes the interconnection of science, technology and society.

These attempts can be classified into those that involve the production of curricula materials for use in the classroom and those involving 'institutional link arrangements'. The 'institutional link arrangements' include visits to industries by students (Bello, Fiffe, Sanfeliz, 1992), work experience in industry or research laboratory for both teachers and students (Tam, 1985), and involvement of students in research projects designed to solve industrial problems (Kanhsuwan, 1986). Other link arrangements are: the institutions of a fund by industries to assist science students and inclusion of industrialists on school science boards (Tam, 1985).

Attempts involving the development of curricula materials and syllabuses with technological (industrial) slant have been designed using the 'science-first' approach or 'applications-first' approach. The 'science-first' approach involves building relevant applications or issues into already existing science curricula materials. Thus, one might teach principles of electrolysis and them bring in the extraction of aluminium to show its application.

The 'applications-first' approach starts with applications or science-related issues from which the relevant science is developed. For example, one might begin with soap manufacture and develop from it scientific ideas such as saponification, bleaching, decolorization, salting out and alkaline hydrolysis.

These curricula approaches are exemplified by some recent curricula materials. The Science and Technology in Society (SATIS) materials (Holman, 1987) developed by the Association of Science Education, in the United Kingdom uses the 'science-first' approach to add relevant applications or issues to concepts in existing science courses. The Science in Ghanaian Society (SGS) project developed in the Department of Science Education of the University of Cape Coast offers applications of science from traditional industries such as palmwine tapping (Yakubu, 1984).

The Salter's Advanced Chemistry developed at the University of York in Britain (Waddington, 1992) and the CHECOM materials developed in the United States (Ware, et. al, 1986) use the 'applications-first' approach to select applications and issues from which the chemistry to be taught is determined.

It seems, however that just like the curriculum development projects in the 60s and 70s, the development of materials based on the science, technology and society framework seems to have been "discussed almost exclusively within the educational community, with little contribution from those in the wider world of work" (Towse and Anamuah-Mensah, 1991).

Perhaps other interested parties with particular expertise should be followed to participate in formulating goals and developing curricula materials for school science education. Teachers may develop curricula materials based on the interaction of science, technology and society. But these may be grossly over simplified because the teachers themselves have little or no industrial and technological experience (Holman, 1987) to help them to place science in its technological context. Industrialists, however, have the 'expertise, and can provide needed technological knowledge'. The teaches are familiar with the scientific concepts taught in schools and also know about the capabilities and interests of their students as well as how learning takes place. Thus, working together the two groups can make the interaction of science and technology with society visible and authentic.

The Science and Technology in Action in Ghana (STAG) project based in the Department of Science Education, University of Cape Coast is attempting in a small way to build bridges over the gap between school science and the applications of science in industry. This is being done by involving industrialists as well as classroom teachers, university lecturers, researches in research institutions, science subject associations and representatives of policy makers in the Ministry of Education in the development of curicula materials for use at the secondary school level. The industrialist as the 'expert' will initially write an account of his industry given the stages in the production of goods and illustrating it with photographs, line drawings and flow diagrams. The accounts would then be studied and turned inside-out in order to weed out much of the technical language. The materials thus produced would then be used during workshops to develop 'teacher-friendly' materials which would be trailled, reviewed and finally published. During the workshop which would involve the participation of industrialists, science teachers among others, information on industrial output, industrial by-products and wastes and their environmental impact would be discussed.

At a later date student materials and videos on the industries would also be developed. The various stages are outlined in the figure below.

So far the first two stages have been executed for eight industries—paints, soaps and detergents, margarine, cement, world processing, soft drinks, cocoa and wheat flour.

It has not been easy getting people in industry to write an account of their enterprise. After initial contacts and visits, it took not less than five visits to get the industries to either write scanty or very technical accounts or to give an oral account. The oral accounts were vetted by personnel from the industry after transcription.

The industrialist had concerns which the project members tried to resolve. There was initial expression of lack of confidence or expertise in writing with can be used in the science classrooms. There was the concern about divulging industrial secrets which would-be competitors can capitalize on. Those who felt strongly about this decided to either not give any written account or give only oral account with or without a tours of the industry. Those who became satisfied with the explanations by the project personnel, wrote very elaborate and much useful account. Others not so well convinced gave scanty accounts which were educationally not useful (Anamuah-Mensah, 1993).

The teachers, on the other hand, doubted the capabilities of the industrialists to write materials that will match the level of their students. However, later on they began to be concerned with how they can transform the technical write-up of the industrialist into a less technical account.

It seems that the industrialists after their initial reluctance became interested in sharing their knowledge which has always remained their own property, in fact a 'secret', with teachers. This is laudable as it will serve (if developed further) not only to open the communication channels between the two groups but also help in bringing industry into the science classroom thereby bridging the gap.

It is hoped that when funding becomes available, other industries would be included and workshops held to develop the final resource materials. It is also hoped that the group dynamics during the workshops would be studied so as to get an insight into the changing concerns of the different groups. In addition, it is expected that the contacts established between industry and school will develop to include 'institutional link arrangement'.

Finally, it is hoped that the project will serve to empower industries to produce materials (not only for the formal school system but) to promote public education and offer a balanced view about industries.

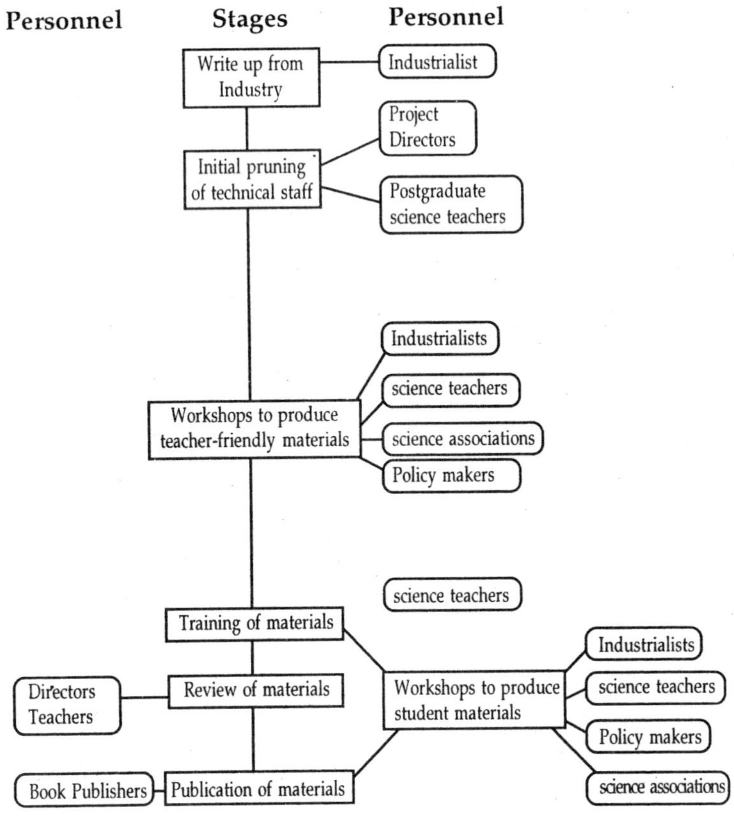

Figure: Stages and personnel involved in the development of industry-based materials

REFERENCES

Anamuah-Mensah, J. (1993). *Bringing Industry in the Science Classroom: Problems, Concerns and Prospects*. Unpublished.

Bello, L.J., Fiffe, N. and Sanfeliz, P. (1992) *How do we Link Industry to the Chemistry Curriculum*. International Newsletter on Chemical Education, 37, 8-9.

Gardner, P. L. (January 1993). *Science and Technology: Rethinking the Relationship*. A paper presented at International Conference on Science Education in developing Countries: From Theory to Practice. Jerusalem, Israel.

Gaskell, P. J. (1982) *Science Education for Citizens: Perspectives and Issues. Science, Technology and Society: Issues for Science Teachers*. Studies in Science Education, 9, 34-46.

Goldstein, P. (1978). *Changing the American Textbook* Lexington, Massachusetts: D.C. Health.

Hannay, N.B. and McGinn, R.E. (1980). *The Anatomy of Modern Technology: Prolegomenon to an Improved Public Policy for the Social Management of Technology*. Daedalus, 109 (1).

Holman, J. (1987). *Introducing Industry and Technology to the Secondary Science Curriculum: The SATIS Approach*. International Newsletter on Chemical Education, 27, 9-11.

Kanhasuwan, L. (1986). *Teaching Industrial Issues in Secondary Schools*. International Newsletter on Chemical Education, 26, 5-7.

Layton, D. (1989). *Science Education and Praxis: the Relationship of School Science to Practical Action*. Studies in Science Education, 19, 43—79.

McConnell, M.C. (1982). *Teaching About Science, Technology and Society at the Secondary School Level in the United States. An Educational Dilemma for the 1980s*. Studies in Science Education, 9, 1-32.

Miller, J.D. (1989, April). *Scientific Literacy*. Paper presented at the Meeting of the American Association for the Advancement of Science. San Francisco, California.

Tam, P. (1985). *Closer Ties Seen Between Chemical Education and Industry in Developing Countries—A Move in the Right Direction*, International Newsletter on Chemical Education, 24, 16-17.

Towse, P. and Anamuah-Mensah, J. (1991). *Science and Technology in Action in Ghana*. Science Education International, June 31-34.

Trachtman, L. E. (1981). *The Public Understanding of Science Effort. A Critique*. Science, Technology and Human Values, 6, (36).

Waddington, D.J. (1992). *Chemical Ideas and the Environment*. International Newsletter on Chemical Education, 38, 15-18.

Ware, S.A. Heikkinen, H. and Pippincott, W.T. (986). *The CHEMCOM Philosophy and Approach*. International Newsletter on Chemical Education, 26, 10-12.

Yager, R.E. (1992). *Viewpoint: What We did not Learn from the 60s about Science Curriculum Reform*. Journal of Research in Science Teaching, 29 (8), 905-910.

Yakubu, J.M (1984). *Science in Ghanaian Society: Teacher's Guide*. Faculty of Education, University of Cape Coast.

8

Video and Teacher Education: Primary School Science Video Teacher Education in Malawi

Harold F. Gonthi

Introduction

In August 1985, the Committee on the Teaching of Science of the International Council of Science Unions, organized a conference in Bangalore, India, on Science and Technology Education and Future Human Needs. The Committee received considerable support of Unesco and the United Nations University.

Corridor discussions at the conference led Vincent Gondwe from Malawi and Gary Knamiller from the University of Leeds, England to consider the possibility of using video for science education.

As a follow-up activity to the Bangalore conference, the two met at the University of Leeds to examine the idea of using video for science education in a more systematic manner. They mapped out the basic approach which started with demonstrating how school science is linked to community science and technology.

Kawaza, a rural village community in Malawi was chosen for this purpose with the assistance of the University of Leeds.

Gondwe and Knamiller took a video tape shot on the life in the Kawaza village. The edited 31 minute long tape shows science-rich technology activities forming part of the daily working lives of the villagers—parents and their children. The commentary urges the audience to consider other such examples in school children's experiences and to think of ways of building on them to make school science and technology meaningful. Thus the Linking Community Science and Technology with School Science Project—a Primary School Science Teacher Education Video Tape Project was borne.

The project is a collaborative effort involving science educators from the University of Leeds and an education institution in Malawi, namely Malawi Institute of Education—the coordinating institution, the Ministry of Education and Culture—supporting the project at the ministerial level, the Malawi National Examinations Board—responsible for examinations, and teachers colleges for primary school teachers.

In 1989 a team of science educators from the University of Leeds and Malawi put together a series of lessons based largely on the content areas as addressed in the Kawaza tape. These lessons incorporate a variety of teaching techniques. The lessons were taught to children in two primary schools and were video-taped as the lessons unfolded.

The Africa Forum for Children's Literacy in Science and Technology, an activity of the Rockefeller Foundation is currently supporting the project.

How is Science Perceived By Children in Schools?

Some years ago when I was involved in a science UNESCO/UNDP curriculum development project, as a counterpart to a science curriculum specialist, we, just like other science educators in the world were talking about making science teaching and learning learner-centred. This consequently called for teaching styles that were different from the ones that were being used before—chalk and talk. I remember vividly the science specialist and I were talking to one senior person in the Ministry of Education who remarking about the teaching strategies we were trying to promote said, "why worry about all these new methods, just tell them". I guess the senior education officer believed in rote memorization. But even rote learning becomes problematic (Savage 1993, p. 4).

Most of us had perhaps gone through this kind of teaching. The teacher taught by telling, we were expected to learn by memorising. It is not surprising many of our colleagues including those of us who survived secondary science and later along university science found science learning difficult. And I am reminded of my physics professor who used to assure us in the physics class what we were going to pass his examinations. After all, he would say, there are all those what are not taking physics—the fact that you are taking it means you can pass and he would mention areas he was going to base his tests on. All this was in an attempt to awaken our interest for physics.

In Malawi, as in many other countries, many children appear to find science difficult and often tedious. There are many causes, one of which is that described above. The other is they perceive the science which they learn in school as having little in common with their everyday lives. The concepts with which they wrestle in class are usually set in unfamiliar scientific contexts. Teaching approaches fail to recognize that pupils bring with them to school significant scientific and technological knowledge based on substantial experience from working with their parents and other adults in their homes and communities.

Teaching is rarely set within such areas of familiarity; indeed it is exceptional for teachers to take the time to find out and build upon children's existing scientific understandings. Additionally, beliefs or even misconceptions are seldom challenged.

Furthermore, teaching methods in science and technology are largely didactic with assessment subsequently emphasizing recalling to the exclusion of other abilities which pupils might have.

The effect on children is ultimately demotivating. Science is seen as remote, hard and abstract. It holds so few attractions that few continue their study of science and technology when offered subject choice.

What Problems do Teachers Meet?

Teachers, particularly in primary schools, meet lots of problems. An interested observer would have a long list of the problems primary school teachers meet in the course of their profession. The most important problem which is often ignored is perhaps the lack of support. This lack of support manifests itself in many ways. Including—lack of moral support, material support as well as ideas they can tap upon.

A primary school teacher is lucky if s/he has a teaching syllabus, enough pupils' books and text books for reference. If the school has a library s/he is lucky if the school head opens it up for the teacher's use. Teacher in-service is rarely heard of. If there is one, the teachers are there to be lectured. Rarely are they allowed to share their frustrations with those oversee them.

If we want teachers to teach effectively and enjoy their teaching profession, we must be seen to support them. Provision of teaching/learning materials is own way of supporting them.

The Philosophy of the Video Teacher Education Project

The major goal of the video teacher education project is to produce video tapes and support materials for use in the training of primary school teachers.

The materials are based on the central idea that Malawian children experience science and technology outside the school in their communities. They bring this extensive knowledge with them to science lessons in school. Therefore it is the job of the teachers to find out what the children already know and to use this as the basis for extending their (children's) knowledge of scientific concepts and acquisition of scientific skills.

In these video segments a variety of strategies are shown. They have been chosen for it is believed that they make the learning of science interesting, enjoyable and above all, effective. The strategies include the use of effective questioning, exploration, investigations, systematic observation, recording, evaluation of results, and group work. Thus, the project has concentrated its efforts, on using activities that children experience in their everyday lives.

The aim is to show student teachers (STs) and provide them an opportunity to practise how to link community science and technology with school science so as to make science lessons for pupils more meaningful and interesting. The project believes that this can only be achieved by using hands on and brains on strategies shown in the video segments.

There are five packages each containing a video segment and written support materials. The video segments are mosquitoes, mushrooms, mbaula-fuel, weevils and bricks.

There is also a sixth resource package that focuses on assessing pupils' and STs understanding of the scientific skills that appear in the five video segments.

The project feels that it can not encourage new approaches to teaching and learning science in primary schools without also offering novel examples of how to assess pupils' knowledge and understanding. It is for this reason that the package on assessment had been developed.

The project recognizes the importance of assessing pupils' knowledge of scientific facts, skills and concepts. In this regard, the assessments package offers examples of good recall type questions which teachers can use across the five segments. However, emphasis has also been given in assessing pupils' activities in skills associated with carrying out scientific investigations. Thus the assessment package provides teachers with specific examples of questions that focus on planning investigations, recording information, analysing data and making inferences based on experimental evidence.

How to Use the Packages

Each video segment shows a teacher carrying out model lessons related to a specific theme. The purpose of the videos are not meant to teach science knowledge content. For example, the mosquito video segment does not systematically present the life cycle of the mosquito. Nor does it list for STs various methods of controlling mosquitoes. It is assumed that STs already know this. The purpose of the video, as said earlier, is to demonstrate a variety of approaches to teaching science using pupils everyday experiences.

Before showing the video segment to the STs, the tutor is expected to prepare the STs to look for the main strategies employed in it. After this the STs should be shown the video segment in its entirety. Then, the video can be used again and again to demonstrate particular points that the tutor wants the STs to focus on. After that the STs should be asked to have demonstration lessons to teach in the similar way. Micro teaching lessons are recommended using both pupils and peer groups. The support materials make specific suggestions for extending activities that require STs to do the investigations presented in the video and ask questions to help pupils observe more critically and so on.

The tutor is expected not to do all the activities suggested. She is free to sample from them as best fits her/his existing programme. The videos are there to hopefully stimulate interest and awareness and to act as starting points for encouraging active learning by STs in the teaching of science to children using their everyday experiences.

The assessment package can be used on its own as a resource for teaching STs how to write good science questions. But perhaps the way to use it most effectively is together with the video segments and their support materials. The project advocates that STs relate these new ideas about teaching science to the process of accessing pupils' abilities in these areas. Indeed, the questions themselves can be used not only as examples of test items but also as interesting and challenging learning activities.

Does the Video have a Change in Teacher Education in Malawi?

The potential of the use of video in teacher education is not new in Malawi. During the first phase of the UNESCO/UNDP curriculum development and teacher education project (1978-1982) video facilities were installed in three of the eight teachers colleges. Its potential was in its use in micro-teaching lessons. Few lessons by the STs were video-taped and the tapes were used for follow up discussions. Perhaps what was lacking was video tapes which were already made to suit the Malawian context. This is where these video tape series try to fill a gap.

Whereas the 'Kawaza' tape was edited and produced at the University of Leeds in England, the five video tape segments have been edited at Chancellor College—University of Malawi. Instead of sending two Malawian project team members to

England to do the editing UNICEF provided the funding to install VHS video-tape editing facilities at the Audio Visual Centre—Chancellor College. This meant that project team members in Malawi were on hand to take an active part in editing, to say nothing of the other advantage of having the equipment in the country. The experience of developing the tapes provided an opportunity to a group of Malawian science educators to acquire knowledge and skills of making video-tapes for educational purposes.

Inset

If the idea of the project are to succeed the project recognizes the importance of making the video project the colleges' own activity. Therefore holding In-set for the college tutors before the video tapes are distributed to the colleges is one of the major activities.

Two types of In-set will be held. The first will be for the key college science tutors. This will be conducted by the project team members. The key tutors will be called to the Malawi Institute of Education for at least 5 days. They will be provided an opportunity to view the tapes and get acquainted with the project philosophy and ideas, identify weaknesses and potentials of the materials. In the second In-set, the key college science tutors will take over from the project team members in orienting their colleagues in the colleges. This In-Set will be college based.

Conclusion

In conclusion, the video teacher education project aims at:

- altering primary school teachers, student teachers, college tutors and other educators to the science and technology experienced by school children in their home communities.
- showing that such scientific experience relates also to school science and to the knowledge and skills valued.
- demonstrating that there is a variety of teaching approaches which can be used to exploit and challenge children's existing knowledge while developing their understanding of abstract concepts and scientific skills.

- showing that such approaches engender an enthusiasm for science in children because they
  - can see the relevance of taught science to the lives outside school and
  - are more actively involved in their own learning.

Since, in the words of Professor Bajah, this is not a 'talkshop' I invite you to watch a selected theme of the project products and hope you will give your constructive criticisms which will be useful for the improvement of the project.

The paper has not tried to dwell on the successes or failures of the project. The paper has concentrated on what is currently happening in an attempt to improve the quality of science and technology education in Malawi.

9

Participating in Science Education Research

Dr. Gilbert O. M. Onwu

Introduction

Educational research is recognized the world over as one of the most effective means of obtaining objective solutions to educational problems, and arguably the only sound basis for effecting educational improvements. It is indeed becoming increasingly accepted as a critical element in the multifarious educational activities aimed at improving the quality of education provided at whatever level.

In this paper an attempt will be made to outline what is believed to be some of the major implications for the improvement of the quality of science education at the basic level emerging from science education research and development. Stated briefly, our position is that science education research and development ought to belong to the teacher (both as a user and as an initiator)—and that there are prospects of making this good in practice. The teacher is the most important resource in science education. No one can lay claim to the same degree of familiarity with classroom conditions that he has. Furthermore, the first indications of success or failure in implementing the curriculum are first known to him, and if that is the case, he must of necessity be equipped with those requisite skills of research (including the appropriate research perspectives and motivation) in his professional development that would enable him to further sustain or enhance the quality of education he provides.

Research and Professional Developments of The Science Teacher

Professional development is something that each science teacher must be involved in—this includes considering one's needs, making decisions about how changes or modifications will occur in some aspects of classroom practice in order to improve learning and evaluating their effectiveness.

In consequence, professional self-development means for the science teacher:

(i) the commitment to the systematic questioning of his own teaching, i.e., what he does, how he does it and the consequences of his doing it;

(ii) the commitment and skills to study his own teaching including the work of other teachers or practitioners in the same field; i.e. knowing how to examine and analyse classroom procedures;

(iii) the concern to question and to test ideas by classroom research procedures.

In short, improvement in the quality of science education depends to a large extent on the capacity of teachers to take a research stance to their own teaching. This means a disposition to examine their own practice critically and systematically (in the light of research findings) in order to improve their teaching.

In general, the aspect of 'feedback mechanisms", "resource and support", and techniques for classroom study which are considered important for successful implementation of programmes and for autonomous professional self-development are alas the ones that seem to be lacking in our science teacher training programmes in colleges of education.

The pre-service training programmes in our colleges of education while emphasizing certain aspects of the academic and professional components of science teacher education would seem not to have given adequate attention to the research element of teacher professionalism. Pre-service education has a part to play no doubt in addressing some of the issues, but what is needed is a recognition of the role teacher participation in science education research can play in improving teaching and learning.

What is Science Education Research?

Science education is about the teaching and learning of science wherever it takes place (at primary, secondary or tertiary level; in industry or in the home).

Science education research is broadly defined here to include any activities that lead to a better understanding of science education problems and that produce findings relevant to programme planning and implementation and/or policy formulation. "Research then includes any activity involving information gathering and analysis from the simplest to the most sophisticated operation" (IDRC).

Students, teachers, curriculum developers and education officials can be considered as research users and researchers. There are people who use exiting knowledge of science education (students and teachers), there are people who develop new methods and approaches (teachers, writers, curriculum developers), and there are people who create new knowledge about the teaching and learning of science (researchers). As with other branches of science (science education is regarded as a branch of science), there are advantages when users developers and researchers work closely together or are even the same people.

To summarize, science education research is aimed at improving the teaching and learning of science, and consequently the researcher will usually also need either to be a developer or user (i.e. a science teacher) or at least be prepared to collaborate closely with science teachers.

We need to make the point however, that while accepting this broad definition of science educational research as appropriate for our immediate goal that of improving the quality of science education, it is neither being suggested that only research which has immediate usefulness of applicability is worthy of respect or support, nor that research in science education is in any way different from that in other subjects. Whether used or unused research—the intellectually honest pursuit and generation of new knowledge and ideas is an essential function of higher education, and where resources permit the acquisition of new knowledge and ideas is an essential function of higher education, and where resources permit the acquisition of new knowledge for its own sake is a legitimate goal of educational research.

Thus research endeavour as conceptualized is not restricted to only the activities of scholars rather it is construed as a human activity involving a systematic way of thinking and behaving that leads to problem solving.

What Does Research Say to the Primary Science Teacher?

Primary science is one of our more recent innovations in primary school education. Today, there has evolved a detailed teaching curriculum—a Core Curriculum for Primary Science delineating expected levels of attainment for precisely specified objectives. The aims of the curriculum are derived from a conceptual view of primary science as simply meaning developing in pupils through self-activity an enquiring mind and a scientific approach to problems. Teachers are expected to be faithful implementers of the intentions of the curriculum developers.

However, in reality observations of pupils and teachers' work in our science classrooms reveal that the intentions of the curriculum developers as contained in the curriculum specifications are often reinterpreted in ways to suit various classroom contexts and also as perceived by the teachers who have the ultimate responsibility of implementing the given curriculum. Teachers adapt the goals, objectives and content of the formal curricula to the specific classroom context. They routinely modify curricula by additions, deletions and changes in sequence and emphasis and often to the detriment of the intentions of the developers.

Part of the problem of the "omnipresent gap between intention and realization" is that our teachers are often ill-prepared (sometimes through no fault of theirs) coming from inadequate subject background, lacking the confidence to attempt non-instructional teaching in the useful methods of scientific enquiry, and indeed often badly tutored or briefed about how this kind of activity work would fit into the overall aims of science education. Overall these problems are if anything more acute in the primary sector where the foundations of an understanding of science is laid.

Given the problems serving science teachers face in translating the aims into action, and the important and far-reaching decisions they are required to make in carrying out managerial responsibility in the classroom, there is the need for them to be provided with opportunities to familiarize themselves with information on the curriculum and curriculum related issues that may suggest modifications and provide a focus for reflection to enable them take appropriate decisions.

This is where knowledge of research becomes relevant. By taking advantage of relevant research findings teachers can improve their ability to make professional decisions concerning how to successfully implement the curriculum.

In sum, what research has to say to the teacher may be construed in terms of feedback which then provided focus for further reflection. Feedback is simply information about a process or experiment that may suggest that changes or adjustments would be desirable. The main purpose of reflection is to uncover assumptions or prevailing beliefs—to get one to think about one's thinking in order to improve. Let's illustrate with a case study.

Case Study 1

A recent study (Okeke and Inomesia 1986) investigated primary science teachers' perception of the teaching of primary science in two states of Nigeria.

The basic questions which the investigation attempted to answer were:

1. What proportion of the primary school teachers have the appropriate perception of the objectives of primary science?
2. What activity/activities during the teaching process do primary school teachers regard as good science teaching?
3. Do the primary school teachers consider primary science as taught now effective? In so why? And if not why not?

The results showed that:

(i) a high proportion of the 310 teachers from 50 schools used for the study demonstrated ignorance of the objectives of science teaching in primary schools. As high as 37.09 per cent of the respondents were unable to state any meaningful objective for the teaching of primary science;

(ii) activities perceived by many of the teachers as indicative of good science teaching were predominantly teacher-centred activities. This is evident in the finding that activities peculiar to the teacher along (talk and chalk method, teacher directed pupil reading of science books, teacher demonstration, etc.) accounted for 59.19 per cent of all activities considered as indicative of good science teaching;

(iii) a good proportion of the teachers (64.5 per cent) were of the view that the teaching of primary science as is presently done in our primary schools is not effective. And 25.8 per cent of the teachers felt that the present teaching activities were alright. About 20 per cent of the respondents were of the view that lack of interest on the part of the teachers and pupils is a strong factor contributing to the preceived ineffectiveness. Another factor which attracted 18.7 per cent of the teachers' positive response is lack of qualified science teachers.

The findings of the study that the present teachers of primary science in Nigeria lack knowledge of objectives and methodology of primary science—even when the Core Curriculum for Primary Science has been published and in use—have great implications for science education at the basic level in the area of teacher education.

Speaking specifically on the aspect of interest in science, it is perhaps pertinent to note that where a teacher is interested in a subject there is the likelihood that he or she would take the trouble to initiate meaningful activities that would be predominantly child-centred aimed at generating and sustaining the child's interest in that subject. On the other hand, it could be argued that one tends to lack interest in what one does not adequately understand its purpose, objectives or goals. The poor knowledge exhibited by the teachers of the objectives of primary science may be the root cause for their lack of interest. Again, these teachers being class-based teach all subjects to their pupils including primary science, and this may well account for the finding that the teachers mostly talk to the children about science, using the traditional "telling" method, instead of engaging them in self-activities that would allow them to experience and do science.

The research has raised issues of teacher preparation and re-training workshops which when tackled can help in the improvement of the quality of science education at the basic level. The beneficiaries of such research should be the teachers themselves and teacher educators.

Teacher As A User of Research

Is contemporary research in science education any use? Most science teachers, whatever their level, will, I am afraid answer in the negative. The results of science education research do in fact remain largely unused.

This is probably because most of the work done in the area has relied on observers—science educators, higher degree students and their teachers, research workers, etc., rather than classroom teachers. And generally speaking these workers have been more interested in building and/or testing a theory of teaching and reporting findings in a form addressed mainly to the research community.

However, this is not true of all the work reported, but there are always indications or traces of the separation (alienation?) of the research worker (from outside) from the teacher.

But the issue of utilization of research results by science teachers is informed, one suspects by certain factors. It all depends on

(i) teachers' attitude to information (whether it is brought relevant or not) and

(ii) the motivation to use available information.

To those two should be add, the manner or format or means by which information is communicated and the recipient's ability to comprehend or make sense of the information.

The views and attitudes of teachers towards educational research has been investigated in the Nigerian context (Ajayi 1982).

Case Study II

The sample for the study comprised 175 graduate teachers (both professional and non-professional) and 20 headmasters drawn from 25 secondary schools located in three states in Nigeria.

The basic questions asked were:

1. What research would secondary school teachers and principals like to see done?
2. Do they think they benefit from the research works in education that have been undertaken?
3. Which is the best method for disseminating research findings to them?
4. How far have they been involved in research projects?
5. To what extent is educational research findings gettings through to them?

Answer to these questions should provide some useful insight into the reasons behind the general apathy towards educational research and development in the country.

The findings showed that:

(i) A majority of the headmasters and teachers had unfavourable and unsavoury attitude towards educational research. While 33 per cent showed a favourable attitude, 67 per cent of the respondents displayed a negative attitude. Female teachers had unfavourable attitude than their male counterparts.

(ii) Most principles (85 per cent) and teachers (9[illegible] per cent) had little or no knowledge of the research findings that had been conducted in the field of education in the areas under study or in their areas of specialization.

(iii) Most teachers (65 per cent) and head masters (65 per cent) would prefer research findings and recommendations being sent either to the Schools Board where teachers could easily have access to them or the summaries of such findings to the head of each institution (school), instead of the present system of reporting them only in journals or stacking them away in the University's library or the researcher's 'cooler'.

(iv) Teachers would prefer researches dealing with teacher training and welfare, teaching methods, and improvement of learning, in that order.

(v) The teachers also complained (in oral interviews) that research findings are published in journals that are not easily accessible to them and that the language and manner of reporting research findings are always too technical with the result that even when they bother to read them they seldom understand what is being said.

From the observations it is evident that research findings are not able to reach or penetrate practitioners in the classroom precisely because of a lack of communication between researchers on the one hand and the intended users on the other hand. Perhaps the simplest explanation is that science teachers do not read the published results and are not sufficiently research-minded to want to use them. Again some of the published research papers use a specialized language which busy teachers have neither the time, nor the inclination to learn. Sometimes this specialized language seems instead to obscure rather than enlighten.

Communicating Research Findings

What action(s) might make science education research more useful to the teacher?

This is basically a question of communication and relevance. Perhaps when thinking about the criteria for determing what strategies or actions might make science education research relevant to the science teacher it many useful to ask answer the following questions:

1. How do researchers see practitioners (teachers) and how do practitioners see researchers?
2. How relevant is the investigation of the teachers' and schools' needs?
3. How do we sensitize the teacher to the need for educational research?
4. What strategy should we evolve to involve schools in the identification of the problems for research?
5. How do we provide feedback to participating schools in a research, ensuring the capacity of the teachers to understand and utilize the information and the possibility for interaction, as well as ensuring anonymity of schools, teachers and students?
6. How do we resolve conflicts arising from the perceptions of researchers and teachers?

Strategies For Bridging the Communication Gap

To help teachers adopt a research-based approach to their teaching help can be given to broaden their view of science education research.

1. Pre-service and in-service activities are needed to help teachers define for themselves research problems and the meanings of action-research in the classroom.
2. Focus on ways of demonstrating research procedures and methods and results to science teachers:
   - Use findings through institutes and facilities of education of the universities—abstracting, reviewing and diffusing findings through in-service training, seminars and workshops.
   - Look at series of researches (on a subject basis) identify the trend, review the researches to identify common findings and develop a model which can then be recommended for use.
3. Address findings of research to School Boards, Ministries of Education, principals, etc., as the case may be.

4. Establish some cooperative acquisition and documentation schemes of result findings (on a subject basis) among institutes and facilities of education of universities, colleges of education, professional associations, etc.

   - Establish a service that distils from research communication, findings that are relevant to the classroom teacher.

5. Look at the possibility of setting up a national journal of science education research available to science teachers and lay audience. The purpose of such a journal would be:

   (i) to concentrate research results on a subject basis so that they would be read by science teachers.

   (ii) to provide an outlet for classroom based research (results would have no more applicability than those in traditional research journals but they would be more likely to stimulate other teachers into making their own investigations) In this regard teacher training institutions would need to encourage their students to undertake project work which should lead to research skills development.

   (iii) to inform teachers about the methodology of classroom based research and to encourage them to do research. Finally more attention should be given to defining research problems. These must be relevant to the teachers and learners of science.

6. Organize workshops, in-service training and seminars designed to encourage user education and involvement of users in generating research information.

We hope that by doing all these we would have at least succeeded in getting information to the potential users. However the problem of utilization still remains because this is primarily in the hands of the curriculum implementer—the teacher.

Teacher as Developer (Researcher)

The science teacher viewed in this role is concerned to understand better his own classroom, to help make informed decision before, during and after a lesson about teaching and learning activities, resources, assessment strategies and to improve the quality of education provided. It is not enough that the teacher's work should be studied they need to study it themselves. So the initial focus of developmental activities could address the things that the teacher does rather than what the student does.

When teachers are researchers or developers they are learners too. As a learner, the teacher has the responsibility of listening to students' ideas and language, of assessing his teacher approach, of interacting with people in the community and his professional colleagues, of locating local resources (people and materials) and of using them to enrich the curriculum so that the learning is useful and appropriate for the students. In effect, the teacher, in an informal way is an action-researcher as he or she is clarifying curriculum issues and problems, collecting data and information, using it to make informed decisions to improve the learning and so on.

A number of action-research models for development occur in the literature. Problem-solving projects are common forms of this type of activity. Action-research models usually involve a cycle of reflecting, planning, collecting data, trying out strategies, getting feedback, modifying plans and continuing on the cycle as summarized diagrammatically below:

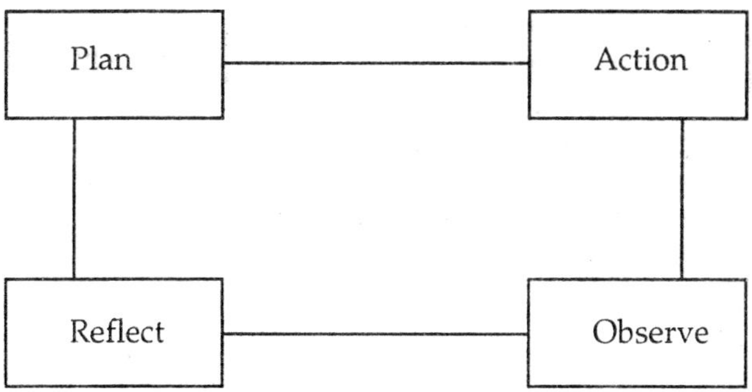

We had earlier on indicated in this paper that reflection is one way for the teacher to obtain feedback for action or for further action. A science teacher working in this tradition could be regarded as sufficiently research-minded.

At the classroom level, reflection (which does not come naturally—it is a learned behaviour) takes three forms and they differ in when they occur.

Reflection—for—action

Reflection—on—action

Reflection—in—action

Reflection-for-action: Traditionally this has been thought of as planning but should include questions about "what will I do?" and "how will I do it?", "why am I doing it the way that I intend to do it?" and "what am I assuming?"

Reflection-on-action: This is essentially an evaluative type of reflection. Apart from the usual questions of "how did the lesson go?" and "did the children understand or learn (and feel) what they were supposed to learn (and feel)?", these should be supplemented by other questions such as "how did I feel trying out those new strategies?", "how do I know that the pupils really understood the topic and were not just kept busy?" and "could I have handled (taught) the topic differently?"

Reflection-in-action: This includes questions that are rarely asked while making quick decisions: "what am I doing?", "why am I doing it like this?", "what if .....". It involves incovering implicit or explicit assumptions while one is teaching. One way of giving oneself time to reflect-in-action in class is to respond to a student's question with another question. This gets the student to say more, given the teacher time to reflect and may even lead to the student reflecting on the situation. It is precisely the development of this kind of systematic thinking strategy for making decisions to improve learning that highlights the role of research endeavour (action-research) in the improvement of the quality of science education.

Constraints

There are constraints that will need to be addressed in say primary teachers or secondary school teachers for that matter, assuming the role of researchers albeit informal ones. These are mainly psychological and social:

(i) **Lack of confidence:** A close examination of one's professional performance is personally threatening particularly if one's subject-matter background is inadequate; and the social climate in which teachers work generally offers little support to who might be disposed to face that threat.

(ii) **Examination Pressure:** These may influence teachers to continue to choose traditional teaching and learning activities that aid rote, not meaningful learning.

(iii) **Large Class Sizes:** Tend to influence teachers to maintain a narrow content view of the curriculum for easier classroom and resource management.

(iv) **Unwillingness to Change:** Teachers may be unwilling to change their perceptions of the curriculum objectives and on such things as appropriate teaching and learning activities. Activities in in-service programmes may need to take this into account by providing opportunities for discussion.

Some Strategies to Help Involve Science Teachers In Action-Research in the Classroom

These are:

1. **part of the pre-service education** programme being a teaching practice of say one term. In this time the student should undertake curriculum projects based on their classroom experience. Such projects would aim to develop the science curriculum on the basis of the classroom/cultural context.

2. **in-service workshops** to help groups of teachers work together to find out what ideas and understanding the pupils are bringing to their science lessons about a series of topics particularly those perceived difficult to

teach, with access to all the necessary published resources. They would then use the information to create a teaching resource within the curriculum specifications.

3. **pre-service/in-service workshops** on the different perceptions and classroom interpretations of the objectives of the official science curriculum. Activities need to focus on the reality of the classroom, for example, the pupils understandings and constructions of scientific ideas and skills, the nature of science and the usefulness of science.

4. **including technology in the science curriculum.** This not only widens the content of the curriculum but also helps teachers reflect on what science curriculum means to them in their cultural context. This is the issue of (cultural) relevance. Ways to assist teachers to include technology in the science curriculum include:

   - encouraging contact between local crafts people (technologists) and teachers so that crafts people can explain the critical aspects of a particular technology;
   - in-service workshops which encourage teachers to identify real life problems in the students' own lives and environment. Science and technology can help solve these personal and societal problems.
   - as a part of pre-service education, teachers being sent to factories, local fabrication workshops, etc., to look for technologies and related scientific knowledge;
   - provision of resource materials, including published texts to illustrate different technologies and the way that science is used to solve a human problem;
   - work experiences where teachers and students have experience in a work situation to raise awareness of the uses of science learning in solving

real problems. (In this approach technologies are ways to solve problems that are based on scientific knowledge and skills).

To conclude, in considering ways of bridging school science and technology in the context of classrooms practice, teachers should be encouraged to look at such issues as how to determine what science and technology is appropriate for their students, the purposes of science and technology education and the appropriate teaching and learning strategies.

REFERENCES

Ajayi, K. (1982). *Attitudes of Teachers and School Administrators to Educational Research in Nigeria*. Paper presented at the Conference on "Priorities in Educational Research", organized by the International Centre for Educational Evaluation (ICEE). Institute of Education, University of Ibadan, 6-10 Sept.

Bajah, S. T (1988). *Science Education at the Classroom. The Challenge of our Time*. Science and Technology Education and the Quality of Life. Kert, Riquarts, ed. Vol. 1.

Begg, A. (1992). *Professional Development: Designing Programmes for High School Mathematics Teachers*. Centre for Science and Mathematics Education Research, University of Waikato, New Zealand.

Federal Ministry of Education *Core Curriculum for Primary Science*. Lagos, Nigeria.

Frazer, M.J. (1977), *Making Chemical Education Research Useful*. A Report of a symposium: Research for the Classroom and Beyond. University of Loughborough, pp. 80-83.

Fullan, M. & Pomfret, A. (1977) *Research on Curriculum and Instruction Implementation*. Review of Educational Research 47 (2), pp. 335-97.

Gounder. T.N. (1992), *Managing Curriculum in the Classroom*. Pacific Curriculum Network. Vol. 1, No. 1, pp. 20-21.

IDRC (1976), *Education Research Priorities: A Collective View Ottawa*

Okeke, E. & Inomesia, E. (1986), *Primary Science Teachers' Perceptions of the Teaching of Primary Science*. Journal of the Science Teachers' Association of Nigeria. (JSTAN), Vol. 25, No. 1, pp. 57-66.

Onwu, G.O. (1989), *Problems of Teaching Primary Science*. A paper presented at the National Workshop on Primary Science Education. The Process Skills of Primary Science. University of Ibadan, Dept of Teacher Education. 26-Nov.-2 Dec.

Onwu, G.O. (1992), *Conducive Classroom Environment for Science, Technology and Mathematics Education, Implications for the Learner.*

A lead paper presented at the Science Teacher Association of Nigeria (STAN) 33rd Annual Conference, Enugu, 17-22 August.

Stenhouse, L. (1975), *An Introduction to Curriculum Research and Development*. Heinneman Education Books, London.

UNESCO-APPEID (1989), *Science for All: Supporting Teacher Change*. Report of a Regional Workshop on Approaches to Teaching and Learning Science For All. Unesco Principal Regional Office for Asia and Pacific. Thailand.

Yoloye, E. A. & Flechsig (1980), *Paradigms of Educational Research in Africa*, Educational Research for Development. Bonu D.S.E. pp. 21-40.

10

Science Camps For Children: A Model for Curriculum Renewal and Change

Shaaban S. Mohammed

Introduction

Schools science provides a useful knowledge base only if it primarily develops the problem solving skills of young boys and girls. Teaching science through investigation, research activities and problem solving and by linking these with a focus on the local environment achieves a better understanding of science as opposed to rote learning of scientific facts and theories for examinations after which learning ends.

For example, we expect school leavers who study the use of measuring instruments to be able to select which one to use; to be able to judge the expected degree of accuracy for a specific situation; and to be able to design an appropriate tool if one is lacking. Too often in practical examinations, pupils show that they cannot use even rulers properly. Other examples abound.

The claim that science teaching in Africa has become too "theoretical" and not "practical" enough has been made repeatedly. This debate conceals a more basic issue, namely that what is called "theoretical" has nothing to do with thoughts and actions of purposeful people, actively theorising about their world. What is introduced in the name of "practicality" too often consists in teaching rigid procedures in a way that permits only one, "right" answer. Such "theory" and "practice" are neither part of science or technology, nor of the work of scientists and technologists. Science education of this kind is just not enough, given the challenges that the peoples of the world, and especially of Africa, currently face.

Woolnough and Allsop (1985, p. 16) argue:

> . . . the pupils should perform experiments with their own hands, and second these experiments should not be the mere confirmation of something previously learned on authority, but the means of elucidating something previously unknown (to them).

Science teaching must divorce itself from the erroneous view of science that is best presented by the teacher (and the syllabus) as the sole owner of knowledge where he or she talks pupils through the lesson. Science teaching must shift more to an inquiry-based approach to teaching.

Science camps for children can provide opportunities, not only for children to work in ways more close to those of the scientist, but also for those responsible for running the camps to work in a similar fashion. Within the protected environment of the camp, resource staff can better find out how the educational system is working and how the energy and commitment for change and improvement can be created. Such camp learning is made in a way that the camp philosophy promulgates, namely by active inquiry and by learning from so-called mistakes. Camp resource staff, however sceptical, can never quite be the same after they have witnessed the excitement and competence of children as they use theory and practise as scientists do to solve problems that have captured them. Thus science camps can become the consciousness of the educational system at work to transform itself. They can become a locus for infection and organic representation of the system. Camps can be a place where changes from chalk and talk teaching can be made and inquiry and learning introduced.

Treneman (1967) and Denny (1986) had this to say about the effectiveness of lecture methods to the facts, the most simple level of knowledge:

> "In a thirty minute talk only 25 per cent of the material heard in the first fifteen minutes could be recalled by adults, even under ideal conditions."

The Zanzibar Science Camps

The Zanzibar Science Camp Project began in 1988. It was established by the Ministry of Education, Zanzibar, with collaboration of the University of Dar-es-Salaam in an attempt to solve problems of science education in the islands. The project would not have been possible without the enthusiastic support of Professor M. Bilal, formerly Dean of Sciences at the University and currently Principal Secretary of Science, Technology and Higher Education, and Professor Bob Lange of Brandeis University, Waltham, Massachussetts, USA.

Project objectives are to:

(i) motivate students and teachers to appreciate science;

(ii) equip teachers with better approaches to teaching science;

(iii) formulate better school science curriculum and support material bearing in mind student's cultural and physical environment:

(iv) bridge the gap between school and the community;

(v) establish effective working relationships between the scientific and educational communities as well as between different departments of the Ministry of Education;

(vi) provide a model for curriculum change that involves participants at all levels in the system, thus promoting a sense of ownership, commitment to change, and development of skills needed to promote inquiry-based learning.

Zanzibar has a typical syllabus and examination driven educational system. The usual comments can be made about its emphasis on "theory" and lack of "practicality". The Zanzibar Camp Project provides participants with an opportunity to develop an inquiry-based learning system that it hopes will be more interesting and empowering to the generation that will be called upon to solve the problems of the next century.

The project is intentionally a locus for problem solving. It is complex enough to have every problem the educational system as a whole has. It is an organic representation of the system, populated by people working within the system and provides sherlter and safety for experimentation and criticism. The project provides repeated opportunities for participants to express dissatisfaction, to see how much better the system could be, and to work practically to make it work better in camps. The camp is not dominated by any imposed structure, rules or traditions and is an arena that permits no trivial arguments against change. The project is itself a constant remainder that trivial arguments against change should have no place in wider system striving to put education truly at the use of the people.

The Zanzibar Science Camp project has evolved from its original conception in 1988 of providing a few secondary school students with an exciting three weak experience of enquiry based science, and supporting mathematics and language learning. Key milestones in the project's development are:

1989 *Inclusion of camper/teachers from each participating school.

*Distribution of kits of supplementary equipment to participating schools;

*Instituting a formal camp Task Force.

1990 *Science festivals held by participating schools for the local community.

*A school follow-up programme by camp resource staff.

*An environmental education programme introduced and involvement of scientists from the National Institute of Marine Science and the Commission of Land and the Environment.

*A computer studies programme introduced.

*An emphasis on attracting female camper/students and resource persons.

1991 *Visit to Mbeya on the mainland to explore possibilities for replication of the project.

*Instituting a Camp Organising Committee.

*Appointment of a full-time project coordinator by the Ministry of Education in the Department of Higher Education, Science and Technology.

*Representatives from Mbeya at the December camp.

*A research seminar concurrent with the December camp.

*Establishment of a science teachers' resource centre in Zanzibar town, with equipment and full-time staff.

*A seminar organized concurrently with the December camp to identify research implications of the project.

1992 *A two-week staff development workshop.

*A much stronger project focus on enquiry science.

*A formal evaluation programme introduced.

*Increased commitment to and planning for implementation of enquiry based, interactive science learning.

All secondary schools in Zanzibar have now attended at least one camp session. In 1993, the project will focus more strongly on expanded resource staff development of teaching/ learning material; model for supporting practising teachers; an intensified pre-service education element; and an environmental education and action programme that links researches with the community; as well as primary teacher education.

Situational Analysis

Most African countries have a rich environment that abounds with phenomena for promoting inquiry learning, particularly when compared with the urban deserts of inner-city schools in industrialized countries. It is with phenomena, not facts, concepts or even processes that inquiry begins. The school compound and nearby bush are homes for plants with their leaves, flowers, seeds, fruits physiologies and ecologies. Pupils' investigations can be as simple as using plant pigments to make dyes and paints, ranging to the complexities of acids and bases, or the necessary conditions for sensitive plants to close their leaves. (In the 1970s, a class of kindergarten children in Sierra

Leone, made this discovery only a few months after it had been confirmed by research biologists). Often pupils do not require the elaborate chemicals, supposedly stocked by secondary school laboratories and the shortage of which is used frequently by teachers to stick to lecture methods of teaching. Familiar material such as flowers, ashes, citrus fruits and so on, often provide a better alternative.

Pupils' Experience

Pupils are themselves an important learning resource for teachers as well as a useful teaching resource. Only if teachers' understand pupils' conceptual view of the word can they hope to bridge those understandings with those of science and scientists. And often, pupils are more effective in helping their peers make the bridge through discussion and cooperation in planning and implementing investigations.

Children bring their own world view to the science classroom, often as a result of their knowledge of the scientific element of the culture of their immediate community.

For example, children have ideas about air. They know it as wind that raises dust, moves tree leaves and can, on occasion, cause great damage. They know air as something that, when deprived of it, animals die, and as something fires need to burn strongly.

Children know that smoke rises and footballs become harder near a fire. Children may have investigated attributes of air as they play with plastic bags, football bladders, paper airplanes and propellers, parachutes and kites. Children can be asked to use their theoretical knowledge gained from their cultural, and increasingly, school background, together with their practical knowledge gained from play, to solve problems that intrigue them. One such problem would be to investigate the water rise when a closed container is placed over a burning candle standing in a dish of water. By using their own conceptual frameworks to investigate this problem, children develop a better understanding of scientists' understanding, than if they are given a lecture together with the traditional, erroneously explained standard demonstration.

Similarly children in Africa have understandings of many aspects of science and technology and are probably closer to the phenomena than children in industrial countries who frequently experience them as black-boxes or only at second hand through print, film or television. Children in Africa frequently are also closer to scientific and technological problem solving processes and principles than their counterparts elsewhere, as they work with adults farming, caring for livestock, making and repairing tools, traps and weapons.

However, traditional science teacher methods used in Africa ignore children's culture, despite rhetoric about the importance of our cultural heritage. The situation in our schools, and current constructivist theories of learning demand a change to more inquiry based ways of teaching.

Science Camps: The Implications for Learning

Participants in the Zanzibar Camp Project have become convinced of the potential that science camps have for implementing change to the benefit of the system and competencies of participating individuals.

Science camps are very effective at generating interest, motivation and commitment. Pupils' delight and excitement are palpable when they are encouraged to investigate familiar phenomena. So too is their boredom, dullness and lack of competence when exploration of their personal interests is replaced by teacher led demonstrations. As one marine research scientist in Zanzibar said after a particularly successful class during the 1992 science camp, "The problem with us teachers is that we must learn to control ourselves. I had no idea that our children were so bright. They were discussing issues in a way that I thought was possible only by scientists and policy makers".

Camps must be designed in ways that permit pupils to investigate, design and construct things that interest them,—and finding out what does interest pupils and in engaging them is in itself a major camp investigation. Children's ideas, like our own when first engaging in an unfamiliar problem, may start simply. But they can develop into work of significant scientific value. The camp environment must accommodate this evolution and world with the reachness of children's ideas. Eleanor Duckworth of Harvard once said, that science teaching/learning should be the having of wonderful ideas.

It is pointless to divorce school learning from children's lives outside of school. Any careful observer can walk down urban streets or through a village and see children busily involved with a number of practical activities.

> "They (children) focus on things I would never dream of looking at."
>
> In Osborne and Freyberg (1990).

Camps are concerned with a more focussed attention to learning through such "hands-on" and "minds-on" learning.

Science camps can be used to broaden children's experience by purposeful visits to places such as ponds, farms, the blacksmith or the local market. These too provide rich sources for science learning that are not usually exploited by our schools. Opportunities to study the sky with clouds, the moon and other heavenly bodies are also not usually provided at school. Children are encouraged to do so at camps, making careful observations, models and predictions. Our experience in Zanzibar has been that children will spend many hours of their free time doing so. They experience science as an active search for meaning that does not necessarily need laboratory materials and standard textbook.

Developmental psychologists such as Piaget claim that children, indeed adults, need concrete experience of concepts before these concepts can be fully understood. These concrete experiences can be provided during camps. Children can see, feel and use materials in a way that forces them to accommodate their conceptual frameworks and understanding to explain new phenomena.

Science Camps as a Metaphor for Change

In Zanzibar, we have grown to see that the real value of science camps is not so much in providing children with an exciting learning experience, but in being a research laboratory for all participants, especially the camp resource staff. Camps provide an opportunity to learn more about learning, both children's and our own,—often it emerges as we plan inquiry-based learning for children that we do not know as much about the subject matter as we thought. Camps provide an opportunity to experiment with and compare different methods of teaching. Camps provide a sheltered background for scientists, teachers and science educators with varying experience, qualifications and starting points to share ideas which can always be resolved by using children as the laboratory. Resource staff have the opportunity and luxury of being able to engage in diagnostic teaching to find out more about how children think. They can experiment with ways to engage all pupils in effective learning, rather than only the usual few high achievers.

> "The most recent developments suggest that improving learning outcomes requires not only the opening of the classroom door to study social interactions, but also requires an insight into individual cognitive processes."
>
> Driver (1985)

As important as providing a laboratory for learning about learning, camps provide an opportunity for resource staff and teachers to express their changing and developing value systems and to strengthen their commitment to inquiry-based teaching/ learning through dialogue. They are able to practice new roles as researchers, innovators, motivators, facilitators, diagnosticians and experimenters. In short, whatever the role of resource staff in their places of work, at camps they become used to viewing these roles in a different light that raises their professionalism and commitment to change.

To summarize, science camps provide an opportunity to transform science teaching and of energising individuals within the system to do so.

REFERENCES

Denny M. (1986) *Science Practicals: What do Pupils think?* European Journal of Science Education: 8, 4, 325-336.

Driver R. (1985) *Changing Perspectives on Science Lessons* in British Journal of Educational Psychology. Monograph series No. 2, Scottish Academic Press.

Matyas M. L. (1985) *Obstacles and Constraints on Women in Science: Preparation and Participation in the Scientific Community* in Kahle, J.B. (ed) Women in Science. The Falmer Press (pp. 77-101).

Roger Osborne and Peter Freyberg (1990) *Learning in Science.* Heinemann.

Woolnough, B. and Allsop T. (1985) *Practical Work in Science.* Cambridge University Press.

11

Project 2000+: Declaration

We, participants in the project 2000+ Forum, meeting at Unesco, Paris, France, from 5-10 July 1993:

1. Recalling the World Declaration on Education for All, in particular its recognition that 'sound basic education is fundamental to the strengthening of higher levels of education and of scientific and technological literacy and capacity and thus to self-reliant development' and, further recalling recent world-wide expressions of concern for the environment and for the quality of human life, especially those contained in Agenda 21, the output of the United Nations Conference on Environment and Development, Rio de Janerio, 3-14 June 1992;

2. Believing that scientific literacy and technological literacy are essential for achieving responsible and sustainable development;

3. Declare our full commitment to the promotion of science and technology education for all keeping with the World Declaration on Education for All, and our readiness to contribute through Project 2000+ to the concerted action set out in the Framework for Action to Meet Basic Learning Needs;

4. Call on governments, industry, public and private sector interests, and education and other authorities in all

countries to:

(a) review critically existing provision for science and technology education at all levels and in all settings with the aim of giving appropriate attention to development and maintenance of learning programmes responsive to the needs of individuals and communities;

(b) assign priority to the development and introduction of programmes leading to scientific literacy and technological literacy for all with the aim of achieving responsible and sustainable development;

(c) take such steps as may be necessary to ensure equity of access for everybody to science and technology education, notably for women and girls, young children and other under-represented groups;

(d) develop appropriate in-school and out-of-school opportunities, programmes, curricula and assessment procedures fro science and technology education responding to the human needs of a scientific and technological society;

(e) ensure and support appropriate pre-service and continuing in-service provisions for those responsible for all forms of science and technology education;

(f) encourage and support evaluation, research and development in science and technology education in both formal and non-formal sectors; and to this end;

(g) establish and support task forces involving partnership with public and private educational bodies and councils; these might include universities and other institutions of higher and further education, research institutions, libraries, interactive science centres, environmental areas and nature reserves as well as public and private bodies active in the fields of agriculture, natural resources, environment, health industry, commerce and the media, and alsc organizations and individuals specially concerned with science and technology education;

(h) recognize the central role of teachers in achieving scientific literacy and technological literacy for everybody, and enhance the status of careers in science and technology education at all levels;

(i) recognize the capital role of institutions of non-formal education, such as museums and scientific centres, of the media (radio, television and the press) and all other out-of-school channels for communicating knowledge of science and technology, in fostering scientific and technological literacy for all; and

develop activities designed to set science and its application in a wider social and cultural environment;

(j) ensure that adequate resources are available to achieve these aims;

5. Urge United Nations Agencies and other inter-governmental organizations to work together to initiate and support programmes which will advance the ability of countries and of populations to shape their own future in a scientific and technological society and which will increase the capacity of counties for designing, planning and implementing scientific literacy and technological literacy programmes;

6. Urge non-governmental organizations active in fields of science and technology education, as well as the social sciences, and professional associations of teachers and educators and educational organizations at all levels to:

enter into partnership with, and make their knowledge and experience available to, United Nations and other inter-governmental bodies as well as establish innovative programmes in a common effort to achieve the goal of scientific literacy and technological literacy for all; and

participate in national, regional and international programmes for the enhancement of scientific literacy and technological literacy for the improvement of the quality of life in all societies and for the achievement of sutainable development;

7. Recommend that UNESCO makes provision, within its Medium Term Plan (1996-2001) in the field of education, and in the context of Project 2000+, for an international programme to develop co-operation among all countries in the field of science and technology education, with particular reference to the promotion of scientific literacy and technological literacy for all:

This programme, conducted in partnership with the relevant and competent governmental and non-governmental organizations and agencies, should focus on regional and subregional co-operation and on strengthening networks for exchange of ideas, information, human and material resources for science and technological education, and actively seek to promote world-wide:

(a) understanding of the nature of, and the need for, scientific literacy and technological literacy in relation to local culture and values and to the social and economic needs, and aspirations of each country and its peoples, and also in accord both with the general aims of education for the all-round development of human personality and with human rights and basic freedoms;

(b) identification of those issues concerning the applications of science and technology which are of special importance for personal, local and national development and their embodiment and educational programmes;

(c) establishment of teaching and learning environments as well as supporting structures conducive to the achievement of scientific literacy and technological literacy for all;

(d) formulation of guidelines for the preparation and continuous professional development of science and technology educators coupled with assistance to countries in giving effect to them;

(e) development of effective communication, both verbal and visual, assessment strategies and evaluation programmes designed to enhance general levels of scientific literacy and technological literacy;

(f) support for the non-formal and informal sector in its own right and support development strategies which will help to stimulate and maintain lifelong scientific literacy and technological literacy;

8. Recommended that by the year 2001 there should be in place appropriate structures and activities to foster scientific literacy and technological for all, in all countries.

Appendix I

CHAIRMAN'S OPENING ADDRESS

By Professor P.N. Lassa (FMAN)

Executive Secretary

National Commission for Colleges of Education

His Excellency, the Executive Governor of Kaduna State, Alhaji Mohammed Dabo Lere,

The Deputy Governor, Mr James Bawa Magaji

The Honourable Secretary for Education and Youth Development, Professor Ben Nwabueze

His Royal Highness, the Emir of Zauzau, Alhaji (Dr) Shehu Idris

The Commonwealth Representative, Professor S.T. Bajah

Representative of the Rockefeller Foundation, Mr Mike Savage

Director of the British Council, Kaduna

Heads of Paratatals

Heads of Units and Divisions

Gentlemen of the Press

Distinguished ladies and gentlemen

It is my pleasure this morning to welcome you all to this important training workshop organised and jointly sponsored by the Commonwealth Secretariat, London and the National Commission for Colleges of Education, Kaduna, Nigeria.

The theme of this training workshop is "Improving the Quality of Science, Technology and Mathematics Education (STME) at the basic level: The Role of Teacher Education in

Nigeria". The vision of this workshop starting today, was initiated by the Commonwealth Conference of Education Ministers in Barbados in 1990 and approved by the Commonwealth Heads of Government in Harare in 1991. At these meetings, the Education Programmes Department of the Commonwealth Secretariat was mandated to pursue programmes that would improve the quality of basic education with respect to Science, Technology and Mathematics Education. The primary focus of the mandate is Teacher Education. Little was I surprised when Professor S.T. Bajah first approached me that the National Commission for Colleges of Education should jointly organize and host the regional workshop.

This a Train the Trainer workshop, which has drawn participants from very highly selected institutions that are under the umbrella of the National Commission for Colleges of Education. Only twenty (20) carefully selected colleges have been invited as the target group, that will be able to train fellow academic and professional colleagues in the Collages of Education for Science, Technology and Mathematics Education (STME). Our aims is to raise the quality of Science, Technology and Mathematics (STME) teachers and products in Africa, behold in the Commonwealth countries. One of the criteria for selecting the participants is an ability to play leadership role in training others. You must therefore, rise to the challenges and opportunities that this workshop provides. I understand that a powerful team of resource people from across the Africa continent have been assembled to take you through the next ten days of rigorous activities. It is my hope that you will take advantage and make the best use of these opportunities, because the future direction of science, technology and mathematics education depends upon you and what you are able to achieve during this workshop.

You all known that science, technology and mathematics have become critical factors of economic and social development. The advances in science and technology have become the index of development. The perception of this workshop of appropriately placed on teacher. The quality of the teachers depends on the qualification and training of the teacher. On the other hand, the quality of teaching depends on the teaching environment and the attitudes of teachers. The teacher is the key resource to science, technology and mathematics education. Any programme that produces excellence and high achievement is taught by qualified and competent teachers. This workshop expects a lot from you.

The Role of the National Commission for Colleges of Education (NCCE)

The National Commission for Colleges of Education, which came into existence by Decree No. 3 of 1989 is mandated among many other things to lay down minimum standards for all programmes of teacher education, among others.

The authoritative position of the National Commission for Colleges of Education (NCCE) is informed by the vision espoused by the National Policy on Education which articulates that the National Certificate of Education (NCE) will ultimately become the minimum basic qualification for entry into the teaching profession in Nigeria. To meet the aspiration of the National Policy therefore, our Colleges of Education, run programmes in science, technology and mathematics education with a view to producing teaches at the NCE level for the 6-3-3-4 system. The Colleges of Education have intensified their admission efforts in these areas of discipline, more qualified teachers are being recruited and facilities for teaching these subjects are being procured. The National Commission for Colleges of Education (NCCE) also has been making efforts in the improvement of Science, Technology and Mathematics Education (STME). This is why we have recently collaborated work with the British Council in introducing the Nigeria Integrated Science Teacher Education Project (NISTEP), to help boost our training efforts in Science, Technology and Mathematics Education (STME) in our Colleges of Education. We are looking forward to more of such opportunities.

Mr. Chairman, and participants, my Commission is leaving no stone unturned in order to realize our desire to produce more qualified and competent teachers in Science, Technology and Mathematics Education (STME) and other school subjects. This workshop in one of such efforts.

I am grateful to the Commonwealth Secretariat for the special honour done to my Commission—the National Commission for Colleges of Education to jointly organize and host this first National-Regional Training Workshop. I am particularly grateful to my long standing friend and colleague Prof. Peter Williams, Director and Professor S.T. Bajah FSTAN, the Chief Project Officer in the Education Programme of the Commonwealth Secretariat, London who championed the cause of this workshop. I wish to thank the Rockefeller Foundation Nairobi, Kenya for sponsoring the International Consultants to this Workshop. I thank you very much for this patronage.

May I also graciously thank the authorities of the Federal Ministry of Education and Youth Development, the Kaduna State Ministry of Education, the National Teachers' Institute, the National Educational Technology Centre and a host of others for their efforts in organising this Workshop.

To our august visitors, the international consultants, I wish you a very pleasant stay in Kaduna, Nigeria. I urge you to avail yourselves of the opportunities to see a little bit of this vast and great country. To the other participants also, I wish and hope that the exposure in this workshop will promote professional and academic cross fertilization of minds, and that at the end you would have met the goals and objectives of the organisers of the workshop and to the utmost satisfaction of your sponsors.

Thank you.

Appendix II

GOODWILL MESSAGE

From Mr Peter Williams
Director
Education Programme
Commonwealth Secretariat
London

Your Excellencies

All Other Protocols observed

Distinguished Guests, Ladies and Gentlemen

After so many uncertainties and postponements, I am delighted that this workshop has at last come to fruition. I am particularly delighted that the Rockefeller Foundation is joining hands with us to support this workshop. I want to express our profound gratitude to the National Commission for Colleges of Education (NCCE) for providing a home for a workshop which I am convinced is as important to you as it is to us.

Science, Technology and Mathematics are key areas of concern in the education of children who will, face the twenty first century. Our whole life pattern is even now gradually being affected by STM and will be more so in the twenty-first century. The approach which we at the Commonwealth Secretariat have adopted is guided by the mandate handed down to our programme at the Eleventh Commonwealth Conference of Ministers of Education held in Barbados in 1991. At that conference, the need to improve the quality of basic education was emphasized and to achieve that, the role of Higher Education was stressed. If teachers who teach science, technology and mathematics at the basic level are well trained or should I say well educated, then there would to a large extent be some assurance that learners will be exposed to challenging STM programmes. And those who prepare the STM teachers in higher institutions must themselves be aware of new strategies of communicating science, technology and mathematics to children. Science I am told is best learnt by experiencing it, and as one of your keynote speakers stressed in his paper, you must practice what you preach.

Here at the Secretariat, we have shown special interest in STME. For years back, we have been involved, in collaboration with UNESCO, in the "Process Approach" to teaching science. After several workshops in that area, we now have a bank of information which we have been sharing with Commonwealth countries. The video film, "Righting the Imbalance", which we hope you can watch before this workshop ends presents our effort in enhancing the participation of girls and women into science.

This two-week workshop in Kaduna is therefore a unique opportunity for all involved to exchange experiences, dialogue on new ideas and then come up with materials that will be of use to STM teachers throughout the Commonwealth. The goal of this workshop, I am reliably informed, is to produce draft monographs in key areas in STM education. I do want to wish you a very challenging period and look forward to the outcome.

Let we at this point also remind you of the approach, which was underscored at the planning meeting in Hertford, England. There it was stated that the CASCADE STRATEGY will be adopted. The cascade strategy involves key teachers (like you) who, having been exposes to a training programme (such as you will be exposed to in the coming weeks), will go back and do likewise, i.e., organise similar in-service programmes for their colleagues either in the same school or under the same educational administration. In other words, the cascade strategy has an in-built MULTIPLIER EFFECT. You cannot therefore adopt a passive stance during this workshop.

In your folder, you will find a number of print materials from our Education Programme. These materials have been selected and given to you gratis to enable you to have an insight into our work. In addition to the print materials, we have made available to you our latest catalogue of available publications. Please study these and do get in touch with us if you find any useful materials among our list.

Distinguished Guests, Ladies and Gentlemen, I want to wish the participants a very busy but fruitful workshop. I am constantly remained that there is a great deal of difference between a TALKSHOP and a WORKSHOP. I am convinced that you will discern the difference in the next few days. I want to conclude by thanking the Executive Secretary of NCCE, Professor Peter Lassa for his letter and the very kind things he had to say about our brief but memorable interaction at the London University Institute of Education. The joy is mine to know that you are today shouldering a gigantic programme of not only formulating policies but also prosecuting projects that will make teachers truly professional. I wish you all a very fruitful workshop and to our Moslem friends BARKA DA SALLAH.

Appendix III

EVALUATION OF THE WORKSHOP BY PARTICIPANTS

1. Twenty participants were originally invited from twenty colleges of education out of fifty-eight colleges of education in Nigeria, but seventeen (17) participants actually turned up. However, sixteen (16) additional participants were registered because of the desire of their organizations to have them in attendance. Out of the fifteen (15), eleven (11) were from the National Educational Technology Centre, Kaduna, while the remaining four were from the Federal Ministry of Education and Youth Development, Special Programmes Unit, Kaduna.

2. In order to improve the conduct of similar workshop in the future, participants were used to complete an evaluation questionnaire. The questionnaire form is attached to an appendix of this annex, which summarises the responses by the participants.

   At the end of the workshop, 26 participants actually returned their forms.

USEFULNESS OF THE ACTIVITIES OF THE WORKSHOP

Q. 1. How useful did you find the different activities to the workshop?

(a) Plenary Session: Setting the Pace

Thirty-five per cent of the participants felt that the activities at the plenary session were very useful, fifty-four per cent felt that the activities were useful, while eleven per cent were of the view that the activities were fairly useful. The implication of the above is that the activities at the plenary have benefical to the participants.

(b) Paper Presentation:

Thirty-one per cent of the participants were of the view that the presentations were very useful, fifty-four per cent felt that it was useful fifteen agreed that the presentation of paper was fairly useful. Nobody felt that the presentation was less useful. In other words, the activities during the paper presentation were generally useful to the participants.

(c) Monograph Group Work:

Seventy-three per cent of the participants felt that the activities during the group work sessions were very useful; twenty-six per cent were of the view that the activities were useful while only four percent felt that the activities of the Group-work were fairy useful. This implies that the activities were very useful to the participants.

(d) Working With Students—FCE Zaria:

Forty-six per cent of the participants felt that activities at the FCE, Zaria were very useful, forty-six per cent were of the view that the activities were useful, four per cent felt that the activities were fairly useful while the remaining four per cent felt the activities were a bit useful. The conclusion from this is that the activities at Federal College of Education, Zaria were generally useful.

(e) Video Film Session:

Nineteen per cent felt that the video session was very useful; forty-two per cent were of the view that the session was just useful; thirty-one per cent were of the opinion that the session was fairly useful; four per cent felt that the session was a bit useful while the remaining four per cent felt that the video session was less useful. The general opinion is that the video session was useful.

(f) Group Presentation:

Twenty-seven per cent of the participants felt that the activities during the group presentation were very useful; fifty-four per cent were of the view that the activities were useful while the remaining nineteen per cent felt that the activities were fairly useful.

2. (a) About eighty-eight (88) per cent of the participants strongly believed in their own contribution towards the achievements of the workshop objectives while the remaining 12 per cent simply agreed.

(b) Resource Person's Usefulness in the Monograph Groups

Forty-six per cent of the participants felt that the resource persons contribution were very useful in the monograph work while 42 per cent were of the view that their (resource person's) contributions were useful while the remaining 12 per cent believed that their contribution were *fairly useful*. The conclusion from this is that the resource persons' contributions were highly useful and beneficial to the participants during the group work.

(c) Participant's Understanding of CASCADE Model of INSET

About 81 per cent of the participants felt that they actually understood the CASCADE Model of INSET while the remaining 19 per cent felt that their understanding of the model is either fair or a bit fair.

(d) Participants' Ability to Play a Leadership Role in the Training of other STME Lectures as a Result of the Workshop

Eighty-two per cent of the participants strongly felt that they can play leadership role in STME as a result of the workshop while the remaining eighteen per cent are partially sure of the ability in this regard.

3. (a) What New Ideas (in any) Did You Learn During the Workshop?

The new ideas acquired during the workshop as stated by the participants are:

(i) Science camps

(ii) Inquiry approach to teaching

(iii) Interactive teaching

(iv) Dialogue teaching

(v) Utilization of community materials

(vi) Use of computer assessment

(vii) Improvization of OHP

(viii) Writing of monographs

(ix) CASCADE method

(b) What Changes (if any) Would You Seriously Consider Changing in your Institution's Training Programme?

The following changes have stated by the participants:

(i) INSET programme participation

(ii) Adequate research funding

(iii) Training the existing staff in the colleges

(iv) Encouragement of more group work in teaching

(v) Incentives should be given to STME teachers

(vi) Forum for all lectures in colleges to come together to consider team teachers.

4. What Additional Topic Areas in STME Would You Have Liked the Workshop to Consider?

The additional topics as suggested by the participants are:

(i) Science library/resource room

(ii) Use of computer in STME

(iii) Micro-teaching organization

5. General Comments on the Workshop

Participants expressed their views about the workshop in different ways: Some described the workshop as innovating, educative, rewarding, successful, satisfactory, highly exposing and informative. Others stated that the workshop was nicely conducted and highly rewarding.

In short, majority of the participants shared the view that the workshop was highly successful.

6. What is it that You Would Have Linked to See Happen in the Workshop that did not happen?

Participants views vary on this question. However, some of their views are as follows:

- Incorporation of practical demonstration of some of the education theories;
- Computer education;
- Production of Modules/Monographs on different areas of STM;
- Emphasis on Technology

7. Any Other General Comments

According to the majority of the participants, everything about the workshop was perfectly done. The workshop had been educative, stimulating and refreshing. The workshop objectives were achieved. The participants commanded the efforts of the consultants and the National Commission for Colleges of Education staff for a job well done.

Finally majority of the participants called for more of such workshops.

Question 1. Table of Analysis

How Useful did you find the different activities of the Workshop?

	Very Useful (5)	Useful (4)	Fairly Useful (3)	A bit Useful (2)	Less Useful (1)	Total
a	9 *30.61	14 *53.85	3 *11.54	0 *0	0 *0	26
b.	8 *30.77	14 *53.85	4 *15.38	0 *0	0	26
c	19 *73.08	6 *26.08	2 *3.84	0 *0	0 *0	26
d	12 *46.15	12 *46.15	1 *3.84	1 *3.84	0	26
e	5 *19.23	11 *42.31	8 *30.77	1 *3.84	1 *3.84	26
f	7 *26.92	14 *53.85	5 *19.23	0 *0	0 *0	26

Note: *percentages
For question under a - f see questionnaire.

Question 2. Analysis Table

	Very Useful (5)	Useful (4)	Fairly Useful (3)	A bit Useful (2)	Less Useful (1)	Total
a	12 *46.15	11 *42.31	2 *7.69	1 *3.84	0 *0	26
b	12 *46.15	11 *42.31	1 *3.84	2 *7.69 *0	0 -0	26
c	2 *7.69	19 *73.08	5 *19.23	0 *0	0 *0	26
d	10 *38.46	12 *46.15	4 *15.39	0 *0 *0	0 *0	26

Note: **percentages*
For question under a - f see questionnaire.